From Stalinism to Pluralism

FROM STALINISM TO PLURALISM

A Documentary History
of Eastern Europe
Since 1945

SECOND EDITION

Edited by
GALE STOKES

New York   Oxford
OXFORD UNIVERSITY PRESS
1996

Oxford University Press

Oxford   New York
Athens   Auckland   Bangkok   Bombay
Calcutta   Cape Town   Dar Es Salaam   Delhi
Florence   Hong Kong   Istanbul   Karachi
Kuala Lampur   Madras   Madrid   Melbourne
Mexico City   Nairobi   Paris   Singapore
Tapei   Tokyo   Toronto

and associated companies in
Berlin   Ibadan

Copyright © 1991, 1996 by Oxford University Press, Inc.

Published by Oxford University Press, Inc.,
198 Madison Avenue, New York, New York 10016

Oxford is a registered trademark of Oxford University Press

Library of Congress Cataloging-in-Publication Data
From Stalinism to pluralism :
a documentary history of Eastern Europe since 1945 /
[edited by] Gale Stokes—2nd ed.
p.   cm.
ISBN 978-0-19-509447-3.—ISBN 978-0-19-509446-6 (pbk.)
1. Europe, Eastern—History—1945–1989—Sources.
I. Stokes, Gale, 1933– .
DJK50.F76   1996   947.08—dc20   95-5924

9

Printed in the United States of America
on acid-free paper

For Roberta

Acknowledgments

The first edition of this book grew out of conversations I had with Michael Henry Heim during several meetings of the Joint Committee on Eastern Europe of the American Council of Learned Societies and the Social Science Research Council, of which we both were members. Without Michael's encouragement and support, as well as his translation help, this book would not have been possible. I would also like to thank Iván Szelényi, also a member of that committee, for providing one of his articles.

Generous grants from Professor Allen Matusow, dean of the School of Humanities, Rice University, helped make it possible to pay for the large number of publication permissions needed in both editions of this book.

I imposed on many other persons with requests for assistance, and I always received gracious and professional responses. I did not always use the materials that others gave me, but without the help of the following people, the book would not have had the shape it does: Joan deBarteleben, Balint Magyar, Andras Kornai, Vid Pečjak, Dimitrij Rupel, Francis Lowenheim, Jan Kubik, Lee Congden, Carole Rogel, Paul Shoup, Ivo Banac, Robert Hayden, Dennison Rusinow, and Margaret Kennel. I would like to thank John Lampe of the Woodrow Wilson Center and Andrew Janos of the University of California at Berkeley for their comments on the original manuscript, and Richard Wolin of Rice University for his observations on the introduction. The students in my undergraduate seminars on postwar Eastern Europe gave me many good suggestions, for which I thank them individually and collectively. In addition, I greatly appreciate the discussion of the original manuscript by the Academic Advisory Council of the East European Program of the Wilson Center. Naturally, all responsibility for what follows is mine alone.

This book, like its predecessor, is intended for student use, although I hope that others will profit from it as well. Therefore, I would very much appreciate hearing suggestions from teachers or other readers for readings that should be included, improvements of the explanatory texts, corrections in the annotations, or any other comments on how the collection might be improved. Please write me directly at the History Department, Rice University, Houston, Texas 77251.

Contents

Contents

From Stalinism to Pluralism

Introduction

The dramatic and unprecedented events that took place in Eastern Europe in 1989 brought the entire post-World War II European settlement seriously into question for the first time since the end of that conflict. Restructurings that in 1985 were inconceivable took place. The turns of Hungary and Poland toward multiparty systems began a process that by the end of the year had toppled the communist regimes in East Germany and Czechoslovakia, forced a fundamental reorganization in Bulgaria, and led to violent upheaval in Romania. Communist parties divested themselves of their constitutionally guaranteed right to an exclusive role in politics, and former oppositionists entered governments to begin the difficult task of restoring devastated economies. The opening of the Berlin Wall brought the question of German reunification to center stage and forced the rethinking of international relationships that only a few years earlier seemed permanent. All of this took place in an atmosphere of anticipation of greater levels of West European integration in 1992 that lent a sense of urgency to the calls of Soviet premier Mikhail Gorbachev for the drawing together of what he called the common European home. In short, after a generation of resignation to a Europe divided between East and West, at the beginning of the 1990s Europeans began to take a fresh look at their future.

The excitement that the new possibilities in Eastern Europe generated was related to the context in which they took place rather than the originality of the initiatives themselves. After all, mixed economies and multiparty systems are the bread and butter of European politics west of the Elbe. But Eastern Europe was a neuralgic point in the great transformation of worldwide politics that took place after World War II. Not only was it the locus of the initial confrontations of the cold war and the place where the politics of superpower rivalry received its initial rehearsal, but it was also the place in which the socioeconomic transformations proposed by the Bolshevik Revolution of 1917 received their fairest test. Because some parts of Eastern Europe were relatively well developed in 1945, both politically and economically, it was there that Leninism found its best opportunity to build a new society.

The history of its failure to do so is suffused with the ghost of Joseph Stalin. East European history after 1945 can be understood as one spasmodic moment of Stalinist appropriation, followed ever since by various forms of de-Stalinization and re-Stalinization. To understand this process and to understand the efforts of East Europeans today to discard completely the Stalinist paradigm that defined their choices for more than a generation, it is important to recognize that Stalinism was not only a system of draconian social controls elaborated by an especially demanding dictator, or as Milan Kundera has suggested, simply the imposition of an Eastern despotism on Western civilizations. In a sense, Stalinism was the reductio ad absurdum of the Enlightenment view that humans, through the proper use of reason, could grasp the laws of human relations, just as Newton had grasped the laws of motion. In contrast with the Christian belief that humans are inherently evil, cursed with original sin that cannot be erased by human agency, Rousseau argued that people are inherently innocent and good but that the organization of society, in which the rich gorged themselves on superfluities while the poor starved, had created a situation in which evil could flourish. God's gift to humankind was not sin, the Enlightenment taught us, but reason, whose proper use could provide the understanding and tools to right the wrongs that the structuring of society around property had created and could produce a system in which everyone shared more or less equally in nature's bounty and in the works of humankind.

In this sense, Karl Marx was a thoroughly Enlightenment thinker who believed that reason could encompass the laws of historical development. Rejecting German philosophy as too abstract, he redesigned Hegel's dialectic to fit what he considered to be real human relations. For Marx, the characteristic that differentiates humans from beasts is that human beings produce goods to meet their needs. In doing so, they perforce create an increasingly complex society marked by the division of labor, private property, and class conflict. Marx believed that he had discovered the true laws of history based on the nature of humanity. The progression of the dialectical struggle between classes would eventually produce, he argued, a society in which no person oppressed another and in which all lived equally unalienated lives.

Marx's claim that his notions were not simply ideas among a family of ideas but, rather, the one true interpretation of human history, coupled with the brilliance of his insights into nineteenth-century phenomena, attracted a significant number of creative European minds. Marx believed that the transcendence of capitalism would come through worldwide revolution, not through the workings of any democratic or representative system, as those were simply the political clothing in which capitalist repression dressed itself.

Like Marx, Lenin believed that human reason could comprehend history and act as the guide to transforming society, but he did not believe that the proletariat, which in Marx's scheme was the class that would achieve unalienated existence, was capable of using its reason without help. Left to its own devices, Lenin thought, the working class would succumb to the economic blandishments of the capitalists, such as higher wages and shorter hours, and thus impede the historical movement toward revolution. Lenin believed that the proletariat needed the guidance of those who comprehended the true direction of history, namely, the intellectuals who correctly understood Marx. The intellectuals he had in mind, of course, were the professional revolutionaries of the Bolshevik wing of the Russian Social Democratic party, or more succinctly, the Communists.

When, therefore, by daring, luck, and force, Lenin and the Communists seized power in Russia, the party undertook to modernize the Soviet Union by imposing its "correct" policies, not by introducing what they considered the empty formalisms of representative government. As early as the Tenth Party Congress in 1921, Lenin insisted that there be no factionalism in the party. For Communists, the party, the vanguard of the proletariat, was the only certain repository of true interpretations of reality.

Stalin pushed this Leninist beginning to its furthest extreme by ruthlessly eliminating not only opponents but even allies and collaborators who might conceivably harbor doubts about the leader's ability to grasp the historical moment. The Communists of Lenin's time spoke about creating a "new Soviet man" by abolishing private property, the basis of capitalist relations, and thus removing the principal cause of evil in society. Stalin went further, following what Robert Tucker has called "Transformism," which is the belief that the leader of the party could, through the force of his understanding, create an equitable and rational economy through centralized economic planning and even new linguistic and biological structures. Stalin's obsession with total control reflected both complex psychological motivations and a confidence that human reason, through Marxism–Leninism, could restructure the world according to its own design.

Among Soviet dissidents and oppositionists, the view that Stalinism was an outgrowth of Enlightenment hubris produced a call to reject reason and return to a pre-Enlightened world. (Alexander Solzhenitsyn was the most notable advocate of this strategy.) In Eastern Europe, however, perhaps because of its closer historical linkages to the historical development of Western Europe, analyses of the totalitarian phenomenon moved in a different direction. Rather than rejecting the Enlightenment, East Europeans began to reconsider how it might be possible to construct a modern society using ethical, political, and economic ideas whose origins lie in a different strain of eighteenth-century rationalism.

The Enlightenment views that East Europeans confronted held that whereas human reason was certainly the underlying hope for betterment, human beings, including kings, remain fallible. Therefore, to ensure that a single individual or group did not exercise tyrannical control over others, it was necessary to create a state in which either the general will of the sovereign people would provide guidance and/or in which the powers of government were balanced in such a way that no one arm of the state could overwhelm and dominate society. If the idea of using reason to impose "correct" solutions on society grew in good measure from the Rousseauian desire to ameliorate the inequalities of wealth, status, and opportunity that characterized both the prerevolutionary regimes and the capitalist ones that followed, the idea of limiting the state reflected the equally powerful eighteenth-century redefinition of freedom. Rather than a specific privilege granted to a subject by his or her sovereign, liberty came to mean a quality of existence in which one was not restrained from pursuing self-interest and, as such, a necessary general condition for the full development of human rationality. A state was necessary to maintain this general condition, but if the freedom of individuals to pursue self-interest was to flourish, this state itself had to be restrained from its normal tendency to usurp power for itself. Freedom, in other words, required a limited state. The Rousseauian vision, on the other hand, seemed to require the fullest use of the powers of the state to impose the necessary redistributions of wealth that would create equality.

The irony of what actually happened in the two hundred years that followed the French and American revolutions is that the measures taken by West European states and the United States based on the notion of preserving liberty—limiting the power of the state and increasing the autonomous voice of the citizens in running that state—turned out to produce not only a new perception of autonomy and freedom among its citizens but more equality as well through the mechanism of economic growth. More or less free to grow in unpredictable ways, capitalism created enormous new wealth. This did not eliminate poverty and inequality, of course, but never in human history has such a large proportion of the population been as healthy, long-lived, and prosperous as it has become in Western democracies in the last one hundred years.

The extraordinarily complex economies of mature capitalism produced equally complex social systems in which the interests of the citizens encompassed a vast plurality of initiatives and aspirations. The states of Western Europe and North America have been able to contain and use this complexity because they have developed political devices that permit public articulation of a bewildering variety of interests. By attempting, in fits and starts and quite imperfectly, to ensure freedom to its populations, Western governments have been able to aggregate interests in such a way as to permit the state to act, while at the same time not destroying the ability of the losers in any given political decision to maintain their dignity. In other words, the political pluralism of the Western democracies matches, however imperfectly, the complexity of their productive forces, and this situation gives the populations of these countries a sense that they are free and that in some way they also are equal. At the very least it offers to those who do not feel that way an opening to attempt to make the changes they think would produce equity.

The restructuring of Eastern Europe according to Stalin's principles of subordination was sudden and complete. In the minds of many who undertook the project, the goal was the creation of modern productive societies in which the injustices of the past would be removed. But the project failed. Stalinism did create a certain perception of equality in East European societies, and it did build the initial elements of a mid-twentieth-century industrial economy based on steel and heavy industry. But the rigidity of the leaderships that claimed the right to control all because they knew all eventually stifled the East European economies, which did not grow with anything near the speed of those of their Western neighbors. Had centralized planning produced a prosperous and productive society, in all likelihood the unrest and changes that occurred in the late 1980s and early 1990s would not have happened. But centralized planning produced shortages, inflation, and debt, not prosperity. The inevitable result was serious discontent and pressure for change.

Until the accession of Mikhail Gorbachev to the leadership of the Soviet Union, that pressure produced some violent and dramatic confrontations, notably the Hungarian Revolution of 1956, the Prague Spring of 1968, and the Solidarity movement of 1980–81, but not any fundamental change. Late in the 1980s, however, Soviet allies in Eastern Europe became much freer to reject the tradition represented by Leninism and Stalinism and to consider creating the kind of pluralism that emerged from the second strain of the Enlightenment. In the minds of East European oppositionists, the impetus behind their criticisms of Stalinism and its successors over the years was primarily ethical, not material. That is, among intellectuals, opposition has always been an issue of ideology, culture, and ethics rather than an issue of economic efficiency. But the implicit purpose of those who proposed regenerating eighteenth-century ideas in twentieth-century costume was to ensure that their countries were not left behind economically. Because any major reform of economic relations had first to loosen the bureaucratic grip of the party on the economic system, the first arena in which dramatic changes took place in these now quite diverse societies was in politics. New elements arising from the dissident movements seized power, formed political parties, conducted elections, and began creating pluralist political systems. The expected economic reforms did not develop with as much clarity, but whether a country adopted a strategy of gradual privatization or a strategy of rapid change, every East European nation opened its doors to private enterprise and foreign investment. By the mid-1990s, East European countries were functioning more and more like their Western counterparts.

The purpose of this book is to bring together in one convenient place some of the most important and interesting documents that suggest how, over the past forty years, East Europeans have made the journey from Stalinism to a new pluralism. The course of this process has dictated the organization of the book. Part I, quite naturally, concerns the imposition of Stalinism on the East European countries in the years that immediately followed World War II. As in the other sections, Part I does not attempt to be comprehensive—there are no documents about the specific events of October–November 1956 in Poland and Hungary, for example—but, rather, it presents a selection of interpretive writings that impart the conceptions (or misconceptions) of those who lived through the era. Because the thrust of the book is to chronicle the transformation of nominally independent European states from a moment of monolithic control to a time of pluralist change, documents concerning developments in the Baltic states, which became part of the Soviet Union in 1941, and Finland, Austria, and Greece, which remained outside the Stalinist orbit, have not been included.

The appeal of Stalinism dropped dramatically with Stalin's death in 1953. Part II concerns the efforts of East European politicians and intellectuals in the fifteen years that followed to find a way to maintain the goals and hopes of socialism, but at the same time to ameliorate Stalinist abuses. The dream of creating a "socialism with a human face" reached its climax in Czechoslovakia in 1968.

Part III is less strictly chronological than Parts I and II are, because it includes selections from as early as 1957 and as late as 1984, but it encompasses a major theme of post-1968 Eastern Europe—the loss of faith that communism, or even politics as such, could provide solutions to the problems posed by modern life, especially modern life lived under a single-party state. Convinced after 1968 that the Soviet Union would never give up its hegemony and that it was hopeless and even irresponsible to act in a way that might bring in Soviet tanks, East Europeans temporarily retreated from politics. All the readings in this part are nonetheless at least implicit critiques of a system that insists on interfering in cultural phenomena, in ethical decisions, and even in ordinary simple pleasures. In contrast with the post-1956 discussions, much of the post-1968 discourse did not use Marxist rhetoric at all. Neo-Stalinism had so devalued the language and categories of Marxism that in the 1970s that language was used less and less, until by the end of the 1980s no self-respecting oppositionist used it at all.

In the 1980s, East Europeans returned to politics. In Poland, Solidarity, by bringing some ten million Poles into its organization, showed the hollowness of the Communist party's claim that it was the historically unique representative of the working class. When Mikhail Gorbachev's programs of reform in the Soviet Union offered the East Europeans an opening, both Poland and Hungary were ready to take advantage of it. Poland conducted Eastern Europe's first free election in forty years, and Hungary opened its doors to East Germans fleeing their country. In short order the Berlin Wall collapsed; Bulgaria turned toward pluralism; Czechoslovakia threw off its communist regime; and Romania executed its dictator. By January 1, 1990, communism in Eastern Europe was finished.

Part IV contains documents concerning this return to politics and also documents of a different kind. The increasingly articulate demands for political change in Eastern Europe rest on a desire for greater freedom of expression, expanded civil liberties, and improved rule by law, all of which are basic goals of the new pluralism, and they also rest on the insight that pluralist political systems have a potential for economic development that centrally organized systems do not. The failure of the Stalinist economic system, including its almost complete lack of concern for environmental issues, drives much of the unrest that challenged communist systems everywhere. In Eastern Europe, economic difficulties have tempted some leaders to play the nationalist card, and so despite claims beginning in the 1940s that nationalities problems had been solved in Eastern Europe, in the 1980s nationalism reemerged, especially in southeastern Europe.

The post-1989 period has been both more violent and less disruptive than expected. The collapse of Yugoslavia into vicious ethnic warfare provided a worst-case example of the costs of inadequate conflict resolution mechanisms. In other parts of Eastern Europe, however, despite several difficult problems, progress toward marketization and pluralization has proceeded apace. Democratic forms now exist in all East European countries, and the private sector provides an increasing proportion of the national product.

Section V contains a representative sample of documents concerning nationalism and the collapse of Yugoslavia. It does not attempt, however, to cover the complex of issues that the collapse of communism created throughout the region, because there are too many of them; it is too early to identify the primary trends; and the circumstances in the various countries are too diverse. The final two documents, however, do point a way to the future while reminding us of what went before. Gorbachev's vision of a common European home, though dated in its detail, provides a positive vision of the future, and his resignation speech reminds us how stultifying the communist system was in the past. Eastern Europe faces difficult new problems, but at least its people now have a fresh opportunity to confront and possibly to solve them.

Some of the documents in this book are printed in their entirety, but most have been condensed, as indicated in the text material for each document. For ease of reading, all ellipses except those appearing in the original text have been eliminated. Spelling, punctuation, and capitalization have been standardized and obvious typographical or grammatical errors have been corrected, but diacritical marks remain as originally published.

Abandonment of the political categories produced by World War II did not begin in earnest until 1985. Only with the dramatic changes of 1989 did the terms *cold war, Iron Curtain,* and *Soviet bloc* lose their grip on the general public, although they had long since been dropped by the specialists who concern themselves with Eastern Europe. The concepts endured because of the drama, intensity, and emotion that accompanied the end of that great war and because they expressed the initial reality of the postwar period: The Western democracies met the Soviet Union over the prostrate body of a destroyed and exhausted Europe. Had the two sides been ideologically compatible, they still would have experienced serious conflicts of interest, especially because the Soviet Union had found itself invaded twice in thirty years through Eastern Europe and was determined to do something about it. But the two sides were not ideologically compatible. The United States matured to the position of power to which its economic strength entitled it in 1945 and sought to make the world safe not only for democracy but also for free trade and commercial prosperity. The Soviet Union, on the other hand, having just survived a close call with destruction, argued that capitalism was in crisis and would soon collapse and that abolition of private property through revolution was essential to creating a better world. The confrontation that resulted, the cold war, dominated international relations for a generation.

The countries of Eastern Europe had little choice in which side they chose in this confrontation—the Red Army occupied them (with the exception of Yugoslavia), and Stalin imposed his will on them (also with the exception of Yugoslavia). For this reason, many East Europeans resented and rejected the term *East* European, pointing out that for centuries they were an integral part of Europe and that the imposition of Stalinism cut them off from their historical connections with Western Europe, subjugating them to an Eastern despotism that was foreign to their history and desires. Whether or not one agrees with this interpretation—for after all the imperial histories of Eastern Europe differ greatly from the histories of the West European states—a full understanding of what it means to be East European would require beginning long before 1945.

We begin, however, not with those histories but with the imposition that was made on top of them, Stalinism, because whatever their previous experience, that is the reality all East Europeans had to confront after World War II. Specifically, we begin with the Yalta Agreements of 1945, which the East Europeans saw as the moment when the West abandoned them. From their viewpoint the rebirth of political pluralism since 1985 was an effort to negate the Yalta system: the joint decision of West and East to sever them from Europe.

Yalta

The conference held in February 1945 at Yalta, which is in the Crimea on the Black Sea, was the second of three meetings among the leaders of the main allies against Hitler in World War II. Joseph Stalin, British Prime Minister Winston Churchill, and U.S. President Franklin Roosevelt met in December 1943 in Teheran, where they worked out the basic agreements that led to a successful conclusion of the war. They met a second time at Yalta and then again in July 1945 at Potsdam (Germany), with the substitution of Harry Truman for the deceased Roosevelt and Clement Attlee for Churchill, whose Conservative party had lost to Labour in the 1945 elections. Of the three, the meeting at Yalta is the best remembered because shortly afterward the wartime alliance began its inevitable breakup and the cold war began. For this reason, and because some thought crucial decisions were (or were not) made there, Yalta became the paradigmatic moment for many East Europeans. For them "Yalta" was shorthand for abandonment by the West, domination by the Soviet Union, interruption of their Europocentric histories, and inclusion in an economic straitjacket.

The two most important goals of the United States at Yalta were to get the Soviets into the war against Japan—as the atomic bomb had not yet been proved and many casualties were expected if Japan had to be invaded—and to obtain Soviet approval for the United Nations, which Roosevelt saw as essential to the preservation of peace in the postwar world. In both of these matters, Roosevelt was successful, as the text of the documents reprinted here shows. For East Europeans, however, and for the many critics of Yalta for years afterward, the most important issues were Churchill's and Roosevelt's acquiescence to a unified Polish government dominated by communists, which sealed the fate of that country, and the Declaration on Liberated Europe, by which the State Department attempted to ensure democratic elections in Eastern Europe after the war.

In the light of the feelings aroused by these issues, it is instructive to read the exchange between Charles E. Bohlen and the U.S. minister counselor to the Soviet Union, George Kennan, contained in Bohlen's description of the conference excerpted in Document 2. Bohlen acted as Roosevelt's interpreter at Yalta and as an adviser to the American delegation.

1

Report of the Crimea Conference (Yalta)

February 11, 1945

The following statement is made by the prime minister of Great Britain, the president of the United States of America, and the chairman of the Council of Peoples' Commissars of the Union of Soviet Socialist Republics on the results of the Crimean Conference:

I

THE DEFEAT OF GERMANY

We have considered and determined the military plans of the three Allied powers for the final defeat of the common enemy. The military staffs of the three Allied nations have met in daily meetings throughout the conference. These meetings have been most satisfactory from every point of view and have resulted in closer coordination of the military effort of the three Allies than ever before. The fullest information has been interchanged. The timing, scope, and coordination of new and even more powerful blows to be launched by our armies and air forces into the heart of Germany from the east, west, north, and south have been fully agreed and planned in detail.

Our combined military plans will be made known only as we execute them, but we believe that the very close working partnership among the three staffs attained at this conference will result in shortening the war. Meetings of the three staffs will be continued in the future whenever the need arises.

Nazi Germany is doomed. The German people will only make the cost of their defeat heavier to themselves by attempting to continue a hopeless resistance.

II

THE OCCUPATION AND CONTROL OF GERMANY

We have agreed on common policies and plans for enforcing the unconditional surrender terms which we shall impose together on Nazi Germany after German armed resistance has been finally crushed. These terms will not be made known

Reprinted from *Foreign Relations of the United States: Diplomatic Papers. The Conferences at Malta and Yalta, 1945* (Washington, D.C.: U.S. Government Printing Office, 1955).

until the final defeat of Germany has been accomplished. Under the agreed plan, the forces of the three powers will each occupy a separate zone of Germany. Coordinated administration and control have been provided for under the plan through a central Control Commission consisting of the supreme commanders of the three powers with headquarters in Berlin. It has been agreed that France should be invited by the three powers, if she should so desire, to take over a zone of occupation and to participate as a fourth member of the Control Commission. The limits of the French zone will be agreed by the four governments concerned through their representatives on the European Advisory Commission.

It is our inflexible purpose to destroy German militarism and Nazism and to ensure that Germany will never again be able to disturb the peace of the world. We are determined to disarm and disband all German armed forces; break up for all time the German general staff that has repeatedly contrived the resurgence of German militarism; remove or destroy all German military equipment; eliminate or control all German industry that could be used for military production; bring all war criminals to just and swift punishment and exact reparation in kind for the destruction wrought by the Germans; wipe out the Nazi party, Nazi laws, organizations, and institutions, remove all Nazi and militarist influences from public office and from the cultural and economic life of the German people; and take in harmony such other measures in Germany as may be necessary to the future peace and safety of the world. It is not our purpose to destroy the people of Germany, but only when Nazism and Militarism have been extirpated will there be hope for a decent life for Germans and a place for them in the comity of nations.

III

REPARATION BY GERMANY

We have considered the question of the damage caused by Germany to the Allied nations in this war and recognized it as just that Germany be obliged to make compensation for this damage in kind to the greatest extent possible. A Commission for the Compensation of Damage will be established. The commission will be instructed to consider the question of the extent and methods for compensating damage caused by Germany to the Allied countries. The commission will work in Moscow.

IV

UNITED NATIONS CONFERENCE

We are resolved upon the earliest possible establishment with our Allies of a general international organization to maintain peace and security. We believe that this is essential, both to prevent aggression and to remove the political, economic, and social causes of war through the close and continuing collaboration of all peace-loving peoples.

The foundations were laid at Dumbarton Oaks.[1] On the important question of voting procedure, however, agreement was not there reached. The present conference has been able to resolve this difficulty.

We have agreed that a Conference of United Nations should be called to meet at San Francisco in the United States on April 25, 1945, to prepare the charter of such an organization, along the lines proposed in the informal conversations at Dumbarton Oaks.

The government of China and the provisional government of France will be immediately consulted and invited to sponsor invitations to the conference jointly with the governments of the United States, Great Britain, and the Union of Soviet Socialist Republics. As soon as the consultation with China and France has been completed, the text of the proposals on voting procedure will be made public.

V

DECLARATION ON LIBERATED EUROPE

We have drawn up and subscribed to a Declaration on Liberated Europe. This declaration provides for concerting the policies of the three powers and for joint action by them in meeting the political and economic problems of liberated Europe in accordance with democratic principles. The text of the declaration is as follows:

The premier of the Union of Soviet Socialist Republics, the prime minister of the United Kingdom, and the president of the United States of America have consulted with each other in the common interests of the peoples of their countries and those of liberated Europe. They jointly declare their mutual agreement to concert during the temporary period of instability in liberated Europe the policies of their three governments in assisting the peoples liberated from the domination of Nazi Germany and the peoples of the former Axis satellite states of Europe to solve by democratic means their pressing political and economic problems.

The establishment of order in Europe and the rebuilding of national economic life must be achieved by processes which will enable the liberated peoples to destroy the last vestiges of Nazism and Fascism and to creat[e] democratic institutions of their own choice. This is a principle of the Atlantic Charter—the right of all peoples to choose the form of government under which they will live—the restoration of sovereign rights and self-government to those peoples who have been forcibly deprived of them by the aggressor nations.[2]

---

[1]In August and September 1944 representatives of the United States, Britain, China, and the Soviet Union met in Washington, D.C., at Dumbarton Oaks—formerly the estate of Mr. and Mrs. Robert Woods Bliss and now a research center for Byzantine studies, pre-Columbian studies, and landscape architecture—in order to draft proposals for creating a permanent international organization to be called the United Nations.

[2]In August 1941 Roosevelt and Churchill issued the Atlantic Charter. They pledged not to seek territorial aggrandizement, affirmed the right of national self-determination, and supported economic collaboration and free trade.

To foster the conditions in which the liberated peoples may exercise these rights, the three governments will jointly assist the people in any European liberated state or former Axis satellite state in Europe where in their judgment conditions require (1) to establish conditions of internal peace, (2) to carry out emergency measures for the relief of distressed people, (3) to form interim governmental authorities broadly representative of all democratic elements in the population and pledged to the earliest possible establishment through free elections of governments responsive to the will of the people, and (4) to facilitate where necessary the holding of such elections.

The three governments will consult the other United Nations and provisional authorities or other governments in Europe when matters of direct interest to them are under consideration.

When, in the opinion of the three governments, conditions in any European liberated state or any former Axis satellite state in Europe make such action necessary, they will immediately consult together on the measures necessary to discharge the joint responsibilities set forth in this declaration.

By this declaration we reaffirm our faith in the principles of the Atlantic Charter, our pledge in the Declaration by the United Nations, and our determination to build in cooperation with other peace-loving nations a world order under law, dedicated to peace, security, freedom, and the general well-being of all mankind.

In issuing this declaration, the three powers express the hope that the provisional government of the French republic may be associated with them in the procedure suggested.

VI

POLAND

We came to the Crimea Conference resolved to settle our differences about Poland. We discussed fully all aspects of the question. We reaffirm our common desire to see established a strong, free, independent and democratic Poland. As a result of our discussions we have agreed on the conditions in which a new Polish provisional government of national unity may be formed in such a manner as to command recognition by the three major powers.

The agreement reached is as follows:

A new situation has been created in Poland as a result of her complete liberation by the Red Army. This calls for the establishment of a Polish provisional government which can be more broadly based than was possible before the recent liberation of western Poland. The provisional government which is now functioning in Poland should therefore be reorganized on a broader democratic basis with the inclusion of democratic leaders from Poland itself and from Poles abroad. This new government should then be called the Polish provisional government of national unity.

M. Molotov, Mr. Harriman, and Sir A. Clark Kerr are authorized as a commission to consult in the first instance in Moscow with members of the present provisional government and with other Polish democratic leaders from within Poland and from abroad, with a view to the reorganization of the present government along the above lines. This Polish provisional government of national unity shall be pledged to the holding of free and unfettered elections as soon as possible on the basis of universal suffrage and secret ballot. In these elections all democratic and anti-Nazi parties shall have the right to take part and to put forward candidates.

When a Polish provisional government of national unity has been properly formed in conformity with the above, the government of the U.S.S.R., which now maintains diplomatic relations with the present provisional government of Poland, and the government of the United Kingdom and the government of the United States will establish diplomatic relations with the new Polish provisional government of national unity, and will exchange ambassadors by whose reports the respective governments will be kept informed about the situation in Poland.

The three heads of government consider that the eastern frontier of Poland should follow the Curzon line with digressions from it in some regions of five to eight kilometers in favor of Poland.[3] They recognize that Poland must receive substantial accessions of territory in the north and west. They feel that the opinion of the new Polish provisional government of national unity should be sought in due course on the extent of these accessions and that the final delimitation of the western frontier of Poland should thereafter await the peace conference.

VII

YUGOSLAVIA

We have agreed to recommend to Marshal Tito and Dr. Subasic that the agreement between them should be put into effect immediately and that a new government should be formed on the basis of that agreement.[4]

---

[3]Early in February 1919 the Supreme Allied Council appointed a commission to report on possible border solutions between Poland and Germany following World War I, and this commission went on to propose a tentative border between Russia and Poland. When the Soviets invaded Poland in 1920, the British prime minister directed his secretary of state for foreign affairs, Lord Curzon, to ask the Soviets to stop at this line, pending the convocation of a Russo–Polish peace conference. Before transmitting the message to the Soviets, the Foreign Office, perhaps under the influence of Lewis Namier, who later became a famous historian and was then on war duty in the Foreign Office, changed the original line to place Lvov in Soviet territory, a point that became important in World War II. Neither the Soviets nor the Poles accepted the proposal, and the Peace of Riga of 1921 established the Polish border far to the east of the Curzon line. In 1939 the Soviet Union seized eastern Poland to a point just beyond the Curzon line as part of its agreement with Hitler, and Stalin made retaining that territory one of his primary war aims. His suggestion at Teheran to accept the Curzon line as the eastern border of postwar Poland and to compensate the Poles with lands taken from eastern Germany by pushing the Polish border westward to the Oder and Neisse rivers was finally agreed to at Yalta, with minor modifications.

[4]In June 1944 Ivan Šubašić, representing the royal Yugoslav government in exile, and Josip Broz Tito, leader of the Yugoslav partisans (communists), agreed, both under pressure from Churchill, to establish a coalition government after the war. Šubašić became foreign minister, and a three-man regency was established until Yugoslavia's postwar system of government could be determined. In 1945, however, with the means of force entirely in their hands, the communists suppressed all other political movements, so that the Yugoslav constitution of November 29, 1945, established a party state on Stalinist principles.

We also recommend that as soon as the new government has been formed, it should declare that

> 1. The Anti-Fascist Assembly of National Liberation (AVNOJ) should be extended to include members of the last Yugoslav parliament (Skupschina) who have not compromised themselves by collaboration with the enemy, thus forming a body to be known as a temporary parliament; and
> 2. Legislative acts passed by the Anti-Fascist Assembly of National Liberation (AVNOJ) will be subject to subsequent ratification by a Constituent Assembly.

There was also a general review of other Balkan question[s].

VIII
MEETINGS OF FOREIGN SECRETARIES

Throughout the conference, besides the daily meetings of the heads of governments and the foreign secretaries, separate meetings of the three foreign secretaries, and their advisers have also been held daily.

These meetings have proved of the utmost value, and the conference agreed that permanent machinery should be set up for regular consultation between the three foreign secretaries. They will, therefore, meet as often as may be necessary, probably about every three or four months. These meetings will be held in rotation in the three capitals, the first meeting being held in London, after the United Nations conference on world organization.

IX
UNITY FOR PEACE AS FOR WAR

Our meeting here in the Crimea has reaffirmed our common determination to maintain and strengthen in the peace to come that unity of purpose and of action which has made victory possible and certain for the United Nations in this war. We believe that this is a sacred obligation which our governments owe to our peoples and to all the peoples of the world.

Only with continuing and growing cooperation and understanding among our three countries and among all the peace-loving nations can the highest aspiration of humanity be realized—a secure and lasting peace which will, in the words of the Atlantic Charter, "afford assurance that all the men in all the lands may live out their lives in freedom from fear and want."

Victory in this war and establishment of the proposed international organization will provide the greatest opportunity in all history to create in the years to come the essential conditions of such a peace.

WINSTON S. CHURCHILL
FRANKLIN D. ROOSEVELT
JOSEPH STALIN

2

The Yalta Negotiations

Charles E. Bohlen

February 1945

We took off from Malta in the middle of the night. Although we had no fighter escort, we flew over Yugoslavia, Bulgaria, and Romania, all of which were occupied in part by Axis troops. We landed about noon at an airfield at Saki which had been hurriedly repaired. Churchill arrived twenty minutes after the president [Franklin D. Roosevelt].

After being welcomed by a greeting party, headed by Molotov, we were offered refreshments, including vodka and champagne, caviar, smoked sturgeon, and black bread. The eighty-mile drive over the mountains to Yalta was made under lowering clouds that spat rain and a little wet snow. The road was lined with troops of at least two Soviet divisions, each soldier standing within sight of the next, for the entire eighty miles. As the presidential car passed (I was in the second car with Stettinius), the soldiers, many of them girls, snapped to the Russian salute—an abrupt move of the arm to put the rifle at a thirty-degree angle from the body. Repeated thousands of times, the salute was impressive. The drive took about five hours. Although the country was mostly uninhabited, we saw signs of destruction—gutted buildings and burned-out Nazi tanks. I believe that the wreckage Roosevelt saw on the drive hardened his view on Germany. "I'm more bloodthirsty than a year ago," he told Stalin when they met.

We arrived at Yalta about 6 P.M. It was already dark, and we were immediately shown to our accommodations in the white granite Livadiya Palace, which had been the summer home of the czars.

At 11 A.M. [the next day], there was a meeting of the top members of the American staff. After the president, who looked much better than at Malta, had said a few suitable words, there was a general discussion of the agenda for the conference.[1] Not much of substance was taken up. Realizing that we were in for

[1]On February 2, 1945, en route to Yalta, Roosevelt stopped off at Malta and met briefly with Churchill. Both attended a meeting of the Combined Chiefs of Staff, which had been in session for some days, but Roosevelt avoided political discussions, so that the meeting had little impact on overcoming the almost complete lack of planning for the Yalta talks.

Reprinted from *Witness to History, 1929–1969*, pp. 173–201, by Charles E. Bohlen, by permission of W. W. Norton & Company, Inc. Copyright © 1973 by W. W. Norton & Company, Inc.

difficult times at the conference, we were businesslike in our discussion. I felt no
great optimism; I do not think other Americans did, either.

Some of my soberness was due to a long letter from George Kennan that I had
received on my arrival at Yalta.[2] Kennan, who six months before had gone to
Moscow as counselor of the embassy, was deeply pessimistic about the future of
Europe. He saw almost no hope of cooperation with the Soviet Union in postwar
Europe. Disputing optimistic statements being made in the flush of military successes, Kennan foresaw unavoidable conflict arising between the Allied need for
stable, independent nations in Europe and a Soviet push to the west. Eloquently, he
argued his case:

> I am aware of the realities of this war, and of the fact that we were too weak to win
> it without Russian cooperation. I recognize that Russia's war effort has been mas-
> terful and effective and must, to a certain extent, find its reward at the expense of
> other peoples in eastern and central Europe.
>
> But with all of this, I fail to see why we must associate ourselves with this
> political program, so hostile to the interests of the Atlantic community as a whole,
> so dangerous to everything which we need to see preserved in Europe. Why could
> we not make a decent and definitive compromise with it—divide Europe frankly
> into spheres of influence—keep ourselves out of the Russian sphere and keep the
> Russians out of ours? That would have been the best thing we could do for
> ourselves and for our friends in Europe, and the most honest approach we could
> have tried to restore life, in the wake of war, on a dignified and stable foundation.
>
> Instead of this, what have we done? Although it was evident that the realities of
> the after-war were being shaped while the war was in progress we have consistently
> refused to make clear what our interests and our wishes were, in eastern and central
> Europe. We have refused to name any limit for Russian expansion and Russian
> responsibilities, thereby confusing the Russians and causing them constantly to
> wonder whether they are asking too little or whether it was some kind of a trap.

As an alternative program, Kennan suggested, in addition to the "partition of
Europe," the following:

> 1. That plans for the United Nations be buried "as quickly and quietly as
> possible," because the only practical effect of creating an international organization
> would be to commit the United States to defend a "swollen and unhealthy Russian
> sphere of power."
> 2. That the American people be corrected of the "dangerously erroneous im-
> pression that the security of the world depends on our assuming some formal
> blanket engagement to use our armed force in some given set of circumstances, as
> set forth in some legal documents." The United States must reserve to itself the
> right to decide where to use armed force.

[2]George Kennan was one of the first American foreign service officers to be trained in the Russian
language and culture. He helped open the Moscow embassy when the United States recognized the
Soviet Union in 1933 and returned as minister counselor in 1944, where he was at the time of writing his
letter to Bohlen, and as ambassador in 1952. His 1947 article in *Foreign Affairs,* which he signed with
the pseudonym X, is considered the essential statement of the postwar American policy of
"containment."

3. That the United States should write off eastern and southeastern Europe unless it possessed the will "to go whole hog" and oppose with all its physical and diplomatic resources Russian domination of the area.

4. That the United States "accept as an accomplished fact the complete partition of Germany" and begin consultations with the British and French about the formation of a Western European federation, which would include West German states.

Because I was so busy, I could write only a hasty reply:

I can't say I have given your letter the attention it deserves, but there is simply not time. As you know, there is a very great deal in your expositions that I agree with. You should know that in this connection the U.S. government is following admittedly a policy of no small risk. But have you ever seriously thought through the alternatives? The "constructive" suggestions that you make are frankly naive to a degree. They may well be the optimum from an abstract point of view. But as practical suggestions they are utterly impossible. Foreign policy of that kind cannot be made in a democracy. Only totalitarian states can make and carry out such policies. Furthermore, I don't for one minute believe that there has been any time in this war when we could seriously have done very differently than we did. It is easy to talk about instruments of pressure that we had in our hands. But the simple fact remains that if we wished to defeat Germany we could never have even tried to keep the Soviet armies out of Eastern Europe and Germany itself. I can never figure out why a piece of paper that you did not get should be regarded as so much more real than those you did get. Isn't it a question of realities and not of bits of paper? Either our pals intend to limit themselves or they don't. I submit, as the British say, that the answer is not yet clear. But what is clear is that the Soyuz [Soviet Union] is here to stay, as one of the major factors in the world. Quarreling with them would be so easy, but we can always come to that.

What I was saying so cryptically to Kennan was that as usual, I agreed in general with his analysis of the situation, but I thought he was far off target in his conclusions. I recall feeling quite strongly that to abandon the United Nations would be an error of the first magnitude. While I had my doubts about the ability of a world organization to prevent big-power aggression, I felt that it could keep the United States involved in world affairs without, as Kennan thought, committing us to use force when we did not want to.

As for the partition of Germany, the domination of Eastern Europe by the Soviet Union, and the general idea of dividing the Continent into spheres of influence, I could not go along with Kennan. To me, acceptance of a Soviet sphere, instead of relieving us of responsibility, would compound the felony. Any formal, or even an informal, attempt to give the Soviet Union a sphere of influence in Eastern Europe would, as soon as the agreement became known, have brought a loud and effective outcry from our own Poles and Czechs.

I had more hope than Kennan that the Yalta Conference might produce some kind of workable agreement. All the subjects were going to be discussed by the three leaders. I do not think that I had any illusions that the end of the war would usher in an era of good feeling between the Allies and the Soviet Union. Like Kennan, I knew too much about the Soviet Union to believe that. At the same time, my contacts with Roosevelt and Hopkins had tempered my realism about Bolshevism with a political fact of life. As hopeless as the outlook seemed, the United States must try to get along with the Soviets. The American people, who had fought a long, hard war, deserved at least an attempt to work out a better world. If the attempt failed, the United States could not be blamed for not trying.

In short, foreign policy in a democracy must take into account the emotions, beliefs, and goals of the people. The most carefully thought-out plans of the experts, even though 100 percent correct in theory, will fail without broad public support. The good leader in foreign affairs formulates his policy on expert advice and creates a climate of public opinion to support it.

Roosevelt, very much a political animal, went to the Yalta Conference keenly aware of American public opinion. With the war almost over in Europe, Americans wanted Soviet help in the final battle against Japan. Thus one major goal for Roosevelt at the conference was to pin down Stalin on the timing and the extent of entering the war in Asia. Roosevelt also realized that he might have scored only a temporary success in gaining public support during the war for an international organization, which he thought was the only device that could keep the United States from slipping back into isolationism. Thus his other major goal was an accord on the United Nations. The other important problems, principally Eastern Europe and Germany, had to be considered against the overriding importance of Roosevelt's two main goals.

The conference, which lasted for eight days, was organized in such a way that there was no orderly discussion and resolution of each problem by the leaders. Instead, issues were brought up, discussed, then shunted off to the foreign ministers or military chiefs or just dropped for a few hours. There was a plenary session of the three leaders every day at 4 P.M. and meetings of the foreign ministers and of the military chiefs every morning. In addition, there were private meetings between any two of the leaders, and discussions by all three at lunch and dinner.

It is a wonder that any agreements could emerge from such confusion. But the constant switch from one subject to another kept tempers cool. It is a matter of fact that despite the difficulties and disappointments, the atmosphere remained pleasant throughout the conference. The good feeling was evident on February 4, at the first Roosevelt–Stalin private meeting before the first plenary session. The two leaders greeted each other as old friends, and in a sense they were, having conferred in Teheran and exchanged many messages during the year. Smiling broadly, the president grasped Stalin by the hand and shook it warmly. Stalin, his face cracked in one of his rare, if slight, smiles, expressed pleasure at seeing the president again.

Underneath this gloss of goodwill, the three leaders were waging a fierce struggle on the shape of the postwar world. The decisions they reached on these questions, while hailed almost universally at the time as great accomplishments, ultimately came under such heavy attack, first from the right and later from the left, that Yalta is undoubtedly the most controversial conference in United States history. From my position at Roosevelt's side, I witnessed almost all the important exchanges with the Soviet Union.

The most difficult question of all at Yalta was Poland. The Soviets realized that since they had physical control over Poland, they could, in the last analysis, do pretty much what they wanted to with that country. On the other hand, they also realized that the British and American governments had a strong interest in Poland. The Western goal was absurdly simple—the right of the Poles to govern themselves, even if they chose a Communist government. The task of the Soviet diplomacy therefore was to retain a tight grip on Poland without causing an open break with the Western powers. In this regard, Stalin displayed a considerable astuteness, an extensive knowledge of the geographic elements of the problem, such as the location of the frontiers, and a tenacity in beating back one Western attempt after another to create conditions for a genuinely democratic government.

A sure clue to the gravity of the problem was Stalin's getting up and walking up and down behind his chair while expounding his points. His best debating skill stood out on the Polish question. When Roosevelt said he wanted the Polish election to be pure, like Caesar's wife, Stalin commented, "They said that about her but in fact she had her sins."

The frontiers of the new Poland, although not what we wanted, did not present a difficult problem. Churchill and Stalin had pretty much settled the issue at Teheran. The president did attempt to get Lvov and the adjacent oil fields returned to Poland, but Stalin refused. Churchill had second thoughts about his hasty giveaway of German land at Teheran. While still favoring the movement of Polish frontiers west, he said it would be a pity to stuff the Polish goose so full of German food that it got indigestion. Stalin brushed aside the argument by asserting that most of the Germans in the affected areas had run away from the advancing Red Army.

The real issue was the composition of the government which was to rule Poland pending the holding of elections. Stalin insisted that the provisional government which he had set up at Lublin should be recognized by London and Washington and that the Polish government in exile in London, which was anti-Communist, should be abandoned.[3] The American and British proposal called for the formation of a new interim government including Mikolajczyk, the peasant party leader with whom I had talked in London, and other moderate Poles abroad, as well as members of the Lublin regime.[4] We opposed the Lublin group as the sole representative because it was a purely Soviet creation.

It was not until the third plenary session, on February 6, that Poland was discussed. Drawing on the Mikolajczyk memorandum that I had given him, the president raised the possibility of creating a council composed of Polish leaders in Lublin and London. Churchill then emphasized how much Poland meant to Britain, which had gone to war to help Poland, and pleaded with Stalin to be magnanimous,

[3]The Lublin Committee refers to the Polish Committee of National Liberation established by Stalin as soon as the Red Army entered Polish territory in July 1944. Early in 1945 Stalin recognized it, along with additions from the Home National Council, another Soviet creature, as the provisional government of Poland. Only when persons representing the Polish government in exile were added in mid-1945 did the Western Allies recognize this government, even though communists and their supporters held sixteen out of the twenty portfolios.

[4]Stanisław Mikołajczyk was leader of the Polish Peasant party (PSL) and premier of the Polish government in exile in 1943–44. The most popular postwar Polish politician, in 1945 he agreed to enter the provisional government of national unity, but in 1947, after the communists used force to dominate the election held in that year, he went into exile.

to accept a solution that would leave Poland independent. The British prime minister asked if a new Polish government might not be formed at Yalta.

The appeal to Stalin's generosity was not, on the face of it, a bad tactic. It flattered his sense of power and gave him an opportunity to show magnanimity. But it did not work in this case. In his reply, Stalin said that he understood that Poland was a question of honor for Britain. But he pointed out that for the Soviets, Poland was a question of life and death as well as honor, because in thirty years it had twice served as an invasion corridor. He was adamant in refusing to budge from full support of the Lublin government. As for Churchill's suggestion that the Big Three create a new Polish government, Stalin cleverly replied, "I am called a dictator and not a democrat, but I have enough democratic feeling to refuse to create a Polish government without the Poles being consulted."

As we left the conference table that day, the Americans and British faced a formidable task in trying to salvage anything on Poland. We were up against a simple fact: the Red Army held most of the country; Stalin had the power to enforce his will. But the President would not give up so easily. That night, he instructed me to draft a letter to Stalin incorporating Mikolajczyk's idea. I composed a letter which, after slight changes, was sent to Stalin. [In this letter Roosevelt suggested that leaders of the various Polish factions come to Yalta to discuss the composition of a provisional government.]

At the fourth plenary session the next day, February 7, Stalin adroitly rejected the Roosevelt proposition and had Molotov introduce the Soviet plan, which was the basis for the final agreement on Poland. This plan called for adding to the Lublin Committee some democratic leaders from Polish émigré circles, with the enlarged temporary regime holding elections as soon as possible. While we could not accept this plan without writing in safeguards, we did see in it the seeds of an acceptable compromise. In a counterproposal the following day, the United States called for a committee of three representatives of the big powers to invite Polish leaders from inside and outside the country to a meeting in Moscow to form an interim government of national unity that would hold free elections for a permanent government. Molotov, while treating the proposal with respect, skillfully stripped away its key points and modified others so that little substance was left.

At Roosevelt's suggestion, the Polish issue was referred to the foreign ministers to work out the details of a compromise. I had occasionally attended the foreign ministers' meetings as an observer when it was certain there was no chance of any Roosevelt–Stalin meetings and sat in on this session on February 9. I did not interpret for Stettinius but did help draft a paper, which I think, in retrospect, went much too far in meeting Molotov's demands. This document proposed that the Lublin group be reorganized into a "fully representative government" based on all democratic forces, including democratic leaders in Poland and abroad. This draft required representatives of the three powers to verify the holding of a free election.

Molotov, as expected, objected to the American draft's call for a "fully representative government" as a repudiation of the Lublin government. His wording was for a reorganization "on a wider democratic basis," implying that the Lublin group was indeed democratic but should be made somewhat more so. He also wished to add to the description of parties allowed to participate in elections the words "non-

Fascist and anti-Fascists," and favored elimination of the responsibilities of the three Allied governments in regard to watching the elections. At a meeting of the American delegation, I warned that the term "anti-Fascist" was too broad, since "Fascist" might easily be interpreted to mean anybody who opposed a Communist government in Poland. The statement was modified to read, "all democratic and anti-Nazi parties."

That evening, at a meeting of the foreign ministers at Stalin's villa, the formula for Poland was finally agreed to. The key paragraphs in the final agreement on Poland, which became a subject of bitter controversy, read as follows:

> A new situation has been created in Poland as a result of her complete liberation by the Red Army. This calls for the establishment of a Polish provisional government which can be more broadly based than was possible before the recent liberation of Western Poland. The provisional government which is now functioning in Poland should be reorganized on a broader democratic basis with the inclusion of democratic leaders from Poland itself and from Poles abroad. This new government should then be called the Polish provisional government of national unity.
>
> Mr. Molotov, Mr. Harriman, and Sir Archibald Clark Kerr [the American and British ambassadors to Russia] are authorized to consult in the first instance in Moscow with members of the present provisional government and with other Polish democratic leaders from within Poland and from abroad with a view to the reorganization of the present government along the above lines. This Polish provisional government of national unity shall be pledged to the holding of free and unfettered elections as soon as possible on the basis of universal suffrage and secret ballot. In these elections all democratic and anti-Nazi parties shall have the right to take part and put forward candidates.

The meaning of these paragraphs, even reread today in the light of what actually happened, is clear. But they were not specific enough and bore the mark of hasty drafting. The number of non-Lublin Poles from within and without Poland is not even indicated. The phrase "in the first instance" seemed clear enough to us at Yalta and still does. But Harriman, Clark Kerr, and Polish émigré representatives soon discovered that the Soviets were interpreting "in the first instance" to mean that the negotiations in Moscow should only be with the members of the Lublin government and not to mean, as the English text clearly indicates, that the first meeting should be in Moscow rather than Warsaw. I do not believe the Soviets put the words "in the first instance" in the agreement with the idea of misinterpreting them later. Rather, I believe the Russians, in studying the text afterward, saw in this phrase a loophole allowing them to promote their own cause. The fact that we did not spot the loophole is another example of the lack of care that the Western Allies occasionally showed in their dealings with the Soviets, to whom even the last comma had meaning. Too often, we were more concerned not to appear to be nit-picking than with defending a position by carefully watching small points.

The next day, the last problem was resolved at a meeting of the foreign ministers with the American withdrawal of its insistence on Allied supervision of the elections. Stettinius, I believe, obtained this concession from the president. I was not present and therefore do not know the details of the conversation.

Roosevelt has been criticized for not doing more for Poland at Yalta. I cannot agree. The concessions that he and Churchill made in their eagerness to avoid a split were perhaps a mistake, but the agreement, although not what the West had wanted, appeared to us, with some doubts, as acceptable. Had it been fully observed, Poland conceivably would be an independent country today.

I do not presume to know what was going on in Roosevelt's mind, but from what he said at Yalta and from his actions there, I feel that he did everything he could to help the Poles. He was not acting out of any sympathy for the London Poles (although he had met and admired Mikolajczyk) and was not trying to install an anti-Soviet regime in Warsaw. He only wanted to give the Polish people, whose country had been overrun and brutalized by the Nazis and who then faced domination by the Soviet Union, the right to choose their own government. He was trying to balance domestic political considerations—strong Polish sentiment in the United States—with his diplomatic goal of maintaining Allied unity by recognizing the Soviet determination to protect its western flank. The compromise failed because Stalin insisted on more than security against attack; he wanted to establish the Soviet system of authoritarian control of every aspect of life in Poland. The Red Army gave Stalin the power he needed to carry out his wishes, regardless of his promises at Yalta. Stalin held all the cards and played them well. Eventually, we had to throw in our hand.

There was one other subject that dealt with our relations with Eastern Europe. This was an American proposal for a Declaration on Liberated Europe. The draft, prepared by the Department of State, called for consultation among the three major powers regarding development in liberated countries to guarantee the establishment of democratic governments. When President Roosevelt presented the proposal on February 10, Stalin, surprisingly enough, had only one amendment to offer. This addition referred to the need to support "those people in these countries who took an active part in the struggle against German occupation." We felt that it was a great mistake to include anything of this kind, because it would give the Soviets an opportunity to push their own followers at the expense of others. Stalin's amendment was turned down, and he did not argue the point.

The declaration was adopted. Had it been implemented by the Soviet Union, it would have radically changed the face of Eastern Europe. Almost all of the protests over Soviet policies in Eastern Europe contained a reference to the declaration. But all Soviet actions, from Vishinsky's forcing of a Communist-dominated government on Romania within a week after the close of the Yalta Conference to moves in Poland, Bulgaria, Hungary, and Czechoslovakia, were made without even a semblance of consultation with Britain or the United States. I have often wondered why Stalin agreed to the declaration.

The closing hours of Yalta were similar to other conferences. There was great confusion and a good deal of irritation and squabbling among members of our own delegation over the wording of the final communiqué.

We finished the job in the middle of the night and then piled into automobiles for the eighty-mile drive back to the airport at Saki. I doubt if anybody was thinking very much about the conference as a whole or assessing its successes and its failures. Although there was a sense of frustration and some bitterness in regard to Poland, the general mood was one of satisfaction.

Each of the three leaders had achieved his major goals. Roosevelt had obtained Stalin's pledge to open a second front against the Japanese and acceptance of a voting formula that would give the United Nations a chance to work. These seemed like immense achievements indeed. Large American casualties in the final assault on Japan might be avoided with Soviet help. As for the United Nations, the agreement meant that Roosevelt had apparently avoided President [Woodrow] Wilson's mistake of waiting until after the war, when isolationist feelings returned, to solve the problems. Churchill had also achieved his goal of creating a counterweight to the Soviet Union on the Continent by building up France. Stalin had fought off the Western Allies' attempts to modify his grasp on Poland, thus ensuring his domination of Eastern Europe, and had struck a profitable bargain in Asia.

In each case, the results could hardly be looked on at that time as triumph or defeat for anyone. Rather, the agreements seemed to us to be realistic compromises between the various positions of each country. Stalin had made a genuine concession in finally agreeing to France as one of the powers occupying Germany. Each country altered its position on the United Nations. The United States and Britain had given in a great deal on Poland, but the plan as finally agreed to could have led to a genuinely democratic government if it had been carried out.

In short, there was hope, as we left Yalta, of genuine cooperation with the Soviet Union on political questions after the war. Kennan's gloomy assessment, which I had read on my first day at Yalta, had not yet proved correct. It would take Stalin's refusal to carry out his bargain on Poland, his disregard of the Declaration on Liberated Europe, and other actions to extinguish our hopes for Soviet cooperation.

Even with all the advantages of hindsight, however, I do not believe that the Western Allies could have walked away from the attempt to reach an understanding with the Soviet Union. Nor do I believe that through harder bargaining we could have struck a better deal with Stalin. Certainly spheres of influence were not the answer. The fault was not the agreements at Yalta but something far deeper. Regardless of all that was said or not said, written or not written, agreed to or not agreed to at the Yalta Conference, there was nothing that could have prevented the breakup of the victorious coalition and the onset of the cold war once Stalin set his course.

Spheres of Influence

Yalta may be the symbol of the abandonment of Eastern Europe by the West, but in fact most of the decisions concerning borders and spheres of influence had been made before then, particularly at Teheran (Iran) regarding Poland, and in a meeting held in Moscow between Churchill and Stalin in October 1944 concerning central and southeast Europe. The next two short readings give a sense of the way in which these decisions were made. The first, again by Bohlen, discusses the initial agreement among the Big Three on postwar Polish borders, whereas the second is Churchill's account of his percentages agreement with Stalin. The Teheran agreement displaced Poland about 150 kilometers to the west. Negotiations between the British and the Soviets in the spring of 1944 preceded the percentages agreement, and much haggling over the exact numbers in the percentages followed the meeting between Churchill and Stalin. Churchill was convinced that Stalin had kept his word in Greece, which was his main concern. In fact, after the preliminary arrangement was concluded in the spring of 1944, the Greek communists suddenly became much more amenable to the reimposition of British influence there. In return, of course, Stalin expected a free hand in Bulgaria and Romania. President Roosevelt was not fully apprised of the final percentages agreement and would not have supported it, as he believed such arrangements should be put off until the peace conference that he fully expected would be held at the conclusion of the war. Churchill's brief account also suggests the great pressure he was putting on the Polish government in exile to reach an accommodation with Stalin.

3

Poland at the Teheran Conference
Charles E. Bohlen
December 1943

At the final plenary session that evening, Roosevelt did not take part in the discussion regarding Poland. As Churchill and Stalin talked over the problem, I noticed that the British and the Russians were working on a map of Poland torn from *The Times* of London. Since we had brought a collection of books with various maps touching on the Polish issue, I asked the president whether he would have any objection to my lending a copy to Stalin and Churchill to make their discussion easier. The president gave me permission, and I took a book over to Stalin, who looked at one map and asked me on what data these lines had been drawn. The map showed the ethnic divisions of eastern Poland. I informed the marshal that as far as I knew, the only data available came from Polish sources. Stalin grunted and took his ever-present red pencil and somewhat contemptuously marked the map to show what would be returned to the Poles and what would be kept for the Soviet Union.

During their discussion, Stalin and Churchill virtually agreed on the future borders of Poland. The frontiers included the Curzon line in the east, with modifications as Stalin had indicated, and the Oder–Neisse line in the west. In other words, the new Poland would give up Poland's eastern areas to Russia in return for parts of eastern Germany. This understanding, which was entirely oral, led to further confusion later on because there were two rivers Neisse, a western and an eastern, and there was no mention of which one they were talking about. The division that Churchill and Stalin agreed to is the one that still exists.

It was a great mistake for Roosevelt to tell Stalin in the private conference of the last day that for electoral reasons he could not take any position on Polish affairs, to say nothing of the error in implying to Stalin, as he did, that the United States would do little for the Baltic countries.[1] By imposing on himself an unnecessary silence

---

[1]According to the terms of the Ribbentrop–Molotov agreement of August 25, 1939, Latvia, Lithuania, and Estonia, which had been independent since 1917 and 1918, were assigned to the Soviet sphere of influence. In 1940 Stalin annexed the three countries as separate republics in the Soviet Union. One of the criticisms of British and American foreign policies both in the early war years and later was that they did not protest this action with sufficient vigor, although the United States never formally recognized the disappearance of these states, and each of the exile governments continued to have a representative

Reprinted from *Witness to History, 1929–1969*, p.152, by Charles E. Bohlen, by permission of W. W. Norton & Company, Inc. Copyright © 1973 by W. W. Norton & Company, Inc.

during the discussion of Polish matters the last day, Roosevelt seemed to give his implied, although unstated, acquiescence to the Churchill–Stalin agreement on Polish frontiers. It is, of course, true that the question of the Polish government, which was subsequently to be a bitter source of controversy at Yalta, did not arise at Teheran.

---

in Washington. After the collapse of the Soviet Union, the three Baltic states reestablished their independence.

4

The Percentages Agreement

Winston S. Churchill

October 9, 1944

We alighted at Moscow on the afternoon of October 9 and were received very heartily and with full ceremonial by Molotov and many high Russian personages. This time we were lodged in Moscow itself, with every care and comfort. I had one small, perfectly appointed house, and Anthony another nearby.[1] We were glad to dine alone together and rest. At ten o'clock that night we held our first important meeting in the Kremlin. There were only Stalin, Molotov, Eden, Harriman, and I, with Major Birse and Pavlov as interpreters. It was agreed to invite the Polish prime minister, M. Romer, the foreign secretary, and M. Grabski, a gray-bearded and aged academician of much charm and quality, to Moscow at once. I telegraphed accordingly to M. Mikolajczyk that we were expecting him and his friends for discussions with the Soviet Government and ourselves, as well as with the Lublin Polish Committee. I made it clear that refusal to come to take part in the conversations would amount to a definite rejection of our advice and would relieve us from further responsibility toward the London Polish government.

The moment was apt for business, so I said, "Let us settle about our affairs in the Balkans. Your armies are in Romania and Bulgaria. We have interests, missions, and agents there. Don't let us get at cross-purposes in small ways. So far as Britain and Russia are concerned, how would it do for you to have 90 percent predominance in Romania, for us to have 90 percent of the say in Greece, and go fifty–fifty about Yugoslavia?" While this was being translated I wrote out on a half-sheet of paper:

Romania	
Russia	90%
The others	10%
Greece	
Great Britain	90%
(in accord with United States)	
Russia	10%

---

[1] "Anthony" is Anthony Eden, British foreign secretary.

Yugoslavia	50–50%
Hungary	50–50%
Bulgaria	
Russia	75%
The others	25%

I pushed this across to Stalin, who had by then heard the translation. There was a slight pause. Then he took his blue pencil and made a large tick upon it, and passed it back to us. It was all settled in no more time than it takes to set down.

Of course we had long and anxiously considered our point, and were only dealing with immediate wartime arrangements. All larger questions were reserved on both sides for what we then hoped would be a peace table when the war was won.

After this there was a long silence. The penciled paper lay in the center of the table. At length I said, "Might it not be thought rather cynical if it seemed we had disposed of these issues, so fateful to millions of people, in such an offhand manner? Let us burn the paper." "No, you keep it," said Stalin.

The Truman Doctrine and the Two-Camp Policy

Postwar antagonisms between the two superpowers became official policy in 1947. A year earlier the Greek communists, frustrated by their lost opportunities in 1944, defied Stalin's deal with Churchill and rose in revolt, supported by Marshal Josip Broz Tito of Yugoslavia. When a weakened Great Britain concluded early in 1947 that it was no longer able to maintain the obligations of empire, which meant in part giving up its support of the conservative Greek government against the communists, President Harry S. Truman concluded that the United States would have to take over the task. In March 1947, in a speech reprinted in part here, he proposed giving assistance to two threatened states, Greece and Turkey, and later that year the United States announced a program of economic aid to Europe that became known as the Marshall Plan. The notion of containing communism informed American foreign policy for the next forty years.

During World War II, Stalin rallied the support of the Soviet peoples by relaxing some of the strict social controls that had characterized the 1930s. When the war ended, many Soviets hoped that their courageous exertions and enormous sacrifices against Hitler would be rewarded by a continuation of this relaxation. Stalin quickly disabused them of this hope. Under the direction of Andrei Zhdanov, the Soviets returned to the strictest regulation of all areas of life, stifling the slightest hint of independent or critical thinking and exalting Stalin to godlike proportions.

In Eastern Europe, however, for the first year or two after the war, Stalin permitted the "peoples' democracies" that the Red Army had imposed on Bulgaria, Romania, and Poland to pursue, within strict limits, moderately varied policies. In Hungary and Czechoslovakia, which remained more or less constitutional states, the communist parties entered an uneasy coalition with the other parties, albeit keeping in their hands control of the police and the army. When the United States followed the enunciation of the Truman Doctrine with the announcement in the summer of 1947 of the Marshall Plan, Stalin evidently decided it was time to tighten his control over Eastern Europe.

In September 1947 the representatives of the communist parties of Eastern Europe met at Szklarska Poręba, a resort town in Poland, where Stalin had his most loyal allies, the Yugoslavs, promulgate the new line. To ensure that it be carried out effectively, the assembled parties created the Communist Information Bureau, or Cominform. The abandonment of all pretense to coalition politics in the peoples' democracies had an immediate impact in consolidating communist rule in Hungary, and within six months Czechoslovakia had become a communist state. The text included here reproduces portions of Zhdanov's speech at Szklarska Poręba. A good example of postwar Stalinist rhetoric, it restates the two-camp theory that was a fundamental part of Stalin's worldview and that Zhdanov propagated on his behalf after the end of World War II.[1] The curious thing is how closely Truman's perception of the postwar world matched Stalin's in this regard.

---

[1] In 1919 Stalin wrote, "The world has split decisively and irrevocably into two camps. The struggle between them is the entire axis of contemporary life" (quoted by Robert C. Tucker, *Stalin as Revolutionary* [New York: Norton, 1973], p. 449). Compare Lenin, who in 1902 wrote, *"The only choice is:* Either bourgeois, or Socialist ideology. There is no middle course" (*State and Revolution* [New York: International Publishers, 1943], p. 41).

5

The Truman Doctrine

Harry S. Truman

March 12, 1947

MR. PRESIDENT, MR. SPEAKER, MEMBERS OF THE CONGRESS OF THE UNITED STATES:

The gravity of the situation which confronts the world today necessitates my appearance before a joint session of the Congress.

The foreign policy and the national security of this country are involved.

One aspect of the present situation, which I wish to present to you at this time for your consideration and decision, concerns Greece and Turkey.

The Greek government has asked for the assistance of experienced American administrators, economists, and technicians to ensure that the financial and other aid given to Greece shall be used effectively in creating a stable and self-sustaining economy and in improving its public administration.

The very existence of the Greek state is today threatened by the terrorist activities of several thousand armed men, led by communists, who defy the government's authority at a number of points, particularly along the northern boundaries. A commission appointed by the United Nations Security Council is at present investigating disturbed conditions in northern Greece and alleged border violations along the frontier between Greece on the one hand and Albania, Bulgaria, and Yugoslavia on the other.

Meanwhile, the Greek government is unable to cope with the situation. The Greek army is small and poorly equipped. It needs supplies and equipment if it is to restore authority to the government throughout Greek territory.

The British government, which has been helping Greece, can give no further financial or economic aid after March 31. Great Britain finds itself under the necessity of reducing or liquidating its commitments in several parts of the world, including Greece.

Greece's neighbor, Turkey, also deserves our attention.

The future of Turkey as an independent and economically sound state is clearly no less important to the freedom-loving peoples of the world than the future of Greece. The circumstances in which Turkey finds itself today are considerably

Reprinted from *A Decade of American Foreign Policy: Basic Documents, 1941–49*, prepared at the request of the Senate Committee on Foreign Relations by the staff of the committee and the Department of State (Washington, D.C.: U.S. Government Printing Office, 1950), pp. 1253–56.

different from those of Greece. Turkey has been spared the disasters that have beset Greece. And during the war the United States and Great Britain furnished Turkey with material aid.

Nevertheless, Turkey now needs our support.

Since the war Turkey has sought additional financial assistance from Great Britain and the United States for the purpose of effecting that modernization necessary for the maintenance of its national integrity.

That integrity is essential to the preservation of order in the Middle East.

The British government has informed us that, owing to its own difficulties, it can no longer extend financial or economic aid to Turkey.

As in the case of Greece, if Turkey is to have the assistance it needs, the United States must supply it. We are the only country able to provide that help.

I am fully aware of the broad implications involved if the United States extends assistance to Greece and Turkey, and I shall discuss these implications with you at this time.

One of the primary objectives of the foreign policy of the United States is the creation of conditions in which we and other nations will be able to work out a way of life free from coercion. This was a fundamental issue in the war with Germany and Japan. Our victory was won over countries which sought to impose their will, and their way of life, upon other nations.

To ensure the peaceful development of nations, free from coercion, the United States has taken a leading part in establishing the United Nations. The United Nations is designed to make possible lasting freedom and independence for all its members. We shall not realize our objectives, however, unless we are willing to help free peoples to maintain their free institutions and their national integrity against aggressive movements that seek to impose upon them totalitarian regimes. This is no more than a frank recognition that totalitarian regimes imposed upon free peoples, by direct or indirect aggression, undermine the foundations of international peace and hence the security of the United States.

The peoples of a number of countries of the world have recently had totalitarian regimes forced upon them against their will. The government of the United States has made frequent protests against coercion and intimidation, in violation of the Yalta agreement, in Poland, Romania, and Bulgaria. I must also state that in a number of other countries there have been similar developments.

At the present moment in world history nearly every nation must choose between alternative ways of life. The choice is too often not a free one.

One way of life is based upon the will of the majority and is distinguished by free institutions, representative government, free elections, guarantees, of individual liberty, freedom of speech and religion, and freedom from political oppression.

The second way of life is based upon the will of a minority forcibly imposed upon the majority. It relies upon terror and oppression, a controlled press and radio, fixed elections, and the suppression of personal freedoms.

I believe that it must be the policy of the United States to support free peoples who are resisting attempted subjugation by armed minorities or by outside pressures.

I believe that we must assist free peoples to work out their own destinies in their own way.

I believe that our help should be primarily through economic and financial aid which is essential to economic stability and orderly political processes.

The world is not static, and the status quo is not sacred. But we cannot allow changes in the status quo in violation of the Charter of the United Nations by such methods as coercion or by such subterfuges as political infiltration. In helping free and independent nations to maintain their freedom, the United States will be giving effect to the principles of the Charter of the United Nations.

It is necessary only to glance at a map to realize that the survival and integrity of the Greek nation are of grave importance in a much wider situation. If Greece should fall under the control of an armed minority, the effect upon its neighbor, Turkey, would be immediate and serious. Confusion and disorder might well spread throughout the entire Middle East.

Moreover, the disappearance of Greece as an independent state would have a profound effect upon those countries in Europe whose peoples are struggling against great difficulties to maintain their freedoms and their independence while they repair the damages of war.

It would be an unspeakable tragedy if these countries, which have struggled so long against overwhelming odds, should lose that victory for which they sacrificed so much. Collapse of free institutions and loss of independence would be disastrous not only for them but for the world. Discouragement and possibly failure would quickly be the lot of neighboring peoples striving to maintain their freedom and independence.

Should we fail to aid Greece and Turkey in this fateful hour, the effect will be far-reaching to the West as well as to the East.

6

The Two-Camp Policy

Andrei Zhdanov

September 1947

The end of the Second World War brought with it big changes in the world situation. The military defeat of the bloc of fascist states, the character of the war as a war of liberation from fascism, and the decisive role played by the Soviet Union in the vanquishing of the fascist aggressors sharply altered the alignment of forces between the two systems—the Socialist and the Capitalist—in favor of Socialism.

What is the essential nature of these changes?

The principal outcome of World War II was the military defeat of Germany and Japan—the two most militaristic and aggressive of the capitalist countries. The reactionary imperialist elements all over the world, notably in Britain, America, and France, had reposed great hopes in Germany and Japan and chiefly in Hitler's Germany: firstly as in a force most capable of inflicting a blow on the Soviet Union in order to, if not having it destroyed altogether, weaken it at least and undermine its influence; secondly, as in a force capable of smashing the revolutionary labor and democratic movement in Germany herself and in all countries singled out for Nazi aggression and thereby strengthening capitalism generally. This was the chief reason for the prewar policy of "appeasement" and encouragement of fascist aggression, the so-called Munich policy consistently pursued by the imperialist ruling circles of Britain, France, and the United States.

But the hopes reposed by the British, French, and American imperialists in the Hitlerites were not realized. The Hitlerites proved to be weaker, and the Soviet Union and the freedom-loving nations stronger than the Munichists had anticipated. As the result of World War II the major forces of bellicose international fascist reaction had been smashed and put out of commission for a long time to come.

Of all the capitalist powers, only one—the United States—emerged from the war not only unweakened but even considerably stronger economically and militarily. The war greatly enriched the American capitalists. The American people on the other hand, did not experience the privations that accompany war, the hardship of occupation, or aerial bombardment; and since America entered the war practically in its concluding stage, when the issue was already decided, her human casualties were relatively small. For the United States of America, the war was

Reprinted from *For a Lasting Peace, for a People's Democracy* [organ of the Cominform], November 10, 1947.

primarily and chiefly a spur to extensive industrial development and to a substantial increase of exports (principally to Europe).

But the end of the war confronted the United States with a number of new problems. The capitalist monopolies were anxious to maintain their profits at the former high level and accordingly pressed hard to prevent a reduction of the wartime volume of deliveries. But this meant that the United States must retain the foreign markets which had absorbed American products during the war, and moreover, acquire new markets, inasmuch as the war had substantially lowered the purchasing power of most of the countries. The financial and economic dependence of these countries on the United States of America had likewise increased. The United States extended credits abroad to a sum of $19,000 million, not counting investments in the International Bank and the International Currency Fund. America's principal competitors, Germany and Japan, have disappeared from the world market, and this has opened up new and very considerable opportunities for the United States. Whereas before World War II the more influential reactionary circles of American imperialism had adhered to an isolationist policy and had refrained from active interference in the affairs of Europe and Asia, in the new, postwar conditions the Wall Street bosses adopted a new policy. They advanced a program of utilizing America's military and economic might, not only to retain and consolidate the positions won abroad during the war, but to expand them to the maximum and to replace Germany, Japan and Italy in the world market.

But America's aspirations to world supremacy encounter an obstacle in the U.S.S.R., the stronghold of anti-imperialist and antifascist policy, and its growing international influence, in the new democracies, which have escaped from the control of British and American imperialism, and in the workers of all countries, including America itself, who do not want a new war for the supremacy of their oppressors. Accordingly, the new expansionist and reactionary policy of the United States envisages a struggle against the U.S.S.R., against the labor movement in all countries, including the United States, and against the emancipationist, anti-imperialist forces in all countries.

Alarmed by the achievements of Socialism in the U.S.S.R., by the achievements of the new democracies, and by the postwar growth of the labor and democratic movement in all countries, the American reactionaries are disposed to take upon themselves the mission of "saviors" of the capitalist system from communism.

The frank expansionist program of the United States is therefore highly reminiscent of the reckless program, which failed so ignominiously, of the fascist aggressors, who, as we know, also made a bid for world supremacy.

Just as the Hitlerites, when they were making their preparations for piratical aggression, adopted the camouflage of anticommunism in order to make it possible to oppress and enslave all peoples and primarily and chiefly their own people, America's present-day ruling circles mask their expansionist policy, and even their offensive against the vital interests of their weaker imperialist rival, Great Britain, by fictious considerations of defense against communism.

The fundamental changes caused by the war on the international scene and in the position of individual countries has entirely changed the political landscape of the world. A new alignment of political forces has arisen. The more the war recedes into the past, the more distinct become two major trends in postwar international policy, corresponding to the division of the political forces operating on the international arena into two major camps: the imperialist and antidemocratic camp, on the one hand, and the anti-imperialist and democratic camp, on the other. The principal driving force of the imperialist camp is the United States of America. Allied with it are Great Britain and France. The existence of the Attlee–Bevin Labour government in Britain and the Ramadier socialist government in France does not hinder these countries from playing the part of satellites of the United States and following the lead of its imperialist policy on all major questions. The imperialist camp is also supported by colony-owning countries, such as Belgium and Holland, by countries with reactionary antidemocratic regimes, such as Turkey and Greece, and by countries politically and economically dependent on the United States, such as the Near Eastern and South American countries and China.

The cardinal purpose of the imperialist camp is to strengthen imperialism, to hatch a new imperialist war, to combat socialism and democracy and to support reactionary and antidemocratic profascist regimes and movements everywhere.

In the pursuit of these ends the imperialist camp is prepared to rely on reactionary and antidemocratic forces in all countries, and to support its former adversaries in the war against its wartime allies.

The antifascist forces comprise the second camp. This camp is based on the U.S.S.R. and the new democracies. It also includes countries that have broken with imperialism and have firmly set foot on the path of democratic development, such as Romania, Hungary, and Finland. Indonesia and Vietnam are associated with it; it has the sympathy of India, Egypt, and Syria. The anti-imperialist camp is backed by the labor and democratic movement and by the fraternal communist parties in all countries, by the fighters for national liberation in the colonies and dependencies, by all progressive and democratic forces in every country. The purpose of this camp is to resist the threat of new wars and imperialist expansion, to strengthen democracy and to extirpate the vestiges of fascism.

In their ideological struggle against the U.S.S.R., the American imperialists, who have no great insight into political questions, demonstrate their ignorance by laying primary stress on the allegation that the Soviet Union is undemocratic and totalitarian, while the United States and Great Britain and the whole capitalist world are democratic. On this platform of ideological struggle—on this defense of bourgeois pseudodemocracy and condemnation of Communism as totalitarian—are united all the enemies of the working class without exception, from the capitalist magnates to the right socialist leaders, who seize with the greatest eagerness on any slanderous imputations against the U.S.S.R. suggested to them by their imperialist masters. The pith and substance of this fraudulent propaganda are the claim that the earmark of true democracy is the existence of a plurality of parties and of an organized opposition minority. On these grounds the British Labourites, who spare no effort in their fight against communism, would like to discover antagonistic classes and a corresponding struggle of parties in the U.S.S.R. Political ignoramuses that they are, they cannot understand that capitalists and landlords, antagonistic classes, and hence a plurality of parties, have long ceased to exist in the

U.S.S.R. They would like to have in the U.S.S.R. the bourgeois parties which are so dear to their hearts, including pseudosocialistic parties, as an agency of imperialism. But to their bitter regret, these parties of the exploiting bourgeoisie have been doomed by history to disappear from the scene.

The laborists and other advocates of bourgeois democracy will go to any length to slander the Soviet regime, but at the same time they regard the bloody dictatorship of the fascist minority over the people in Greece and Turkey as perfectly normal, they close their eyes to many crying violations even of formal democracy in the bourgeois countries, and say nothing about the national and racial oppression, the corruption and the unceremonious abrogation of democratic rights in the United States of America.

The "Truman Doctrine," which provides for the rendering of American assistance to all reactionary regimes which actively oppose the democratic peoples, bears a frankly aggressive character. Its announcement caused some dismay even among circles of American capitalists that are accustomed to anything. Progressive public elements in the United States of America and other countries vigorously protested against the provocative and frankly imperialistic character of Truman's announcement.

The unfavorable reception which the "Truman Doctrine" was met with accounts for the necessity of the appearance of the "Marshall Plan," which is a more carefully veiled attempt to carry through the same expansionist policy.

The vague and deliberately guarded formulations of the "Marshall Plan," amount in essence to a scheme to create a bloc of states bound by obligations to the United States and to grant American credits to European countries as a recompense for their renunciation of economic, and then of political, independence. Moreover, the cornerstone of the "Marshall Plan" is the restoration of the industrial areas of Western Germany controlled by the American monopolies.

It is the design of the "Marshall Plan," as transpired from the subsequent talks and the statements of American leaders, to render aid in the first place, not to the impoverished victor countries, America's allies in the fight against Germany, but to the German capitalists, with the idea of bringing under American sway the major sources of coal and iron needed by Europe and by Germany and of making the countries which are in need of coal and iron dependent on the restored economic might of Germany.

In view of the fact that the majority of the leaders of the Socialist parties (especially the British Labourites and the French Socialists) are acting as agents of United States imperialist circles, there has devolved upon the Communists the special historical task of leading the resistance to the American plan for the enthrallment of Europe and of boldly denouncing all coadjutors of American imperialism in their own countries. At the same time, Communists must support all the really patriotic elements who do not want their countries to be imposed upon, who want to resist enthrallment of their countries to foreign capital, and to uphold their national sovereignty. The Communists must be the leaders in enlisting all antifascist and freedom-loving elements in the struggle against the new American expansionist plans for the enslavement of Europe.

The chief danger to the working class at this present juncture lies in underrating its own strength and overrating the strength of the enemy. Just as in the past the Munich policy untied the hands of the Nazi aggressors, so today concessions to the new course of the United States and the imperialist camp may encourage its inspirers to be even more insolent and aggressive. The Communist parties must therefore head the resistance to the plans of imperialist expansion and aggression along every line—state, economic, and ideological; they must rally their ranks and unite their efforts on the basis of a common anti-imperialist and democratic platform, and gather around them all the democratic and patriotic forces of the people.

Stalinists

One of the participants in the Szklarska Poręba meeting was Jakub Berman, a member of the top leadership of the Polish United Workers' [Communist] party that Stalin and the Red Army imposed on Poland in 1945 and 1946. Berman was a "Muscovite," as were many of the new leaders in the communist states of Eastern Europe, in the sense that he had spent much of World War II in the Soviet Union. He remained in power until 1956. In 1980, under the relatively relaxed conditions of Solidarity Poland, Teresa Torańska conducted a series of interviews with several old-line Polish communists, including Berman. The remarkable thing is not that Berman remained unrepentant, or that after forty years he still repeated Zhdanov's arguments, but that he was not alone in the early postwar period in his enthusiasm for the new regime. Many were fed up with the squabbling of interwar parliaments, the narrow religious or nationalistic views of the old politicians, and the economic backwardness of their countries. Berman's justifications and passions reflect the worldview of the men and women who imposed Stalinism for what seemed to them good reasons.

Those who were not enthusiastic about the new system, however, were legion. Eventually, sometimes after bitter and even armed struggle, opponents who were not killed had to give in or emigrate. One who did the latter was Czesław Miłosz, who left Poland in 1951 and has written in the West ever since. Winner of the Nobel Prize for literature, Miłosz's first substantial work in the West was his description of what he called The Captive Mind. *In the following selection he discusses the many guises that accommodation to the harsh realities of the new regime could take.*

43

7

The Case for Stalinism

Jakub Berman

After World War II (interview conducted in the early 1980s)

On 21 April 1945, when you signed the treaty of friendship, mutual aid, and postwar cooperation with the Soviet Union, which was supposed to provide a "guarantee of the independence of the new democratic Poland," as well as "assure its strength and well-being," you could have included a clause requiring the release of all Poles from Soviet prisons and camps, could you not?
It wasn't a question of us or of the Soviet Union in that treaty. It was drawn up as a compromise with the coalition against Hitler. But what exactly are you getting at?

At the fact that you brought yet another disaster upon this nation.
That's not true. We brought it liberation.

Did you?
Yes, we did. We didn't come to this country as its occupiers, and we never even imagined ourselves in that role. After all the disasters that had befallen this country, we brought it its ultimate liberation, because we finally got rid of those Germans, and that counts for something. I know these things aren't simple. We wanted to get this country moving, to breathe life into it; all our hopes were tied up with the new model of Poland, which was without historical precedent and was the only chance it had had throughout its thousand years of history; we wanted to use that chance 100 percent. And we succeeded. In any case we were bound to succeed, because we were right; not in some irrational, dreamed-up way we'd plucked out of the air, but historically—history was on our side.

So how did they vote [in the referendum of 1946]? PSL statistics show, on a necessarily fragmentary scale, that in 2,004 out of the 11,070 voting districts, 83.54 percent of the vote was against you.[1]

[1]The PSL (*Polskie Stronnictwo Ludowe*) was the Polish Peasant party, which Mikołajczyk organized in 1945 on the basis of a tradition of Polish populism that began in 1895. The Referendum of 1946 asked Polish voters three questions: (1) Are you in favor of a senate? (2) Do you favor land reform and nationalization of basic industries while maintaining the rights of private enterprise? and (3) Are you for

I can't say. Probably it was like that in some districts, while in others we had a majority.

Why didn't you at least reveal this fact?
My dear lady, you can't, not if you want to stay on. If we'd had an alternative—if we win, we stay, if we lose, we hand over power—then of course you can tell the whole truth. But here we were compelled by the situation: in an election, we can't go by the criterion of a majority, because there isn't anyone we can hand over power to. There wasn't then and there isn't now.

I don't understand.
Well, whom would you have had us hand over power to? To Mikolajczyk, perhaps? Or to those even more to the right of him? Or to the devil knows who else? You'll be telling me in a moment it would have been democratic if we had. So what? Who needs that kind of democracy? And we can no more have free elections now than we could ten or twenty years ago, even less so, because we'd lose. There's no doubt of that. So what's the point of such an election? Unless, of course, we wanted to behave like such ultrademocrats, such perfect gentlemen, that we took off our top hats and bowed and said: Fine, we're going to get some rest, go ahead and take power.

Well?
Well what [shouting]? Well what? Why do you say "well"?

Because that's just what you should do, exactly that.
I don't want to be rude.

Well, then, I will: You're hated here.
Miss Toranska, politics isn't something you do for pleasure, and it's not something you do in order to be loved and understood. I know things are bad now, but there are some prospects that we'll make them better. We will make them better, I'm deeply convinced of it. We'll find a way out of the situation, despite all its zigzags and contortions. Maybe not in my lifetime, but we will. It's not at all true that Poland is doomed to destruction, to total destruction.

But you're considered to be the cause of all the evil that has befallen this nation, don't you see that?
That's the result of mental backwardness, yes, backwardness [shouting]! You can't live by nineteenth-century concepts. Two great powers arose, and spheres of influence were defined and agreed. We found ourselves in the Soviet sphere of influence, which was lucky for us, because it helped in implementing a number of changes,

---

the Oder–Neisse line, the new western frontier that compensated Poland for losses to the Soviets in the east? Because most Poles favored the second and third questions, Mikołajczyk asked for a no vote on the first question as a symbolic protest against communist repression. In many places proposition 1 lost heavily, but the official tally released by the Communist-dominated government showed it winning handily. Efforts of the Peasant party to make public the true results were suppressed. In any event, the senate was abolished. Forty-three years later, when the roundtable agreements of 1989 reestablished the senate and provided for Poland's first free and open election since World War II, the opposition candidates from Solidarity won ninety-nine of the one hundred available seats.

although I agree that it also introduced many restrictions—no one's denying their existence. They had to meet with resistance on the part of a population raised on and accustomed to an entirely different set of ideas. But don't people undergo a process of evolution? Don't they change when reality contradicts their ideas?

You really don't see?
It's certainly true that people here are weighed down by complexes which the Czechs, the Romanians, and even the Hungarians don't have, because they didn't experience either the geographical or the social perturbations that we went through: But clinging to absurdities, imagining that we live on the moon instead of on the Oder and the Vistula, is completely ridiculous. It's on a different planet that you can reflect, or meditate, or write poetry, not here. Here we have a different world, different threats, different dangers, and different prospects. Was it plausible at any moment to imagine that Poland would be again the country it had been between the wars? In this configuration? With this distribution of forces? Surely that's inconceivable. You have to be deaf and blind not to see that we, the Polish communists, rescued Poland from the worst.

Certainly, this sovereignty of ours became stronger, greater, and more independent after Stalin's death—that's why I introduced the division into the years before his death and the years after—but even then, during his lifetime, we tried to ensure the greatest possible autonomy and independence for Poland. That was what the Polish road to socialism was about; that was how we understood it.

But you didn't ensure it!
That's not true. There were indeed attempts, after 1949, to check our independence to some extent, and our efforts to retain it in full were stifled by the extraordinary pressure of the cold war atmosphere and by a genuine threat from America, but even then we tried not to allow Polish affairs to suffer. For what was happening was that America had decided to appropriate the whole of Europe for herself. She wanted to invest in Europe (hence the Marshall Plan) in order to make it dependent on her. Her aim was for us and the other countries of the Eastern bloc to break away from the Soviet Union. Such were her intentions, and neither the Soviet Union nor we—we all the less—could agree to this, because for us it would probably have ended in disaster from the point of view of the state, quite apart from the ideological point of view. For us to break away from the Soviet Union would have meant losing the recovered territories, and Poland would have become the duchy of Warsaw. Yes, that's right, the duchy of Warsaw. There's no other possibility that I can see.

And who was supposed to take these western territories away from us? America?
The Germans, naturally. Because America immediately placed her bets on Germany and made efforts to unite it, and if she had succeeded, a victorious Germany would have been created, and thus an aggressive and greedy Germany, ten times worse than it is now, just as Hitler's Germany turned out to be worse than Wilhelmian Germany. It would have posed a complicated problem for us, and maybe even a new threat, for a united Germany would have become a pro-American Germany and thus hostile to the Soviet Union and to us. And the existence of a pro-American center

bordering on the Soviet Union would lead to an inevitable clash, because the whole of Europe would be in danger of being subordinated to America. In such a situation we would immediately be the first to foot the bill, since we would be the first to be exposed to the dangers of such a clash. We're in the middle, after all; we'd be crushed to bits, and then the recovered territories would be taken away from us. The whole Adenauer strategy was directed toward taking the recovered territories away from us at the appropriate moment, and that's what would have happened, I've no doubt at all about that.[2] Because, look: It's been so many years since the war, and yet the issue of Vilnius and Lvov is still alive in Polish society, so how alive must the issue of our western territories be in Germany.[3] Germans lived en masse on those territories; millions, millions of Germans were born and raised there. I'm convinced that if circumstances were favorable they would claim that land back, without, of course, giving anything in return.

Or take someone like Michnik![4] Why is Michnik speaking out against Yalta? What would we have done without Yalta? What would we be? A duchy of Warsaw. At best. That's actually where the lack of logic and the disastrous thinking of the extremists lie: They don't realize that everything they do is a threat to the shape of Poland, narrowing it down to a duchy of Warsaw. Where's the sense in that? Was there any deeper political thought there? If there was, it was harmful and base, but mostly it was all just thoughtless, leading nowhere and only attesting to the narrowness of Solidarity's mentality. It began with a very noble and worthwhile surge of enthusiasm, flowing from healthy sources and healthy roots, but from correcting mistakes, from renewal, from creating new principles, where did it finally lead? To the same thing all over again. To firing up dreams, by then somewhat muted and calmed, of French sovereignty, absolute independence, semi-independence, quarter-independence, who the hell knows what else. It was probably different in different circles, and all of them, unaware of the consequences, went on the rampage together! Following the intelligentsia. Their position—the position adopted by a broad section of the Polish intelligentsia—is something that causes me enormous pain. After all, these are sensible, rationally thinking people, so what is their aim, what do they want?

Independence, Mr. Berman.
That's stupidity [shouting], lunacy, utter lunacy! We're living in a different epoch, a different age! Maybe after World War I you could still go around dreaming up various plans, as Mr Pilsudski did, although they weren't very happily conceived,

[2]Konrad Adenauer, the Christian Democratic chancellor of the Federal Republic of Germany from 1949 to 1963, was a strong anticommunist and pursued a hostile policy toward the Soviet Union and its satellites, particularly the German Democratic Republic. He did not recognize the legitimacy of Poland's new borders. German policy changed in 1969 when the Social Democrats under the leadership of Willy Brandt took power. See Document 24.

[3]Vilnius, today the capital of Lithuania, was part of Poland from 1921 to 1939, as was Lvov, an ethnically mixed city whose past is well reflected in the various spellings of its name: Lviv (Ukrainian), Lwów (Polish), Lvov (Russian), and Lemberg (German–Hapsburg).

[4]From his participation in the student movement of 1968, Adam Michnik was one of the foremost oppositionists in Poland. See Document 38.

either, but after the second war that was absurd.[5] The world *has* changed, can't you see that? There aren't any sovereign states any more, only semisovereign ones. The degree of dependence can be lesser òr greater, but it's always there. Look at what France, that great power, is doing. It's maneuvering. De Gaulle still had sufficient character and strength of will to force through a more independent political line, but not Mitterand—he's marching in file, because that's how the world is and that's how you have to see it.[6] And no amount of maneuvering will get round that—don't count on it. And thinking that we'll sit down in our little corner and smile a little at each in turn is stupidity; it shows ignorance of geography and of elementary political principles. Poland can only be either pro-Soviet or pro-American; there's no other possibility.

There isn't [shouting]! Poland can't be uprooted from the Soviet bloc. How? Uproot it and then where would you put it? On the moon? Poland lies on the road between the Soviet Union and Western Europe, and its position is clear: either/or. There are no half-shades, because Poland can't float in the air. So the objective reality is this: Either America succeeds in building up enough ferment here to overthrow us, whereupon intervention will naturally ensue because the overriding interests of the Soviet Union require it, and there will be so much bloodshed that all the nation will be drained of blood, which is no solution for anyone; or the whole bloc will be destroyed and Poland will become the duchy of Warsaw; or a third world war will break out, and part of Europe or the whole of it will be laid waste. There are no other prospects that I can see, and I don't understand why Polish society and the Polish intelligentsia doesn't see them. I try to enter into their mentality and understand why they're provoking trouble, aggravating problems that are past. And I always reach the same conclusion: Various pains, ailments, and restrictions are blocking their view, and because of that they are unable to distinguish between major and secondary issues. But they will see them, and grasp them, they have to see them, probably after I die, because things being as they are now, *rebus sic stantibus* [since this is the way things stand], the system is doomed to remain; you can improve it, moderate and soften it, but exist it must, and instead of wondering how to overthrow it we should muster our strength and effort to save the

---

[5]Józef Piłsudski (1867–1935) was the national hero of Polish independence during and after World War I. He spent five years in Siberia as a czarist prisoner and as a young man was a socialist. Before World War I he realized that the conflict he saw coming could lead to Polish independence, and he began a military organization. As an ally of the Central Powers, Poland did achieve independence in 1917, but when Piłsudski took that independence seriously and would not subordinate his troops to the Germans, he was arrested. Returning to Warsaw in 1918 as a hero, he became president of Poland from 1918 to 1922 and led the Polish army in its successful efforts to repel the Soviet invasion of 1920. In 1926 he effected a coup d'état and remained the power behind the government until his death in 1935. Not really a socialist in his mature years, he opposed the exclusive nationalism of the National Democrats under Roman Dmowski but at the same time preferred a centralized government to a fully democratic one.

[6]Charles de Gaulle was the leader of the Free French during World War II and head of the French government from 1958 to 1969. He was noted for his adamant pursuit of French national grandeur. François Mitterand, leader of the French Socialist party, became president of France in 1981. In the 1970s the Socialist party overtook and passed the Communist party in electoral popularity, so that by the time of this interview Mitterand had reduced the French communist party to a minor role in French politics.

Poland we have created, a Poland which, for all its faults and mistakes, is a power, and finally rid ourselves of those absurd myths and unrealistic hopes, because they're *contra naturam* [against nature].

Contra naturam, *Mr. Berman, is what the current state of affairs is.*
Exactly! Gomulka also finally understood that his popularity was only the result of dreams and illusions.[7] Maybe he didn't see it immediately; perhaps he didn't see it fully until 1957, or maybe even not until 1958, I don't know, but I think it partly got through to him during the rally in front of the Palace of Culture. It gave him a great shock, because he finally saw both sides of the situation. On the one hand he knew certain dams had been breached, and it was a good thing that they had, but on the other hand he also saw that they would break more and more visibly and might end up undermining the whole postwar structure which is the basis of our presence in the western territories and of our existence as a state. Why? Because some people were asking themselves who was a good Pole and who wasn't, and others proceeded to act. We want to bring back the National Democratic party, they shouted; we want to reactivate the Labor party, shouted others; we want this reform and that reform.[8] Gomulka was lost in all this. He launched into self-criticism, some of it right and some not, because he lacked the feel and understanding to distinguish between them. And since, in addition, his outlook was narrow, he did some silly things. And since he also lacked organizational talent and had many faults and a number of failings, as well as being too conceited and placing too much faith in arithmetical calculations, he managed to alienate several wise people who were devoted to the party; he had a stupid fear of the old intelligentsia; and he stepped up the pace at the cost of any reforms. But what was the reason for all this? Concern, fear, and terror. Because he finally saw, with full clarity, that a mood of independence had swept the country like a wave and that he had to stop it because he wouldn't be able to control it and in the end it would sweep him away. Like an ocean.

How long do you intend to fight against it?
Sixty years, a hundred years if need be [bangs his fist on the table]. Until we defeat it!

You didn't manage it in 150 years.
But we will [shouting]! The nation must mold itself into its new shape. It must.

No.
But my dear lady. I understand that for a nation to be able to shift to a new set of values, a new shape, it has to experience a breakthrough of a kind it has never

---

[7]Wladisław Gomułka was a lifelong party activist and head of the Polish United Workers' party from 1956 to 1970. His appointment in 1956 was popularly received because he had been removed from office in 1948 for "Titoist deviations," that is, for having reservations about some aspects of the Stalinist program for Poland. His popularity waned fairly quickly, and by the time he left office in 1970 he was reviled.

[8]The National Democratic party was Poland's largest right-wing party before World War II. Under the leadership of Roman Dmowski it advocated a policy of narrow Polish nationalism, including anti-Semitism. The Labor party was the most conservative of the centrist parties seeking worker support in the 1930s, but it was relatively small.

known throughout its thousand years of history. One can't erase 150 years of oppression and struggle with Russia from memory all at once, because they left a profound mark on the national consciousness. No other country has to bear the burden of such experiences. Neither the Czechs nor the Hungarians nor the Romanians can be compared to us in that regard. The Czechs did experience change of a sort, but qualitatively it was not as staggering as what we went through. The Hungarians lost Transylvania after the Second World War, a wound which probably aggravates them still, but they also gained a lot: stability and a certain degree of wealth. Nor was the history of Romania as dramatic as ours. We are doomed to shoulder the enormous load of the experience of a thousand years, and therefore the process of breaking away from tradition and coming to love our new shape is not an easy one, and it can't take place smoothly, slowly and flexibly: It has to cause jolts, which will appear and return in one form or another from time to time. Especially as all these Jagiellonian illusions, combined with dreams of a great eastward expansion, continue to live in the Polish consciousness, because they were cultivated for centuries in various circles; every generation has been brought up on them and continues to be brought up on them, in spite of great efforts on our part.[9] So they can't be erased overnight, and things can't be set straight by even the most carefully edited history textbooks or the most skillfully written articles—not that they were very intelligent, and they certainly should have made more mention of things they passed over. But it's a dream, an illusion, to think that a consciousness that had shaped itself over centuries can be changed in the space of thirty or forty years with the aid of one lecture or another or a film or a book. Teachers may be disappointed to see that the effort they've invested has had no effect, but it has had none because it couldn't have an immediate effect. But without placing my faith in the magical power of words I am nonetheless convinced that the sum of our actions, skillfully and consistently carried out, will finally produce results and create a new Polish consciousness; because all the advantages flowing from our new path will be borne out, must be borne out, and if we're not destroyed by an atomic war and we don't disappear into nothingness, there will finally be a breakthrough in mentality which will give it an entirely new content and quality. And then we, the communists, will be able to apply all the democratic principles we would like to apply but can't apply now, because they would end in our defeat and elimination. It may happen in fifty years or it may happen in a hundred; I don't want to make prophecies, but I'm sure it will happen one day.

Thank you.

9 "Jagiellonian illusions" refers to territorial pretensions based on the holdings of the medieval and early modern dynasty of Poland and Lithuania. Founded in 1386 by the marriage of the Lithuanian king Jogaila to the Polish queen Jadwiga, at its peak the Jagiellonian dynasty reigned over Hungary, which extended to the Adriatic Sea, Bohemia, and Moravia in central Europe, Poland and Lithuania on the Baltic, and White Russia and the Ukraine, which reached almost to the Black Sea. The line died out in 1572.

8

Ketman

Czesław Miłosz
1951–52

What is Ketman?[1] I found its description in a book by Gobineau entitled *Religions and Philosophies of Central Asia*. Gobineau spent many years in Persia (from 1855 to 1858 he was a secretary in the French legation, from 1861 to 1863 he was French minister), and we cannot deny his gift for keen observation, even though we need not necessarily agree with the conclusions of this rather dangerous writer. The similarities between Ketman and the customs cultivated in the countries of the New Faith are so striking that I shall permit myself to quote at length.

The people of the Mussulman East believe that "he who is in possession of truth must not expose his person, his relatives, or his reputation to the blindness, the folly, the perversity of those whom it has pleased God to place and maintain in error." One must, therefore, keep silent about one's true convictions if possible.

"Nevertheless," says Gobineau, "there are occasions when silence no longer suffices, when it may pass as an avowal. Then one must not hesitate. Not only must one deny one's true opinion, but one is commanded to resort to all ruses in order to deceive one's adversary. One makes all the protestations of faith that can please him; one performs all the rites one recognizes to be the most vain; one falsifies one's own books; one exhausts all possible means of deceit. Thus one acquires the multiple satisfactions and merits of having placed oneself and one's relatives under cover, of not having exposed a venerable faith to the horrible contact of the infidel, and finally of having, in cheating the latter and confirming him in his error, imposed on him the shame and spiritual misery that he deserves.

"Ketman fills the man who practices it with pride. Thanks to it, a believer raises himself to a permanent state of superiority over the man he deceives, be he a minister of state or a powerful king; to him who uses Ketman, the other is a miserable blind man whom one shuts off from the true path whose existence he does

[1]In Arabic *ketman* means hidden. The custom Miłosz refers to is the Shi'ite tradition of *Taqiyya*, or religious dissimulation while maintaining mental reservation, which "is considered lawful in Shi'ism in situations where there is overwhelming danger of loss of life or property and where no danger to religion would occur thereby" (Moojan Momen, *An Introduction of Shi'i Islam* [New Haven: Yale University Press, 1985], p. 183).

not suspect; while you, tattered and dying of hunger, trembling externally at the feet of duped force, your eyes are filled with light, you walk in brightness before your enemies. It is an unintelligent being that you make sport of; it is a dangerous beast that you disarm. What a wealth of pleasures!"

Ketman in its narrowest and severest forms is widely practiced in the people's democracies. As in Islam, the feeling of superiority over those who are unworthy of attaining truth constitutes one of the chief joys of people whose lives do not in general abound in pleasures. "Deviations," the tracing of which creates so many troubles for the rulers, are not an illusion. They are cases of accidental unmaskings of Ketman, and those who are most helpful in detecting deviations are those who themselves practice a similar form of Ketman. Recognizing in other acrobats the tricks they themselves employ, they take advantage of the first occasion to down an opponent or friend. Thus they protect themselves; and the measure of dexterity is to anticipate by at least one day the similar accusation which could be leveled against them by the man they denounce. Since the number of varieties of Ketman is practically unlimited, the naming of deviations cannot keep pace with the weeding of a garden so full of unexpected specimens of heresy. Every new commentary on the precepts of the New Faith proclaimed by the Center multiplies the internal reservations of those who are externally the most faithful. It is impossible to enumerate all the forms of Ketman that one can discover in the people's democracies. I shall try, however, to proceed somewhat in the manner of a naturalist determining major groups and families.

National Ketman is broadly diffused throughout the masses, and even the upper brackets of the party in the various dependent states are not free of it. Because Tito, like Sadra, announced his heresy to all the world, millions of human beings in the people's democracies must employ exceedingly ingenious means of masking themselves.[2] Instructive displays of condemnation of those who wished to follow the national road to socialism in individual Eastern capitals taught the public what kind of phrases and reflexes can expose one to reproach for harboring this fatal tendency. The surest safeguard is to manifest loudly one's awe at Russia's achievements in every field of endeavor, to carry Russian books under one's arm, to hum Russian songs, to applaud Russian actors and musicians enthusiastically, etc. A writer who has not consecrated a single work to outstanding Russian figures or to Russian life, but has confined himself to national themes, cannot consider himself entirely safe. The chief characteristic of the people who practice this Ketman is an unbounded contempt for Russia as a barbaric country. Among the workers and peasants it is most often purely emotional and based on observation of either the soldiers of the liberating army, or (since during the war a great many were in areas directly administered by the Russians) of Russians in their daily life.

The Ketman of Revolutionary Purity is a rare variety, more common in the large cities of Russia than in the people's democracies. It is based on a belief in the "sacred fire of the revolutionary epoch of Lenin" which burns in such a poet as

[2]Sadra was a disciple of the medieval philosopher Avicenna. Miłosz describes him (in a portion of the text omitted here) as a good example of Ketman.

Mayakovski.[3] Mayakovski's suicide in 1930 marked the end of an era distinguished by the flowering of literature, the theater, and music. The "sacred fire" was dampened; collectivization was introduced mercilessly; millions of Soviet citizens perished in slave labor camps; a ruthless policy toward non-Russian nations was established. Literature became flat and colorless under the influence of imposed theories; Russian painting was destroyed; Russian theater, then the foremost in the world, was deprived of freedom to experiment; science was subjected to directives from party chiefs. A man who reasons thus hates Him with all his heart, holding Him responsible for the terrible lot of the Russian people and for the hatred they inspire in other nations.

Still, he is not altogether sure whether He is necessary or not. Perhaps in extraordinary periods such as the present the appearance of a tyrant must be considered desirable. Mass purges in which so many good communists died, the lowering of the living standard of the citizens, the reduction of artists and scholars to the status of yesmen, the extermination of entire national groups—what other man would dare undertake such measures? After all, Russia stood firm against Hitler; the revolution weathered the attack of enemy armies. In this perspective, His acts seem effective and even justified, perhaps, by an exceptional historical situation. If He had not instituted an exceptional terror in the year 1937, wouldn't there have been more people willing to help Hitler than there actually were? For example, doesn't the present-day line in scholarship and art, no matter how at odds it may be at times with common sense, effectually raise Russian morale in the face of the war that threatens? He is an infamous blot on the bright New Faith, but a blemish we must tolerate for the moment. And indeed we must even support Him. The "sacred fire" has not gone out. When victory is achieved, it will burst forth again with its old strength, the bonds He imposed will fall away, and relations between nations will operate on new and better principles. This variety of Ketman was widespread if not universal in Russia during the Second World War, and its present form is a rebirth of an already once-deceived hope.

Aesthetic Ketman is born of the disparity between man's longings and the sense satisfactions the New Faith offers. A man of taste cannot approve the results of official pressure in the realm of culture no matter how much he applauds the latest verses, how many flattering reviews he writes of current art expositions, nor how studiously he pretends that the gloomy new buildings coincide with his personal preferences in architecture. He changes completely within the four walls of his home. There one finds (if he is a well-situated intellectual) reproductions of works of art officially condemned as bourgeois, records of modern music, and a rich collection of ancient authors in various languages. This luxury of splendid isolation is pardoned him so long as his creative work is effective propaganda. To protect his position and his apartment (which he has by the grace of the state), the intellectual is prepared to make any sacrifice or compromise, for the value of privacy in a society

[3]Vladimir Mayakovski (1893–1930) was a vigorous spokesman for the Bolsheviks from 1917 until the time of his suicide in 1930. In 1924 he wrote a three-thousand-line elegy on Lenin's death, and Stalin called him "the best and most talented poet of our Soviet epoch."

that affords little if any isolation is greater than the saying "my home is my castle" can lead one to surmise. Two-way television screens installed in private homes to observe the behavior of citizens in seclusion belong as yet to the future. Hence, by listening to foreign radio stations and reading good books, he profits from a moment of relaxation, that is, of course, if he is alone, for as soon as guests arrive the play begins anew.

Professional Ketman is reasoned thus: Since I find myself in circumstances over which I have no control and since I have but one life and that is fleeting, I should strive to do my best. I am like a crustacean attached to a crag on the bottom of the sea. Over me storms rage and huge ships sail, but my entire effort is concentrated upon clinging to the rock, for otherwise I will be carried off by the waters and perish, leaving no trace behind. If I am a scientist I attend congresses at which I deliver reports strictly adhering to the party line. But in the laboratory I pursue my research according to scientific methods and in that alone lies the aim of life. If my work is successful, it matters little how it will be presented and toward whose glory. Discoveries made in the name of a disinterested search for truth are lasting, whereas the shrieks of politicians pass. I must do all they demand, they may use my name as they wish, as long as I have access to a laboratory and money for the purchase of scientific instruments.

If I am a writer, I take pride in my literary achievements. Here, for example, is my treatise on Swift, a Marxist analysis. This type of analysis, which is not synonymous with the Method or the New Faith, makes possible a keen penetration into historical events. Marx had a genius for observation. In following him one is secure against attack, for he is, after all, the prophet, and one can proclaim one's belief in the Method and the New Faith in a preface fulfilling much the same function as dedications to kings or czars in times past. Here is my translation of a sixteenth-century poem, or my novel whose scene is laid in the distant past. Aren't they of permanent value? Here are my translations from Russian. They are viewed with approbation and have brought me a large sum of money, but certainly Pushkin is a great poet, and his worth is not altered by the fact that today his poems serve Him as a means of propaganda. Obviously I must pay for the right to practice my profession with a certain number of articles and odes in the way of tribute. Still one's life on earth is not judged by transitory panegyrics written out of necessity.

Skeptical Ketman is widely disseminated throughout intellectual circles. One argues that humanity does not know how to handle its knowledge or how to resolve the problems of production and division of goods. The first scientific attempts to solve social problems, made in the nineteenth century, are interesting but not precise enough. They happened, however, into the hands of the Russians who, unable to think otherwise than dogmatically, raised these first attempts to the dignity of dogma. What is happening in Russia and the countries dependent upon her bespeaks a kind of insanity, but it is not impossible that Russia will manage to impose her insanity upon the whole world and that the return to reason will occur only after two or three hundred years. Finding oneself in the very midst of an historical cyclone, one must behave as prudently as possible, yielding externally to forces capable of destroying all adversaries. This does not prevent one from taking pleasure in one's observations, since what one beholds is indeed unprecedented. Surely man has never before been subjected to such pressure; never has he had to writhe and wriggle so to adapt himself to forms constructed according to the books but obviously not to his size. All his intellectual and emotional capacities are put to the test.

Whoever contemplates this daily sight of repudiation and humiliation knows more about man than an inhabitant of the West who feels no pressure other than that of money. The accumulating of this store of observations is the activity of a miser who counts his treasure in secret. Since this Ketman is based on a total lack of belief in the Method, it helps one conform externally to the obligatory line by allowing for complete cynicism and therefore for elasticity in adjusting oneself to changing tactics.

Metaphysical Ketman occurs generally in countries with a Catholic past. Most examples of it within the Imperium are found in Poland. This Ketman depends upon a *suspended* belief in a metaphysical principle of the world. A man attached to this Ketman regards the epoch in which he lives as antimetaphysical, and hence as one in which no metaphysical faith can emerge. Humanity is learning to think in rationalistic and materialistic categories; it is burdened with immediate problems and entangled in a class war. Other-worldly religions are crumbling, living through a period of crisis, and, what is worse, serving to defend the obsolete order. This does not mean that mankind will not return to a better and purified religion in the future. Perhaps the New Faith is an indispensable purgatory; perhaps God's purpose is being accomplished through the barbarians, i.e. the Center, who are forcing the masses to awaken out of their lethargy. The spiritual fare these masses receive from the New Faith is inferior and insufficient. Still one must commend the Center for breaking new ground and for demolishing externally splendid but internally rotten facades. One should cooperate in this task without betraying one's attachment to the Mystery. All the more so because the Mystery has no possibility of appearing in literature, for example and because neither the language nor the ideas at the disposal of contemporary man are ripe enough to express it.

Ethical Ketman results from opposition to the ethics of the New Faith, which is based on the principle that good and evil are definable solely in terms of service or harm to the interests of the revolution. Since exemplary behavior of citizens in their interrelations aids the cause of socialism, great emphasis is placed upon individual morality.

"The development of a new man" is the key point in the New Faith's program. Demands made upon party members are exceedingly harsh. One exacts of them no small degree of abstinence. As a result, admission to the party is not unlike entrance into a religious order, and the literature of the New Faith treats this act with a gravity equal to that with which Catholic literature speaks of the vows of young nuns. The higher one stands in the party hierarchy, the more attentively is one's private life supervised. Love of money, drunkenness, or a confused love life disqualify a party member from holding important offices. Hence the upper brackets of the party are filled by ascetics devoted to the single cause of revolution. As for certain human tools, deprived of real influence but useful because of their names, even if they belong to the party one tolerates or sometimes encourages their weaknesses, for they constitute a guarantee of obedience. The general ethical ideal of the New Faith is puritanical. If it were feasible to lodge all the citizens in cells and release them only for work or for political meetings, that would undoubtedly be most desirable. But alas, one must make concessions to human nature. Procreation is possible only as a result of sexual relations between men and women, and one must take this inconvenience into account.

The "new man" is conditioned to acknowledge the good of the whole as the sole norm of his behavior. He thinks and reacts like others; is modest, industrious, satisfied with what the state gives him; limits his private life to nights spent at home; and passes all the rest of his time amidst his companions at work or at play, observing them carefully and reporting their actions and opinions to the authorities. Informing was and is known in many civilizations, but the New Faith declares it a cardinal virtue of the good citizen (though the name itself is carefully avoided). It is the basis of each man's fear of his fellowmen. Work in an office or factory is hard not only because of the amount of labor required but even more because of the need to be on guard against omnipresent and vigilant eyes and ears. After work one goes to political meetings or special lectures, thus lengthening a day that is without a moment of relaxation or spontaneity. The people one talks with may seem relaxed and careless, sympathetic and indignant, but if they appear so, it is only to arouse corresponding attitudes and to extract confidences which they can report to their superiors.

The inhabitants of Western countries little realize that millions of their fellowmen, who seem superficially more or less similar to them, live in a world as fantastic as that of the men from Mars. They are unaware of the perspectives on human nature that Ketman opens. Life in constant internal tension develops talents which are latent in man. He does not even suspect to what heights of cleverness and psychological perspicacity he can rise when he is cornered and must either be skillful or perish. The survival of those best adapted to mental acrobatics creates a human type that has been rare until now. The necessities which drive men to Ketman sharpen the intellect.

Whoever would take the measure of intellectual life in the countries of Central or Eastern Europe from the monotonous articles appearing in the press or the stereotyped speeches pronounced there would be making a grave error. Just as theologians in periods of strict orthodoxy expressed their views in the rigorous language of the church, so the writers of the people's democracies make use of an accepted special style, terminology, and linguistic ritual. What is important is not what someone said but what he wanted to say, disguising his thought by removing a comma, inserting an "and," establishing this rather than another sequence in the problems discussed. Unless one has lived there one cannot know how many titanic battles are being fought, how the heroes of Ketman are falling, what this warfare is being waged over. Obviously, people caught up in this daily struggle are rather contemptuous of their compatriot political émigrés. A surgeon cannot consider a butcher his equal in dexterity; just so a Pole, Czech, or Hungarian practiced in the art of dissimulation smiles when he learns that someone in the emigration has called him a traitor (or a swine) at the very moment when this traitor (or swine) is engaged in a match of philosophical chess on whose outcome the fate of fifteen laboratories or twenty ateliers depends. They do not know how one pays—those abroad do not know. They do not know what one buys and at what price.

The Expulsion of Yugoslavia

To observers in 1947 and 1948 the Cominform appeared to be a platform from which Stalin's most loyal ally, Yugoslavia, could point the way to proletarian internationalism for the other parties. The Yugoslavs were given the task of making the most extreme speeches against coalition politics at Szklarska Poręba, and the Cominform's newspaper was published in Belgrade. In retrospect, however, it seems likely that Stalin gave them the leading role in the Cominform only to set them against the other parties for the purpose of eventually bringing them down. For when the Cominform convened in June 1948 in Bucharest for its second meeting, the world was astonished to hear that Yugoslavia had been excluded from the fraternal brotherhood of socialist states—excommunicated.

The controversy that led to this totally unexpected result reached its climax in an exchange of letters between Stalin and the Yugoslav party in the spring of 1948. The Yugoslavs, under the leadership of Josip Broz Tito, had conducted their own successful communist revolution as an outgrowth of their resistance to Nazi occupation in World War II, and they were justifiably proud of that accomplishment. Loyal Stalinists, they were nonetheless frustrated by heavy-handed Soviet attempts to exploit them economically and to spy on them militarily, and what is more, they said so in a series of letters to Stalin beginning early in 1948. "No matter how much each of us loves the land of Socialism, the U.S.S.R.," the Yugoslavs said, "he can, in no case, love his own country less." This is precisely the position that Stalin refused to accept.

The following excerpts begin with the Soviet reaction to the first Yugoslav letter and continue with the Yugoslav answer, the Soviet response, and the final Yugoslav statement. In the last extract the Cominform calls on the "healthy elements" in Yugoslavia to overthrow Tito and his colleagues.

9

The Tito–Stalin Correspondence
March–June 1948

I
SOVIET PARTY TO TITO (MARCH 27, 1948)

In your letter you express the desire to be informed of the other facts which led to Soviet dissatisfaction and to the straining of relations between the U.S.S.R. and Yugoslavia.[1] Such facts actually exist, although they are not connected with the withdrawal of the civilian and military advisers. We consider it necessary to inform you of them.

(a) We know that there are anti-Soviet rumors circulating among the leading comrades in Yugoslavia, for instance that "the CPSU is degenerate," "great-power chauvinism is rampant in the U.S.S.R.," "the U.S.S.R. is trying to dominate Yugoslavia economically," and "the Cominform is a means for control of the other parties by the CPSU," etc. These anti-Soviet allegations are usually camouflaged by left phrases, such as "socialism in the Soviet Union has ceased to be revolutionary" and that Yugoslavia alone is the exponent of "revolutionary Socialism." It was naturally laughable to hear such statements about the CPSU from such questionable Marxists as Djilas, Vukmanovic, Kidric, Rankovic, and others.[2] However, the fact remains that such rumors have been circulating for a long time among many high-ranking Yugoslav officials, that they are still circulating, and that they are naturally creating an anti-Soviet atmosphere which is endangering relations between the CPSU and the CPY.

We readily admit that every Communist party, among them the Yugoslav, has

---

[1]On March 18, 1948, the Soviets informed the Yugoslavs that they were withdrawing their military advisers because they were "surrounded by hostility." On March 20 Tito wrote Molotov expressing amazement at this move and denying that the Yugoslavs had shown any "lack of hospitality and lack of confidence" toward the Soviet experts.

[2]At this time Milovan Djilas was chief party propagandist; Svetozar Vukmanović-Tempo, a less important figure than the other three, was head of political affairs for the Yugoslav National Army; Boris Kidrić was Tito's main economic adviser; and Aleksandar Ranković headed the state security apparatus. Surprisingly, Edward Kardelj, later the main party theorist of self-administration, is mentioned only later.

Excerpted from *The Soviet–Yugoslav Dispute: Text of the Published Correspondence*, pp. 58–65, published by Oxford University Press for the Royal Institute of International Affairs, London. Copyright © by Royal Institute of International Affairs.

the right to criticize the CPSU, even as the CPSU has the right to criticize any other Communist party. But Marxism demands that criticism be aboveboard and not underhanded and slanderous, thus depriving those criticized of the opportunity to reply to the criticism. However, criticism by the Yugoslav officials is neither open nor honest; it is both underhanded and dishonest and of a hypocritical nature, because, while discrediting the CPSU behind its back, publicly they pharisaically praise it to the skies. Thus criticism is transformed into slander, into an attempt to discredit the CPSU and to blacken the Soviet system.

We do not doubt that the Yugoslav party masses would disown this anti-Soviet criticism as alien and hostile if they knew about it. We think this is the reason why the Yugoslav officials make these criticisms in secret, behind the backs of the masses.

Again, one might recall that when he decided to declare war on the CPSU, Trotsky also started with accusations that the CPSU was degenerate, was suffering from the limitations inherent in the narrow nationalism of great powers. Naturally he camouflaged all this with left slogans about world revolution. It is well known, however, that Trotsky himself became degenerate and, when he was exposed, crossed over into the camp of the sworn enemies of the CPSU and the Soviet Union. We think that the political career of Trotsky is quite instructive.

(b) We are disturbed by the present condition of the CPY. We are amazed by the fact that the CPY, which is the leading party, is still not completely legalized and still has a semilegal status. Decisions of the party organs are never published in the press, neither are the reports of party assemblies.

Democracy is not evident within the CPY itself. The Central Committee, in its majority, was not elected but coopted. Criticism and self-criticism within the party does not exist or only barely exists. It is characteristic that the personnel secretary of the party is also the minister of state security. In other words, the party cadres are under the supervision of the minister of state security. According to the theory of Marxism, the party should control all the state organs in the country, including the ministry of state security, while in Yugoslavia we have just the opposite: the ministry of state security actually controlling the party. This probably explains the fact that initiative among the party masses in Yugoslavia is not on an adequate level.

It is understandable that we cannot consider such a Communist party organization to be Marxist–Leninist, Bolshevik.

The spirit of the policy of class struggle is not felt in the CPY. An increase in the capitalist elements in villages and cities is in full swing, and the leadership of the party is taking no measures to check these capitalist elements. The CPY is being hoodwinked by the degenerate and opportunist theory of peaceful absorption of capitalist elements by a socialist system, borrowed from Bernstein, Vollmar, and Bukharin.[3]

---

[3]Stalin considered these men counterrevolutionary renegades. Eduard Bernstein (1850–1932), a German radical who was a close friend of Friedrich Engels, invoked the wrath of his Social Democratic colleagues at the turn of the century when he abandoned the idea that capitalism was at the point of imminent collapse and the view that the proletariat should seize power by force. As a young man, Georg von Vollmar (1850–1922) was a radical. After 1890, however, as the leader of the Bavarian Social

According to the theory of Marxism–Leninism, the party is the leading force in the country, has its specific program and cannot merge with the nonparty masses. In Yugoslavia, on the contrary, the People's Front is considered the chief leading force, and there was an attempt to get the party submerged within the front.[4] In his speech at the Second Congress of the People's Front, Comrade Tito said: "Does the CPY have any other program but that of the People's Front? No, the CPY has no other program. The program of the People's Front is its program."

It thus appears that in Yugoslavia this amazing theory of party organization is considered a new theory. Actually, it is far from new. In Russia forty years ago a part of the Mensheviks proposed that the Marxist party be dissolved into a nonparty workers' mass organization and that the second should supplant the first; the other part of the Mensheviks proposed that the Marxist party be dissolved into a nonparty mass organization of workers and peasants, with the latter again supplanting the former. As is known, Lenin described these Mensheviks as malicious opportunists and liquidators of the party.

II

YUGOSLAV RESPONSE (APRIL 13, 1948)

In answering your letter of March 27, 1948, we must first of all emphasize that we were terribly surprised by its tone and contents. We feel that the reason for its contents, that is, for the accusations and attitudes on individual questions, is insufficient knowledge of the situation here. We cannot explain your conclusions otherwise than by the fact that the government of the U.S.S.R. is obtaining inaccurate and tendentious information from its representatives, who, because of lack of knowledge, must obtain such information from various people, either from known antiparty elements or from various dissatisfied persons. . . . We cannot understand why the representatives of the U.S.S.R. have not insisted on confirming such information with responsible people in our country, that is, on verifying such information with the CC of the CPY or the government. We regard the issuing of such information as antiparty work and antistate because it spoils the relations between our two countries.

No matter how much each of us loves the land of socialism, the U.S.S.R., he can, in no case, love his own country less, which also is developing socialism—in this concrete case the FPRY—for which so many thousands of its most progressive people fell.[5] We know very well that this is similarly understood in the Soviet Union.

Democrats, he pursued a policy of cooperation with other parties seeking reform and became one of Bavaria's most popular political figures. Nikolai Bukharin (1888–1938) was at the same time one of the most important intellectual forces of Bolshevism and the most famous victim of Stalin's purges of 1936–38.

[4]The People's Front was a mass organization of some seven million people in 1948. In contrast with the practice in other communist states, all of whom had similar mass organizations, in Yugoslavia the party's policies were advanced in the name of the People's Front rather than directly by the party. In 1953 the front became the Socialist Alliance of Working People of Yugoslavia.

[5]The initials stand for the Federal People's Republic of Yugoslavia.

Your letter of March 27 states that we are making anti-Soviet criticisms and criticisms of the CPSU. It states that this criticism is being made among the leaders of the CPY. It further states that this criticism is being carried on behind the backs of the mass of the party members; that this criticism is dishonorable, underhanded, hypocritical, etc. The names of Djilas, Vukmanovic, Kidric, and Rankovic are mentioned, and it is said that there are some others. Thus, the letter mentions the names of some of the best-known and most popular leaders of New Yugoslavia, who have proved themselves in many difficult situations faced by our party.

It is very difficult for us to understand how such serious accusations can be advanced without mentioning their source. It is even more amazing to compare statements by our leaders with the one-time statements of Trotsky. The letter quotes parts of alleged statements, for example, "the CPSU is degenerate," "the U.S.S.R. is trying to dominate Yugoslavia economically," "great-power chauvinism is rampant in the U.S.S.R.," "the Cominform is a means for control of the other parties by the CPSU." Further "these anti-Soviet allegations are usually camouflaged by left phrases, such as 'socialism in the U.S.S.R. has ceased to be revolutionary,' that only Yugoslavia is the true exponent of 'revolutionary socialism.' "

On the basis of this and similar information, gathered over a long period from various suspicious sources, tendentiously attributed to the leading men of the new Yugoslavia as if it were theirs, and thus presented to the leaders of the U.S.S.R., it is without doubt possible to draw wrong conclusions and describe them as anti-Soviet statements. However, we feel that on the basis of unidentified persons and suspicious information, it is incorrect to draw conclusions and make accusations like those brought in the letter against men who have performed invaluable services in popularizing the U.S.S.R. in Yugoslavia and won priceless renown in the war of liberation. Is it possible to believe that people who spent six, eight, ten, and more years in prison—among other things because of their work in popularizing the U.S.S.R.—can be such as shown in your letter of March 27? No. But these are the majority of the present high-ranking leaders of the new Yugoslavia, who on March 27, 1941, led the masses through the streets against the antipopular regime of Cvetkovic-Macek, which signed the anti-Comintern pact and desired to harness Yugoslavia to the Fascist Axis wagon.[6] They are the same people who in 1941 organized the uprising against the Fascist invader, deeply believing in the Soviet Union. They are the same people who, at the head of the insurgent Yugoslav people, with gun in hand, fought under the most difficult conditions on the side of the Soviet Union as the only true ally, believing in the victory of the U.S.S.R. in the darkest days, just because they believed and believe today in the Soviet system, in Socialism.

---

[6]In August 1939, after tortuous negotiations, Dragiša Cvetković, a rightist Serb who was prime minister of Yugoslavia, and Vladko Maček, leader of the Croatian Peasant party, signed an agreement granting many of Croatia's long-term demands for autonomy within Yugoslavia. At the same time, the two men formed a joint government. On March 25, 1941, Cvetković signed the Tripartite Pact, aligning Yugoslavia with Germany. Almost immediately a military coup overthrew the government, and crowds jubilantly celebrated in Belgrade's streets. Communists participated in this popular outburst but in no sense organized or inspired it. Even though the new government assured Hitler it would continue its adherence to the Tripartite Pact, the angry Führer attacked on April 6, and Yugoslavia collapsed within two weeks.

Such people cannot work "to blacken the Soviet system" because that would mean betraying their convictions, their past. We feel that these people should not be judged on the basis of dubious information but on the basis of their long revolutionary activity.

III

SOVIET ANSWER (MAY 4, 1948)

We feel that behind the attempts of the Yugoslav leaders to clear themselves of the responsibility for straining Soviet–Yugoslav relations lies a lack of desire by these comrades to admit their mistakes and their intention to continue an unfriendly policy toward the U.S.S.R.

Lenin says:

> The attitude of a political party toward its mistakes is one of the most important and most significant criteria of the seriousness of the party and the fulfillment of its obligations toward its class and toward the working masses. To admit errors frankly, to discover their cause, to analyze the situation which has been created by these errors, to discuss measures for correcting them—that is the sign of a serious party, that is the fulfillment of its obligations, that is the education of the class and the masses.

Unfortunately, we must state that the leaders of the CPY, who will not admit and correct their errors, are crudely destroying this principal directive of Lenin.

Tito and Kardelj, in their letter, speak of the merits and successes of the CPY, saying that the CC of the CPSU earlier acknowledged these services and successes but is now supposedly silent about them.[7] This, naturally, is not true. No one can deny the services and successes of the CPY. There is no doubt about this. However, we must also say that the services of the Communist parties of Poland, Czechoslovakia, Hungary, Romania, Bulgaria, and Albania are not less than those of the CPY. However, the leaders of these parties behave modestly and do not boast about their successes, as do the Yugoslav leaders, who have pierced every one's ears with their unlimited self-praise. It is also necessary to emphasize that the services of the French and Italian CPs to the revolution were not less but greater than those of Yugoslavia. Even though the French and Italian CPs have so far achieved less success than the CPY, this is not due to any special qualities of the CPY, but mainly because after the destruction of the Yugoslav partisan headquarters by German paratroopers, at a moment when the people's liberation movement in Yugoslavia was passing through a serious crisis, the Soviet army came to the aid of the Yugoslav people, crushed the German invader, liberated Belgrade, and in this way created the conditions which were necessary for the CPY to achieve power.[8] Unfor-

---

[7]Edvard Kardelj (1910–79) was the organizer of the partisan uprising in Slovenia in 1941 and one of the three or four leading Yugoslav communists for thirty years after the war. He was the party's main theorist of self-management.

[8]One of Stalin's worst mistakes in his dealings with the Yugoslavs was to denigrate their war effort. Whereas much of the leadership of the other East European parties spent the war in the Soviet Union, the

tunately the Soviet army did not and could not render such assistance to the French and Italian CPS. If Comrade Tito and Comrade Kardelj bore this fact in mind they would be less boastful about their merits and successes and would behave with greater propriety and modesty.

The conceit of the Yugoslav leaders goes so far that they even attribute to themselves such merits as can in no way be justified. Take, for example, the question of military science. The Yugoslav leaders claim that they have improved on the Marxist science of war with a new theory according to which war is regarded as a combined operation by regular troops, partisan units, and popular insurrections. However, this so-called theory is as old as the world and is not new to Marxism. As is known, the Bolsheviks applied combined action of regular troops, partisan units, and popular insurrections for the entire period of the civil war in Russia (1918–21), and applied it on a much wider scale than was done in Yugoslavia. However, the Bolsheviks did not say that by applying this method of military activity, they produced anything new in the science of war, because the same method was successfully applied long before the Bolsheviks by Field Marshal Kutuzov in the war against Napoleon's troops in Russia in 1812.

However, even Field Marshal Kutuzov did not claim to be the innovator in applying this method because the Spaniards in 1808 applied it in the war against Napoleon's troops. It thus appears that this science of war is actually 140 years old, and what they claim as their own contribution is actually the contribution of the Spaniards.

Besides this, we should bear in mind that the services of any leader in the past do not exclude the possibility of his committing serious errors later.[9] We must not close our eyes to present errors because of past services. In his time Trotsky also rendered revolutionary services, but this does not mean that the CPSU could close its eyes to his crude opportunist mistakes which followed later, making him an enemy of the Soviet Union.

IV

FINAL YUGOSLAV POSITION (MAY 17, 1948)

We received your letter of May 4, 1948. It would be superfluous to write of the discouraging impression created on us by this letter. It has convinced us of the fact that all our explanations, though supported by facts showing that all the accusations against us were the result of wrong information, are in vain.

Yugoslav leaders fought and suffered with their resistance movement in the mountains of Yugoslavia. The Red Army did cut across the northeast corner of the country, and tens of thousands of Yugoslavs died in the last months of the war under Red Army command. But the Yugoslav leaders could call on a strong memory of sacrifice and sense of purpose born of implacable and successful resistance to Nazism in a way no other East European leaders could.

[9] Stalin believed that "no enemy is so evil and dangerous, so important to expose and so deserving of harsh treatment, as one who has worn the mask of a friend." As Robert C. Tucker puts it, "The word 'mask' . . . came readily to his lips" (Tucker, *Stalin as Revolutionary*, p. 453). Compare Rudolf Slánský's comments of December 1949 in Document 11, as well as the blameless careers of both Slánský and Rajk prior to their being purged.

We do not flee from criticism about questions of principle, but in this matter we feel at such a disadvantage that it is impossible for us to agree to have this matter decided now by the Cominform. Even before we were informed, the nine parties received your first letter and took their stand in resolutions. The contents of your letter did not remain an internal matter for individual parties but were carried outside the permissible circle, and the results are that today, in some countries such as Czechoslovakia and Hungary, not only our party but our country as a whole is being insulted, as was the case with our parliamentary delegation in Prague.

The results of all this have been very serious for our country.

We desire that the matter be liquidated in such manner that we prove, by deeds, that the accusations against us are unjust. That is, we will resolutely construct socialism and remain loyal to the Soviet Union; remain loyal to the doctrine of Marx, Engels, Lenin, and Stalin. The future will show, as did the past, that we will realize all that we promise you.

V

EXPULSION FROM THE COMINFORM (JUNE 28, 1948)

The Information Bureau considers that the basis of these mistakes made by the leadership of the Communist party of Yugoslavia lies in the undoubted fact that nationalist elements, which previously existed in a disguised form, managed in the course of the past five or six months to reach a dominant position in the leadership of the Communist party of Yugoslavia, and that consequently the leadership of the Yugoslav Communist party has broken with the internationalist traditions of the Communist party of Yugoslavia and has taken the road to nationalism.

Considerably overestimating the internal, national forces within Yugoslavia and their influence, the Yugoslav leaders think that they can maintain Yugoslavia's independence and build socialism without the support of the people's democracies, without the support of the Soviet Union. They think that the new Yugoslavia can do without the help of these revolutionary forces.

Showing their poor understanding of the international situation and their intimidation by the blackmailing threats of the imperialists, the Yugoslav leaders think that by making concessions they can curry favor with the imperialist states. They think they will be able to bargain with them for Yugoslavia's independence and, gradually, get the people of Yugoslavia oriented toward these states, that is, toward capitalism. In this they proceed tacitly from the well-known bourgeois–nationalist thesis that "capitalist states are a lesser danger to the independence of Yugoslavia than the Soviet Union."

The Yugoslav leaders evidently do not understand or, probably, pretend they do not understand, that such a nationalist line can only lead to Yugoslavia's degeneration into an ordinary bourgeois republic, to the loss of its independence and to its transformation into a colony of the imperialist countries.

The Information Bureau does not doubt that inside the Communist party of Yugoslavia there are enough healthy elements, loyal to Marxism–Leninism, and to the international traditions of the Yugoslav Communist party and to the united socialist front.[10]

Their task is to compel their present leaders to recognize their mistakes openly and honestly and to rectify them; to break with nationalism, return to internationalism; and in every way to consolidate the united front against imperialism.

Should the present leaders of the Yugoslav Communist party prove incapable of doing this, their job is to replace them and to advance a new internationalist leadership of the party.

The Information Bureau does not doubt that the Communist party of Yugoslavia will be able to fulfill this honorable task.

[10]There were in fact a significant number of supporters of the Cominform resolution in Yugoslavia, but Tito suppressed them. The most important of them passed through a concentration camp as horrible as anything Stalin constructed, Goli otok (Naked island). One of the reasons that the controversy escalated in the spring of 1948 was that after the initial exchange of letters Tito had arrested two former members of the Central Committee who supported Stalin. Sreten Žujović was suspected of passing information to the Russians, and Andrija Hebrang opposed the strongly worded answers to Stalin's letters.

The Purge Trials

With the creation of the Cominform and the subsequent expulsion of Yugoslavia from it, transformation of the communist states of Eastern Europe on the model of Stalin's Soviet Union began in earnest. The now-unopposed communist parties extended their influence and control to the lowest local level of government, re-organized the education system, eliminated private property, began a program of forced industrialization, collectivized agriculture (although with varying degrees of success), and "unmasked Titoist spies."

The first prominent "Titoist spy" was László Rajk, Hungarian foreign minister in 1948. Rajk joined the party as a young man and became political commissar of the Hungarian Battalion in the Spanish civil war. Interned by the French, he escaped in 1941 and became leader of the underground Hungarian Communist party, a role that probably hurt rather than helped him, as he was not a "Mus-covite" and therefore, to Stalin, was suspect. After the war Rajk rose to become minister of interior, where he ruthlessly brought the Hungarian Smallholders party under communist control. Despite this obviously loyal career, in 1949 Rajk ran afoul of the need to unmask a traitor. What better proof of the depth of his perfidy than his spotlessly loyal record? Tortured and promised a reprieve, Rajk confessed to all the absurd charges against him, the tone and direction of which are captured in the excerpt of the prosecutor's summation that follows. After being convicted, Rajk was quickly executed. Seven years later the party posthumously rehabilitated him and ceremonially reburied him as a "martyr of the party."

Perhaps the most disgusting purge took place in Bulgaria, where prosecutors ridiculed Traicho Kostov, who had been one of the party's most vigorous leaders and who had been deformed by injuries suffered when he jumped from a window to escape from jail years earlier. In Czechoslovakia the purges were the most exten-sive. There in 1952 the party's General Secretary Rudolf Slánský was convicted of the usual preposterous charges and executed. Almost twenty years later, during the Prague Spring of 1968, a commission of inquiry investigated Slánský's trial. Its report gives a good idea of how the purge trials originated and operated. Early in 1990, in an exquisite gesture of contempt, Václav Havel's newly installed Czecho-slovak government sent Slánský's son, also named Rudolf, to the Soviet Union as its ambassador.

10
The Trial of László Rajk

September 1949

Honored People's Court, it is obvious that the conspirators having the aim of restoring capitalism, the introduction of a bloodthirsty dictatorship on the fascist pattern, the betrayal of the independence of the country, and colonization on behalf of the imperialists, concentrated their attention and effort to weaken and dissolve that political force, that great party, which was the architect of the victories of the working people in Hungary, whose political determination and fighting spirit foiled all the attempts of reaction at home and abroad.

It is no accident that Rajk, Tibor Szőnyi, and their company were ordered by their imperialist bosses from [Allen] Dulles to [Aleksandar] Rankovich and Tito to make the party of the Hungarian Communists, the Hungarian Working People's party, unfit for the fight.[1] For the enemy has also learned that the party is the guardian and the defender of the people, democracy, and the people's republic and learned, too, that in order to stab the people's democracy, it is necessary to liquidate those leaders who are at the head of the party, the best defenders of the cause of the Hungarian working class, of our working people, and at the same time the firm pillars of our people's democratic government.

So it is no accident that an organic and definite part of the plan directed at the overthrow of our people's democracy was the annihilation of the most important leaders of the Hungarian Working People's party, "to render them harmless," and first of all, the murder of Mátyás Rákosi, Ernő Gerő, and Mihály Farkas.[2] It is easy to understand that the millions of masses of our working people were especially outraged by this vile plan of the conspirators, feeling instinctively that the man who wants to lift his bloodstained hand against the leader of our party and people, Mátyás Rákosi, is, at the same time, also an assassin of the power, the development, and the prosperity of the people.

Honored People's Court. In connection with this trial the speakers of the West-

---

[1]Allen Dulles was the head of the American intelligence branch at the end of World War II, and Aleksandar Ranković was the head of Yugoslav internal police and intelligence services.

[2]Rákosi (1892–1971) was active in the Soviet regime of Béla Kun in 1919 and spent World War II in the Soviet Union. He was first secretary of the Hungarian Communist party from 1945 to July 1956, when he was replaced by Gerő (1898–1980), also a lifelong member of the party. Gerő lasted only until October 25, 1956, when János Kádár replaced him. Farkas, noted for his brutalities during the purge period, headed the national defense and the secret police.

Reprinted from *László Rajk and His Accomplices Before the People's Court* (Budapest, 1949), pp. 264–65, 268–69, 271–73.

ern imperialist circles cast doubt on the objectiveness of the administration of justice in the Hungarian democracy, pretending that this trial is, in essence, not the trial of László Rajk and his company but that it is actually Tito and his associates who are in the dock. I do not deny that there is a great deal of truth in this. For by rights, not only those who personally committed the crime should be placed in the dock, but their instigators, too. It is true and right that the Hungarian People's Court, passing sentence on László Rajk and his gang of conspirators, should also pass sentence, in a political and moral sense, on the traitors of Yugoslavia, the criminal gang of Tito, Rankovich, Kardelj, and Djilas. The international significance of this trial lies particularly in the fact that we are passing sentence also on the Yugoslav deserters and traitors to democracy and socialism. We are exposing their duplicity, their perfidy, their intrigues, against democracy and socialism, their plans and acts of assassination. This trial has exposed the Titoites, the great majority of the present members of the Yugoslav government in their role of allies of the American imperialists and of common agents of the imperialist intelligence organizations.

There were two stages in the policy of the Tito clique. During the first stage, when the fight between bourgeois reaction and people's democracy in the East European countries was as yet undecided and one could still count on reaction getting the upper hand in the struggle of the forces in the peoples' democracies, the Tito clique remained in reserve, did not yet show their teeth, and did not yet come forward openly as the anti-Soviet storm troops of American imperialism. They appeared as these storm troops only in the second stage of development in East Europe when the democratic and socialist forces had already won a decisive victory in these countries and the organization of the anti-Soviet, proimperialist political forces could no longer be entrusted to the defeated groups of open reaction.

Fitting in with these two periods, the Tito gang attempted, up to the resolution of the Information Bureau, to hinder the peaceful development of the peoples' democracies in a so-called peaceful manner, and only later did they take to using terrorist and putsch methods.

Just as Yugoslavia was still in reserve in the years immediately after the war and only later became the open storm troops of imperialism, so in the same way Rajk did not immediately, in the first stages of Hungarian democratic development, come into prominence but remained an instrument in the hands of reaction at home and abroad. Only later, after the decisive victories of the Hungarian working class and after the routing of the different reactionary forces, did he come into prominence, and as the Tito clique's candidate for the post of prime minister he became, if only temporarily, the head of Hungarian reaction. The Titoites and their imperialist bosses did not turn to Rajk because of his beautiful eyes but because they could no longer turn to Ferenc Nagy and [Cardinal József] Mindszenty.[3] But they did not abandon the reactionary kulaks and clerical reactionary forces once they had put their cards on Rajk.

---

[3]Ferenc Nagy was a leader of the Smallholders party after World War II and prime minister of Hungary from 1946 to 1947. József Cardinal Mindszenty (1892–1975), primate of Hungary since 1945, was arrested both by the Béla Kun regime in 1919 and by the fascist Hungarian regime of 1944, for opposing totalitarianism. In 1948, when he refused to secularize Catholic schools, he was arrested again and convicted of treason. Released by the revolution of 1956, after the Soviet invasion he took refuge in the American legation, which he did not leave until 1971.

A necessary accessory of such gangster methods and the gangster program was the gangster art of lurking in the dark, pretence, political disguise, and duplicity. Rankovich gave Rajk lessons in this art. He explained to him Tito's so-called ingenious reorientation plan, how they would orientate the masses of the Yugoslav people stage by stage against the Soviet Union and the peoples' democracies. This gangster art of camouflage they prepared to use in Hungary also, where the new Rajk government wanted to issue a manifesto after the putsch about its unchanged "friendship" toward the Soviet Union, at the same time offering their mediating services in the conflict between the Soviet Union and Yugoslavia. In preparing Rákosi's murder, in preparing the country for subjection, abandoning the path of Soviet–Hungarian friendship, Rajk and his band at the same time prepared to deceive the Hungarian working people.

To throw dust in the eyes of the Hungarian working people, he wanted to extend a fascist, murderous hand, dipped in communist blood, in friendship to the Soviet Union.

American imperialism was the instigator and executor behind Tito's and Rankovich's entire political program and "putsch" plans! The American and British intelligence services purchased Tito and his clique even during the war against Hitler, to prevent the national and social liberation of the peoples of southeastern Europe, to isolate the Soviet Union, and to prepare the third world war. The anti-Soviet plan for the Balkan bloc was born not in Tito's head but in the intelligence offices of Washington and London. The putsch in Hungary, planned by Tito and his clique to be put into action by Rajk's spy ring, cannot be understood out of the context of the international plans of the American imperialists. Let us remember what Rajk said about the timing of the armed putsch. By this he meant the selection of a favorable moment from the point of view of world politics, that is, of a moment when the Soviet Union would be tied down, in order to allow free hands for the Yugoslav adventurers to carry out their internal and external armed intervention against the Hungarian People's Republic.

At the trial of a conspiracy against the state, in my opinion, it is the deeds of the accused which are decisive. Psychological motives are very unimportant. It is not difficult, however, to explain the psychological development of the accused either. Why did they become traitors? Because they were cowardly and vacillating, because they were not able to make any sacrifices. Why did they not desist from their trade of treachery later? For the same reason that they started it: They were in the hands of their masters; they were afraid of exposure; they had not enough courage to come out with their soiled past themselves. Why do they confess? Why don't they deny, or why don't they defend themselves? Because they have been exposed, because they know that they cannot help themselves by a denial. There is no regret in them, only fear of punishment. Their confessions are the results not of regret but of their exposure.

Precisely because of this, Honored People's Court, there is no extenuating circumstance. There are no extenuating circumstances, only aggravating circumstances. Our people demand death for the traitors and I, as the representative of the prosecuting authority, identify myself with this demand. The head of the snake which wants to bite us must be crushed. We must defend the achievements of our democracy, our national independence, and our peaceful building work from traitors

11

The Slánský Trial

Events of 1949–52 (report written in 1968)

The main buildup of the major political trials started in our country early in 1949. Yet the situation at home, the distortion of party work and violations of the law . . . could not in themselves have given cause for the fabricating of such large-scale political trials as those in which the Czechoslovak party became involved in the early 1950s. Throughout 1949 the party leadership still adhered to the view expressed by [Czechoslovak President Klement] Gottwald that they had all known each other over many years of joint work, and that in a legal party, as the Czechoslovak Communist party had been before the war, there were no grounds for such conspiracies as were supposed at that time to exist in Hungary, Poland, and Bulgaria. A big part in the concocting of cases against top men in the party and government of Czechoslovakia was played by international factors—the Cominform policies that assumed the existence of an international imperialist conspiracy against the socialist countries, the specific political and ideological pressures exerted from without, notably Hungarian, Polish, and Soviet insistence that an extensive conspiracy, or even the center of an international plot, was located in Czechoslovakia. In the course of time these ideas came to be accepted by the Czechoslovak party leaders, and in other quarters, especially Security.

The state in which the party found itself is best illustrated by a speech made by [General Secretary of the Czechoslovak Communist party Rudolf] Slánský at a meeting of Prague activists in the Lucerna Hall on 7 December [1949]. Referring to the experience gained from the trials in the other countries, he said:

> Nor will our party escape having the enemy place his people among us and recruiting his agents among our members. . . . Aware of this, we must be all the more vigilant, so that we can unmask the enemies in our own ranks, for they are the most dangerous enemies.

At this gathering Slánský also outlined ways of seeking and finding the enemies. The first thing was to take a good hard look at those who voiced incorrect views, because that was the way that "the true bourgeois–nationalist face" of a spy revealed itself. Secondly, it was necessary to examine how political tasks were carried out, because difficulties, irregularities and muddles could be signs of deliberate sabotage. Lastly, a daily check on party functionaries was needed, with special attention to their past, because "dark spots" in their lives could be misused by enemy agencies.

Slánský's speech provided a complete justification for extensive security work inside the Communist party and for the general attitude of suspicion; it could not but have the gravest consequences. By the end of 1949 the course of events abroad and the trend of party policy had produced a state of affairs where it was no longer possible to halt the process of distortion in the party and in State Security. Lack of success in the investigations led not to any reassessment of the original assumptions but, on the contrary, to a compounding of the blunders. Under these conditions the preparation of the political trials entered upon a new and more dangerous phase.

Further steps by the Czechoslovak authorities were taken in an atmosphere of psychosis about an imminent threat to the republic and the entire socialist camp—an atmosphere further poisoned, probably, by fear that they might be labeled as allies of the Titoists for preventing a final "unmasking" of these "enemies." On 16 September [1949] Gottwald and Slánský requested Malenkov to send to Czechoslovakia, as advisers, men acquainted with the handling of the Rajk case.[1] The request was granted and on 23 September two Soviet experts, Likhachev and Makarov, arrived in Prague.

With the arrival of the Soviet advisers, changes took place in the work done by Czechoslovak Security. Preparations for political trials now assumed massive proportions. An entirely new *modus operandi* was introduced; the investigation of genuine offences in the light of verified evidence was replaced by the search for enemies, primarily inside the Communist party. Political views expressed not only in deeds but also in words or intentions, fulfilled or otherwise, and also confessions of imaginary "hostile acts" now served as evidence. By variously combining such testimony from prisoners, the security officers were able to fabricate hostile groups and treasonable offenses. Once a man was detained, therefore, his confessions could provide the starting point for further investigations and convictions. Hence everything was done to extract "confessions" and depositions. The inhuman methods used, involving a carefully worked out system of physical and mental coercion, have been described in numerous books and newspaper articles.

Often a sincerely self-critical admission of error or a single obscure point in a *curriculum vitae* was enough for a man to be denounced and arrested, or the cause could be mere tittle-tattle or slander, a fabrication or provocation. Special attention was paid to anybody even remotely suspected of holding Trotskyist or nationalist views (the latter being automatically taken to be anti-Soviet), to people of Jewish extraction (denounced as Zionists), and to anyone who had spent some time in the Western countries or lived in a "bourgeois environment." In a word, an arrested man was assumed to be guilty, and the interrogators had merely to "make" a case out of him and secure his conviction. The purpose of the interrogation was to break the victim at all costs, to extract a confession irrespective of whether he had

---

[1]Georgi Malenkov was perhaps Stalin's closest adviser from 1948 to 1953. In 1949 he was deputy chairman of the Council of Ministers and secretary of the Central Committee.

committed an offense or not. To achieve this, all kinds of mental and physical coercion and brute force were permissible. The usual method was an endless interrogation of the victim, with the officers working in shifts so that he or she received only a minimum of rest; to this was added beatings, torture by hunger and thirst, confinement in the dark chamber, the inculcation of fear about the fate of the prisoner's family, subtly staged confrontations, the use of stool pigeons, the bugging of cells, and many other refinements.

The situation was complicated by growing rivalry and mistrust in the relations between the Control Commission and State Security. Some of the commission's staff gradually became convinced that quite a number of top people in State Security lacked the necessary ability and determination to discover the Czechoslovak Rajk, that they were even covering up political sabotage and that they wanted to break free from party control—indeed, to impose their own control on the party. Towards the end of 1950 suspicion turned against [Karel] Šváb, the man whom the party leadership had appointed to a top post in State Security. Two of the Control Commission staff were installed in the central Security office to collect information about leading people there.

These facts indicate that in the second half of 1949 a truly paradoxical situation was taking shape. On the initiative of the top men in the party, a section had been established for hunting enemies in the party; while operating in parallel with this, in the shape of the Party Control Commission, was a party section that included Security methods in its repertoire of techniques used for unmasking enemies among the Communists employed in State Security. It is easy to understand how in the early 1950s, when both organizations took a hand in preparing and carrying through the political cases and the trials, there were often sudden switches, with the hunter becoming the hunted, the prosecutor the accused, and the interrogator the interrogated.

The large-scale arrests of Communists late in 1950 and early in 1951 were a sure sign that yet another wave of political repression was on the way. Top men in the party, in Security, and in military and industrial posts suddenly found themselves in prison, and a similar fate befell many people at lower levels. A selected group of prisoners was held for some weeks in a hurriedly improvised prison at Koloděj House near Prague. Many witnesses have confirmed that the brutality of the interrogations at this place was the worst known up to that time. On the recommendation of the Soviet advisers and with their most active participation, people were subjected to nonstop questioning, beaten, and tormented by hunger and thirst. Prisoners were kept in damp cellars with earthen floors where they suffered frostbite on their hands and feet.

In these conditions the interrogators managed to get most of their victims to "confess" to sabotage or to make statements about other people. But while they extracted a lot of "damaging findings," the interrogators and their advisers had to admit that the "evidence" was not very conclusive and that it failed to confirm their view of Šling and Švermová as the leaders of a conspiracy. Anxious lest the scheme publicly announced at the Central Committee meeting in February should come to nothing, and impatient at the slow progress, some of the staff suggested to Gottwald and Slánský that the ringleader must be someone in a higher position than Šling.

At this point the name of Rudolf Slánský began to appear with increasing frequency in statements by prisoners. Some mentioned him in self-defense, saying truthfully that they had been posted to responsible positions at his suggestion or that they had acted with his knowledge or consent, or even on his orders. Others named him because—rightly or wrongly—they thought him responsible for agreeing to their arrest.

Slánský's name had been mentioned during the February interrogations at Koloděj, but since the inquiries were still directed against Šling, these remarks attracted little attention and, in obedience to a political ruling about the names of prominent people, were not recorded.[2] Nevertheless, the minister of national security and the Soviet advisers were informed, either by word of mouth or in written reports.

Before long, however, these anti-Slánský statements began to attract greater attention as offering a possible way out of the impasse reached by the investigation. Moreover, by the spring of 1951 several statements accusing Slánský of definite offenses had been made by detainees in the Ruzyň Prison. For the most part they had been obtained by interrogators and others who were so dissatisfied with the restrictions on direct questions about Slánský that they went so far as to go behind the backs of the Ministry of National Security and the Soviet advisers and state their views at the embassy of the U.S.S.R.

The idea of turning the inquiry against Slánský was also encouraged by the fact that at this time Zionism was regarded as a major weapon in the imperialist conspiracy against the socialist camp. Moreover, after Šváb's arrest his place at the head of the department handling the search for enemies in the party was taken by [A.] Keppert, a man described in a report made in 1963 as notorious for his "rabid anti-Semitism."

On his fiftieth birthday, 31 July, Slánský was awarded the highest Czechoslovak decoration (the Order of Klement Gottwald for the Building of Socialism) and a letter of congratulation from the party's Central Committee; at the last moment Gottwald deleted some of the superlatives contained in the draft, and the words that Slánský was among Gottwald's most faithful colleagues. No birthday greetings came from Moscow, however, although that was the message he seemed most concerned to receive.

At the very time when the press was carrying laudatory articles about Slánský and when the letters and telegrams of congratulation were pouring in, Artur London and Karel Šváb were writing their statements in the Ruzyň Prison "convicting" Slánský of espionage and subversion. The [Soviet] advisers Galkin and Yesikov then got Doubek and Košťál to write a second report on the whole affair.[3] Early in August the four of them used this document in order to persuade Minister Kopřiva to agree that direct questioning about Slánský should proceed.[4] Kopřiva consulted

[2]Otto Šling, head of the party in Brno and member of the Central Committee, was the original target of the investigations that eventually led to Slánský. Tried and executed with Slánský, he was rehabilitated in 1963 but not reinstated in the party.

[3]Bohumil Doubek was head of the investigations section of State Security, and Karel Košťál was one of that agency's interrogators.

[4]Ladislav Kopřiva was minister of national security.

Gottwald at his residence in Lány and returned with the news that the president had received the reports in all seriousness, and considered that all possible means should be used to discover the head of the conspiracy. This indirect answer was enough; orders were immediately issued for renewed interrogation of certain prisoners.

At a Central Committee meeting in September Slánský was subjected to searching criticism: His misjudgments in making appointments had given an opening to the enemy; he had elevated the party apparatus above governmental bodies (the theory of the second center of power); and he had failed to appreciate the fundamental question, "where is the actual seat of government?" Gottwald clearly took his speech largely from material received via Kopřiva from the interrogators and the Soviet advisers. Slánský made a self-critical statement, which was sent with a confidential letter from the Central Committee to all party branches. He was appointed a deputy prime minister, and Zápotocký was supposed to pay special attention to him.[5] At about the same time one of the Soviet advisers was arranging for all the material against Slánský and others to be assembled, after which he left with it for Moscow.

The criticism and demotion of Slánský evoked a powerful response. The general feeling expressed at meetings and in resolutions was that Gottwald had opened the door to the correction of errors in party work; there was appreciation for the fact that he had not hesitated to criticize even his closest associate of many years' standing. Gottwald's prestige grew, and Communists, especially, pinned their hopes on him as the wave of universal suspicion mounted once more. Slánský's self-criticism was received with approval in some quarters, in others with mistrust; not a few voices declared that he had been treated too lightly, that he had not told the party everything, and that he might well be the hidden enemy in the top party leadership.

The Slánský case took a new and decisive turn when [Anastas] Mikoyan made a sudden visit to Prague on 11 November [1951] in his capacity as a member of the Soviet Politburo. He brought with him a personal message from Stalin to Gottwald, differing substantially from the standpoint of July. Stalin now insisted on Slánský's immediate arrest, because, it seemed, he might escape at any moment to the West.

The summer and autumn were spent also in making the final organizational and personnel preparations and in drafting the indictment. The prosecutors, judges, and defense counsel underwent special briefing before the trial, each being assigned his precise role. They had to promise to adhere faithfully to the documents provided by the interrogators and to follow the scenario of the proceedings.

Meanwhile, on the instructions of the advisers, the accused were memorizing the statements they were to make in court. Although by now they were broken men, to make sure all went well their parts were tape-recorded in advance—a lesson gleaned from the trial of Kostov who, once in court, retracted his previous statements, whereupon he was forbidden to speak and his prepared testimony was read out.[6] Extracts from the recordings were actually played to the party presidium!

---

[5]Antonín Zápotocký, who spent the war in a German concentration camp, was prime minister from 1948 to 1953.

[6]Traicho Kostov was the Bulgarian equivalent of Rajk and Slánský. He was the only "Titoist spy" to repudiate his confession in open court, but he was hanged anyway.

Immediately before the trial, [Karol] Bacílek held personal talks with the accused (except Slánský), suggesting to them that by keeping to the agreed procedure in court they might earn lighter sentences, appealing to their loyalty to the party, in whose interest the trial had to take place, and promising that their families would be cared for.

The indictment underwent several changes. The first two versions were drafted on instructions from the Soviet advisers and amended according to their wishes. When the Political Secretariat discussed the document on 13 November there was no opposition. Some criticism, not directed against the substance of the indictment, was voiced by Čepička and Gottwald; the former considered the indictment weak from the professional point of view, and the evidence for an attempt to assassinate Gottwald seemed to him unconvincing.[7] Gottwald expressed the view that "activity in the party ought not to be a matter for prosecution." Yet both made it quite clear that they agreed with the charges against Slánský, and this was implicit in their other criticisms. Gottwald, for instance, thought it necessary to show Slánský's "deception, hypocrisy and lying." Judging from the minutes of the meeting, a sharp attack on Slánský and others was made by [Václav] Kopecký, who found it necessary to point out that "Westerners" and Jews were liable to become agents of American imperialism.[8] A pragmatic approach to the affair betrayed fears that the trial might undermine confidence in the Five Year Plan. A commission was appointed to make the final draft of the indictment, the final editing being done by Gottwald who, in addition to minor amendments, deleted passages accusing Slánský of propagating a Czechoslovak road to socialism.

A decision about the sentences was also taken about this time, though there is no record of where and when. However, the customary procedure was followed—a decision was made and handed down by the Minister of Justice to the prosecutors and the court. That this decision was taken by the political leadership is indicated in a statement made by Čepička in 1963: "Discussion of the verdicts was conducted in an atmosphere of great responsibility on the part of all, not excluding Gottwald, and I think it did not last long."

On 20 November 1952 the trial began—staged according to a scenario and timetable prepared in advance. Only once did the prosecutor leave out a question, and the accused, having memorized his sequence of questions and answers, reply to the question he should have been asked, instead of the one actually put to him.

Before the proceedings ended, instructions had already been given for handling any appeals that might be lodged. They were to be heard on 4 December and were to confirm the verdicts. A remarkable feature, apart from the decision that the appeals should be heard in one day, was that the Political Secretariat decided upon so important a matter without meeting to discuss it; the members merely telephoned their agreement with the arrangements proposed.

The trial was given full radio and press publicity. From the moment it started, the party and other organizations were mobilized for action. Thousands of resolutions poured in to the Central Committee, the president, and the State Court.

---

[7]Alexej Čepička was deputy prime minister.

[8]"Westerners" refers to persons who were not in the Soviet Union during the war.

Thousands of death sentences were passed in factories, offices, and other places of work before the court had even delivered its verdict. And yet there were individuals who had doubts and warned against giving way to irrational moods and passions. Clearly, the long indictment and the clockwork precision of the proceedings had caused some misgivings.

The verdicts, delivered on 27 November 1952, found the accused guilty of multiple charges of high treason, espionage, sabotage and military treason: Slánský, Geminder, Frejka, Frank, Clementis, Reicin, Šváb, Margolius, Fischl, Šling, and Simone were sentenced to death; London, Löbl, and Hajdů to life imprisonment. No appeals were lodged, and the pleas for clemency were rejected. On 3 December 1952 eleven of the fourteen accused went to the scaffold [including Slánský].

II

The Marxist Critique

Brief though Stalin's direct rule over Eastern Europe was, lasting five years in Czechoslovakia and only slightly longer elsewhere, the history of the region since his death in 1953 can be read as an effort to maintain, modify, or overthrow the system he established there. The initial relaxation that followed his death produced the Polish October and the Hungarian Revolution, which together defined the limits the new Soviet leadership was willing to tolerate—a certain amount of national communism in Poland and Yugoslavia, but no overt challenges to Soviet hegemony or to the leading role of the communist parties. Within these limits, however, a good deal of rethinking of the Marxist viewpoint was possible. Steeped in Leninism, intellectuals in Eastern Europe in the decade after the Hungarian Revolution sought to redefine Marxism, while several regimes drifted from strict reliance on Soviet and Stalinist models. In Poland, Gomułka permitted the peasantry to retain most of its private holdings. János Kádár, at first reviled as the man who came to power over the bodies of Hungarian revolutionaries, proved to be a flexible and original leader. Hewing closely to the Soviet line in international and party affairs, he introduced a New Economic Mechanism (NEM), which for a while at least seemed to create improved economic conditions. Even Romania resisted Soviet Premier Nikita Khrushchev's efforts to coordinate the economies of the East European countries through Comecon (Council for Mutual Economic Assistance, or CMEA), the Soviets' rickety response to the European Community. The most transformed country was Yugoslavia, which began to decentralize, opened its borders to permit more than a million Yugoslavs to work in Western Europe in the 1960s as *Gastarbeiters*, and began economic reforms that by the 1970s had brought considerable prosperity. The culmination of these "winds of change" as they were called at the time, however, was not a general evolution toward a hybrid system, but the Prague Spring, a brief outpouring of Czech reformism that brought on an invasion of Warsaw Pact forces in August 1968.

The readings in this part begin with the Hungarian Revolution and end with the announcement of the Brezhnev Doctrine in 1968. During this period of search for a path to socialism that would not be Stalinist, few in Eastern Europe openly challenged the Marxist framework. Reform, renewal, and improvement were the themes, not outright rejection or disgust. Even the theorists of the Hungarian Revolution of 1956 began with strictly Marxist premises, although for a few climactic days many Hungarians went beyond them. We begin with two selections from the literature of that revolution.

The Hungarian Revolution

After Stalin's death in March 1953 the new Soviet leadership began to pursue an ameliorative policy toward Eastern Europe. In 1955, for example, Nikita Khrushchev and Georgi Malenkov, party leader and head of state, respectively, visited Belgrade and apologized to Tito for expelling Yugoslavia from the Cominform in 1948. In Hungary the Soviet leadership moved to end the Stalinist practice of placing the offices of both prime minister and general secretary in the hands of one man. Imre Nagy became Hungary's new prime minister in 1953 while Mátyás Rákosi retained his party position. Nagy, who had spent the years between 1929 and 1944 in the Soviet Union, quickly attempted to set Hungary on what the Soviets called a "New Course," permitting peasants to leave cooperatives, lessening the influence of the security services, and rationalizing Hungary's unbalanced heavy industry policy. But by 1955, in a series of internal maneuvers, Rákosi forced him out. Between this ouster and his reemergence as prime minister during the Hungarian Revolution of October–November 1956, Nagy wrote a lengthy study based on his complete confidence in Marxian analysis, but in effect strongly condemning the communist practices of his day. When the revolution of 1956 failed, the Soviets seized Nagy by trickery and, after holding him in Romania, secretly executed him and buried him in an unmarked grave, in this way making him a national martyr. In June 1989, 250,000 Hungarians attended Nagy's ceremonial reburial in Budapest.

The second reading in this section is part of a talk presented to the Petőfi Circle in the summer of 1956 by György Lukács. The Petőfi Circle, named after the great Hungarian poet of national resistance in 1848, produced a good deal of the intellectual agitation that led to the Hungarian Revolution of 1956. Lukács was the greatest philosophical interpreter of Stalinism, a creative Marxist thinker who nonetheless always considered the party to be right. Inspired by the Twentieth Party Congress of the Soviet party, held in 1956, at which Khrushchev exposed Stalin's "cult of personality," Lukács's speech criticizes the silences of Stalinism and calls for a return to true Leninism. Lukács became minister of culture in the brief revolutionary regime of 1956, even though in principle he opposed the free expression of ideas. Held in Romania with Imre Nagy, in 1957 he returned to Budapest, where he died in 1971.

12

Reform Communism

Imre Nagy
1955–56

Marxism is a science that cannot remain static but must develop and become more perfect. It is impossible that Marxism in its development should not become enriched with new experiences, new knowledge; therefore certain Marxist theories and conclusions must necessarily change as time passes. There must be changes by adding new theories and conclusions to conform with the new historical demands of the times. "Marxism does not recognize unchangeable conclusions and theories that are binding for every era and time," Stalin wrote in the Marr debate.

One must keep in step with the rapidly changing economic, social, political, and cultural situation. As a matter of fact Marxism–Leninism must be the first to point out the further development of vital, basic needs in international relations, in revolutionary transformation, in the future of socialism.

Therefore Marxism–Leninism has not been completed with the scientific theories and results attained thus far. The further development of Marxism–Leninism and its enrichment through the additions of new theories did not cease with the death of Marx, Engels, and Lenin.

The scientific theories of Marxism–Leninism, its theoretical statements, their further development in conformity with changing social–economic trends on the basis of the teachings of the masters—there is the historic role and duty of every communist and workers' party. The forms, methods, and means of attaining this were not prescribed by Marx, nor did he tie the hands of the leaders of the socialist revolution or himself in attaining this goal. He foresaw that during the period of development the ever changing situation would bring about new problems. It was from this that the Lenin directive sprang: that the science for which Marx laid down the cornerstone through his teachings about the dictatorship of the proletariat must be expanded in all directions, in order that it keep pace with life. The theory of Marx—as Lenin stated—gives general guiding principles, which must be utilized in Britain in another fashion than in France, in France differently than in Germany, and in Germany in another way than in Russia.

Since the death of Lenin a rigid dogmatism has been the rule, based on the application and further development of Marxism–Leninism and upon the theory of scientific socialism. This has caused serious theoretical mistakes, which have had

Reprinted from Imre Nagy, *On Communism* (New York: Praeger, 1957), pp. 4–8, 80–84.

repercussions in social development on a worldwide scale as well as on the struggle between the two systems, and finally on the fate of socialism itself.

As a result of the Stalinist monopoly over the science of Marxism–Leninism, ideas became prevalent in communist and workers' parties that the only way of building socialism through "proper" methods, ways, and means were those practiced in the Soviet Union. Leninist teachings dealing with the application of Marxism–Leninism to characteristic situations in the Soviet Union were forced into the background. The existence of the Soviet Union, its development and strengthening, have had a decisive historical significance on the development of socialism all over the world. This is the basic theory of scientific socialism. Of course it cannot be denied that the Communist party of the Soviet Union has had the most experience in the pioneering application of Marxism–Leninism, which means that the Communist party of the Soviet Union is the one that is destined to play the most important role in further development of Marxist–Leninist teachings. But from all this it does not necessarily follow that the application of Marxism–Leninism to Soviet situations should constitute a general law, which would be everywhere applicable, regardless of characteristic Soviet situations, as the only correct and binding theory. This could cause serious difficulties in the development of socialism on a worldwide scale.

"All nations will arrive at socialism—this is inescapable—but they will not arrive there in a completely identical fashion. Each will lend its own characteristics to one or another form of democracy, or one or another form of the dictatorship of the proletariat, or to the changes and the pace at which socialist life will be finally accomplished," stated Lenin.

The great importance of these individual traits is especially pointed up by the following words of Lenin:

> As long as there are national and governmental differences between nations and peoples—and we know that these differences will be apparent for a very, very long time to come, even after the attainment of the dictatorship of the proletariat on a worldwide scale—there will be a need for the tactical unity of the international movement of the world's communist workers. This will not demand the elimination of various differences, or the end of specific national characteristics, but the validation of basic communist theories (soviet power and the dictatorship of the proletariat), in conformance with national and governmental differences. It is necessary in each individual country to seek out, to study, find, and recognize those national characteristics, those characteristic elements which, from a national standpoint, may lead to the concrete solution of the central international problem, to the victory over opportunism and leftist doctrinairism, to overthrowing the rule of the bourgeoisie, and to the creation of the Soviet republic and the dictatorship of the proletariat: This is the chief aim in the leading (and not only the leading) countries at the present time.

Lenin is speaking of the same thing when he says that the road leading to socialist economy is generally well known, and he rounds out this declaration by the following:

But the concrete ways and means of achieving this change are necessarily very diverse and they must so remain, since they depend upon conditions upon which the creation of socialism and progress toward it begins. All these local differences, as well as the characteristics forms of the economy, the way of life of the population, the degree of their preparedness, and all plans directed toward realizing the road to socialism must be reflected in the attempts for bringing socialism about.

Lenin brought this to the attention of Hungarians during the first days of the Soviet republic, when he told us in a direct radio message:[1] "It cannot be questioned that under the characteristic conditions of the Hungarian revolution it would be wrong merely to imitate our Russian tactics in every detail."

A people's democracy is the only characteristic form that has thus far been recognized by the dogmatic explanation of Marxism–Leninism in attaining socialism through the transition from capitalism to socialism. But the peoples' democracies are treated as similar, utilizing identical methods, prescribing for their development identical forms and pace, not recognizing the diversity of differences in conditions, although it is clearly apparent that socialism is different in its development in the Soviet Union, China, Yugoslavia, or Hungary.

Such rigid, dogmatic interpretations of Marxism–Leninism and its application prevent the "working out" of the characteristic forms of socialism.

The Third Congress of the Hungarian Workers' party confirmed the thesis that the June resolution of the Central Committee had opened a new course in the building of socialism in Hungary.[2] A correct definition of the concept, essence, and character of the New Course is of great importance because the unclear definition of the essence of the New Course is responsible for certain views, according to which the New Course is tantamount to an anti-Marxist, rightist deviation. Such views and the charge of anti-Marxism are incorrect and completely unfounded. A study of Marxism–Leninism will reveal that the classics of scientific socialism alternately used the expressions of "course" (*étape*) and "period," meaning the same thing. The principle and concept of a "New Course" is, therefore, not in contradiction with the theory of Marxism–Leninism. Stalin divided the New Economic Policy (NEP) into two "courses" or "periods," emphasizing that strategic tasks did not change in the former or in the latter course.

For an exact Marxist–Leninist theoretical definition of the New Course, needed to avoid misinterpretations or to refute them, and for amending the incomplete and inadequate statements concerning the New Course voiced at the Third Congress of

[1]The Soviet Republic of 1919 refers to the revolutionary regime of Béla Kun, which assumed power on March 21, 1919. Kun instituted a radical regime of socialization, alienated the peasantry by not carrying out land reform, and lost the support of nationalists by acceding to Allied demands to give up Slovakia, which the Hungarians had just taken back from the occupying Czechs. His regime, which was repressive and bloody, lasted 133 days and was followed by an even bloodier conservative reaction.

[2]Imre Nagy assumed the position of premier in June 1953. Accordingly, the Central Committee of the Hungarian Workers' party adopted a resolution of changed party policy implicitly criticizing the Stalinist policies of Mátyás Rákosi, who remained first secretary of the party. Nagy announced this "New Course" in a speech on July 4, 1953, and it was routinely confirmed, as all resolutions of the Central Committee were at that time, by the Third Congress of the party in 1954.

the HWP, it must be established that the New Course initiated by the June 1953 resolution of the Central Committee did not set new strategic tasks for the party.[3] The former strategic task—laying the economic foundations of socialism and building socialism in Hungary—had been left untouched. Therefore, the policy of the New Course had been directed toward the solution of the old strategic task by changing and improving the former bad tactics. The New Course gives expression to this tactical change. Arguments on the terminology and charges of anti-Marxism are only forms in the fight against the important economic and political measures stipulated by the June resolution.

The main strategic task, the party's strategy, is based on historic "turns" and embraces whole periods. Therefore during the period of transition from capitalism to socialism the strategy and its main goal remain unchanged. At the same time, however, there are definite changes within the given periods, which are best expressed by the word *course*. Within the unchanged principal strategic direction, these changes are expressed in new tactics. Thus, in the *étapes* of development, *within* the strategy, there can be and definitely will be changes. Such a change, in Hungary, was the New Course, the new tactic.

One of the main characteristics of the transitional period is the struggle between capitalist and socialist elements. Within the transitional period, the economic and political goals of the New Course were determined by these same basic tasks. The economic policy of the New Course is, therefore, the proper application of the teachings of Marxism–Leninism to the specific Hungarian conditions, on the basis of specific traits in the transitional period and the objective needs of building socialism in the field of socialist transformation and development of the people's economy.

In the transitional period, during the struggle between socialist and capitalist elements, it is of utmost importance that

1. The party and the state rely in all their activities on a scientific basis, and, first of all, on a knowledge of the law of harmonizing the forces of production with a proper ratio between the various types of production.

2. The party's economic policy must be so directed as to increase the forces of production and to develop the people's economy in a proportionate and planned way. Increase of the forces of production and a planned, proportionate developing of agriculture in the field of building socialism will ensure the realization of the basic law of socialism (raising the standard of living) and the realization of uninterrupted, augmented secondary production on the basis of the most modern technical achievements.

3. The party's economic policy must be founded on the principles of proletarian internationalism and the pursuit of a lasting peace, peaceful coexistence, and economic competition of different systems. Furthermore, trade agreements between the two systems (communist and capitalist) must serve the improvement of international division of labor as well as the expanding of the socialist world market.

[3]HWP stands for the Hungarian Workers' party, or the communists. After the revolution of 1956, the party changed its name to the Hungarian Socialist Workers' party, and in 1989 it became simply the Hungarian Socialist party.

4. The party's economic policy must take into account the requirements of national and international security based on the Leninist principles of peaceful coexistence, which makes disarmament and reduction of war expenditures possible and also makes it possible that the latest achievements of science and technology be employed for the purpose of peaceful construction and improvement of well-being and of the standard of living.

5. The party's economic policy must take into account that in the world, as well as in the peoples' democracies within the socialist bloc, many socioeconomic formations or sectors, or the remnants of these, exist side by side during the transitory period.

6. The NEP policy must be carried out unconditionally, as it means the establishment of increasingly closer relations in the exchange of goods between the city and the village, between socialist industry and the system of small holdings producing for the market, facilitating the switch to a socialist system of agricultural farms producing on a large scale.

These basic requirements and specific traits of the transitional period's economic policy were either nonexistent in Hungary or were realized only in part—partly because our economic policy lacked a scientific basis in Marxist–Leninist analysis and also because, as a consequence, we simply copied the Soviet methods applied at a much later stage in the building of socialism, thus skipping whole stages of development. That is the reason why Hungary needed a New Course in the building of socialism—to make it possible that basic principles and requirements of transitional period could fully assert themselves, leaving room for characteristic and specific traits arising from concrete conditions and at the same time assuring the most effective ways, forms, and methods of developing socialism. But for the very same reason the New Course cannot be simply "abolished" or "suspended," because such action would deprive the country of the possibility of a successful and easy way of building socialism, and one requiring the least possible sacrifices from the population.

One of the main tasks of the New Course in Hungary was to make it possible that basic principles of general validity and normal development of the transitional period, which previously had been completely suppressed or just partly realized, could fully assert themselves.

Another task was giving the green light to specific ways and forms arising from Hungarian conditions in the building of the people's economy on a socialist basis, in order to create conditions for basic principles of universal validity as well as for the concrete and wide application of new ways and forms created by specific conditions during the period of transition. It had to guarantee democratism in the country and the party; far-reaching activities and creative initiative of the masses; observance of regulations by party organization in the party and of human rights and duties and citizens' rights in state life as stipulated by the constitution; and it had to advance the activities of leading organs to the platform of legality.

It was a serious shortcoming of the New Course that in many important fields it brought about only half-solutions. The economic policy of the New Course showed serious shortcomings because of the resistance of the party and state organs, especially in the field of economy, and also because objective economic laws were not always correctly applied as a result of not having been scientifically analyzed, and because specific Hungarian conditions were not clearly defined. The main error was not that we established the New Course in Hungary for building socialism but, rather, the fact that we did not follow this course consistently and fully. This, on the other hand, makes us draw the logical conclusion that the New Course must not be liquidated but, rather, should be fully realized, eliminating its shortcomings and paying great attention to those specific tasks that are necessitated by specific conditions in Hungary. Lenin laid special emphasis on the latter problem.

These teachings of Lenin were, unfortunately, all but forgotten in Hungary. One of the most important ideological tasks awaiting Hungarian Communists is to revive these teachings and apply them to the specific Hungarian conditions.

13

Contemporary Problems of Marxist Philosophy
György Lukács (translated by Michael Henry Heim)
June 15, 1956

Esteemed Comrades! Viewing the situation after the Twentieth Congress, we see that in abstract terms there have never been such prospects for the spread of Marxism–Leninism on a worldwide scale as those afforded by the Twentieth Congress.[1] The Twentieth Congress offers exciting possibilities that call for more than a short campaign; I dare say it will take all of us—and here I have in mind the young people rather than myself—a lifetime to realize the possibilities unleashed now, and this should give every one of us new spirit and enthusiasm.

Colossal possibilities stand before us, but—and here we have the other side of the question—what is the situation of Marxism today in Hungary? And I hope the comrades will not take it amiss—certain quotations have given the impression that I am quite blunt and outspoken—and now I wish to speak my mind quite bluntly. I venture to suggest that Marxism has never been in such ill repute among the citizens of our country as it is now; I venture to suggest that it is in worse repute than it was in the Horthy period.[2] Why? Because in the Horthy period at least a small group of people risked their lives to get hold of a work by Marx or Lenin and because a part of the intelligentsia opposed Marxism with animosity, with hatred, but with a certain fear—a feeling that it was something terrifying, perhaps dangerous, perhaps even good—and a certain respect. The last seven or eight years have been enough to destroy this good feeling and not only, I would add, among nonparty intellectuals but also—though of course secretly, under cover, on the sly—among party intellectuals.

Allow me to illustrate this phenomenon with an anecdote that many of you

---

[1] At the Twentieth Congress of the Communist party of the Soviet Union, held in February 1956, party leader Nikita Krushchev shocked the communist world by revealing Stalin's crimes. Krushchev characterized Stalin's "cult of personality" as an aberration from party principles and called for a return to Leninist practices.

[2] Admiral Miklós Horthy (1868–1957) led the army of the right against the Hungarian Soviet Republic of Béla Kun, and, as regent for the restored Hungarian king who never returned to his throne, dominated Hungarian politics until his removal by the Germans in 1944. Conservative and anticommunist, Horthy's regime was increasingly rigid, but it never acceded to the most monstrous demands of the Nazis.

Taken from György Lukács, *Curriculum vitae*, ed. János Ambrus (Budapest: Magvető kiado, 1982), pp. 159–67.

doubtless know. A university student was being examined in Marxism–Leninism. He was a bright student and did very well on the examination, answered every question, received a grade of "Excellent" naturally, and when his fellow students congratulated him out in the corridor he stopped them with a wave of the hand and said, "What is this Marx stuff? Utter nonsense. Only Heidegger and Huxley are worth reading."[2]

Things have come to such a pass because of a type of Marxist education bearing a certain analogy to the mistakes that have occurred in our industrial development. I will not go into details about that here, but everyone knows what disastrous results the one-sided, quantity-based development of industry has led to; I will not go into details, nor should I, as it is not my field. But in the area of ideology, too, we took to the assembly line; we began mass-producing philosophers with no knowledge, no ability to think, no culture. I do not blame the individual philosophers so much as the system that produced them. There are those among the young who complain of having no time. But why have they no time? Because the teacher who trained them as philosophers did not consider it necessary for a philosopher to know anything.

Let me again refer to personal experience. I have heard any number of complaints from the intelligentsia in this regard. Even party members who have attained a relatively high level of party education and participated in "individual study" are forced to fight for permission to read, say, the first volume of *Capital* in its context. It may no longer be the case, but a few years ago individual study for a philosopher consisted in reading the *Anti-Dühring* from page 40 to page 70, Feuerbach from page 80 to page 85, and so on, and not for anything in the world could a person be induced to read a work through in its context.

It is clear, comrades, that if this is how we mass-produced our philosophers they could have little knowledge or even—hats off to the few exceptions—thirst for knowledge, because the Marxism they were taught was nothing but an assignment to find the quotation from Lenin or, even better, Stalin relevant to an issue at hand, whatever was "politically correct." In point of fact, all it did was train people in the reading of coffee grounds.

Allow me to tell a story in this connection, a story that took place in the Soviet Union about twenty-five years ago. When I first arrived in Moscow, there was a debate in progress about the works of a Menshevik economist by the name of Rubin. I was very interested and asked a friend about it. The friend, a young Hungarian communist studying at the "Red Professoriate," immediately told me that Comrade Varga was correct in criticizing Rubin's rightist views but had then himself committed a leftist error, which a certain Comrade Ivanov corrected but had then himself . . . and so on.[3] In the end I told the young Hungarian comrade that that was all well and good but I wanted to know what economic issues were under debate. He

[2]Martin Heidegger (1889–1976), one of the most original twentieth-century philosophers, contended that Western thought had suffered a great fall, creating "a highly inauthentic way of being." His postwar reputation has suffered because of his support of the Nazis. Thomas Henry Huxley (1825–95) was Darwin's most vigorous supporter in the decade following publication of *The Origin of the Species* and was well known as an agnostic.

[3]Isaak Rubin was a minor Russian economist, whereas Eugen Varga (1879–1964) was one of the most famous Marxist economic thinkers. Varga was a member of the government of Kun's Hungarian

was unable to come up with an answer. Or, rather, he was able to enumerate all the rightist and leftist errors occurring in the debate and would probably have been able to categorize them according to the prevailing party line, but he had no interest whatever in the essence of the debate.

There we have it, the main problem, the issue at hand: What is our relationship to the intelligentsia? Comrade Jánossy was correct to note a certain accommodation process going on.[4] It is not limited to philosophers, however; scholars in all fields stick rigidly to their humanistic, positivistic, or other comparable views, come up with the two or three quotations from Stalin—and they are not hard to find—that will make them acceptable to the bureaucracy in charge and then go merrily on their way, never to be bothered again by anyone. Yet this greatly damages the credibility of Marxism in the eyes of the intelligentsia.

Now I think that what I said before—about our being in an extremely unfavorable, difficult position—will seem less of a paradox. We are in a much more difficult position than the Soviet Union, because although the dogmatism of the Stalinist period has doubtless caused setbacks in the development of the Soviet Union, we must not forget that there a fairly broad cross section of society experienced Stalinism firsthand, whereas here in Hungary, as legal historians with their penchant for scholasticism are wont to say, *glossant glossarum glossas,* or glosses of glosses are glossed, and it made us one of the leading countries of Stalinism.

Let us not forget this, comrades. I have neither the means nor the intention to go digging around in old newspapers, but if we go back a few years we shall find pronouncements in which we boast of standing at the forefront of Stalinism. Of course we must forget this today, and anyone who happens upon that sort of quotation speaks with the voice of the enemy. I must admit I am not enough of a philologist to judge; I can only say that in the current situation we Hungarians may well have more ground to cover than anyone, more battles to fight, if we wish to reestablish Marxism's reputation, put an end to the antipathy that has grown up around it, create confidence in it.

We cannot build socialism and a socialist culture if we cannot convince our intelligentsia that using dialectical and historical materialism in their own individual fields is as essential from their perspective as from ours. This is the task we must face, and if I have been highly critical up to now, it has not been out of pessimism but to give every honest Marxist a sense of the enormity of the task and of the spirit fired by the great possibilities the Twentieth Congress holds forth for coming to grips with this error, the consequence of seven or eight years of development, by means of zealous, hard work. It will not happen overnight; it cannot be taken care of with a speech or a burst of enthusiasm. It will require a long, hard struggle on the

Soviet Republic, after which he spent twenty years working in Moscow. Disgraced by Stalin and Zhdanov in 1947, he was rehabilitated in 1959. The Institute of the Red Professors was founded in 1921 as an agency of the Agitation and Propaganda Section of the Central Committee to train specialists in the social sciences. Led through the 1920s by the historian M. N. Pokrovsky, it became a number of separate institutes in the 1930s.

[4]Lajos Jánossy was a well-known atomic scientist who returned to Hungary from Dublin in 1950 to take a professorship at Budapest University.

part of us all, of every Marxist, each in his own area, and the precondition for the hard, unremitting struggle is that we each examine our own baggage and arsenal to see how capable it is of confronting an intellectual in our field, whether it can provide genuine answers to his questions, demonstrate that he can solve his own problems better with the help of Marxism than without it. Without this kind of propaganda we shall make no headway in the world. I will not enter into the "philosophical debate," but the problem behind that debate, behind the entire period in question, is that in our day-to-day practice we have let agitation devour propaganda, and bad propaganda throttles scholarly research. We must recognize we have gone about it the wrong way round: Without good research there is no good propaganda, and without good propaganda there is no good agitation. We must recognize that a scholarly formulation of the problems of Marxism in all areas is the precondition for good propaganda and good agitation.

But here again we have the political connection between the problems of the Twentieth Congress and the problems of the recent past. In the Soviet Union during the Stalin period I remember seeing posters showing an express train whisking us off to Communism, but I might also refer to the large number of works by not un-talented writers, works that take place in the present and conclude by showing most of the characters with one foot in communism, which was passé even before the Twentieth Congress. And what is the result? What stands behind it? If we are only a step away from communism, it should mean that we are fully prepared for it ideologically and morally to say nothing of economically, that our scholars have formulated the major problems, and that all we need do in each case is apply the ready-made doctrines to that given case. Here we have the worldview roots of what we call dogmatism, citationology, and much else.

What is the situation really like, then? More than fifty years ago, shortly before his death, Engels wrote of the great task Marxists had ahead of them in formulating the major problems of history, science, logic, and so on, and in another letter written at about the same time he speaks mockingly of young Marxists who use historical materialism as an excuse for not studying history. Since that time the proletariat has taken power; the material preconditions for a genuinely scientific elaboration of Marxism as called for by Engels and later, repeatedly, by Lenin in the *Philosophical Notebooks* have come into being. The great historical crime of Sta-linism consists in failing to make use of them, impeding their development, thwart-ing trends that would have promoted such an elaboration of Marxism. If we look closely at all fields of knowledge from the point of view directly concerning us here, we must recognize that we still have no Marxist logic, we still have no Marxist aesthetics, we still have no Marxist ethics, we still have no Marxist theory of education, we still have no Marxist psychology, and so on.

This does not mean that we should build up these branches of knowledge from nothing: Without the great works of the classics, without the methodological foun-dation they have created, without their formulation of many issues we should be unable to take even a single step forward. Nor does it mean, however, that if we gather together all the statements Marx, Engels, and Lenin ever made about aesthet-ics, to speak of my own field, then these statements will constitute a ready-made Marxist aesthetics. No aesthetics can be constructed without them, but *we* are the ones, this generation, the current generation, who must construct it. The same holds, of course, for the rest of the branches of knowledge. This is not meant to discourage anyone, comrades; on the contrary, I deeply feel our responsibility not only to the proletariat of the world but to all mankind. The fact that history has imposed vast and grand tasks upon us must provide the courage and spirit for not merely a few individuals but for the total body of Marxists roused and spurred on to true Marxism by the Twentieth Congress to create a unified whole of all Marxist branches of knowledge. Not in three months, not a year. No, this is what might be called the work of a generation.

All this brings up many concrete questions and issues in connection with the current situation of Marxism, by which I mean our relations with both party intellectuals who have become alienated from Marxism—because they do exist—and intellectuals outside the party. I think that if we lay our main emphasis on Marxist research and seek out problems, dig problems out from behind the facts, we shall be able to work with the intelligentsia; we shall not lord it over them as if we had the wisdom of the world at our fingertips, or answer, if they ask how we feel Piero della Francesca should be judged, like the Marxist who had heard his name for the first time and immediately replied that he was an ideologue of the Siena petty bourgeoisie (though he was not even from Siena).[5]

We must make a radical break with this way of doing things, comrades. It is harmful not only to the development of Marxism but to the building of trust in Marxism. If we work on these issues with our serious, honest intellectuals—by which I mean not merely the elite but also the vast number of engineers working in factories and dealing with the plan and attendant economic issues, I mean university students, and there are vast numbers of them—we can and must win them over to Marxism.

Second, no matter how self-evident it sounds, we must introduce democratization and the possibility for debate. As a member of the executive board of the Academy of Sciences I can state that I do not know how many years it is—let us shamefully admit it—since a true spirit of debate has made itself felt in any field whatever. Let me explain immediately why I am ashamed. Why did it fail to make itself felt? We must recognize that before the Twentieth Congress no debate was even possible. We always said debate was necessary, and now I shall take the liberty of telling you something I heard during a discussion at quite a high level. What I heard was that debate is an excellent thing and people should be encouraged to speak their minds, because then we can come down on them like a ton of bricks. Under such circumstances there can be no debate: We mustn't think intellectuals are stupid, after all. They have not heard this story from me, because I am a disciplined party member and have not told it until now. Still, I say with Lenin that an entire social class cannot be duped. Intellectuals knew perfectly well that debate was impossible, and it is now our task to pave the way, step by step, for genuine, concrete debate in every branch of knowledge, art, and literature.

Finally, I wish to address a third issue, a danger whose signs I see only here and

---

[5]Piero della Francesca (1420–92), a painter who used the new technique of perspective with great subtlety, is today recognized as a major contributor to the Italian Renaissance.

there but one I feel called upon to bring to the comrades' attention. The Twentieth Congress has replaced Stalinism with the Leninist method, but it must really be the Leninist *method*. To use once more the bluntness for which I am known, Lenin can be turned into as much of a figure of citationology and dogmatism as Stalin. And even if, both at home and abroad, it is as yet no more than a sporadic tendency, I am convinced that there are certain forces ready to steer the Twentieth Congress in this direction, and it is the duty of every communist—his duty to the socialist revolution, his duty to the honor of Marxism, which binds us as Marxist philosophers and intellectuals—to take up arms against it from the very start. Because the Twentieth Congress will lead to the truly great results within its grasp only if we renew Lenin's spirit, Leninist dialectics, and the Leninist method.

Let me give just one example. Earlier I spoke of philosophers produced on the assembly line. "Less but better" was Lenin's last will and testament, so to speak, in the field of economics. Leninism and Lenin's entire philosophical method are diametrically opposed to the cultural assembly line. What we must concentrate on is a genuine renewal of Lenin's method; it is our most important task. With Lenin's help we shall come to know Marx and Engels anew and through them the entire development and history of world culture. Only then will the grand possibilities held forth by the Twentieth Congress be realizable here in Hungary. And should we prove weak, should other forces, forces wishing to turn Leninism into nothing more than Stalinism with a different key signature, triumph, then the Twentieth Congress will run aground much as the brilliant initiatives of the Seventh Comintern Congress in the 1930s failed to lead to the results the worldwide workers movement had reason to expect of it in 1935.[6] I hope that the Twentieth Congress will not cause a similar disappointment and that we are truly on the threshold of a new flowering of Marxism and the Marxist workers' movement.

[6]At its Seventh Congress, held in 1935, the Communist International adopted the Popular Front policy by which European communists were encouraged to seek electoral coalitions with social democrats, whom until that point they had reviled as "social fascists."

Self-Management

The first communist regime to seek out a non-Stalinist path to socialism, and for many years the most successful, was the Yugoslav. Stung by Stalin's expulsion in 1948, Tito and his colleagues, who had matured in the 1930s adoring Stalin, tried at first to show themselves even more orthodox than the master by beginning a ruthless (and unsuccessful) collectivization of agriculture. Fairly quickly, however, they realized they had an opportunity to create a new kind of socialism, and in the early 1950s they began to experiment with workers' self-management. In the first reading, Milovan Djilas describes, perhaps in a self-serving way, how he and his colleagues first introduced the idea.

In 1958 the League of Communists of Yugoslavia formally adopted self-management as the underlying principle of its program. In the decades that followed, the party introduced the principle into the constitution and into every aspect of public life, decentralizing economic functions to the extent that after Tito's death in 1980 the central government lost control of the levers of economic policy. Beginning in the 1960s, the Yugoslavs opened their borders and made a serious effort to introduce market elements into their system, making it for about twenty years a positive and hopeful model for reform Marxists throughout the world.

The flaw in the Yugoslav system was that the party, having made self-management its underlying philosophy, did not intend thereby to relinquish its leading political role. Previewing the problems that Mikhail Gorbachev faced in the late 1980s, the Yugoslav communists hoped to maintain political control while encouraging initiative and democracy. The following excerpts from the party program of 1958, which give party members torturous advice on how to be both authoritative and democratic, hint at the paradoxical (and ultimately unsuccessful) nature of this policy.

14

The Origins of Self-Management in Yugoslavia
Milovan Djilas
Events of Spring 1950

Just what is Yugoslavia's program of "self-management"? What are the prospects of its finding a solution to the social and nationality troubles now besetting Yugoslavia?

The idea of self-management was conceived by Kardelj and me, with some help from our comrade Kidrič. Soon after the outbreak of the quarrel with Stalin, in 1949, as far as I remember, I began to reread Marx's *Capital*, this time with much greater care, to see if I could find the answer to the riddle of why, to put it in simplistic terms, Stalinism was bad and Yugoslavia was good. I discovered many new ideas and, most interesting of all, ideas about a future society in which the immediate producers, through free association, would themselves make the decisions regarding production and distribution—would, in effect, run their own lives and their own future.

The country was in the stranglehold of the bureaucracy, and the party leaders were in the grip of rage and horror over the incorrigibly arbitrary nature of the party machine they had set up and that kept them in power. One day—it must have been in the spring of 1950—it occurred to me that we Yugoslav communists were now in a position to start creating Marx's free association of producers. The factories would be left in their hands, with the sole proviso that they should pay a tax for military and other state needs "still remaining essential." With all this, I felt a twinge of reservation: Is not this a way for us communists, I asked myself, to shift the responsibility for failures and difficulties in the economy onto the shoulders of the working class, or to compel the working class to take a share of such responsibilities from us? I soon explained my idea to Kardelj and Kidrič while we sat in a car parked in front of the villa where I lived. They felt no such reservation, and I was able all too easily to convince them of the indisputable harmony between my ideas and Marx's teaching. Without leaving the car, we thrashed it out for little more than half an hour. Kardelj thought it was a good idea, but one that should not be put into effect for another five or six years, and Kidrič agreed with him. A couple of days later, however, Kidrič telephoned me to say that we were ready to go ahead at once with the first steps. In his impulsive way he began to elaborate and expound on the whole

Excerpt from *The Unperfect Society: Beyond the New Class*, pp. 220–23, by Milovan Djilas, copyright © 1969 by Harcourt Brace & Company, reprinted by permission of the publisher.

conception. A little later, a meeting was held in Kardelj's cabinet office with the trade union leaders, and they proposed the abolition of the workers' councils, which up to that time had functioned only as consultative bodies for the management. Kardelj suggested that my proposals for management should be associated with the workers' councils, first of all in a way that would give them more rights and greater responsibilities. Shortly there began the debates on the issues of principle and on the statutory aspects, preparations that went on for some four or five months. Tito, busy with other duties and absent from Belgrade, took no part in this and knew nothing of the proposal soon to introduce a workers' council bill in the parliament until he was informed by Kardelj and me in the government lobby room during a session of the National Assembly. His first reaction was: Our workers are not ready for that yet! But Kardelj and I, convinced that this was an important step, pressed him hard, and he began to unbend as he paid more attention to our explanations. The most important part of our case was that this would be the beginning of democracy, something that socialism had not yet achieved; further, it could be plainly seen by the world and the international workers' movement as a radical departure from Stalinism. Tito paced up and down, as though completely wrapped in his own thoughts. Suddenly he stopped and exclaimed: "Factories belonging to the workers—something that has never yet been achieved!" With these words, the theories worked out by Kardelj and myself seemed to shed their complications and seemed, too, to find better prospects of being workable. A few months later, Tito explained the Workers' Self-Management Bill to the National Assembly.

15

The Challenge of Self-Management

1958

Assigning an indispensable and important role to the state in the first stages of socialist construction, and also aware of state-ist deformation which this role may cause in the development of socialist relations, the Yugoslav communists believe that the state, that is, its administrative apparatus and measures, is not at all the main instrument of socialist construction and solution of the inner contradictions of socialist development. The state apparatus cannot be the decisive, permanent and all-embracing factor in the development of new social relations. The Yugoslav communists must not, nor do they wish to, become a power through the use of the state apparatus instead of through the working class and working people. Only the social and economic interest of the working class, of the working people who produce with the social means of production, and socialist consciousness based on that interest can be the basic, permanent motive power of social progress.

The communists do not renounce their leading social role. Social consciousness plays the decisive part in the solution of the contradictions of socialist development. But the leading socialist forces can be victorious only if they act in accordance with the objective laws of development and with the needs of society in general; and in particular, if they act in accordance with the social and economic interests of the working class, that is, the working people who produce with the social means of production.

In the struggle for further strengthening of socialism, the communists must constantly verify their political line through their increasing responsibility to the broad masses of the working people. Taught by practice and by contradictions which appear in socialist development, they must educate the working masses so that these may be able increasingly, more and more directly and independently, to manage society, think like socialists and act in practice like socialists, until each individual citizen learns how to manage the affairs of the social community.

The relationship between the communists and the working masses, accordingly, cannot be either that prevailing between a governing party and the governed or that between the teacher and the pupil. This relationship must appear more and more as a relationship between equals. Therefore the individual best qualified and most capable in the realization of common interests earns the highest confidence. In the struggle for the progress of socialism in all fields of social life, the communists and

Reprinted from Stoyan Prebichevich, trans., *Yugoslavia's Way: The Program of the League of the Communists of Yugoslavia* (New York: All Nation's Press, 1958), pp. 120–22, 173–74.

the leading socialist forces generally must develop their own action primarily through the life, work, and social action of the working people themselves.

In other words, they must strive to fight for the advance of socialism and in this struggle to establish their leadership less and less through their own power and more and more through the direct power of the working people—producers with the social means of production—in all the varied organs of social self-management. In doing so, the communists must struggle for all factors of socialist development to be active, for this activity to be socialistic, educating and training ever broader masses for socialist management. Through such activity the communists and the leading socialist forces protect themselves against bureaucratization and at the same time steadily raise the social consciousness of the working people, striving all along toward gradual reduction and abolition of the antagonism between the government and the governed, between the leaders and the followers, between the state and the citizens.

Simultaneously, the communists will continue the struggle for keeping key positions of state authority in firm revolutionary hands—positions on which depend further development of socialist society and defense of that society against the various internal and foreign antisocialist forces. The great socialist, democratic, humane, and peaceful goals that the Yugoslav socialist society has set itself can be achieved most quickly and least painfully if the enemies of socialism are allowed no opportunity to bring obstacles and disturbances into our internal social life.

The communists will pay particular attention to the development of workers' councils. Workers' councils are democratic economic–political organs of social self-management through which direct producers independently manage enterprises and take a decisive part in the development of the forces of production—within a single coordinated social economic plan and in accordance with the general interests of the community, expressed in a single coordinated economic system. The motive power of the activity of the direct producers in workers' councils, aimed at more productive labor and faster development of the forces of production, is their desire continuously to improve their living conditions and the general material standard of the social community through better individual work, better operation of the enterprise, and faster general economic progress of the social community; and to develop freely their individual creative abilities and inclinations, in harmony with the general interests of the working people.

Workers' councils are neither representatives of the owner nor the collective owner of the means of production. They manage the means of production on behalf of the social community and in their work are stimulated by their own material and moral–political aspirations. Just for this reason, they are the most suitable social–economic instrument of struggle against both bureaucratism and selfish individualism.

Workers' self-management is the expression and confirmation of the social character of ownership of the means of production. It is also the basic form of the direct participation of the working people in managing the economy. On this foundation, social production is most directly connected with the actual needs of the people, and products of human labor become objects of both social acquisition and personal acquisition by the worker. Social relations in production and distribution, and gradually in all basic spheres of society, receive an increasingly developed socialist substance.

Managing the social means of production from which he was separated in the class society, the producer now takes his active place in society. He becomes more and more aware that the realization of his individual economic and social interest directly depends on a higher productivity of his own work, on an increase of production of the working collective, and on a further development of the productive forces in the commune and in the whole country. Therefore workers' councils give and will continue to give ever-new incentives to the production and economy, which will make possible accelerated development of the forces of production. In these circumstances, the producer himself, and the working man generally, gradually determines the further process of liberation of man and humanization of social relations.

The New Class

Milovan Djilas's early life was a heroic communist success story. Born to poverty in Montenegro, he participated in the sectarian struggles of the 1930s and emerged from the National Liberation Struggle, as the Yugoslavs called it, as one of the three or four most powerful men in Yugoslavia, perhaps even second in line after Tito himself. But elevation to high political office did not blunt Djilas's sense of injustice. In 1954, when he began to criticize the extravagant life-styles of the new leadership and even to call for the introduction of opposition politics, Tito expelled him from the party and sent him into disgrace. Unbowed, Djilas responded with a study entitled The New Class, *which argued that Stalinism had not destroyed class domination but simply substituted the state and its party bureaucracy for the bourgeoisie. Tito sent him to jail for the book, but from that point, in and out of jail, Djilas continued to write as his quixotic conscience dictated, until eventually he repudiated communism entirely.*

16

The New Class

Milovan Djilas
1955–56

Everything happened differently in the U.S.S.R. and other communist countries from what the leaders—even such prominent ones as Lenin, Stalin, Trotsky, and Bukharin—anticipated. They expected that the state would rapidly wither away, that democracy would be strengthened. The reverse happened. They expected a rapid improvement in the standard of living—there has been scarcely any change in this respect, and in the subjugated East European countries, the standard has even declined. In every instance, the standard of living has failed to rise in proportion to the rate of industrialization, which was much more rapid. It was believed that the differences between cities and villages, between intellectual and physical labor, would slowly disappear; instead these differences have increased. Communist antic-ipations in other areas—including their expectations for developments in the non-communist world—have also failed to materialize.

The greatest illusion was that industrialization and collectivization in the U.S.S.R., and destruction of capitalist ownership, would result in a classless soci-ety. In 1936, when the new [Soviet] constitution was promulgated, Stalin an-nounced that the "exploiting class" had ceased to exist. The capitalist and other classes of ancient origin had in fact been destroyed, but a new class, previously unknown to history, had been formed.

It is understandable that this class, like those before it, should believe that the establishment of its power would result in happiness and freedom for all men. The only difference between this and other classes was that it treated the delay in the realization of its illusions more crudely. It thus affirmed that its power was more complete than the power of any other class before in history, and its class illusions and prejudices were proportionally greater.

This new class, the bureaucracy, or more accurately the political bureaucracy, has all the characteristics of earlier ones as well as some new characteristics of its own. Its origin had its special characteristics also, even though in essence it was similar to the beginnings of other classes.

Other classes, too, obtained their strength and power by the revolutionary path, destroying the political, social, and other orders they met in their way. However, almost without exception, these classes attained power *after* new economic patterns had taken shape in the old society. The case was the reverse with new classes in the communist systems. It did not come to power to *complete* a new economic order but to *establish* its own and, in so doing, to establish its power over society.

In earlier epochs the coming to power of some class, some part of a class, or of some party, was the final event resulting from its formation and its development. The reverse was true in the U.S.S.R. There the new class was definitely formed after it attained power. Its consciousness had to develop before its economic and physical powers, because the class had not taken root in the life of the nation. This class viewed its role in relation to the world from an idealistic point of view. Its practical possibilities were not diminished by this. In spite of its illusions, it represented an objective tendency toward industrialization. Its practical bent emanated from this tendency. The promise of an ideal world increased the faith in the ranks of the new class and sowed illusions among the masses. At the same time it inspired gigantic physical undertakings.

Because this new class had not been formed as a part of the economic and social life before it came to power, it could only be created in an organization of a special type, distinguished by a special discipline based on identical philosophic and ideological views of its members. A unity of belief and iron discipline was necessary to overcome its weaknesses.

The roots of the new class were implanted in a special party, of the Bolshevik type. Lenin was right in his view that his party was an exception in the history of human society, although he did not suspect that it would be the beginning of a new class.

To be more precise, the initiators of the new class are not found in the party of the Bolshevik type as a whole but in that stratum of professional revolutionaries who made up its core even before it attained power. It was not by accident that Lenin asserted after the failure of the 1905 revolution that only professional revolutionaries—men whose sole profession was revolutionary work—could build a new party of the Bolshevik type. It was still less accidental that even Stalin, the future creator of a new class, was the most outstanding example of such a professional revolutionary. The new ruling class has been gradually developing from this very narrow stratum of revolutionaries. These revolutionaries composed its core for a long period. Trotsky noted that in prerevolutionary professional revolutionaries was the origin of the future Stalinist bureaucrat. What he did not detect was the beginning of a new class of owners and exploiters.

This is not to say that the new party and the new class are identical. The party, however, is the core of that class, and its base. It is very difficult, perhaps impossible, to define the limits of the new class and to identify its members. The new class may be said to be made up of those who have special privileges and economic preference because of the administrative monopoly they hold.

As in other owning classes, the proof that it is a special class lies in its ownership and its special relations to other classes. In the same way, the class to which a member belongs is indicated by the material and other privileges which ownership brings to him.

As defined by Roman law, property constitutes the use, enjoyment, and disposition of material goods. The communist political bureaucracy uses, enjoys, and disposes of nationalized property.

If we assume that membership in this bureaucracy or new owning class is predicated on the use of privileges inherent in ownership—in this instance nationalized material goods—then membership in the new party class, or political bureaucracy, is reflected in a larger income in material goods and privileges than society should normally grant for such functions. In practice, the ownership privilege of the new class manifests itself as an exclusive right, as a party monopoly, for the political bureaucracy to distribute the national income, to set wages, direct economic development, and dispose of nationalized and other property. This is the way it appears to the ordinary man who considers the communist functionary as being very rich and as a man who does not have to work.

The ownership of private property has, for many reasons, proved to be unfavorable for the establishment of the new class's authority. Besides, the destruction of private ownership was necessary for the economic transformation of nations. The new class obtains its power, privileges, ideology, and its customs from one specific form of ownership—collective ownership—which the class administers and distributes in the name of the nation and society.

The new class maintains that ownership derives from a designated social relationship. This is the relationship between the monopolists of administration, who constitute a narrow and closed stratum, and the mass of producers (farmers, workers, and intelligentsia) who have no rights. But that is not all, since the communist bureaucracy also has complete monopolistic control over material assets.

Every substantive change in the social relationship between those who monopolize administration and those who work is inevitably reflected in the ownership relationship. Social and political relations and ownership—the totalitarianism of government and the monopoly of ownership—are being more fully brought into accord in communism than in any other political system.

To divest communists of their ownership rights would be to abolish them as a class. To compel them to relinquish their other social powers, so that workers may participate in sharing the profits of their work—which capitalists have had to permit as a result of strikes and parliamentary action—would mean that communists were being deprived of their monopoly over property, ideology, and government. This would be the beginning of democracy and freedom in communism, the end of communist monopolism and totalitarianism. Until this happens, there can be no indication that important, fundamental changes are taking place in communist systems, at least not in the eyes of men who think seriously about social progress.

The ownership privileges of the new class and membership in that class are the privileges of *administration*. This privilege extends from state administration and the administration of economic enterprises to that of sports and humanitarian organizations. Political, party, or so-called general leadership is executed by the core. This position of leadership carries privileges with it. In his *Stalin au pouvoir*, published in Paris in 1951, Orlov states that the average pay of a worker in the U.S.S.R. in 1935 was 1,800 rubles annually, while the pay and allowances of the secretary of a rayon committee amounted to 45,000 rubles annually. The situation has changed since then for both workers and party functionaries, but the essence remains the same. Other authors have arrived at the same conclusions. Discrepancies between the pay of workers and party functionaries are extreme; this could not be hidden from persons visiting the U.S.S.R. or other communist countries in the past few years.

Other systems, too, have their professional politicians. One can think well or ill of them, but they must exist. Society cannot live without a state or a government, and therefore it cannot live without those who fight for it.

However, there are fundamental differences between professional politicians in other systems and in the communist system. In extreme cases, politicians in other systems use the government to secure privileges for themselves and their cohorts, or to favor the economic interests of one social stratum or another. The situation is different with the communist system where the power and the government are identical with the use, enjoyment, and disposition of almost all the nation's goods. He who grabs power grabs privileges and indirectly grabs property. Consequently, in communism, power or politics as a profession is the ideal of those who have the desire or the prospect of living as parasites at the expense of others.

Membership in the Communist party before the revolution meant sacrifice. Being a professional revolutionary was one of the highest honors. Now that the party has consolidated its power, party membership means that one belongs to a privileged class. And at the core of the party are the all-powerful exploiters and masters.

For a long time the communist revolution and the communist system have been concealing their real nature. The emergence of the new class has been concealed under socialist phraseology and, more important, under the new collective forms of property ownership. The so-called socialist ownership is a disguise for the real ownership by the political bureaucracy. And in the beginning this bureaucracy was in a hurry to complete industrialization, and hid its class composition under that guise.

No class is established by deliberate design, even though its ascent is accompanied by an organized and conscious struggle. This holds true for the new class in communism, but it also embodies some special characteristics. Since the hold of the new class on economic life and on the social structure was fairly precarious, and since it was fated to arise within a specific party, it required the highest possible degree of organization, as well as a consistent effort to present a united, balanced, class-conscious front. This is why the new class is better organized and more highly class conscious than any class in recorded history.

This proposition is true only if it is taken relatively; consciousness and organizational structure being taken in relation to the outside world and to other classes, powers, and social forces. No other class in history has been as cohesive and singleminded in defending itself and in controlling that which it holds—collective and monopolistic ownership and totalitarian authority.

On the other hand, the new class is also the most deluded and least conscious of itself. Every private capitalist or feudal lord was conscious of the fact that he belonged to a special discernible social category. He usually believed that this category was destined to make the human race happy and that without this category chaos and general ruin would ensue. A communist member of the new class also believes that without his party, society would regress and founder. But he is not conscious of the fact that he belongs to a new ownership class, for he does not consider himself an owner and does not take into account the special privileges he enjoys. He thinks that he belongs to a group with prescribed ideas, aims, attitudes, and roles. That is all he sees. He cannot see that at the same time he belongs to a special social category: the *ownership* class.

The new class instinctively feels that national goods are, in fact, its property, and that even the terms *socialist, social,* and *state* property denote a general legal fiction. The new class also thinks that any breach of its totalitarian authority might imperil its ownership. Consequently, the new class opposes *any* type of freedom, ostensibly for the purpose of preserving "socialist" ownership. Criticism of the new class's monopolistic administration of property generates the fear of a possible loss of power. The new class is sensitive to these criticisms and demands depending on the extent to which they expose the manner in which it rules and holds power.

This is an important contradiction. Property is legally considered social and national property. But, in actuality, a single group manages it in its own interest. The discrepancy between legal and actual conditions continuously results in obscure and abnormal social and economic relationships. It also means that the words of the leading group do not correspond to its actions and that all actions result in strengthening its property holdings and its political position.

This contradiction cannot be resolved without jeopardizing the class's position. Other ruling, property-owning classes could not resolve this contradiction either, unless forcefully deprived of monopoly of power and ownership. Wherever there has been a higher degree of freedom for society as a whole, the ruling classes have been forced, in one way or another, to renounce monopoly of ownership. The reverse is true also: Wherever monopoly of ownership has been impossible, freedom, to some degree, has become inevitable.

In defending its authority, the ruling class must execute reforms every time it becomes obvious to the people that the class is treating national property as its own. Such reforms are not proclaimed as being what they really are but, rather, as part of the "further development of socialism" and "socialist democracy." The groundwork for reforms is laid when the discrepancy mentioned above becomes public. From the historical point of view the new class is forced to fortify its authority and ownership constantly, even though it is running away from the truth. It must constantly demonstrate how it is successfully creating a society of happy people, all of whom enjoy equal rights and have been freed of every type of exploitation. The new class cannot avoid falling continuously into profound internal contradictions; for in spite of its historical origin it is not able to make its ownership lawful, and it cannot renounce ownership without undermining itself. Consequently, it is forced to try to justify its increasing authority, invoking abstract and unreal purposes.

This is a class whose power over men is the most complete known to history. For this reason it is a class with very limited views, views which are shaky because they are based on falsehoods. Closely knit, isolated, and in complete authority, the new class must unrealistically evaluate its own role and that of the people around it.

Having achieved industrialization, the new class can now do nothing more than strengthen its brute force and pillage the people. It ceases to create. Its spiritual heritage is overtaken by darkness.

While the revolution can be considered an epochal accomplishment of the new class, its methods of rule fill some of the most shameful pages in history. Men will marvel at the grandiose ventures it accomplished and will be ashamed of the means it used.

When the new class leaves the historical scene—and this must happen—there will be less sorrow over its passing than there was for any other class before it. Smothering everything except what suited its ego, it has condemned itself to failure and shameful ruin.

Marxian Opposition in Poland

In Poland the rule of the "Muscovites" began to unravel in March 1956 with the death of the general secretary of the Polish United Workers' party, Bolesław Bierut. In June the workers of Poznań took to the streets to protest economic conditions and had to be put down by force. After a series of negotiations inspired by the crisis, Khrushchev finally acquiesced in the selection of Władisław Gomułka as first secretary of the party. Gomułka was one of the few Polish communists to survive Stalin's purges of the 1930s and one of even fewer to spend the war underground in Poland. Because he harbored doubts about the wisdom of collectivizing the fiercely independent Polish peasantry and about imposing Soviet models on a country with such a long history of confrontation with Russia, in 1948 he had been imprisoned for "right-wing bourgeois nationalism." His return to power in October 1956 indicated that Khrushchev was willing to tolerate a certain degree of "national communism," albeit within a commonwealth of socialist states led by the Soviet Union.

Popular at the beginning as a Polish patriot, by 1970 Gomułka had become reviled as a man who had conducted attacks on the church, permitted a surge of anti-Semitism, administered an economic decline, put down a student revolt, and finally, in 1970, suppressed shipyard strikes with scores of deaths. One of the first indications of dissatisfaction with his regime came as early as 1964 when a furor broke out over a letter that thirty-four prominent writers sent to Prime Minister Józef Cyrankiewicz demanding "a change in Polish cultural policies in the spirit of rights guaranteed by the Constitution." Despite the innocuousness of the letter, the writers found themselves in serious trouble, although with one exception, no one was imprisoned.

More fundamental was a thesis written by two University of Warsaw graduate students, Jacek Kuroń and Karol Modzelewski. The two students claimed that the new class of workers created by industrialization could best create a workers' revolution through plural workers' parties, although they opposed parliamentary regimes. When the authorities would not permit them to defend their thesis, they wrote a second version, Open Letter to the Party, portions of which appear here, and for which they received jail terms. Both men were important figures in Solidarity politics, and when Solidarity formed a government in 1989, Modzelewski was elected senator from Wrocław and Kuroń became minister of labor.

17

The Kuroń-Modzelewski Open Letter to the Party

Jacek Kuroń and Karol Modzelewski

Early 1965

According to a widely held opinion, the present regime and its first leaders, brought into the country by the Red Army, had no economic and social base and were only able to establish themselves in a situation where real national sovereignty was lacking. Thus, the *causes* of the formation of the bureaucratic system are put outside Polish boundaries, and the causes of what happens outside Poland holds little interest for the proponents of this view. They are interested in the effects only, in the present state of things interpreted as the *"raison d'état"* of Poland. The nationalist ideology, thus despite appearances, helps to solidify the social relationships on which the rule of the bureaucracy is based.

We do not dispute the role played by external circumstances in the abolition of capitalism in our country: the weakness of authentic independent revolutionary elements, the decisive role of the Red Army, our government's very great dependence on the Soviet bureaucracy—long since elevated into a ruling class—the situation in the international workers' movement.

All this, of course, effectively accelerated the process of bureaucratization. However, we believe that this process was objectively conditioned by the country's level of economic development and by its economic and social structure; this holds true for czarist Russia as well as for the Poland of the interwar period, and for the great majority of countries in our camp. This process was conditioned as well by the relative international isolation of these countries (since the large industrial powers remained capitalist). When capitalism was abolished in these countries, they were backward, with meager industry and a great unused surplus of manpower evidencing itself in unemployment and, most of all, rural overpopulation. Their economies were, in one way or another, under the domination of the capitalists of the advanced imperialist nations.

In such countries, only industrialization could bring real improvement in the material, social, and cultural conditions of life of the rural and urban masses and ensure progress for society as a whole. Industrialization, therefore, is in the interests of the entire society and constitutes the principal task of the new governments which abolished capitalism in the interests of the workers and ruled in their name.

Reprinted from George Lavan Weissman, ed., and Gerald Paul, trans., *Revolutionary Marxist Students in Poland Speak Out* (New York: Merit Press, 1968), pp. 39–43, 65, 68–69, 75–78.

With industrial capacity low, the economic surplus (the difference between production and current total consumption, that is, the basis of accumulation) was also low. Aid from the developed capitalist countries could not be expected. To the contrary, the mechanism of the world market makes the underdeveloped countries exporters of food and raw materials and brings their economies under the domination of the capital of the imperialist powers which control the world market, thus holding back industrialization and perpetuating underdevelopment. Independence from the mechanism of the international capitalist market was therefore essential to development. Industrialization had to be accomplished rapidly or not at all.

Enormous reserves of unemployed manpower were the basis for development. Therefore industrialization was of necessity carried out through employment of these reserves and by the rapid construction of new productive forces. (This is what is called the extensive method of economic development.) Furthermore, the increase in employment could not be accompanied by a rapid increase in consumption because this would entail a diminution of the already meager economic surplus, making impossible rapid development of the productive apparatus and employment of still unused manpower, thus putting a brake on industrialization. The maximum increase in employment and production had to be brought about while keeping consumption at the lowest possible level. The aim was the maximum economic surplus—thus production for production's sake. This aim expressed the needs of industrializing the country as long as the construction of the industrial base was incomplete; therefore, for a certain time, production for production's sake corresponded to the demands of economic development and to the interests of society as a whole.

In the course of industrialization there was a massive influx of unemployed manpower from the countryside into the industries being built, an increase in the size of the working class, the higher technical cadres, the intellectuals, and an explosion in the number of technocrats. At the same time the need to restrict consumption forced a significant cut, in comparison to prewar standards, in the salaries of the technocrats, intellectuals, and office workers; similarly the restriction of workers' wages to a very low level was regarded by the older workers as a wage cut; finally, a policy tending forcibly to deprive the peasants of agricultural surpluses beyond the basic needs of their families and their farms.

Thus, industrialization, although it represented the interest of the society as a whole, did not correspond to any of the various interests of any class or social group considered separately. The natural aspiration of each group in society, of the peasants as peasants, of the workers as workers, of the plant managers as plant managers—and not as individuals who had lately improved their financial and social circumstances or had reasonable hope of so doing—was the greatest possible increase in their individual incomes, and the improvement of the material and social position of their own group—hence, in any event, a tendency to maximum consumption.

On the contrary, however, the needs of industrialization required production for the sake of production. Industrialization was a *raison d'être*, a primary goal of the new state. It pursued this end despite the specific interests of the other classes and social strata, indeed to a certain extent, against them. Against the peasants, forcibly deprived of their agricultural surplus and constantly threatened with expropriation en masse, against the workers—whose wages were kept at the lowest possible level—and even lower, against the intellectuals and the technocrats. The achievement of such industrialization required that they be deprived of any opportunity of expressing their special interests and of struggling to defend or fulfill them.

Concentrating all political decisions, as well as control over the means of production and the collective product, in the hands of the new state required that production be freed from regulation by the market, and that the opportunities for the workers, technocrats, or peasants to act on their own initiative be as strictly limited as possible. The "one-party" system was introduced to meet these requirements. All other groups in society were prevented from having their own parties—first and foremost, the working class—by placing all organizations under state tutelage, by reinforcing the apparatus of constraint against the producers, by concentrating all news and propaganda media exclusively in the hands of an all-powerful elite, by eliminating the freedom of artists and intellectuals to create, and by establishing a centralized system of economic management. All this was accompanied by massive police terror.

The elite, in thus concentrating in its hands alone social and political power, as well as power over the productive process and the division of the product created (i.e., ownership), made industrialization its class interest and, in a sense, its personal interest. It made "production for production's sake" its class goal and the basis for consolidating and extending its rule.

This elite was thus transformed into a new ruling class, "the central political bureaucracy," and the state it ruled into a bureaucratic class dictatorship. It can be said, therefore, that the needs of industrializing an underdeveloped country gave birth to the bureaucracy as a ruling class; it alone could answer these needs, since in the conditions of the country's underdevelopment, it alone adopted industrialization—production for production's sake—as its class interest.

We have already seen that the class goal of the bureaucracy is production for production and that this goal corresponds to the interests of economic development in an underdeveloped country in the first phase of its industrialization, that is, when the industrial base is being constructed. The length of this phase is determined primarily by the degree to which the economy is saturated by industry at the start of intensive industrialization. In Poland, the end of this period came in the second half of the 1950s. In 1956, the productive apparatus was already three times larger than in 1949, and in 1960, four times larger.

Suppose that after having completed the essential tasks of this phase, the bureaucracy maintains its class rule as well as the same class goal. Let us consider the situation which flows from this hypothesis: A mass industrial base has been built; the forced investment of the preceding years has permitted the development of industrial capacity and the employment of idle manpower at breakneck speed. Production for production is characterized by the attempt to limit, as far as possible, all growth in production to Sector A.[1] It seeks to convert all growth in production

---

[1] Soviet Marxists divided the economy into two sectors: Sector A contained industries making products that were used in further production, such as steel and machine tools, and Sector B contained

into new means of production. Therefore, continuing this tendency, when the economy is "saturated" by industry, signifies that the expanded means of production must be used exclusively—aside from a certain increase in consumption which is absolutely necessary but kept as small as possible—to create new means of production, to enlarge the productive apparatus. In other words, the growth of industrial capacity must be followed by the growth in the share of the national income allotted to capital accumulation.

Intensive industrialization cannot take place under conditions of equilibrium. Since the economic surplus is small, industry cannot be built up all at once without distortions. The disproportions, which appear in the course of the rapid increase in productive capacity, create the necessity for supplementary investments and lead to the still further enlargement of capital accumulation fund.

Suppose that the productive apparatus which has increased many times over due to industrialization must be fully utilized; this means that the conditions must be created for full utilization of the enlarged industrial capacity. This would entail— under the hypothesis of the maintenance of production for production—such an increase in accumulation that consumption would be pushed below the socially necessary minimum. On the other hand, it must not be forgotten that such phenomena as full employment, the development of an industrial civilization, and the raising of the cultural level of society go hand in hand with an increase in consumption needs deemed essential by that society. In these conditions, reducing consumption below the essential level threatens the system with economic, social, and political catastrophe. Therefore, it is impossible to push consumption back down below this level and, consequently, equally impossible to raise the rate of accumulation so as to permit total utilization of the increased industrial capacity.

Thus the low level of overall consumption, in the last analysis, limits production itself. The bureaucratic system is not exempt from this law. However, this limitation is not brought about by the difficulties of realizing the value created on the market, but by direct restriction of enlarged reproduction. Keeping production as the goal of production after the construction of the industrial base has been completed—under conditions of industrial "saturation"—*creates a contradiction between the already developed industrial capacity and the low level of consumption.* This contradiction is the cause of an underutilization of industrial capacity, of waste of the economic surplus, and it puts a brake on economic development. Therefore, it is the source of a crisis.

It is clear that the crisis is getting worse, as not only the material conditions of the workers but also their social and cultural condition deteriorate. This situation is reinforcing the enslavement of the workers in the shops; it is depriving them of the chance to satisfy even their minimum desires within the framework of the present productive and social relationships.

The crisis is forcing the workers to stand up against the bureaucrats and the system in order to defend the present level of their material and cultural existence.

The bureaucracy will not concede one zloty of its own free will. In any case, given the crisis and the lack of economic reserves, it has nothing more to concede to

---

industries making products that were simply consumed, such as clothing and food. By emphasizing Sector A, they believed they could sustain rapid growth.

pressure. Under these circumstances, any large-scale strike action will inevitably turn into a political conflict with the bureaucracy. This is the only way the workers can change their conditions. Today, in the epoch of the universal crisis of the system, the workers' interests lie in revolution: in the abolition of the bureaucracy and the production relationships associated with it, in taking control of their own labor and its product—control of production—into their own hands, that is, in establishing an economic, social, and political system based on workers' democracy. The interests of the majority of wage earners, because of their proletarian situation, are parallel to those of the workers.

This general crisis of social relations flows from the fact that the productive relations, on which the power of the bureaucracy is based, have become an obstacle to the development of the economy and the source of its crisis and that all segments of society are without hope of progress or of satisfying their minimum class interests within the framework of the system. Thus, no more than the economic crisis can be overcome on the basis of present productive relations can the general social crisis be overcome within the framework of present social relations, which only aggravate the crisis; it can be overcome only by the abolition of the prevailing production and social relationships. *The only road to progress is through revolution.*

In the circumstances of the system's general crisis, the bureaucracy is isolated in society. No class in society will rally to its side; at most, the rich peasantry and the petty bourgeoisie will remain neutral. But only the workers, as a result of the conditions of their life and labor, sense the need of abolishing the bureaucracy. As we have already seen, the primary sources of the economic and social crisis lie in the production relations in the heavy industry sector, that is, in the relations between the workers and the central political bureaucracy actualized in the process of production. This is why the working class must be the principal and leading force in the revolution. The revolution which will abolish the bureaucratic system, therefore, is in essence proletarian.

It is often said that the powerful state apparatus, with all of the modern means of material coercion at its command, is in itself a sufficient prop for the ruling class and enables it to maintain itself over the long run even in the total absence of social support. The essence of this argument, despite its seemingly modern form, is a misunderstanding as old as class society and the state. In October 1956, we saw how the powerful machine of coercion in Hungary became impotent, toppled, and evaporated in the space of a few days. The workers produce and transport arms, fill the ranks of the army, and create the entire material power of the state. If the walls of the prisons, barracks, and arsenals remain standing over long periods, it is not only because they are made of solid materials but because they are protected by the hegemony of the ruling class, the authority of the government, fear and resignation before the social order in power. The existence of these psychological walls permits the government to install itself securely behind brick walls. The social crisis strips the regime of its hegemony, its authority; it brings the overwhelming majority into conflict with it, and finally it arrays the working class against the ruling bureaucracy. The inevitable deepening of the crisis undermines the psychological walls, which are the government's real protection. A revolutionary situation causes them to collapse, and then the brick walls are no longer an obstacle. The economic and social crisis cannot be overcome within the limits of the bureaucratic system. *Revolution is inevitable.*

We have shown that revolution is the gravedigger of the old society. At the same time, it is the creator of the new. The question now before us is whether the working class, which by its very nature is the principal and leading force of revolution, is capable of offering a valid program.

This would be true if the program is advanced by the social class whose particular interest is most in accord with the needs of economic development and satisfaction of the needs of other classes and social layers—in other words, whose program permits the realization of the interests of society as a whole. The class interest of the workers requires the end of bureaucratic ownership of the means of production. This doesn't mean that workers' wages must be equal to the total value of the product of their labor. The level of development of productive forces in modern society creates the necessity of a division of labor permitting the existence of nonproductive sectors supported by the material product of the workers.

1. The present level of productivity implies a social division of labor in which the function of production is separate from that of management. There must be workers and managers. In the process of production, the working class is not destined to manage but to produce. In order to manage, it must organize itself and be organized by its state.

2. This is why it is necessary for the working class to organize, in addition to workers' councils in factories, delegations from plants throughout the country. That is, it must organize *councils of workers' deputies* with a central council of deputies at their head. Under this system of councils, the working class would set the goals of social production, would make the necessary decisions, and supervise carrying out the plan at every step. At each level the councils would become the instruments of economic, political, executive, and legislative authority. They would be truly elective bodies for the voters, organized on the basis of factories. Voters would be able to recall their representatives and replace them at any moment, without regard to regular election dates. Workers' delegations would become the framework of the proletarian state.

3. If workers' delegates in the central council of deputies had before them only a single project for the distribution of national income presented by the government or by the leadership of a single party, their role would be limited to that of a perfunctory vote. As we have shown, monopolistic power cannot have a proletarian character. That automatically becomes a dictatorship over the working class, a bureaucratic organization serving to atomize workers and keep them and all of society in subjection.

In order for the system of councils to become the expression of the will, of the thinking, of the activity of the working masses, *the working class must organize itself into more than one party*. What does a plurality of parties mean in practice? The right of every political group recognized by the working class to publish its own newspaper, to present its program via the modern information media, to organize cadres, to carry on political campaigns—in brief, to be a party. The existence of more than one workers' party requires freedom of speech, press, assembly, *the end of preventive censorship*, complete freedom of scientific research, of literary and artistic creation. Without freedom of expression for different currents of thought in the press, in scientific research, in literary and artistic experimentation, without complete freedom to create, there is no workers' democracy.

For the same reasons, we oppose parliamentary regimes. The experience of the last twenty years shows that they are no guarantee against dictatorship and that, even in the most perfect forms, they are not governments of the people. In the parliamentary system, the parties only fight to be elected: The moment the vote is cast, the electoral platforms can be thrown into the wastebasket. In parliament, the deputies feel themselves bound only to the party leadership which named them as candidates. Voters are grouped in arbitrary election districts according to purely formal criteria. This atomizes them. The right to recall deputies is a complete fiction. Participation of citizens in political life amounts to nothing more than reading statements of the leaders in the press, listening to them on the radio, and seeing them on TV—and, once every four or five years, voting to choose the party to govern them. The rest takes place by virtue of a mandate, without the voters' participation. Furthermore, parliaments only exercise legislative power. The executive apparatus holds the only real power, the power over those who control the material force, that is, the power over surplus values.

Therefore the parliamentary system is one in which the working class, and the entire society, finds itself deprived of all influence on government—by virtue of voting. To formal voting every four or five years, we counterpose the permanent participation of the working class, organized in a system of councils, political parties and unions: Workers would assume the correction and supervision of political and economic decisions at all levels.

In the capitalist system, the bourgeoisie, which controls the surplus value, is above parliament. In the bureaucratic system, the untrammeled rule of the central political bureaucracy lies behind the parliamentary fiction. In the system of workers' democracy, if representation of the entire body of citizens takes a parliamentary form, the working class will be above parliament, organized in councils and controlling the material base of the existence of society, namely, the product of labor.

4. The working class cannot decide on the division of the labor product directly; it can only do so through its central political representation. Furthermore, the working class is not absolutely homogeneous in regard to its class interests. Conflicts between the decisions of workers' delegations and the interests and tendencies of workers in particular factories and particular sectors of the working class are inevitable. The mere fact of separation between management and production holds within it the possibility of the development of an elected power with a certain amount of independence, and this holds true as much at the factory level as at the state. If workers were deprived—above and beyond the right to vote—of the possibility of self-defense against the decisions of their representational system, the system would degenerate and act against the interests of those it is supposed to represent. If the working class were deprived of the possibility of defending itself against the state, workers' democracy would become a fiction. The possibility of defense must be guaranteed by *trade unions absolutely independent of the state with the right to organize economic and political strikes*. The different political parties would fight to maintain the proletarian character of trade unions in seeking to exert influence over them.

The *Praxis* Group

Although Marx's Economic and Philosophical Manuscripts of 1844 *appeared in a complete version first in 1932, they did not enter fully into the consciousness of Marxian thinkers until after World War II. The emphasis on "self-estrangement," or alienation, in these manuscripts led some to argue that the young Marx was more relevant to the problems of the industrializing world than was the older Marx of* Capital, *or than the Engels who had codified Marx's views. This turn to the younger Marx took place in the West as well as in Eastern Europe and produced the hope in the 1960s that it might be possible to create a non-Stalinist Marxism that would perform the ideological function of informing political action while at the same time sustaining fundamental human values.*

One of the most important groups of East European thinkers involved with this effort to create "socialism with a human face" was the group of Yugoslav philosophers who published the journal Praxis *in Zagreb from 1964 to 1974. Because* Praxis *appeared in a Western-language version as well as in a Serbo-Croatian edition, it became an international forum for innovative Marxian critiques of the modern condition that attracted authors from many countries. After many difficulties the journal lost its state stipend in 1974 and had to cease publication. In the following selection a Belgrade philosopher, Mihailo Marković, presents a thumbnail sketch of the emergence of the* Praxis *group and a brief overview of the group's basic position. In the late 1980s and early 1990s, Marković became a prominent adviser of the Serbian president, Slobodan Milošević.*

18

The *Praxis* Group

Mihailo Marković

Retrospective published in 1975

Marxist philosophy in Yugoslavia emerged with the rise of the socialist revolutionary movement before and during World War II. All the preceding history of Yugoslav philosophy is to an insignificant measure relevant for contemporary philosophical thought. Two important spiritual sources in the past however are (1) a very old tradition of resistance to sheer force, expressed especially in beautiful epic poems about struggles for liberation against the Turks and other foreign invaders, and (2) nineteenth-century socialist thought which combined a general revolutionary orientation with a concrete approach to existing backward, rural society in the south Slavic countries of that time.

School philosophy was not very attractive to the young generation that took part in the liberation war and struggle against Stalinism after 1948. With few exceptions professors of philosophy in Yugoslav universities were mere followers, epigones of influential European trends. Socially committed philosophical thought was needed, yielding a capacity to deal with and settle grave social issues. Marxism seemed the only existing philosophy that was likely to satisfy that need.

For a brief time, until 1947, the only interpretation of Marxism that was available was "dialectical materialism" in the form elaborated by Soviet philosophers. But very soon, even before the conflict with Stalinism in 1948, the most gifted students of philosophy in the universities of Belgrade and Zagreb began to doubt whether what they found in the fourth chapter of the *History of the Communist Party of the Soviet Union (Bolsheviks)* was really the last word in revolutionary philosophy. It sounded superficial, simplified, and dogmatic, and it altogether lacked any criticism of the existing forms of socialist society.

The 1950s was a period of reinterpretation of Marx's philosophy and modern science, a period of building up the theoretical foundations of a new philosophy which, while remaining in the tradition of Marx, was sharply opposed to rigid, dogmatic schemes of *Diamat* and at the same time tended to incorporate the most important achievements in post-Marxian philosophy and culture.

A thorough study of the classical works of Marxism, especially of Marx's early

Reprinted from Mihailo Marković, "Marxist Philosophy in Yugoslavia: The Praxis Group," in Mihailo Marković and Robert S. Cohen, *Yugoslavia: The Rise and Fall of Socialist Humanism* (London: Bertrand Russell Peace Foundation, 1975), pp. 14–18, 20–21, 26–27, 30–33, 37–40, by permission of Spokesman (Nottingham, England).

manuscripts, in a new perspective, led to the rediscovery of a profound and sophisticated humanist philosophy which, for a long time, has been either ignored or dismissed by a great many Marxist philosophers as being Hegelian. It became clear that the problems which the Young Marx was grappling with—praxis, the conflict of human existence and essence, the question of what constitute true needs and basic human capacities, alienation, emancipation, labor and production, and other concerns, expressed at that time, far from being sins of youth—underlay all his mature work and, furthermore, remain even now the living, crucial issues of our time and indeed of the whole epoch of transition.

A fortunate circumstance in those formative years after 1948 was the fact that the new, postwar generation quickly found suitable forms for a collective intellectual life. In 1950 the Serbian Philosophical Society was created. Later similar philosophical societies emerged in all the other republics. Since 1958 there has also been a Yugoslav Philosophical Association. During the decade of the 1950s, dozens of philosophical conferences were held on problems which were considered essential at that time: the nature of philosophy, the relationship between philosophy and science, ideology, truth, alienation, the young and old Marx, Marxist humanism. These discussions were led in complete freedom and sincerity, in an atmosphere of genuine dialogue among spokesmen of several different Marxist orientations. A basic polarization occurred between those who continued the line of orthodox Marxism, which is to say, a mere defense and justification of the classical writings of Marx, Engels, and Lenin; and those who radically opposed any orthodoxy, insisting on the further development of what is, in our time, still living and revolutionary in the classical sources.

The former orientation laid emphasis on the philosophy of the natural sciences, trying to employ recent achievements in that field to confirm an Engelsian conception of *Naturphilosophie*. Outside the domain of their interest remained Marx's critique of the political economy and especially the early humanistic writings of Marx. Therefore the basic philosophical problem remained for them the relation of matter and mind. The main objective of their research programme was the establishment of the most general laws in nature, society, and human thought. This in fact was the program of the whole orientation of dialectical materialism.

The latter orientation rejected "dialectical materialism" as a dogmatic and essentially conservative orientation which at best leads to a generalization and systematization of existing scientific knowledge but does not contribute to the creation of a critical epochal consciousness capable of directing practical social energy toward the liberation and humanization of the world. From this point of view the basic philosophical problem is the historical human condition and the possibilities for radical universal emancipation.

Within this humanist orientation there was from the beginning a clear distinction between those who tended to develop *Marxism as a critical science* and those who construed it as essentially a revolutionary *utopia*. From the former standpoint the essential limitation of dogmatism was the ideologization of Marx's doctrine. In order for this to be demystified it was necessary not only to return to classical sources and to reinterpret them but also to develop a high degree of objectivity and criticism in dealing with contemporary problems, to reestablish the unity of theory and practice, and to mediate the a priori philosophical vision of man as a "being of praxis" and communism as a dealienated human community—with concrete knowledge about existing historical conditions and tendencies. According to this view Marx had transcended pure philosophy and created an all-embracing critical social theory. Such an approach required the development of a general method of critical inquiry: dialectic.

From the latter standpoint it was believed that the essential philosophical limitation of dogmatism was a positivist reduction of philosophy to a *quasi*-objective science. It is the nature of science to divide, fragment, quantify, reduce man to an object, study equilibrium rather than change, see changes only as variations of a fixed pattern. It was considered desirable, therefore, to sharply separate philosophy from science, to put philosophy into brackets as insufficiently relevant for the study of human alienation and emancipation. According to this view the philosophical thought of Marx expressed in his early writings was in fact utopian thought about the future, about what *could be*. Such an utopian thought is radical due to its implicit invitation to abolish existing reality. Scientific knowledge, on the other hand, remains within the boundaries of actually existing objects—that is the source of its conformism.

Since 1963 *Praxis* philosophers established that both forms of economic and political alienation still existed in Yugoslav society, that the working class was still exploited—this time by the new elites: bureaucracy and technocracy—that the market economy will inevitably reproduce capital–labor relations; that self-management exists only at the microlevel in enterprises and local communities and organizations, and that consequently its further development requires a gradual withering away of professional politics and the formation of workers' councils at the regional, republican, and federal level; that the basic precondition for a really participatory democracy was at first a radical democratization and, later, the withering away, of the party.

In the period 1963–1968 an attempt was made to mobilize loyal party theoreticians to oppose these critical views with ideological countercriticism. But few able scholars were available, and the counterarguments were weak. "How can the working class," asked these official spokesmen, "being the ruling class in socialism, exploit itself?" Marx's critique of the market economy, they alleged, did not hold valid for a socialist market economy. "The attack on bureaucracy" they held "is an anarchistic assault on organized society." Any critique of the existing form of self-management they saw as a critique of self-management in principle. Integrated self-management at the republican and federal level was held to be a form of statism. Democratization of the party, in the sense of allowing minorities to continue to express and justify their ideas, amounted in their view to a demand that factions be allowed within the party, and so on.

The year 1968 was a turning point. Students' mass demonstrations in Belgrade on June 2 and 3, and the occupation of all buildings of the universities in Belgrade June 3–10, followed by similar events in Zagreb and Sarajevo, opened up the greatest political crisis in Yugoslav postwar society and produced a permanent fear that philosophical critical theory under certain conditions might inspire a mass practical movement.

A series of measures were undertaken in order to thoroughly reduce the field of activity of *Praxis* philosophers. Most of those who were members of the party were expelled, or their organizations were dissolved. They were eliminated from important social functions. Funds for philosophical activities, journals, and other publications were cut off or became extremely scarce. Demands were expressed by top leaders that those philosophers who had exerted a "corrupting," "ideologically alien" influence on students, more specifically those from the University of Belgrade, had to be ousted from the university.

The *Praxis* group is composed of individual philosophers who not only specialize in different fields but also differ in certain basic conceptions. They must not be treated therefore as a homogeneous philosophical school. What unites them is much more a practical attitude than a theoretical doctrine, which does not exclude the possibility of formulating certain basic views which could be endorsed by all.

The orthodox, *Diamat,* view that the central philosophical problem is the relation of matter and mind has been generally rejected as abstract, ahistorical, dualistic. The central problem for Marx was how to realize human nature by producing a more humane world. The fundamental philosophical assumption implicit in this problem is that man is essentially a being of *praxis,* that is, a being capable of free creative activity by which he transforms the world, realizes his specific potential faculties, and satisfies the needs of other human individuals. Praxis is an essential possibility for man, but under certain unfavorable historical conditions its realization may be blocked. This discrepancy between the individual's actual existence and potential essence, that is, between what he is and what he might be, is *alienation.* The basic task of philosophy is to critically analyze the phenomenon of alienation and to indicate practical steps leading to human *self-realization,* to *praxis.*

Praxis has to be distinguished from the purely epistemological category of *practice.* The latter refers simply to any subject's activity of changing an object, and this activity can be alienated. The former is a normative concept and refers to an ideal, specifically human activity which is an end in itself, a statement of basic values and at the same time a standard of criticism of all other forms of activity.

Praxis must also not be identified with *labor* and *material production.* The latter belong to the sphere of necessity; they are necessary conditions for human survival and must involve division of roles, routine operations, subordination, hierarchy. Work becomes *praxis* only when it is freely chosen and provides an opportunity for individual self-expression and self-fulfillment.

How may we conceive of potential human faculties? They must be universal; otherwise a general standard of criticism would be lacking, and philosophy would have to be relativized—which is absurd. On the other hand, if they are unchangeable, history would lose all meaning and would be reduced to a series of changes in the realm of mere phenomena. The only solution is to conceive of universal faculties as latent dispositions which are the product of the whole previous history and which can be slowly modified or even replaced by some new future ones—depending on actual life conditions over a long period of time.

But is human nature constituted only by "positive" faculties such as creativity, capacity for reasoning, for communication, sociability, and so on? How may we justify such an optimistic view? And how may we account for the tremendous amount of evil in human history? Again, the only solution is to somewhat modify Marx's optimism and to introduce an idea of polarity of human nature. As a result of millennia of life in class society man has also acquired some "negative" latent dispositions such as aggressiveness, egoistic acquisitiveness, will to power, destructive drives. All these enter into a *descriptive* concept of human nature which can be tested by historical evidence. Which of the conflicting latent dispositions will prevail and what sort of character will be formed in each individual case depend upon the social surroundings, upon the actual historical conditions. Thus when a philosopher builds up a selective *normative* concept of human nature he implicitly commits himself to a way of life, to the creation of such life conditions under which certain desirable (positive) latent dispositions entering his normative concept may prevail, while certain undesirable (negative) dispositions would be blocked or slowly modified assuming socially acceptable forms.

On these grounds it becomes possible to distinguish between *true genuine needs* and *false, artificial* ones, or between a true and an illusory *self-realization*. The concept of truth in this context is much more general than the customary epistemological concept. One of its dimensions is adequacy to actual reality (the descriptive concept of truth). Another dimension is adequacy to an ideal standard, to an essential possibility (the normative concept of truth).

A philosophy based on the notion of *praxis* will naturally pay special attention to deriving practical consequences from its principles; furthermore, these consequences essentially will be steps that have to be undertaken in order to make true the idea of man as essentially a *being of praxis*.

Under what social conditions, in what kind of social organization can human activity become the objectification of the individual's most creative capacities and a means of satisfying genuine individual and common needs?

This question is much more general than the one usually asked by Marxists who ignore the philosophical roots of Marx's economic and political criticism. All questions about specific social institutions, such as private property, capital, the bourgeois state, and so on boil down to the fundamental issue: What happens to man; what are his relationships to other human beings, does he actualize or waste all the wealth of his potential powers?

In this radical perspective (*radical* because the root, *radix*, of all issues is man) the basic purpose of critical inquiry is the discovery of those specific social institutions and structures which cripple human beings, arrest their development, and impose on them patterns of simple, easily predictable, dull, stereotyped behavior.

Thus while it is in the nature of Marxist theory to offer "a relentless criticism of all existing reality"—a characterization of the *Praxis* group approach which infuriates bureaucracy—this criticism does not invite destruction but the *transcendence* of its object.

The practical form of transcendence in history is *revolution*. The defining characteristics of a social revolution are neither use of violence, nor overthrow of a government and seizure of political power, nor economic collapse of the system. Already Marx spoke of a possible peaceful social revolution in England, Holland, and America. He also made very clear, explicit statements about seizure of power being only the first episode of a long process of social revolution, about political revolution (as distinguished from social revolution) having a "narrow spirit" and leading necessarily to the rule of an elite. That economic collapse is also not a necessary condition of revolution follows from Marx's description of economic transition measures which a new proletarian government has to undertake after successful seizure of power. These measures are cautious and gradual, intended to preserve the continuity of economic functioning.

From this point of view none of the twentieth century socialist revolutions has so far been completed; what has taken place so far in Russia, China, Cuba, Yugoslavia, and elsewhere were only initial phases or abortive attempts. Private ownership of the means of production was not transcended by really social ownership but modified into state and group property. Professional division of labor still largely exists, and work is equally long, monotonous, stultifying, and wasteful as in capitalism. The market is no longer the exclusive regulator of production; it has been supplemented by state planning but this latter way of regulating production is still far from being very rational and democratic, and it still preserves a good deal of profit motivation. The bourgeois state was not transcended by a network of self-management organs but was only modified into a bureaucratic state which allows a greater (in Yugoslavia) or a lesser (in Russia) degree of participatory democracy in atomic units of social organization. The party as a typically bourgeois type of political organization tends to be perpetuated. It is true, the social composition of the rank-and-file membership of the "communist" party shows a shift toward the working class, but the organization is even more authoritarian, and ideological indoctrination even more drastic. The fact that there is only one such organization which monopolizes all political power is hardly an advantage over bourgeois pluralism. Real supersession of political alienation will materialize only when all monopolies of power are dismantled, when authoritarian and hierarchical organizations such as the state and party gradually wither away and are replaced by self-governing associations of producers and citizens at all social levels.

This whole conception is labeled "anarcho-liberal" by some politicians who speak in the name of Marx and of the Yugoslav League of Communists. The irony of the situation is that these are the ideas of Marx, ideas with which the Yugoslav League of Communists attracted the best minds of a generation of partisans and rebels against Stalin's domination. These are the ideas explicitly formulated in the 1958 program of that same League of Communists.

The mortal sin of the *Praxis* group seems to be in taking these ideas seriously.

The Prague Spring

Early in 1968 Alexander Dubček replaced Antonín Novotný as secretary general of the Communist party of Czechoslovakia. The change came not because of public pressure for reform, but because of dissatisfaction within the party over Novotný's neo-Stalinist failures. Dubček began to permit criticism from the public and to consider reform. Already by March 1968, public discussion, censored less and less, was becoming unusually forthright. In April the party proclaimed its Action Program, which stated that "if party resolutions and directives fail to express correctly the needs and potentialities of the society, they must be altered." When critics began to question even the legitimacy of the Communist party, the Soviet Union became alarmed. Ominous troop maneuvers and high-level meetings failed to slow the momentum toward reform, and so on August 27, 1968, armies of the Warsaw pact invaded Czechoslovakia and reinstalled a Stalinist-style regime. Until November 1989, Czechoslovakia was one of the most politically regressive countries in Eastern Europe.

The first of the following two readings is part of an article by Zdeněk Mlynář, who, while a student in the Soviet Union, was a close friend of Mikhail Gorbachev. Assigned by the Czechoslovak party in 1967 to draft policy recommendations to the party congress planned for 1970, Mlynář unexpectedly concluded that a pluralist system would be best. In 1967 Mlynář thought of himself as a reform communist, not a democrat, but it is clear from this statement of May 1968 that his notion of socialism comes perilously close to democratic pluralism. He left the party as a consequence of the Soviet invasion and in 1977 emigrated. During the 1980s he lived in Vienna as the leader of the opposition in exile.

The second reading is Ludvík Vaculík's "Two Thousand Words." Published in four Prague newspapers on June 27, 1968, just before the beginning of a special party election process, and signed by many other public figures, this plea inspired both widespread support in the Czechoslovak public and serious concern among the Soviets. One author has called it "probably the most important single document of the revival process." Actually about 2,700 words in length in English translation, it is printed here in full.

19

Towards a Democratic Political Organization of Society

Zdeněk Mlynář

May 5, 1968

The basic problem is the position of man in socialism. This may sound like a very abstract idea to some people, but what I mean is a very concrete thing which is felt in everyday life. Socialist man is not a private owner, and therefore the stimuli which are created by private property relations have disappeared. If in these conditions we try to keep people, either as individuals or as members of a certain group, in the position of *objects overwhelmingly directed from above,* one tendency will be more and more in evidence: People will begin to separate the pursuit of their own private interests and needs from the pursuit of the collective, group, and social interests.

They understand anyway that they have no influence over the collective interest and will therefore leave this to other anonymous creatures (we know the expression "Let them decide and solve the problem"). But people do realize that they can have a direct influence on their own private circumstances and therefore use their initiative to find ways and means of ensuring the best standard of living *for themselves,* from their material conditions to the amount of free time they have.

The traditional utopian ideal of collectivism as the basis for a new social order was turned under the old political system into a situation where *official collectivism* has become just a hollow-sounding phrase. It is now a cloak under which a person can build his atomized private life or produce the most favorable conditions for his own individual "survival." And thus, one of the most characteristic features of the breakdown of the official ideology of the old political system is the huge disparity between the formal political activity of nearly every "upright citizen" and the *completely different values* for which this same citizen increasingly shows a preference in his private life. It was mere "window dressing" for a citizen who was part of some organization to go to the right meetings and take part in various activities, to present himself at elections and vote without being forced to do so for the prescribed candidate, when in reality he increasingly expended his most important activity and talent on his private interests, regardless of whether this activity was connected with the formally professed fetish of "the social good" or not. And so we were led to the phenomenon which we can see today, that the people who are really the most "honest," those who are devoted to the ideas of collectivist communism, and so forth, *objectively* perform in some situations the socially negative role of sectarians. And incidentally it is these facts which will be among the strongest barriers the democratization process will come up against. . . .

Unless there is a change in the position of people in the political system, this state of affairs will not change; without an alteration in people's economic relationships (which the new system should be trying to create), an efficient and dynamic socialist economy cannot be created. . . . And only in this way will people begin to turn their initiative, activity, and talent away from advancing their own private affairs, toward the goal of the social whole, to the search for ways to satisfy their own needs and interests *in harmony with* the whole development of society. . . .

Of course, this is a thesis, a premise. But it is one which does hold some water. It is based on a concept of socialism as a social order which will preserve the *active forces in European capitalist development* . . . the necessary independence and subjectivity of the human individual. It is in conflict with other conceptions of socialism which do not have this end in view and which are based on the historical conditions of the development of other civilizations, for instance of the East, as we can clearly see in the Chinese conception of socialism.

In general, it has been suggested here that *more than one* kind of political organ must be created. The political system which is based on this principle is called a *pluralist system,* and it would therefore be true to say that an experiment is going on in Czechoslovakia to create a pluralist society for which there is at present no real analogy among the socialist states.

A pluralist political system is quite often identified just with the existence of a large number of political parties. But I do not think this is really right, and all the less so for a socialist society. It is very easy to understand why this question is so much discussed at the moment in Czechoslovakia. . . .

What is clear above all is that the direct fusion of the Communist party with the state, and the idea of the leading role of the Communist party . . . is one of the critical points of the old system. So a guarantee is needed to make it possible for this to happen again. Therefore, the fundamental problem of the development of socialism is thought to be the formation of an opposition. Some people think that it is even necessary for an opposition party to be *outside the National Front* and to be created immediately, because even the whole idea of the National Front as a platform for dispute between the different political interests seems to some people a kind of fraud, when they take into account what the National Front has stood for in the last twenty years.

I am not one of those people who think that the idea of the development of the National Front as outlined in the Action Program . . . is the last word on the theory and practice of Marxism or of socialism.[1] But I do think that the idea of a model of,

---

[1] A key moment in the development of the Prague Spring was the publication on April 9 of the party's Action Program. One of the more interesting parts of the program was its suggestion that the National Front, which was the mass agent of the party, was the place where those who wished to criticize the regime could articulate their views and thereby have some influence. The opposition rejected this effort to ward off the creation of political parties.

for instance, two political parties, which would operate on something like the principle of the well-known system of opposition in Great Britain, is not only not out of the question but, on the contrary, has its own logic and virtues. There is nothing antisocialist in principle in this idea as a *mechanism* of governing, just as there is nothing antisocialist in the mechanism of the so-called division of power. . . .

When I look at our current social situation, the present state of the political system, and the practical possibilities for it to be transformed, it does not seem to me that the attempt to create political parties outside the National Front, parties which would put forward programs and a platform of opposition and attempt to win state power at elections . . . would be a guarantee of our democratic development.

I don't want to frighten anyone by saying this, but I should like to state the fact that there is enough scope in the situation as it is at the moment for all the other forces in this society, given maintenance of the principle of the National Front, to oppose the tendency to a monopoly. And I say, "the principle of the National Front" on purpose, not wanting it to continue on its present basis. The possibility of the independent development of political parties themselves cannot be ruled out. It could take place by their being reconstructed, integrated with other groups, or by the constitution of a new party, *but this should be on the basis of the existence of a National Front.*

20

Two Thousand Words to Workers, Farmers, Scientists, Artists, and Everyone

Ludvík Vaculík

June 27, 1968

The life of this nation was first of all threatened by the war. Then still more bad times followed, together with events which threatened the spiritual health and character of the nation. Most of the people of Czechoslovakia optimistically accepted the socialist program, but its direction got into the wrong people's hands. It would not have mattered so much that they did not possess enough experience as statesmen, have enough practical knowledge or intellectual training, if they had at least had more common sense and humanity, if they had been able to listen to other people's opinions, and if they had allowed themselves to be replaced as time passed by more capable people.

After the war people had great confidence in the Communist party, but it gradually preferred to have official positions instead of the people's trust, until it had only official positions and nothing else. This has to be said: Communists among us know that it's true, and their disappointment about the results is just as great as that of others. The incorrect line of the leadership turned the party from a political party and ideological grouping into a power organization which became very attractive to power-hungry egotists, reproachful cowards, and people with bad consciences. When they came into the party, its character and behavior began to be affected. Its internal organization was such that good people, who might have maintained its development for it to have fitted into the modern world, could not wield any influence at all without shameful incidents occurring. Many communists opposed this decline, but not in one single case did they have any success in preventing what happened.

The conditions in the Communist party were the model for and the cause of an identical situation in the state. Because the party became linked with the state it lost the advantage of being able to keep its distance from the executive power. There was no criticism of the activity of the state and economic organizations. Parliament forgot how to debate: The government forgot how to govern and the directors how to direct. Elections had no significance, and the laws lost their weight. We could not trust representatives on any committee, and even if we did, we could not ask them to do anything, because they could accomplish nothing. What was still worse was that we could hardly trust each other anymore. There was a decline of individual and communal honor. You didn't get anywhere by being honest, and it was useless expecting ability to be appreciated. Most people, therefore, lost interest in public affairs; they worried only about themselves and about their money. Moreover, as a result of these bad conditions, now one cannot even rely on money. Relationships between people were harmed, and they didn't enjoy working any more. To sum up, the country reached a point where its spiritual health and character were both threatened.

We are all of us together responsible for the present state of affairs, and the communists among us are more responsible than others. But the main responsibility rests with those who were part of, or the agents of, uncontrolled power. The power of a determined group was conveyed, with the help of the party apparatus, from Prague to every district and community. This apparatus decided what one might or might not do: It directed the cooperatives for the cooperative workers, the factories for the workers, and the National Committees for the citizens. No organizations actually belonged to their members, not even the communist ones.

These rulers' greatest guilt, and the worst deception they perpetrated, was to make out that their arbitrary rule was the will of the workers. If we were to continue to believe this deception, we would have now to blame the workers for the decline of our economy, for the crimes committed against innocent people, for the introduction of the censorship which made it impossible for all this to be written about. The workers would now have to be blamed for the wrong investments, for the losses in trade, for the shortage of flats. Of course, no sensible person believes in such guilt on the part of the workers. We all know, and especially every worker knows, that in actual fact the workers made no decisions about anything. Someone else controlled the voting of the workers' representatives. While many workers had the impression that they were in control, a specially educated group of party officials and officials of the state apparatus ruled. In fact, they took the place of the overthrown class and themselves became the new aristocracy.

In all fairness, we should say that some of them were aware of what was going on a long time ago. We can recognize these people now by the fact that they are redressing wrongs, correcting mistakes, returning the power of making decisions to the party members and the citizens, and limiting the authority and the number of the apparatchiks.[1] They are with us in opposing the backward, obsolete views among the party membership. But many officials are still defending themselves against changes, and they still carry a lot of weight. They still have means of power in their hands, especially in the districts and in the small communities, where they may use these instruments secretly and without any risk to themselves.

Since the beginning of the year, we have been taking part in the revival process of democratization. It began in the Communist party. Even noncommunists, who until

---

[1]An apparatchik is a member of the *apparat*, or (party) bureaucracy. Apparatchik is therefore a derogatory term for a small-minded and obstructive (party) bureaucrat whose main goal is simply retaining his slot in the system.

recently expected no good to come from it, recognize this fact. We should add, however, that the process could not have begun anywhere else. After all, only the communists could for twenty years lead anything like a full political life; only the communists were in a position to know what was happening and where; only the opposition within the Communist party were privileged enough to be in contact with the enemy. The initiative and efforts of democratic communists are therefore only a part of the debt which the party as a whole owes to noncommunists, whom it has kept in a position of inequality. No thanks, therefore, is due to the Communist party, although it should probably be acknowledged that it is honestly trying to use this last opportunity to save its own and the nation's honor.

The revival process hasn't come up with anything very new. It is producing ideas and suggestions, many of which are older than the errors of our socialism and others which came up to the surface after being in existence underground for a long time. They should have come out into the open a long time ago, but they were suppressed. Don't let's kid ourselves that these ideas are now winning the day because truth has a force and strength. The fact that they are now winning is much more because of the weakness of the old leadership, which apparently had to be weakened beforehand by twenty years of unopposed rule during which no one interrupted it. Obviously, all the faults hidden in the very foundations and ideology of this system had to mature before they could be seen properly developed.

Let us not, therefore, underestimate the significance of criticism from the ranks of writers and students. The source of social changes lies in the economy. The right word carries significance only if it is said in conditions which have already been duly prepared. And by duly prepared conditions in our country we have to understand our general poverty and the complete disintegration of the old system of rule, in which politicians of a certain type quite calmly compromised themselves, but at our expense. So you can see that truth is not victorious here, truth is what remains when everything else has gone to pot. We have no reason to be patting ourselves on the back, but there is reason to be a little more optimistic.

We turn to you in this optimistic moment because it is still being threatened. It took several months for many of us to believe that we really could speak out, and many people still do not believe it. But nevertheless, we have spoken out, and such a huge number of things have come out into the open that somehow we must complete our aim of humanizing this regime. If we don't, the revenge of the old forces would be cruel. So we are turning now mainly to those who have been waiting. This moment will be a decisive one for many years to come.

The summer is approaching, with its holidays, when, as is our habit, we shall want to drop everything and relax. We can be quite sure however that our dear adversaries will not indulge in any summer recreations, that they will mobilize all their people, and that even now they are trying to arrange for a calm Christmas! So let us be careful about what happens, let's try to understand it and respond to it. Let's give up this impossible demand that someone above us must always provide us with the only possible interpretation of things, one simple conclusion. Every single one of us will have to be responsible for arriving at his own conclusions. Commonly accepted conclusions can only be arrived at by discussions, and this requires the freedom of expression which is actually our only democratic achievement of the last year.

In the future, we shall have to display personal initiative and determination of our own.

Above all, we shall have to oppose the view, should it arise, that it is possible to conduct some sort of a democratic revival without the communists or possibly against them. This would be both unjust and unreasonable. The communists have well-constructed organizations, and we should support the progressive wing within them. They have experienced officials, and last but not least, they also have in their hands the decisive levers and buttons. Their Action Program has been presented to the public. It is a program for the initial adjustment of the greatest inequalities, and no one else has any similarly concrete program. We must demand that local Action Programs be submitted to the public in each district and each community. By doing so, we shall have suddenly taken very ordinary and long-expected steps in the right direction. The Czechoslovak Communist party is preparing for the Congress which will elect a new Central Committee. Let us demand that it should be better than the present one. If the Communist party now says that in the future it wants to base its leading position on the confidence of the citizens and not on force, then we should believe what it says as long as we can believe in the people it is sending as delegates to the district and regional conferences.

Fears have recently been expressed that the democratization process has come to a halt. This feeling is partly caused by the fatigue brought on by the worrying times and partly because the times of surprising revelations, resignations from high places, and intoxicating speeches of a quite unprecedented bravery are now past. The conflict of forces, however, has merely become hidden to a certain extent. The fight is now being waged about the content and form of laws, over the kind of practical steps that can be taken. And we must also give the new people, the ministers, prosecutors, chairmen and secretaries, time to work. They have the right to this time so that they can either prove their worth or their worthlessness. One cannot expect any more of the central political organs than this. They have, after all, shown that they are responsible enough.

The practical quality of the future democracy depends on what becomes of the enterprises and what will happen in them. In spite of all our discussions, it is the economists who control things. We have to find good managers and back them up. It is true that, in comparison with the developed countries, we are all badly paid, and some are worse off than others.

We can demand more money—but although it can be printed, it will be worth less. We should instead demand that directors and chairmen explain to us the nature and extent of the capital they want for production, to whom they want to sell their products and for how much, what profit they can expect to make, and the percentage of this profit that is to be invested in the modernization of production and the percentage to be shared out.

Under quite superficially boring headlines, a very fierce struggle is going on in the press about democracy and who leads the country. Workers can intervene in this struggle by means of the people they elect to enterprise administrations and councils. As employees, they can do what is best for themselves by electing as their representatives on trade union organs their natural leaders, capable and honest people, no matter what their party affiliation is.

If at the moment we cannot expect any more from the central political organs, we must achieve more in the districts and smaller communities. We should demand the resignation of people who have misused their power, who have damaged public property, or who have acted in a dishonest or brutal way. We have to find ways and means to persuade them to resign, through public criticism, for instance, through resolutions, demonstrations, demonstration work brigades, collections for retirement gifts for them, strikes, and picketing their houses. We must however, reject improper or illegal methods, since these might be used as weapons against Alexander Dubček.

We must so strongly condemn the writing of insulting letters that if some official still receives one, then we shall know that he has written it to himself. Let us revive the activity of the National Front. Let us demand that the meetings of the National Committees should be held in public. And let us set up special citizens' committees and commissions to deal with subjects that nobody is yet interested in. It's quite simple, a few people get together, elect a chairman, keep regular minutes, publish their findings, demand a solution, and do not allow themselves to be intimidated.

We must turn the district and local press, which has degenerated into a mouthpiece for official views, into a platform for all the positive political forces. Let us demand that editorial councils composed of members from the National Front be set up, and let us found other newspapers. Let us establish committees for the defence of the freedom of the press. Let us organize our own monitoring services at meetings. If we hear strange news, let's check on it ourselves, and let's send delegations to the people concerned and, if need be, publish their replies. Let us support the security organs when they prosecute real criminal activity. We do not mean to cause anarchy and a state of general instability. Let's not quarrel amongst ourselves; let's give up spiteful politics. And let's show up informers.

The recent apprehension is the result of the possibility that foreign forces may intervene in our internal development. Face to face with these superior forces, the only thing we can do is to hold our own and not indulge in any provocation. We can assure our government—with weapons if need be—as long as it does what we give it a mandate to do, and we must assure our allies that we will observe our alliance, friendship, and trade agreements. But excited accusations and ungrounded suspicions will make our government's position much more difficult and cannot be of any help to us. After all, we can ensure equal relations only by improving our internal situation and by carrying the process of revival so far that one day at elections we will be able to elect statesmen who will have enough courage, honor, and political talent to establish and maintain such relations. This, of course, is the problem of the government of every small country in the world.

This spring, as after the war, we have been given a great chance. We have once again the opportunity to take a firm grip on a common cause, which has the working title of socialism, and to give it a form which will much better suit the once good reputation that we had and the relatively good opinion that we once had of ourselves. The spring has now come to an end, and it will never return. By winter we will know everything.

And so we come to the end of our statement to workers, farmers, officials, artists, scholars, scientists, technicians, everybody. It was written at the suggestion of the scientists.

The Brezhnev Doctrine

The brutal Soviet response to socialist humanism in Czechoslovakia came during a period of hopes for relaxation of the two-camp policy and the cold war. During the 1960s, Western analysts, noting the outbreak of conflict between China and the Soviet Union, the tendency of Romania to go its own way in foreign policy, the increasing openness of Yugoslavia, and the stirrings of reform in Czechoslovakia, began to speak of "winds of change blowing through Eastern Europe" and of "polycentrism." Such positions became more difficult to maintain after the invasion of Czechoslovakia. A few months after that chilling event, Soviet leader Leonid Brezhnev told a meeting of the Polish United Workers' party that when a transition to socialism took place anywhere, the Soviet Union considered that transition irreversible, and he pledged to back up that view with force. Although the Soviets maintained that there never was such a thing as a Brezhnev Doctrine, until the mid-1980s most observers, East and West, believed that Brezhnev's statement constituted a fundamental principle of Soviet policy toward the communist states of Eastern Europe.

21

The Brezhnev Doctrine

Leonid Brezhnev
November 12, 1968

The might of the socialist camp today is such that the imperialists fear military defeat in the event of a direct clash with the chief forces of socialism. Needless to say, as long as imperialism exists, the danger of war that imperialist policy entails can on no account be disregarded. However, it is a fact that in the new conditions the imperialists are making increasingly frequent use of different and more insidious tactics. They are seeking out the weak links in the socialist front, pursuing a course of subversive ideological work inside the socialist countries, trying to influence the economic development of these countries, attempting to sow dissension, drive wedges between them and encourage and inflame nationalist feelings and tendencies, and are seeking to isolate individual socialist states so that they can then seize them by the throat one by one. In short, imperialism is trying to undermine socialism's solidarity precisely as a world system.

The experience of the socialist countries' development and struggle in these new conditions during the past few years, including the recently increased activity of forces hostile to socialism in Czechoslovakia, reminds the communists of socialist countries with fresh force that it is important not to forget for one moment certain highly important, time-tested truths.

If we do not want to retard our movement along the path of socialist and communist construction, if we do not want to weaken our common positions in the struggle against imperialism, we must, in resolving any questions of our domestic and foreign policy, always and everywhere, maintain indestructible fidelity to the principles of Marxism–Leninism, display a clear-cut class and party approach to all social phenomena, and deal a resolute rebuff to imperialism on the ideological front without making any concessions to bourgeois ideology.

When petit-bourgeois leaders encounter difficulties, they go into hysterics and begin to doubt everything without exception. The emergence of difficulties makes the revisionists ready to cancel out all existing achievements, repudiate everything that has been gained, and surrender all their positions of principle.

Reprinted from "Speech to the Fifth Congress of the Polish United Workers' Party (November 12, 1968)," *Current Digest of the Soviet Press* 20 (46), 1968: 3–5, by permission of *The Current Digest of the Soviet Press*. Translation copyright © 1968 by *The Current Digest of the Soviet Press*, published weekly in Columbus, Ohio. Reprinted by permission of the *Digest*.

But real communists confidently clear the path ahead and seek the best solutions to the problems that have arisen, relying on socialist gains. They honestly acknowledge the mistakes made in a given question and analyze and correct them so as to strengthen the positions of socialism further, so as to stand firm and refrain from giving the enemies of socialism one iota of what has already been won, what has already been achieved through the efforts and struggle of the masses. (*Prolonged applause.*) In short, it can confidently be said that if the party takes a firm stand on communist positions, if it is faithful to Marxism–Leninism, all difficulties will be overcome.

Experience shows most convincingly the exceptional and, one might say, decisive importance for successful construction of socialism that attaches to ensuring and constantly consolidating the leadership role of the Communist party as the most advanced leading, organizing, and directing force in all societal development under socialism.

Socialist states stand for strict respect for the sovereignty of all countries. We resolutely oppose interference in the affairs of any states and the violation of their sovereignty.

At the same time, affirmation and defense of the sovereignty of states that have taken the path of socialist construction are of special significance to us communists. The forces of imperialism and reaction are seeking to deprive the people first in one, then another socialist country of the sovereign right they have earned to ensure prosperity for their country and well-being and happiness for the broad working masses by building a society free from all oppression and exploitation. And when encroachments on this right receive a joint rebuff from the socialist camp, the bourgeois propagandists raise the cry of "defense of sovereignty" and "noninterference." It is clear that this is the sheerest deceit and demagoguery on their part. In reality these loudmouths are concerned not about preserving socialist sovereignty but about destroying it.

It is common knowledge that the Soviet Union has really done a good deal to strengthen the sovereignty and autonomy of the socialist countries. The CPSU has always advocated that each socialist country determine the concrete forms of its development along the path of socialism by taking into account the specific nature of their national conditions. But it is well known, comrades, that there are common natural laws of socialist construction, deviation from which could lead to deviation from socialism as such. And when external and internal forces hostile to socialism try to turn the development of a given socialist country in the direction of restoration of the capitalist system, when a threat arises to the cause of socialism in that country—a threat to the security of the socialist commonwealth as a whole—this is no longer merely a problem for that country's people, but a common problem, the concern of all socialist countries. (*Applause.*)

It is quite clear that an action such as military assistance to a fraternal country to end a threat to the socialist system is an extraordinary measure, dictated by necessity; it can be called forth only by the overt actions of enemies of socialism within the country and beyond its boundaries, actions that create a threat to the common interests of the socialist camp.

Experience bears witness that in present conditions the triumph of the socialist system in a country can be regarded as final, but the restoration of capitalism can be considered ruled out only if the Communist party, as the leading force in society, steadfastly pursues a Marxist–Leninist policy in the development of all spheres of society's life; only if the party indefatigably strengthens the country's defense and the protection of its revolutionary gains, and if it itself is vigilant and instills in the people vigilance with respect to the class enemy and implacability toward bourgeois ideology; only if the principle of socialist internationalism is held sacred, and unity and fraternal solidarity with the other socialist countries are strengthened. (*Prolonged applause.*)

Let those who are wont to forget the lessons of history and who would like to engage again in recarving the map of Europe know that the borders of Poland, the GDR and Czechoslovakia, as well as of any other Warsaw Pact member, are stable and inviolable. (*Stormy, prolonged applause.*) These borders are protected by all the armed might of the socialist commonwealth. We advise all those who are fond of encroaching on foreign borders to remember this well!

The Brezhnev Doctrine threw into doubt the possibility of creating "socialism with a human face" in Eastern Europe. It appeared that any changes undermining the dominant position of the ruling parties would be met by Soviet force, as it had been in 1956 and 1968. At the same time, however, the very possibility of legitimizing the exercise of power by means of Leninist rhetoric faded, for the Czechoslovak invasion had made it quite clear that the ideology's staying power was due not to any correct interpretation of history, but to raw force. Whereas East Europeans came to believe that Leninist regimes were intellectually bankrupt, they recognized at the same time that these bankrupt regimes would be able to maintain themselves in power as long as the Soviet Union would support them, which seemed likely to be a very long time. Frustrated by Soviet domination but aware of the dangers of direct confrontation, many simply retreated from politics. This retreat was the most damaging kind of critique that thinking people could make of regimes that insisted that all participate in public life. For many intellectuals, real life, autonomous being, the space in which hope was possible, retreated to inside the family, to the ethical sphere, and, especially in Poland, to religion and the church. Public life, the grand arena in which, since the French Revolution, humans have hoped to remake society for their own purposes, was revealed as hollow, empty, full of bombastic rhetoric, but devoid of meaning. The regimes continued talking about real existing socialism, reform, and the masses, but people stopped believing it.

There is no specific moment when one can say this realization hit everyone. As the Ferenc Münnich Society of the late 1980s in Hungary demonstrated, there were some who continued to believe in the Stalinist system. And many opponents, such as Czesław Miłosz or the fifty thousand Hungarians that fled the Soviet armies in 1956, had no difficulties expressing their dissatisfactions. From the new life of exile they turned every shade of political coloration that suited them, except Leninist. But for those who stayed in Eastern Europe, the 1970s, or the period from the Prague Spring to Solidarity, was a time when disillusionment became conscious. No one spoke of "socialism with a human face" any more, but many spoke of moral issues, ethics, human rights, culture, and even, in the case of György Konrád, antipolitics, the complete rejection of politics as an appropriate mode of social behavior. This section ends with Konrád's analysis. It begins with Leszek Kołakowski's disturbing parable of modern ethics from almost thirty years earlier.

The Clerks

One of the aspirations of modern totalitarian regimes was to coordinate all public activity under the control of the ruling party, from bridge clubs through fraternal organizations to labor unions. Any participation in public life became participation in party life, or put the other way around, to be able to participate in public life, one had to accept the domination of the party. One device many East Europeans used to evade this imposition was simply to do the minimum possible to remain in good standing at the workplace and then to build a weekend cottage in the country, devote a great deal of time to gardening, or become an alcoholic. Those with entrepreneurial abilities and ambitions found "hiding places," as Iván Szelényi puts it, where they could remain in a "parking orbit" until the possibilities for enterprise improved. Among oppositionists, however, the retreat from politics involved a number of more thoughtful strategies, ranging from promoting ethical behavior or cultural enrichment to the nonpolitical pursuit of human rights.

Even before the Czechoslovak invasion of 1968 made it seem imperative to escape from politics, at least temporarily, there were those who thought in these ways. One of them was the Polish philosopher, Leszek Kołakowski. An orthodox Marxist as a very young man, in the 1950s Kołakowski became interested in Kantian ethics. In 1957 he published several articles on the relationship between the individual and society in a book entitled Philosophy and Everyday Life. *The debate between the Clerk and the Anticlerk reprinted in its entirety here is taken from that book. The term* Clerk *as Kołakowski used it originated with Julien Benda, in his* La Trahison des clercs *(Paris, 1927). By Clerk, Benda meant a critically thinking individual, or intellectual. The treason of the intellectuals, according to Benda, is that in the twentieth century they abandoned critical thinking and became the advocates of political hatreds. No longer seekers after truth, the intellectuals became the rationalizers of modern politics. In Kołakowski's cautionary debate, the Clerk returns to his true function as critical thinker.*

The term intelligentsia *is itself of East European origin, and the role of the critical thinker in society has been a constant matter of speculation among East Europeans. In the 1970s György Konrád and Iván Szelényi contended—using Marxian categories that still retained their vitality in Hungary—that under postwar conditions in Eastern Europe the intelligentsia had become a class. Szelényi characterized the book as a "friendly debate" with Milovan Djilas's view that under state socialism the bureaucracy had become a dominant class. Konrád and Szelényi did not necessarily mean that intellectuals as individuals always succeeded, as the second part of the excerpt indicates, but they implied, echoing Benda's point, that the formation of the intelligentsia into a class ultimately would crown the treason of the clerks with success: the achievement of political power. More recently, Szelényi modified his view somewhat, noting that the bureaucrats blunted the intelligentsia's drive toward class power by being more stubborn than anticipated and by being more flexible toward private business, which permitted the workings of the second economy to create a new stratum of small entrepreneurs.*

22

The Debate of the Clerks

Leszek Kołakowski

September 1957

CLERK: You are saying that at a given moment in history the specific interests of the working class become identical with the interests of mankind as a whole, that they not only retain all human values but are alone capable of salvaging them. Yet what evidence can you offer in support of this view except vague historical–philosophical speculation? Why should I abandon, on the spot, the noblest values of human existence in the name of this speculative dialectic of the future?

Our experience so far does not justify such optimism. On the contrary, it teaches us that those specific interests, as you understand them, have frequently been realized in opposition to universal human values. There are examples: one, two, thousands! Though you may represent a given historical reality, by what right do you demand that I approve it morally merely because it is a reality? I refuse to support any form of historical existence on the basis of its inevitability—for which I see no evidence at this time.

If crime is the law of history, is that sufficient reason for me to become a criminal myself? Why? You won't allow me to measure your moves against the yardstick of absolute values because in your opinion these are sheer fabrication. Yet on the other hand, you speak of universal human values that are presumably, by the same token, absolute. You therefore quietly introduce absolute axioms into your doctrine, though in a vague and equivocal form, only to destroy them immediately with an equally ambiguous historical relativism.

You come to me with this baggage and expect me to renounce all the best that civilization has created because your eschatology promises to return it intact after some unspecified lapse of time. You demand unlimited moral credit for your historiosophy and your history, although both reveal their bankruptcy at every step. It is not you who stand for the philosophy of responsibility—you who recklessly agree to sacrifice everything to the Moloch of immediate reality in the unsubstantiated hope that all will be restored. He who is really willing to shoulder responsibility for the treasures history has discovered and produced will defend them at any cost, even at the price of disengaging himself from current struggles, if the only way to preserve these values lies outside the field of battle.

ANTICLERK: It is, nevertheless, worth noting that you can save these values only by saving your own skin. Also, it is peculiar that while you cast doubt on my historical arguments, you fail to see what direction the other side of history is taking. There is no longer room for doubt. Over there, books are burned on pyres. What have you done to save them? Do you think it is enough for you to learn them by heart? Over there, people's guts are ripped out and their faces trampled on by hobnailed boots. What did you do to prevent it? Do you think preaching to armed soldiers about universal love will do any good? Or do you believe you'll extinguish those fires by repeating the Ten Commandments?

CLERK: Pyres burn on both sides of Mount Sinai. Will counting them give you a feeling of moral superiority? That would be a cheap victory. You persist in telling me that the threat to human freedom is so great that in order to combat it one must renounce liberty. You keep harping on Saint-Just's slogan: "No freedom for the enemies of freedom."[1] I am willing to agree up to a point; but I must know who determines the friends and foes of freedom. It is always someone committed to one of the camps. This is like a trial in which one person is simultaneously plaintiff, judge, prosecutor, and policeman.

My involvement, which is constantly forced down my throat, must be based on an absolute faith in this man and his present and future intentions. In other words, I must place more confidence in him than I am willing to accord myself. Why should I prevail upon myself to place such complete trust in a man who insists on acting as the court even while he is a party to the proceedings? That is to deny the eternal and most elementary principle of justice. He will not allow the conflict between him and his adversary to be settled by anyone but himself. Yet in order to render a just verdict a judge must be impartial, unbiased, when he takes over his duties—that is to say, he discharges his functions properly only when he applies the same criteria of abstract justice to both parties to the dispute. Yet you refuse me this right, claiming that I must first be on your side before I can form a just opinion, that I have the right to be a judge only when I am one of the contenders.

To vindicate this shocking rule you have, it is true, a theory all your own, that no third force can exist in a society torn by class antagonisms. This theory renders the role of judge, as conceived by modern jurisprudence, altogether impossible. You regard this theory as self-evident and demand that I accept it. If I reject it and desire to act as a judge in the dispute, you automatically place me in your opponents' camp. Because I recognize the possibility of a third force, I am immediately classified an antagonist and as such deprived of the moral right to assess the merits of your case—for then I am part of the controversy. I can avoid this only if I accept your theory of the nonexistence of a third force and espouse your point of view: I can judge and understand you only if I am one of you. Don't you see you're arguing

---

[1]Louis-Antoine de Saint-Just (1767–94) was the youngest (twenty-six years old) member of Robespierre's Committee of Public Safety and one of the most fanatical. He fully supported the use of terror to create a republic of virtue. After sending many colleagues to the guillotine, he himself perished by that means in 1794.

just like Søren Kierkegaard, who said that in order to understand Christianity one had to believe in it?[2]

You are saying the same thing: To appreciate you, one must first accept your reasoning. Surely you are aware that this demand is unacceptable to any rational being in the world; rationalism means, among other things, abstaining from making a choice until all the arguments are weighed. But your postulate bids me accept your thinking before I am given the right to examine it. The entire experience of European culture warns me against this manifestation of total irrationality. I do not deny that your method may win you many adherents, but please note that you cannot win them by intellectual means. Your position is completely "impermeable"; it cannot be penetrated by rational thinking for it repels a priori all criticism as an intrinsically hostile act necessarily launched—consciously or unconsciously—from the opposing camp. Sensible human beings will find your theory of the nonexistence of a third force fundamentally irrational and indigestible.

And if you continue to argue that I protect myself together with those unalterable cultural values you scoff at, and if on those grounds you wish to show me up as an escapist enamored of himself, then my answer is that I've no intention of becoming a scoundrel merely to demonstrate that I do not care whether or not I have the reputation of being an honest man.

ANTICLERK: Your defense is your indictment.

CLERK: I am not defending myself. Why do you always divide the world into prosecutors and defendants?

ANTICLERK: I didn't invent this world. One must face its horrors without wailing. You accuse us revolutionaries of splitting the world in two and of insisting that people commit themselves to only one side. There is as much point in this as there is in upbraiding meteorologists for hail and tornadoes. The entire history of mankind supports our argument. Another proof is the actual effectiveness of our social action, which is based precisely on this interpretation of conditions.

CLERK: History proves everything the historian chooses to deposit in it beforehand. You analyze history on the basis of a ready-made diagram and then announce triumphantly that this same diagram emerged from your analysis, forgetting to add that you put it there in the first place. And the practical efficacy of this interpretation has not been proven. The extent to which a given movement is truly effective historically can be measured only when its time is over, after the event. By claiming that for the first time in history you are free of the limitations a man's era imposes on his outlook, you fall prey to the same mystification you rightly discern in your predecessors.

ANTICLERK: *In qua mensura mensi fueritis, remetietur vobis.* (As you mete out unto others, so it shall be measured unto you.) You are saying that we are drunk with our alleged freedom from historical limitations, while you are truly free, since you pretend to rule over a world of eternal values that transcend history and are not subject to its pressures. We, on the contrary, recognize clearly the relativity of

[2]Søren Kierkegaard (1813–55) is regarded as the founder of existentialist thought. Through his criticism of the Danish church he also propagated a severe form of Christianity. The nature of his concerns are indicated by some of his titles: *Either/Or; The Concept of Dread, Fear and Trembling;* and *Sickness unto Death.*

values, and what is more, we are the only ones who have acquired the ability to think historically, and this enables us to observe the present in its continuous flow.
CLERK: Yes, you *proclaim* the general principle of historicism, but I cannot see that you practice it. I would not reproach you for this or even for your inconsistency if you accepted what I propose as an alternative possibility—namely, the recognition of values that cannot be canceled under any conditions and whose negation is evil regardless of circumstances. But you act differently. Your relativism hides behind a mask of fictitious immutability. Your values change fundamentally every day, and daily they are pronounced final. This is the worst form of relativism, because it inters historical thinking (whose worth I do not deny) as well as the unalterable and lasting achievements of mankind. It is a peculiar cult that professes monotheism but changes its god daily.

Ours is a strange discussion. It rather closely parallels Romain Rolland's fictional dialogue between Carnot and Lavoisier.[3] A certain naïveté in that drama does not conceal the analogy. Carnot demands that the other sacrifice the present for the sake of the future. Lavoisier replies that to sacrifice the truth, self-respect, and all other human values to the future is tantamount to sacrificing the future. I cannot disagree with him. Since I do not share your faith, as optimistic as it is unsubstantiated, regarding the predictability of things to come, I never know what effects our present actions will have in the future. Therefore I cannot agree with the idea of offering up great moral and cognitive values on the altar of uncertain future objectives. However, I do know that the means used necessarily imprint their stigma on the final results.
ANTICLERK: You have been duped by the mendacious picture that liberal politicians always paint of the revolutionary movement so as to make it loathsome. We are not engaged in constructing an eschatology that devours the present. In fact, the present benefits from the revolution, and thanks to this, it is possible to renounce some potentials for the sake of a better future instead of exploiting them fully now. All the measures that shock you so are in every instance a defense against a greater evil. Remember that in politics a choice between two evils is far more common than a choice between absolute good and evil. And that is a premise of reality that neither one of us created.
CLERK: I will never believe that the moral and intellectual life of mankind follows the laws of economic investments: expecting a better tomorrow because of saving today, lying so that truth may triumph, taking advantage of crime to save nobility. I know that sometimes we have to choose between two evils. But when both possibilities are extremely evil, I will do my utmost to refrain from making a choice. In this way I do choose, be it only man's right to make his own evaluation of the situation in which he finds himself. This is no small matter.

[3]Romain Rolland (1866–1944) is no longer read in the West, although he won a Nobel Prize for literature in 1915. Because he supported the Soviet Union in the 1930s, he was published and read widely in postwar Eastern Europe. Lazare-Nicholas-Marguerite Carnot (1753–1823) was the member of the Committee of Public Safety in charge of military affairs, and he was on the committee when it sentenced Antoine-Laurent de Lavoisier (1743–94) to death as part of a purge of former tax officials. France's greatest eighteenth-century scientist, Lavoisier destroyed the theory of phlogiston through his research into the nature of oxygen, and he also was an innovative participant in the revolution.

ANTICLERK: Nevertheless, reverting to your example, history proved Carnot right.

CLERK: I hadn't noticed.

ANTICLERK: In that case, to continue our conversation we must reinterpret the whole history of the world—an impossible task, especially if we have to wait until it is done before we make a choice that must be made at once.

CLERK: You have something there. Since we are forced to take a stand on current changes, we obviously cannot wait upon the uncertain outcome of historiosophical discussions, which can remain nebulous for a hundred years. This being so, our choice is always best if it is determined by that particle of certainty we do possess. Lasting moral values, continuously evolving up to now, are the surest support available if reality demands that we make a choice, which, after all, is also of a moral nature. In any case, they are more trustworthy than any historiosophy. And that, ultimately, is why I will stick to my opinion.

ANTICLERK: Whatever happens?

CLERK: Whatever happens.

23

Intellectuals as a Class

György Konrád and Iván Szelényi

Written between December 1973 and September 1974

In this essay we argue that under contemporary Eastern European state socialism, for the first time in the history of mankind, the intelligentsia is in the process of forming a class. Intellectuals there are a dominant class *in statu nascendi* [in a state of growing].

We, too, are intellectuals, members of the class that is the object of our investigation; consequently our task is self-critical.

Marxist sociology of knowledge was the first major step toward the intelligentsia's critical examination of itself, for it made relative the "objectivity" of knowledge by discovering that all knowledge is existentially based and that intellectuals, who create and preserve knowledge, act as spokesmen for different social groups and articulate particular social interests. This essay is an invitation to our fellow intellectuals to go on to a new stage of this critical self-examination.

In its search for the existential bases of knowledge the sociology of knowledge, whether Marxist or non-Marxist, has usually assumed that intellectuals have been neutral instruments in the hands of different social forces. The question of what effect the interests of intellectuals, as intellectuals, had on the knowledge they cultivated was never asked. It was assumed that they had no effect. We believe that the Eastern European intellectual vanguard abused our epistemological innocence and, while pretending to carry out the "historical mission of the proletariat," in fact gradually established its own class domination over the working class.

Ever since Marx it has been a commonplace of the sociology of knowledge that knowledge in general, and our knowledge of society in particular, is determined by the conditions in which it arises and expresses, directly or indirectly, a variety of interests in society. Yet Georg Lukács, in the critical and philosophical works of his Marxist period, was the first and up to now the only writer to attempt a full elaboration of Marx's rather sketchy theory of the intellectual superstructure of society.[1] Lukács saw the culture of the past two centuries as a changing mixture of apology for the bourgeoisie, criticism of it, and bourgeois self-criticism. He ap-

[1]For Lukács, see Document 13.

plied, with considerable sophistication, a rather simple scheme of values according to which developing capitalism was progressive until 1848 but thereafter became retrograde, particularly after the Russian Revolution of 1917. Before 1848 a critical attitude, rationalism, coherence, wholeness, and humanism predominated in our culture; afterward apology, irrationalism, disintegration, decadence, and anti-humanism. In this paradigm creative artists and scholars had no appreciable autonomy vis-à-vis the owners of capital and the social structure of capitalism, which were decisive.

It was Gramsci who quite properly drew from the work of Marx and Lukács the conclusion that every social class needs its own intelligentsia to shape its ideology and that intellectuals must choose which social class they are going to become an organic part of.[2] Since those tenets of Marxism which relate to the sociology of knowledge and the social position of the intelligentsia are based, like the fundamental principles of Marxism generally, on an analysis of capitalist society, it is understandable that for Marxist thinkers the notion of defining the intelligentsia as a class has never even arisen, for intellectuals are neither owners of capital nor proletarians. Kautsky and Lenin pointed out that on one hand the intellectual resembles the proletarian by reason of his social position, since he lives by selling his labor and so is often exploited by the power of capital; but on the other hand he differs substantially from the worker, for the intellectual performs mental work, often managerial work directing the efforts of other workers, and thanks to his higher income lives in a manner comparable to that of the bourgeois.[3]

As a result Marxism regards the intelligentsia—like a number of other classes, for example, the petty-bourgeoisie—as a *stratum* situated between the fundamental classes and with that relieves itself of the trouble of offering a more precise definition. Thus the classics of Marxism did not even attempt to make the connection between social knowledge and the position of the intelligentsia into a subject of study. It was Gramsci who first made the attempt, dissatisfied as he was with a tautological description of intellectual activity which asserted that an intellectual is someone who does intellectual work, a banality tantamount to saying that a worker is someone who does physical work. His was a more sophisticated approach. Gramsci ascribed to intellectual activity an independent structural position in the ensemble of social relations. Its function was to formulate the interests and ideologies of the fundamental social classes. But even Gramsci did not ask whether the position of the intellectuals differs in different social systems and, if it does, how far their social position, and the changes it undergoes, determines the character of the culture they produce.

All these analyses created the impression that the intellectuals, the social bearers of culture, left on their works no trace of their own historically determined existence

---

[2]Antonio Gramsci (1891–1937) founded the Italian Communist party. During eleven years in Mussolini's prisons he wrote *Letters from Prison*, which became influential in the 1970s and 1980s, particularly through its analysis of cultural hegemony.

[3]Karl Kautski (1854–1938) knew Friedrich Engels and wrote the Erfurt program of the reunited German Social Democratic party in 1891. He opposed a minority socialist dictatorship and therefore was considered a renegade by the Bolsheviks, but unlike some of his militant colleagues Kautsky remained antiwar throughout World War I.

or of the interests which sprang from it, as if this peculiar agent were a mere transmitter which lent no modifications of its own to the ideologies it conceived. The intelligentsia, in this view, were mere technicians formulating ideologies determined by the interests of other classes; it would never have occurred to them to create a class culture corresponding to their own interests. And even if it had, the notion would have been an impossible one, for they could have learned from their own works that the intelligentsia itself, as a class, did not even exist.

There is nothing wrong with the proposition that under free-market conditions our social consciousness is determined by the major class interests in society and that the intellectuals as a social stratum always form the intelligentsia of some class; thus each social class has its own intellectuals. In the social history of the twentieth century, however, decisive changes are evident: the consolidation of early forms of socialism in Eastern Europe, the emergence of state-monopoly capitalism in the developed industrial countries, and most recently the first signs of the technocratic global hegemony of multinational economic organizations. All of these changes critically influence the position of intellectuals in the social structure.

We find it natural that a sociology of knowledge devoted to describing free-market capitalism should not even have raised the possibility that intellectuals could have their own interests, distinct from those of other social groups. Their subordination to other social classes was far more conspicuous, and for that reason their growing tendency to gain autonomy escaped attention. That tendency was manifest in two principal areas: the bureaucratization of the state, and the socialist labor movement. These phenomena did not go completely unnoticed; Max Weber called attention most clearly to the first, Mikhail Bakunin to the second.[4] We cannot any longer avoid discussion of the separate and distinct interests of the intelligentsia in planned economies dedicated to rational economic growth, which redistribute the greater part of the national income through the state budget, restricting consumption and investment in agriculture and the infrastructure so that a large portion of the national income will be made available for rapid industrialization. These are the socialist economies of Eastern Europe. On the basis of the more detailed analysis which follows we place them in the category of rational-redistributive economies. In light of the emergence of the class position of this purposeful agent of redistribution we must reconsider the social role of the intellectuals, and the consequences it entails for their function of generating knowledge.

To anticipate one of the basic ideas of our study, we believe that the conditions under which society's knowledge is acquired are crucial when the social group which undertakes to create, preserve, and transmit both culture and social goals comes to function as a class and so subordinates its cognitive activity to its own class interests. Indeed the question must arise: Is self-knowledge possible at all if the intelligentsia becomes a class? How far the intelligentsia under early socialism, or under the forms of postindustrial state-monopoly capitalism now appearing, is a

[4]Max Weber (1864–1920) had a profound influence on sociological thought in the twentieth century, particularly concerning questions of legitimacy, the elaboration of ideal types, and the relationship between protestantism and capitalism. Mikhail Bakunin (1814–76) was the most flamboyant of the nineteenth-century anarchists, remembered in part for his statement "the passion for destruction is also a creative passion."

ruling class in the traditional sense is, by comparison, almost of secondary importance. However that may be, according to our initial thesis the transformation of the intelligentsia into a class, principally in the rational-redistributive economies, has indeed meant that in the industrially backward agrarian societies of Eastern Europe the intelligentsia, organized into a government-bureaucratic ruling class, has taken the lead in modernization, replacing a weak bourgeoisie incapable of breaking with feudalism.

A scientifically ordered society held great attractions for the Eastern Europe intelligentsia, as did the fact that intellectuals were being called upon for their expert knowledge in the construction of the new social order. They were exhilarated at the opportunity to help eliminate the obstacles which had hitherto prevented the creation of a new society, whether they were obsolete feudal privileges or the first chaotic features of an emerging capitalism; once these were overcome the age of planned rationality would open before them. That was why socialist society was able to rely from the first on the loyalty of the technical intelligentsia, even though they did not for a moment pretend to be adherents of Communist doctrine or of the dictatorship of the proletariat. They sensed that socialist redistribution placed in their hands a power incomparably greater than any they had ever had before. An engineer from a small factory could advance to a position where he might supervise the investment of billions. An architect accustomed to designing private villas could go on to draw the plans for giant industrial complexes or whole sections of cities. An economist who once had to be content with a well-paid but not very influential consular post or, at best, a university professorship could now be the head of a planning office with a budget in the billions. A poet who once paid for the publication of his verses out of the proceeds of a clerical job could now live in a one-time chocolate manufacturer's villa and see his poems published in editions of tens of thousands and recited on revolutionary holidays in hundreds of factory and village houses of culture. A librarian who used to rejoice if he could interest a few readers in his favorite books could now command from his post high in the ministry that libraries be organized in every factory and village with funds from his budget and could determine their contents, at the same time removing from existing collections not only books which offended ideologically but also any which went against his literary taste.

The humanist intellectuals felt themselves just as much called to disseminate the cultural values of socialism as the economists and technicians did to redistribute the national income. On the eve of the socialist revolution the Eastern European intellectuals longed for the chance to free themselves from the control of laymen, the humiliating necessity of serving untutored landowners and manufacturers. From now on the people with the requisite professional knowledge would be the ones to make the decisions. It gratified them to think that knowledge, not property, would legitimize the right to make decisions. They saw in socialism the advent of a society more genuinely based on the performance principle than bourgeois society had turned out to be. The intellectuals hailed their new situation as the realization of their own transcendence. They could finally rise above the service of particular interests, the role assigned to them in bourgeois society, and undertake to serve the universal interests of the new collective owners, the whole working people, and ultimately even the goals of world history. And even where their actual work did not change, it still acquired a transcendent meaning: It was ennobled, elevated from a money-making profession into a calling.

These characteristics of the Eastern European intelligentsia help explain why in most of those countries the socialist revolution was not heralded by peasant seizures of land or worker occupation of factories, or enforced by waves of strikes; on the contrary, communist and other left intellectuals divided the land among the peasants and explained to the workers that nationalization was a good thing. On the eve of the socialist revolutions the intellectuals lined up en masse behind the Communist parties. The older technocrats, after soberly weighing their interests, accepted their new status with a dignity befitting expert professionals; the radicalized young, organized into militant shock troops under charismatic leaders, lent to events the appearance of a broad revolutionary upheaval. They streamed into the party and, once there, rose rapidly through the ranks of a greatly expanded officialdom, eventually reaching the comfortably upholstered seats of power, where like their older colleagues they could hurry from conference to conference in black limousines. Thus the scene of revolutionary conflict shifted with almost magical rapidity from the streets to the conference tables of the ministries.

It was this high-hearted intelligentsia which was now forced to submit to the cathartic experience of the political elite's monopolistic rule. It had to learn that the road to class power was longer and more painful than it at first believed. The ruling elite which had formed in the meantime, just as quickly and almost imperceptibly, ousted large numbers of intellectuals from power. Those who remained were converted from revolutionaries or technical experts into apparatchiks. Intellectuals who realized in time which way the wind was blowing were allowed to go on working in peripheral, low-ranking positions, where they languished under onerous political controls and under the authority of technically inept superiors. Those who gave any sign of not accepting the ruling elite's monopoly of power were declassed, expelled from the ranks of the intellectual class.

This rapid turn of events, almost too rapid to follow, did not, of course, manifest its dramatic logic in the life of every single individual. Who wound up where was in many cases a matter of sheer luck, the work of a sometimes comically absurd combination of circumstances. One man would be expelled from the party and lose his job because his father had owned an apartment house, another because his half-brother was an officer in the American army or because he had been too friendly with a superior convicted of treason, because his correspondence with a French friend put him under suspicion of treason, because an ambitious informer turned him in for some innocent remark, or because he spoke admiringly of Freud, Mondrian, or Camus (or slightingly of a celebrated Soviet novel).[5] It was not their

---

[5]All three of these men seriously threatened the Stalinist view of the world. Sigmund Freud (1856–1939) opened up the investigation of unconscious motivations that lie outside the control of the individual, let alone the state. Piet Mondrian (1872–1944) completely abandoned the concept of subject matter in painting, reducing his work to the simplest harmonies of line and color, and therefore may be considered the ultimate antagonist of socialist realism. Albert Camus (1913–60), who won the Nobel Prize for literature in 1957, originally was sympathetic to the left, but his investigations of the finality of death and of isolation and estrangement led him eventually to reject the pretensions of revolutionaries in his book *The Rebel*.

fault that they were excluded from their class; they came to that end not because of any criticism they made of the ruling elite but simply because circumstances quite beyond their control made it possible to suppose that they were not unwaveringly committed to the interests of the elite.

Shouldered aside from political power, the intellectuals once again began to regard their work less as a calling and more as a profession. The fiery lecturer on political economy became a careful econometrician, the empire-building academic administrator a laboratory researcher, the university party secretary a solid historian. The great majority of the intellectual class saw that there was no place for them in the ruling elite, gave up their political ambitions, and acknowledged the political leadership of the ruling elite. If at heart they did not accept the elite's monopoly of power and only waited for the first opportunity to question it, for the time being they had no desire to enter the elite either, or even to replace it, but simply, by throwing their gradually increasing professional weight into the balance, to arrive at a reasonable compromise with the ruling elite. By the late 1950s and early 1960s the conditions had ripened on both sides for such a compromise, at once cynical and deeply heartfelt.

The Sphere of Culture

For many East European thinkers the proper sphere of human engagement always remained cultural and artistic, not political, and the appropriate style of discourse traditional, not Marxist. In a single-party state, of course, any effort to establish freedom of expression quickly becomes political. In Czechoslovakia before 1968 censorship sharply restricted the ability of writers to express their views directly, but several authors still managed to publish works that were good literature and at the same time thoughtful assessments of the Czechoslovak situation. Ludvík Vaculík's The Axe, *published in 1966, describes a cover-up of official bungling that resulted in a woman's suicide. A reporter pays the price for this bungling because he decided, before the suicide occurred, to write about the woman in an article that, as he put it, "could be printed, but would nevertheless allow me to preserve some modicum of integrity." The following year Milan Kundera's novel* The Joke *related the tragic consequences of a young man's incautious postcard to his girlfriend in which he said, "Optimism is the opium of the people. A healthy atmosphere stinks of stupidity. Long live Trotsky."*

Later, when someone described The Joke *as "a major indictment of Stalinism," Kundera responded, "Spare me your Stalinism, please.* The Joke *is a love story." Nevertheless, in February 1967 the Novotný government considered it necessary to reaffirm its restrictive policy in the arts. In June, Vaculík and Kundera responded. In his speech to the Fourth Congress of the Union of Czechoslovak writers, which follows, Kundera suggested that culture is a more significant sphere of endeavor than politics, thereby assigning a rather different role to the intelligentsia than did Konrád and Szélenyi in their analysis.*

24

A Nation Which Cannot Take Itself for Granted
Milan Kundera
June 1967

In spite of the fact that no nation has existed forever, and the very idea of the nation is a relatively recent one, most nations nevertheless take their existence for granted as a gift from God, from nature, from time immemorial. Nations feel their culture, their political system, and their frontiers as their own personal affairs, as questions and problems. But national existence itself is for them something that they never think to question. The unhappy, uneven history of the Czech nation, which has even come perilously close to death's door, has made it impossible for us to allow ourselves to be lulled into this false sense of security. The existence of the Czech nation has never been a matter to be taken for granted, and it is this fact which is its central predicament.

It is seen most clearly at the beginning of the nineteenth century, when a handful of intellectuals made an attempt to resurrect the half-forgotten Czech language and, in the next generation, an almost extinct nation as well. This resurrection was the result of deliberate intention, and every choice is a matter of deciding between the pros and the cons. The intellectuals of the Czech Revival, although they made a positive decision, also knew the weight of the arguments against them. . . .

For the great European nations, with their so-called classical history, the European context is something natural. But the Czechs have been through periods of wakefulness and periods of sleep, and several vital phases in the evolution of the European spirit have passed them by. They have had to appropriate, acquire, and create the European context for themselves over and over again. For the Czechs have never been able to take anything for granted, neither their language nor their being a part of Europe. And the nature of their Europeanness is their eternal conundrum: either leave the Czech language to stultify and become a mere European dialect and Czech culture a mere European folklore, or the Czechs must become one of the European nations with all that this entails.

Only the second choice can guarantee real life for the Czechs, but it is an extraordinarily difficult choice for a nation which all through the nineteenth century had to devote most of its energy to building its foundations, from secondary education to an encyclopedia. Yet as early as the beginning of the twentieth century, and especially in the period between the two world wars, a cultural flowering occurs which is without any doubt the greatest in Czech history. In the short space of twenty years there grew up a whole pleiad of men of genius, who in a bewilderingly short space of time raised Czech culture for the first time since the days of Comenius on to a European level, as a self-sufficient entity.

This great period, which was so brief and so intense and which we still feel nostalgia for today, was quite naturally a period of adolescence rather than of maturity. Czech letters were still in a predominantly lyrical style, at an early stage of development, which needed nothing more than a long, peaceful, and uninterrupted period of time. For such a fragile culture to be interrupted for almost a quarter of a century first by occupation and then by Stalinism, for it to be isolated from the rest of the world, to destroy its many rich internal traditions and to lower it to the level of fruitless propaganda, all this was a tragedy which threatened to thrust the Czech nation once more, and this time decisively, back into the suburbs of European culture. If in the last few years Czech culture has again been developing, if today it is without any doubt the most successful of our national activities, if many outstanding works of art have been created and certain cultural activities, such as the Czech cinema, are experiencing the greatest flowering in the whole of their history, then this is the most important national event in the past few years.

But is the nation, as a community aware of what is happening? Is it aware of the fact that an opportunity has presented itself of carrying on from the point at which interwar literature was interrupted, during its promising adolescence? And that this is a chance that will not be repeated? Is it aware that the fate of its culture is the fate of the nation? Or has the Revivalists' view that without strong cultural values our national existence cannot be guaranteed lost its validity today?[1]

The position of culture in national life has certainly changed since the time of the Revival, and the danger of our being suppressed as a nation hardly threatens us today. But nevertheless, I don't think even today that our culture has completely lost its meaning for us as a means of protecting the nation and justifying its existence. In the second half of the twentieth century great prospects of integration have been opened up. Mankind's evolution has for the first time been united in a single world history. Small units blend with larger ones. International cultural efforts are being concentrated and united. Mass traveling is developing. All this makes a few world languages all the more important, and the whole of life becomes more and more international, and the influence of the languages of small nations all the more limited. . . .

It is a priority for the whole community to become fully aware of the importance of our culture and literature. Czech literature, and this is yet another of its oddities, is not at all aristocratic; it is a plebeian literature addressing itself to a broad section of the public. Its strength and its weakness can be found in this fact. It is strong in

---

[1]The Czech Revival occurred in the late eighteenth and first half of the nineteenth centuries. Technically, the Revivalists were the first handful of scholars and concerned nobility that began standardizing the Czech language late in the eighteenth century. They were followed by the Awakeners, who created literary Czech and established the foundations of Czech historiography in the decades prior to the revolutions of 1848. Modern Czech national consciousness began during the Revival.

that it has a well-established hinterland in which its words echo powerfully, but weak in that it is not emancipated enough and too dependent on the public, on their receptivity and education, and it seems all the time to doubt the strength of its own convictions, its own cultural level. Sometimes today I become very frightened when I think that our civilization is losing that European character which was so close to the hearts of the Czech Humanists and Revivalists. Greek and Roman and antiquity and Christianity, the two basic sources of the European spirit which created the conditions for the development of Czech culture, have almost vanished from the consciousness of the young Czech intellectual, and this is a loss which can never be replaced. It has to be remembered that an iron continuity exists in European thought which is more powerful than every revolution and every idea, which has created its own vocabulary, its own terminology, its own myths and themes, without a knowledge of which European intellectuals cannot communicate. Recently I read a shattering document about the knowledge of world literature possessed by future teachers of Czech, and I wouldn't like to imagine what their knowledge of general world history is like. Provincialism doesn't only have its impact on the nation's literary achievements, but is a problem of the nation's whole existence, especially its schooling, its journalism and so on.

A little while ago, I saw a film called *Daisies*.[2] It concerned two splendidly repulsive girls, supremely satisfied with their own cute limitations and merrily destroying everything which they didn't understand. It seemed to me then that I was watching a profound and very topical parable about vandalism. What is a vandal? He certainly isn't an illiterate peasant who burns a hated landowner's castle in a fit of anger. A vandal, as I observe him around me, is socially secure, literate, self-satisfied, and with no very good reason for trying to get his own back on somebody. A vandal is an arrogant, limited person, who feels good in himself and is willing at any time to appeal to his democratic rights. This arrogant limitedness thinks that one of its basic rights is to change the world into its own image, and because the world is too big for it to understand, it chooses to change the world by destroying it. In exactly the same way, a youngster will knock the head off a sculpture in a park because it seems to insult him by being bigger than he is, and he'll do it with great satisfaction, because any act of self-assertion satisfies man.

People who live only in the immediate present, unaware of historical continuity and without culture, are capable of transforming their country into a desert without history, without memory, without echoes, and without beauty. Vandalism today is not just something that is fought by the police. When representatives of the people or the relevant officials decide that a statue or a castle, a church, an old lime tree, is pointless and order it to be removed, that is just another form of vandalism. There's no substantial difference between legal and illegal destruction and there is not a great deal of difference between destruction and prohibition. In the chamber a certain Czech deputy recently demanded, in the name of twenty-one deputies, a ban on two serious, "difficult" films, one of them, by an irony of fate, *Daisies*, a parable about vandals. He uncompromisingly denounced both films and at the same

---

[2]Věra Chytilová directed *Daisies*, which remains one of the classics of the remarkable wave of excellent Czech films that appeared between 1963 and 1968.

time declared quite explicitly that he didn't understand them. There is no real contradiction in such an attitude as this. The biggest sin of these two works was that they were above the heads of those who did not like them and thus insulted them.

In a letter to Helvetius, Voltaire wrote a wonderful sentence: "I don't agree with what you say, but I will fight to the death to defend your right to say it." This expresses the basic ethical principle of modern cultural life. If we return in history to a time when this principle did not apply, then we are taking a step from the modern age into the Middle Ages. Any suppression of views, especially any violent suppression of incorrect views, tends eventually to militate against truth, because truth can only be arrived at by a free and equal dialogue. Any infringement of freedom of thought and speech, however discreet the means and however subtle the name for such censorship, is a scandal in the twentieth century and inhibits and shackles the flourishing of our literature.

But one thing is beyond dispute: If a flowering of our art has occurred, it is due to the fact that intellectual freedom has been broadened. The fate of Czech literature is at this moment vitally dependent on the extent of our intellectual freedom. I know that when they hear the word *freedom* some people immediately get their backs up and object that the freedom of socialist literature must surely have its limits. We know that every sort of freedom has its limits, limits which are determined for instance by the level of contemporary knowledge, education, prejudice and so on. Except that no new period has ever tried to define itself in terms of its own limitations! The Renaissance did not define itself by the limiting naïveté of its rationalism, for this was apparent only in historical perspective. Romanticism defined itself by saying that it went beyond and outside the limits set by classical canons and by making a new discovery which it was able to master outside those limits. And so also the words *socialist literature* will have no real meaning until they mean a similar liberating act of transcendence.

The trouble is that in our country it is always considered to be a greater virtue to guard frontiers than to cross them. The most diverse, transient sociopolitical circumstances are supposed to justify the various limitations which are put on spiritual freedom. But the only great politics are those which place the interests of the age before transient interests. And the greatness of Czech culture is the vital interest of the age for the Czech nation.

This is even more true in that today the nation has quite exceptional opportunities open to it. In the nineteenth century, our nation was living on the periphery of world history. In this century, however, it is living right in the very center. As we know quite well, the fact of being in the center of the world's stage is not always a matter of milk and honey. But on the miraculous soil of art this hardship becomes a source of great wealth. Even the bitter experience of Stalinism can be turned paradoxically into something of unique value.

I don't like it when people equate "fascism" with "Stalinism." Fascism, based on a quite open antihumanism, created a situation which was fairly simple from the moral point of view: It left humanistic principles and virtues untouched because it appeared as their antithesis. Stalinism, however, was the heir of the great humanist movement, which even within the Stalinist disease preserved many of its original attitudes, ideas, slogans, expressions, and dreams. To see such a humanistic movement turning into something exactly the opposite before one's own eyes, taking along with it the last traces of human virtue, replacing love for mankind with cruelty to people, love for truth with a renunciation of it, and so on, to watch this process going on, opens up incredible insights into the most fundamental aspects of human values and virtues. What is history, and what place has man in history, and anyway, what is man? None of these questions can be answered in the same way after that experience as before it. No one could emerge from this period of history the same as he was when it began. And of course, it isn't just a question of Stalinism. The whole story of this nation from democracy, fascist slavery, and Stalinism to socialism (coupled with its unique national problem) has something quintessential in it, something which makes the twentieth century what it is. This experience perhaps means that we are able to pose more meaningful questions, to create more meaningful myths, than people who have not gone through this anabasis. This nation has perhaps been through more than many other nations have during this century, and if its genius has been alert during that time, it may well know more than most others as well. This greater knowledge could change into a liberating crossing of previous boundaries, into the ability to surpass the limits of previous knowledge about man and his destiny, and thus give significance, maturity, and greatness to Czech culture. For the time being these are just possibilities, just chances, but there have been many works appearing in the past few years which show that these chances are very real.

But again I have to put the question: Is our nation aware of these possibilities? Does it know that these are *its* chances? Does it realize that historical opportunities don't occur twice? Does it realize that to lose these chances means to lose the twentieth century for the Czech nation?

"It is universally recognized," wrote Palacký,[3] "that it was the Czech writers who would not allow the nation to perish but resurrected it and gave a noble purpose to its endeavors." Czech writers took on the responsibility for the very existence of their nation and they bear it still today, because the standard of Czech letters, their greatness or insignificance, courage, or cowardice, provincialness or their wide humanistic outlook determine to a considerable extent what is to be the answer to our most important national question. Is it worthwhile for the nation to exist at all? Is it worth having a language? And these terribly fundamental questions, which lie at the root of the existence of the contemporary nation, are still waiting for a conclusive answer. That is the reason why everyone who through his bigotry, his vandalism, his philistinism and his narrow-mindedness sabotages the cultural revolution which has largely already begun, is sabotaging the very existence of this nation.

---

[3]František Palacký (1798–1876) is considered by Czechs to be the "father of the nation." A historian, he believed that the nation was the carrier of ideas and progress. In 1848 he wrote a famous letter from Prague to the Frankfurt parliament in which he stated: "I am not a German. . . . I am a Czech of Slavic blood," which shocked the parliament, as it considered Prague a German city. For additional remarks by Kundera on Palacký, see Document 37.

Human Rights

Curiously, the increased possibilities for making human rights a public matter in the 1970s grew out of the concerns of the Soviet Union for its geopolitical security. When the Allies found it impossible to agree on a German peace treaty to end World War II, the two halves of occupied Germany went their own ways. In 1949 the Soviets established the German Democratic Republic as a counterweight to the Federal Republic of Germany, which adopted a constitution of its own in that year. Almost from that moment the Soviets, fearing that West Germany could always seek reunification as the representative of the "real" Germany, began calling for a wide-ranging conference on European security at which the Western powers would accept the permanence of East Germany and agree definitively to the new borders of Poland.

Until 1969, however, the main stumbling block to this possibility was the resistance of West Germany's ruling party, the Christian Democrats, led by Konrad Adenauer. In 1969, however, a few days after Willy Brandt's Social Democrats took power on their own for the first time, Brandt introduced a new Ostpolitik, *which in 1970 led to treaties with the Soviet Union and with Poland, and in 1973 to full mutual recognition between East and West Germany. Portions of the speech in which Brandt introduced his new policy are excerpted here.*

The clearing of this roadblock led in 1973 to the convening of the Conference on Security and Cooperation in Europe in Helsinki. In return for the acceptance of postwar European borders, the Western powers at the conference demanded the addition of a series of clauses to the Final Act that guaranteed certain human rights. Conservatives in most Western countries argued that the Helsinki accords simply condoned an illegitimate Soviet domination over Eastern Europe, but in practice the Soviets' acceptance of the clauses on human rights, and the creation of an ongoing process for review of the agreements, gave the Western powers unprecedented opportunities to question internal policies in the Soviet Union and Eastern Europe. This section includes the portions of the Final Act that achieved both the Soviet aim of strategic security and the Western aim of guaranteeing human rights. The full act, which is quite lengthy, goes into considerable detail concerning precisely what human rights are to be protected.

If Leonid Brezhnev believed that the human rights provisions of the Helsinki accords would remain a dead letter, as had the Yalta Declaration on Liberated Europe, he was quickly disappointed. Even in the Soviet Union itself Helsinki Watch groups formed to monitor human rights abuses, and a similar organization connected with the Catholic church quickly appeared in Poland. The best-known initiative in Eastern Europe was Charter 77. The charter, which is reprinted here, was signed eventually by some fifteen hundred Czechs and Slovaks, as well as by many intellectuals from other countries. Consistent with the spirit of opposition in the 1970s, it does not call for political action, nor does it create an organization. It simply asks all who are interested in human rights to do what they can. Despite severe repression, the movement continued its work in Czechoslovakia right up to the fall of the single-party regime late in 1989.

25

Ostpolitik
Willy Brandt
October 28, 1969

This government works on the assumption that the questions which have arisen for the German people out of the Second World War and from the national treachery committed by the Hitler regime can find their ultimate answers only in a European peace arrangement. However, no one can dissuade us from our conviction that the Germans have a right to self-determination just as has any other nation. The object of our practical political work in the years immediately ahead is to preserve the unity of the nation by ending the present deadlock in the relationship between the two parts of Germany.

The Germans are one not only by reason of their language and their history, with all its splendor and its misery; we are all at home in Germany. And we still have common tasks and a common responsibility: to ensure peace among us and in Europe.

Twenty years after the establishment of the Federal Republic of Germany and of the GDR, we must prevent any further alienation of the two parts of the German nation—that is, arrive at a regular *modus vivendi* and from there proceed to cooperation. This is not just a German interest; it is of importance also for peace in Europe and for East-West relations. . . .

The federal government will continue the policy initiated in December 1966, and again offers the Council of Ministers of the GDR negotiations at government level without discrimination on either side, which should lead to contractually agreed cooperation. International recognition of the GDR by the Federal Republic is out of the question. Even if there exist two states in Germany, they are not foreign countries to each other; their relations with each other can only be of a special nature.

Following up the policy of its predecessor, the federal government declares that its readiness for binding agreements on the reciprocal renunciation of the use or threat of force applies equally with regard to the GDR.

The federal government will advise the United States, Britain, and France to continue energetically the talks begun with the Soviet Union on easing and improving the situation in Berlin. The status of the city of Berlin under the special responsibility of the four powers must remain untouched. This must not be a hindrance to seeking facilities for traffic within and to Berlin. We shall continue to ensure the viability of Berlin. West Berlin must be placed in a position to assist in improving the political, economic, and cultural relations between the two parts of Germany. . . .

The federal government will promote the development of closer political cooperation in Europe with the aim of evolving step by step a common attitude in international questions. Our country needs cooperation and coordination with the West and understanding with the East. The German people need peace in the full sense of that word also with the peoples of the Soviet Union and of the European East. We are prepared to make an honest attempt at understanding, in order to help overcome the aftermath of the disaster brought on Europe by a criminal clique. . . .

In continuation of its predecessor's policy, the federal government aims at equally binding agreements on the mutual renunciation of the use or threat of force. Let me repeat: This readiness also applies as far as the GDR is concerned. And I wish to make it unmistakably clear that we are prepared to arrive with Czechoslovakia—our immediate neighbor—at arrangements which bridge the gulf of the past. . . .

Today the federal government deliberately abstains from committing itself to statements or formulae going beyond the framework of this statement, which might complicate the negotiations it desires. It is well aware that there will be no progress unless the governments in the capitals of the Warsaw Pact countries adopt a cooperative attitude.

26

The Helsinki Accords
August 1, 1975

The states participating in the Conference on Security and Cooperation in Europe,

Reaffirming their objective of promoting better relations among themselves and ensuring conditions in which their people can live in true and lasting peace free from any threat to or attempt against their security;

Convinced of the need to exert efforts to make détente both a continuing and an increasingly viable and comprehensive process, universal in scope, and that the implementation of the results of the Conference on Security and Cooperation in Europe will be a major contribution to this process;

Considering that solidarity among peoples, as well as the common purpose of the participating states in achieving the aims as set forth by the Conference on Security and Cooperation in Europe, should lead to the development of better and closer relations among them in all fields and thus to overcoming the confrontation stemming from the character of their past relations, and to better mutual understanding;

Mindful of their common history and recognizing that the existence of elements common to their traditions and values can assist them in developing their relations, and desiring to search, fully taking into account the individuality and diversity of their positions and views, for possibilities of joining their efforts with a view to overcoming distrust and increasing confidence, solving the problems that separate them and cooperating in the interest of mankind;

Recognizing the indivisibility of security in Europe as well as their common interest in the development of cooperation throughout Europe and among themselves and expressing their intention to pursue efforts accordingly;

Recognizing the close link between peace and security in Europe and in the world as a whole and conscious of the need for each of them to make its contribution to the strengthening of world peace and security and to the promotion of fundamental rights, economic and social progress and well-being for all peoples;

Have adopted the following [Parts I and II have been omitted]:

Reprinted from *Conference on Security and Cooperation in Europe: Part II*. Hearings before the Subcommittee on International Political and Military Affairs of the [House] Committee on International Relations (Washington, D.C.: U.S. Government Printing Office, 1975), pp. 120, 122–24.

III
INVIOLABILITY OF FRONTIERS

The participating states regard as inviolable all one another's frontiers as well as the frontiers of all states in Europe, and therefore they will refrain now and in the future from assaulting these frontiers.

Accordingly, they will also refrain from any demand for, or act of, seizure and usurpation of part or all of the territory of any participating state.

IV
TERRITORIAL INTEGRITY OF STATES

The participating states will respect the territorial integrity of each of the participating states.

Accordingly, they will refrain from any action inconsistent with the purposes and principles of the Charter of the United Nations against the territorial integrity, political independence, or the unity of any participating state, and in particular from any such action constituting a threat or use of force.

The participating states will likewise refrain from making each other's territory the object of military occupation or other direct or indirect measures of force in contravention of international law, or the object of acquisition by means of such measures or the threat of them. No such occupation or acquisition will be recognized as legal [Parts V and VI have been omitted].

VII
RESPECT FOR HUMAN RIGHTS AND FUNDAMENTAL FREEDOMS, INCLUDING THE FREEDOM OF THOUGHT, CONSCIENCE, RELIGION, OR BELIEF

The participating states will respect human rights and fundamental freedoms, including the freedom of thought, conscience, religion or belief, for all without distinction as to race, sex, language, or religion.

They will promote and encourage the effective exercise of civil, political, economic, social, cultural, and other rights and freedoms, all of which derive from the inherent dignity of the human person and are essential for his free and full development.

Within this framework the participating states will recognize and respect the freedom of the individual to profess and practice, alone or in community with others, religion or belief acting in accordance with the dictates of his own conscience.

The participating states on whose territory national minorities exist will respect the right of persons belonging to such minorities to equality before the law, will afford them the full opportunity for the actual enjoyment of human rights and fundamental freedoms, and will, in this manner, protect their legitimate interests in this sphere.

The participating states recognize the universal significance of human rights and fundamental freedoms, respect for which is an essential factor for the peace, justice, and well-being necessary to ensure the development of friendly relations and cooperation among themselves as among all states.

They will constantly respect these rights and freedoms in their mutual relations and will endeavor jointly and separately, including in cooperation with the United Nations, to promote universal and effective respect for them.

They confirm the right of the individual to know and act upon his rights and duties in this field.

In the field of human rights and fundamental freedoms, the participating states will act in conformity with the purposes and principles of the Charter of the United Nations and with the Universal Declaration of Human Rights. They will also fulfill their obligations as set forth in the international declarations and agreements in this field, including, inter alia, the International Covenants on Human Rights, by which they may be bound.

VIII
EQUAL RIGHTS AND SELF-DETERMINATION OF PEOPLES

The participating states will respect the equal rights of peoples and their right to self-determination, acting at all times in conformity with the purposes and principles of the Charter of the United Nations and with the relevant norms of international law, including those relating to territorial integrity of states.

By virtue of the principle of equal rights and self-determination of peoples, all peoples always have the right, in full freedom, to determine, when and as they wish, their internal and external political status, without external interference, and to pursue as they wish their political, economic, social, and cultural development.

The participating states reaffirm the universal significance of respect for and effective exercise of equal rights and self-determination of peoples for the development of friendly relations among themselves as among all states; they also recall the importance of the elimination of any form of violation of this principle.

27

Charter 77
January 1, 1977

In the Czechoslovak Collection of Laws, no. 120 of 13 October 1976, texts were published of the International Covenant on Civil and Political Rights, and of the International Covenant on Economic, Social, and Cultural Rights, which were signed on behalf of our Republic in 1968, were confirmed at Helsinki in 1975 and came into force in our country on 23 March 1976. From that date our citizens have the right, and our state the duty, to abide by them.

The human rights and freedoms underwritten by these covenants constitute important assets of civilized life for which many progressive movements have striven throughout history and whose codification could greatly contribute to the development of a humane society.

We accordingly welcome the Czechoslovak Socialist Republic's accession to those agreements.

Their publication, however, serves as an urgent reminder of the extent to which basic human rights in our country exist, regrettably, on paper only.

The right to freedom of expression, for example, guaranteed by Article 19 of the first-mentioned covenant, is in our case purely illusory. Tens of thousands of our citizens are prevented from working in their own fields for the sole reason that they hold views differing from official ones and are discriminated against and harassed in all kinds of ways by the authorities and public organisations. Deprived as they are of any means to defend themselves, they become victims of a virtual apartheid.

Hundreds of thousands of other citizens are denied that "freedom from fear" mentioned in the preamble to the first covenant, being condemned to live in constant danger of unemployment or other penalties if they voice their own opinions.

In violation of Article 13 of the second-mentioned covenant, guaranteeing everyone the right to education, countless young people are prevented from studying because of their own views or even their parents'. Innumerable citizens live in fear that their own or their children's right to education may be withdrawn if they should ever speak up in accordance with their convictions. Any exercise of the right to "seek, receive, and impart information and ideas of all kinds, regardless of frontiers, either orally, in writing or in print" or "in the form of art," specified in Article 19, paragraph 2 of the first covenant, is punished by extrajudicial or even judicial sanctions, often in the form of criminal charges as in the recent trial of young musicians.

Reprinted from H. Gordon Skilling, *Charter 77 and Human Rights in Czechoslovakia* (London: Allen & Unwin, 1981), pp. 209–12.

Freedom of public expression is repressed by the centralized control of all the communications media and of publishing and cultural institutions. No philosophical, political, or scientific view or artistic expression that departs ever so slightly from the narrow bounds of official ideology or aesthetics is allowed to be published; no open criticism can be made of abnormal social phenomena; no public defense is possible against false and insulting charges made in official propaganda; the legal protection against "attacks on honor and reputation" clearly guaranteed by Article 17 of the first covenant is in practice nonexistent; false accusations cannot be rebutted, and any attempt to secure compensation or correction through the courts is futile; no open debate is allowed in the domain of thought and art. Many scholars, writers, artists, and others are penalized for having legally published or expressed, years ago, opinions which are condemned by those who hold political power today.

Freedom of religious confession, emphatically guaranteed by Article 18 of the first covenant, is systematically curtailed by arbitrary official action; by interference with the activity of churchmen, who are constantly threatened by the refusal of the state to permit them the exercise of their functions or by the withdrawal of such permission; by financial or other measures against those who express their religious faith in word or action; by constraints on religious training; and so forth.

One instrument for the curtailment or, in many cases, complete elimination of many civic rights is the system by which all national institutions and organizations are in effect subject to political directives from the apparatus of the ruling party and to decisions made by powerful individuals. The constitution of the republic, its laws, and other legal norms do not regulate the form or content, the issuing or application of such decisions; they are often only given out verbally, unknown to the public at large and beyond its powers to check; their originators are responsible to no one but themselves and their own hierarchy; yet they have a decisive impact on the actions of the lawmaking and executive organs of government, and of justice, of the trade unions, interest groups and all other organizations, of the other political parties, enterprises, factories, institutions, offices, schools, and so on, for whom these instructions have precedence even before the law.

Where organizations or individual citizens, in the interpretation of their rights and duties, come into conflict with such directives, they cannot have recourse to any nonparty authority, since none such exists. This constitutes, of course, a serious limitation of the right ensuing from Articles 21 and 22 of the first-mentioned covenant, which provides for freedom of association and forbids any restriction on its exercise, from Article 25 on the equal right to take part in the conduct of public affairs, and from Article 26 stipulating equal protection by the law without discrimination. This state of affairs likewise prevents workers and others from exercising the unrestricted right to establish trade unions and other organizations to protect their economic and social interests and from freely enjoying the right to strike provided for in paragraph 1 of Article 8 in the second-mentioned covenant.

Further civic rights, including the explicit prohibition of "arbitrary interference with privacy, family, home, or correspondence" (Article 17 of the first covenant), are seriously vitiated by the various forms of interference in the private life of citizens exercised by the Ministry of the Interior, for example, by bugging telephones and houses, opening mail, following personal movements, searching homes, setting up networks of neighborhood informers (often recruited by illicit threats or promises), and in other ways. The ministry frequently interferes in employers' decisions, instigates acts of discrimination by authorities and organizations, brings weight to bear on the organs of justice, and even orchestrates propaganda campaigns in the media. This activity is governed by no law and, being clandestine, affords the citizen no chance to defend himself.

In cases of prosecution on political grounds the investigative and judicial organs violate the rights of those charged and of those defending them, as guaranteed by Article 14 of the first covenant and indeed by Czechoslovak law. The prison treatment of those sentenced in such cases is an affront to human dignity and a menace to their health, being aimed at breaking their morale.

Paragraph 2, Article 12 of the first covenant, guaranteeing every citizen the right to leave the country, is consistently violated, or under the pretense of "defense of national security" is subjected to various unjustifiable conditions (paragraph 3). The granting of entry visas to foreigners is also handled arbitrarily, and many are unable to visit Czechoslovakia merely because of professional or personal contacts with those of our citizens who are subject to discrimination.

Some of our people—either in private, at their places of work, or by the only feasible public channel, the foreign media—have drawn attention to the systematic violation of human rights and democratic freedoms and demanded amends in specific cases. But their pleas have remained largely ignored or been made grounds for police investigation.

Responsibility for the maintenance of civic rights in our country naturally devolves in the first place on the political and state authorities. Yet, not only on them: Everyone bears his share of responsibility for the conditions that prevail and accordingly also for the observance of legally enshrined agreements, binding upon all citizens as well as upon governments. It is this sense of coresponsibility, our belief in the meaning of voluntary citizens' involvement and the general need to give it new and more effective expression that led us to the idea of creating Charter 77, whose inception we today publicly announce.

Charter 77 is a free informal, open community of people of different convictions, different faiths, and different professions united by the will to strive, individually and collectively, for the respect of civic and human rights in our own country and throughout the world—rights accorded to all men by the two mentioned international covenants, by the Final Act of the Helsinki conference, and by numerous other international documents opposing war, violence, and social or spiritual oppression, and which are comprehensively laid down in the United Nations Universal Declaration of Human Rights.

Charter 77 springs from a background of friendship and solidarity among people who share our concern for those ideals that have inspired, and continue to inspire, their lives and their work.

Charter 77 is not an organization; it has no rules, permanent bodies, or formal membership. It embraces everyone who agrees with its ideas, participates in its work, and supports it. It does not form the basis for any oppositional political activity. Like many similar citizen initiatives in various countries, West and East, it seeks to promote the general public interest. It does not aim, then, to set out its own programs for political or social reforms or changes, but within its own sphere of activity it wishes to conduct a constructive dialogue with the political and state authorities, particularly by drawing attention to various individual cases where human and civil rights are violated, by preparing documentation and suggesting solutions, by submitting other proposals of a more general character aimed at reinforcing such rights and their guarantees, and by acting as a mediator in various conflict situations which may lead to injustice and so forth.

By its symbolic name Charter 77 denotes that it has come into being at the start of a year proclaimed as the Year of Political Prisoners—a year in which a conference in Belgrade is due to review the implementation of the obligations assumed at Helsinki.

As signatories, we hereby authorize Professor Dr Jan Patočka, Václav Havel, and Professor Jiří Hájek to act as the spokesmen for the charter. These spokesmen are endowed with full authority to represent it vis-à-vis state and other bodies, and the public at home and abroad, and their signatures attest the authenticity of documents issued by the charter. They will have us, and others who join us, as their coworkers, taking part in any needful negotiations, shouldering particular tasks and sharing every responsibility.

We believe that Charter 77 will help to enable all the citizens of Czechoslovakia to work and live as free human beings.

Ethics and Antipolitics

One of the most important figures in the Charter 77 movement was Václav Havel, a noted playwright of the theater of the absurd. Imprisoned after the charter appeared, Havel was forced to break off with the movement for a short while, but during the 1980s he became one of the most steadfast advocates of the proposition that the Czechoslovak government should follow its own laws regarding human rights and change those that did not accord with the international agreements it had signed. Havel spent considerable time in jail for eloquently advocating his position, but with the fall of the old regime this moral steadfastness made him Czechoslovakia's most popular public figure and the well-nigh unanimous choice for president of the new republic. For Havel, the important questions are not so much political as ethical. How might it be possible to live a life that is not a lie when all public life is built on lies? Not living the lie is what constitutes "The Power of the Powerless," as he argues in the portions of his essay from the 1970s reprinted here. Havel dedicated his essay to Jan Patočka, a prominent philosopher who, at the age of seventy, provided spiritual and moral inspiration for Charter 77. Questioned at length after publication of the charter, Patočka collapsed and died. Ludvík Vaculík attributed Patočka's death to a "moral illness—the disease of civil liberty."

György Konrád goes even further than Havel in his rejection of the political. For Konrád all power is antihuman. His book Antipolitics, *excerpts of which appear here, does not sustain a coherent argument, is not very practical, and wanders from topic to topic in short bursts of energy, but it remains a powerful plea for the autonomy of simple everyday humanity in a world saturated with politics.*

28

The Power of the Powerless

Václav Havel

1979

The manager of a fruit and vegetable shop places in his window, among the onions and carrots, the slogan: "Workers of the World, Unite!" Why does he do it? What is he trying to communicate to the world? Is he genuinely enthusiastic about the idea of unity among the workers of the world? Is his enthusiasm so great that he feels an irrepressible impulse to acquaint the public with his ideals? Has he really given more than a moment's thought to how such a unification might occur and what it would mean?

I think it can safely be assumed that the overwhelming majority of shopkeepers never think about the slogans they put in their windows, nor do they use them to express their real opinions. That poster was delivered to our greengrocer from the enterprise headquarters along with the onions and carrots. He put them all into the window simply because it has been done that way for years, because everyone does it, and because that is the way it has to be. If he were to refuse, there could be trouble. He could be reproached for not having the proper "decoration" in his window; someone might even accuse him of disloyalty. He does it because these things must be done if one is to get along in life. It is one of the thousands of details that guarantee him a relatively tranquil life "in harmony with society," as they say.

Obviously the greengrocer is indifferent to the semantic content of the slogan on exhibit; he does not put the slogan in his window from any personal desire to acquaint the public with the ideal it expresses. This, of course, does not mean that his action has no motive or significance at all or that the slogan communicates nothing to anyone. The slogan is really a *sign,* and as such it contains a subliminal but very definite message. Verbally, it might be expressed this way: "I, the green-grocer XY, live here and I know what I must do. I behave in the manner expected of me. I can be depended upon and am beyond reproach. I am obedient and therefore I have the right to be left in peace." This message, of course, has an addressee: It is directed above, to the greengrocer's superior, and at the same time it is a shield that protects the greengrocer from potential informers. The slogan's real meaning, there-fore, is rooted firmly in the greengrocer's existence. It reflects his vital interests. But what are those vital interests?

Let us take note: If the greengrocer had been instructed to display the slogan, "I am afraid and therefore unquestioningly obedient," he would not be nearly as indifferent to its semantics, even though the statement would reflect the truth. The greengrocer would be embarrassed and ashamed to put such an unequivocal statement of his own degradation in the shop window, and quite naturally so, for he is a human being and thus has a sense of his own dignity. To overcome this complication, his expression of loyalty must take the form of a sign which, at least on its textual surface, indicates a level of disinterested conviction. It must allow the greengrocer to say, "What's wrong with the workers of the world uniting?" Thus the sign helps the greengrocer to conceal from himself the low foundations of his obedience, at the same time concealing the low foundations of power. It hides them behind the facade of something high. And that something is *ideology*.

Ideology is a specious way of relating to the world. It offers human beings the illusion of an identity, of dignity, and of morality while making it easier for them to *part* with them. As the repository of something "suprapersonal" and objective, it enables people to deceive their conscience and conceal their true position and their inglorious *modus vivendi*, both from the world and from themselves. It is a very pragmatic, but at the same time an apparently dignified, way of legitimizing what is above, below, and on either side. It is directed toward people and toward God. It is a veil behind which human beings can hide their own "fallen existence," their trivialization, and their adaptation to the status quo. It is an excuse that everyone can use, from the greengrocer, who conceals his fear of losing his job behind an alleged interest in the unification of the workers of the world, to the highest functionary, whose interest in staying in power can be cloaked in phrases about service to the working class. The primary excusatory function of ideology, therefore, is to provide people, both as victims and pillars of the post-totalitarian system, with the illusion that the system is in harmony with the human order and the order of the universe.

The smaller a dictatorship and the less stratified by modernization the society under it, the more directly the will of the dictator can be exercised. In other words, the dictator can employ more or less naked discipline, avoiding the complex processes of relating to the world and of self-justification which ideology involves. But the more complex the mechanisms of power become, the larger and more stratified the society they embrace, and the longer they have operated historically, the more individuals must be connected to them from outside, and the greater the importance attached to the ideological excuse. It acts as a kind of bridge between the regime and the people, across which the regime approaches the people and the people approach the regime. This explains why ideology plays such an important role in the post-totalitarian system: That complex machinery of units, hierarchies, transmission belts, and indirect instruments of manipulation which ensure in countless ways the integrity of the regime, leaving nothing to chance, would be quite simply unthinkable without ideology acting as its all-embracing excuse and as the excuse for each of its parts.

If an entire district town is plastered with slogans that no one reads, it is on the one hand a message from the district secretary to the regional secretary, but it is also something more: a small example of the principle of social *autototality* at work. Part of the essence of the post-totalitarian system is that it draws everyone into its sphere of power, not so they may realize themselves as human beings, but so they may surrender their human identity in favor of the identity of the system, that is, so they may become agents of the system's general automatism and servants of its self-determined goals, so they may participate in the common responsibility for it, so they may be pulled into and ensnared by it, like Faust with Mephistopheles. More than this: so they may create through their involvement a general norm and, thus, bring pressure to bear on their fellow citizens. And further: so they may learn to be comfortable with their involvement, to identify with it as though it were something natural and inevitable and, ultimately, so they may—with no external urging— come to treat any noninvolvement as an abnormality, as arrogance, as an attack on themselves, as a form of dropping out of society. By pulling everyone into its power structure, the post-totalitarian system makes everyone instruments of a mutual total-ity, the autototality of society.

Everyone, however, is in fact involved and enslaved, not only the greengrocers but also the prime ministers. Differing positions in the hierarchy merely establish differing degrees of involvement: The greengrocer is involved only to a minor extent, but he also has very little power. The prime minister, naturally, has greater power, but in return he is far more deeply involved. Both, however, are unfree, each merely in a somewhat different way. The real accomplice in this involvement, therefore, is not another person, but the system itself.

The fact that human beings have created, and daily create, this self-directed system through which they divest themselves of their innermost identity is not therefore the result of some incomprehensible misunderstanding of history, nor is it history somehow gone off its rails. Neither is it the product of some diabolical higher will which has decided, for reasons unknown, to torment a portion of humanity in this way. It can happen and did happen only because there is obviously in modern humanity a certain tendency toward the creation, or at least the tolera-tion, of such a system. There is obviously something in human beings which responds to this system, something they reflect and accommodate, something within them which paralyzes every effort of their better selves to revolt. Human beings are compelled to live within a lie, but they can be compelled to do so only because they are in fact capable of living in this way.

In highly simplified terms, it could be said that the post-totalitarian system has been built on foundations laid by the historical encounter between dictatorship and the consumer society. Is it not true that the far-reaching adaptability to living a lie and the effortless spread of social autototality have some connection with the gener-al unwillingness of consumption-oriented people to sacrifice some material certain-ties for the sake of their own spiritual and moral integrity? With their willingness to surrender higher values when faced with the trivializing temptations of modern civilization? With their vulnerability to the attractions of mass indifference? And in the end, is not the grayness and the emptiness of life in the post-totalitarian system only an inflated caricature of modern life in general? And do we not in fact stand (although in the external measures of civilization, we are far behind) as a kind of warning to the West, revealing to it its own latent tendencies?

Let us now imagine that one day something in our greengrocer snaps, and he stops putting up the slogans merely to ingratiate himself. He stops voting in elections he knows are a farce. He begins to say what he really thinks at political meetings. And he even finds the strength in himself to express solidarity with those whom his conscience commands him to support. In this revolt the greengrocer steps out of living within the lie. He rejects the ritual and breaks the rules of the game. He discovers once more his suppressed identity and dignity. He gives his freedom a concrete significance. His revolt is an attempt to *live within the truth*.

The bill is not long in coming. He will be relieved of his post as manager of the shop and transferred to the warehouse. His pay will be reduced. His hopes for a holiday in Bulgaria will evaporate. His children's access to higher education will be threatened. His superiors will harass him, and his fellow workers will wonder about him. Most of those who apply these sanctions, however, will not do so from any authentic inner conviction but simply under pressure from conditions, the same conditions that once pressured the greengrocer to display the official slogans. They will persecute the greengrocer either because it is expected of them, or to demonstrate their loyalty, or simply as part of the general panorama, to which belongs an awareness that this is how situations of this sort are dealt with, that this, in fact, is how things are always done, particularly if one is not to become suspect oneself. The executors, therefore, behave essentially like everyone else, to a greater or lesser degree: as components of the post-totalitarian system, as agents of its automatism, as petty instruments of the social autototality.

Thus the power structure, through the agency of those who carry out the sanctions, those anonymous components of the system, will spew the greengrocer from its mouth. The system, through its alienating presence in people, will punish him for his rebellion. It must do so because the logic of its automatism and self-defense dictates it. The greengrocer has not committed a simple, individual offense, isolated in its own uniqueness, but something incomparably more serious. By breaking the rules of the game, he has disrupted the game as such. He has exposed it as a mere game. He has shattered the world of appearances, the fundamental pillar of the system. He has upset the power structure by tearing apart what holds it together. He has demonstrated that living a lie is living a lie. He has broken through the exalted facade of the system and exposed the real, base foundations of power. He has said that the emperor is naked. And because the emperor is in fact naked, something extremely dangerous has happened: By his action, the greengrocer has addressed the world. He has enabled everyone to peer behind the curtain. He has shown everyone that it *is* possible to live within the truth. Living within the lie can constitute the system only if it is universal. The principle must embrace and permeate everything. There are no terms whatsoever on which it can coexist with living within the truth, and therefore everyone who steps out of line *denies it in principle and threatens it in its entirety*.

Individuals can be alienated from themselves only because there is *something* in them to alienate. The terrain of this violation is their authentic existence. Living the truth is thus woven directly into the texture of living a lie. It is the repressed alternative, the authentic aim to which living a lie is an inauthentic response. Only against this background does living a lie make any sense: It exists *because* of that background. In its excusatory, chimerical rootedness in the human order, it is a response to nothing other than the human predisposition to truth. Under the orderly surface of the life of lies, therefore, there slumbers the hidden sphere of life in its real aims, of its hidden openness to truth.

The singular, explosive, incalculable political power of living within the truth resides in the fact that living openly within the truth has an ally, invisible to be sure, but omnipresent: this hidden sphere. It is from this sphere that life lived openly in the truth grows; it is to this sphere that it speaks and in it that it finds understanding. This is where the potential for communication exists. But this place is hidden and therefore, from the perspective of power, very dangerous. The complex ferment that takes place within it goes on in semidarkness, and by the time it finally surfaces into the light of day as an assortment of shocking surprises to the system, it is usually too late to cover them up in the usual fashion. Thus they create a situation in which the regime is confounded, invariably causing panic and driving it to react in inappropriate ways.

The profound crisis of human identity brought on by living within a lie, a crisis which in turn makes such a life possible, certainly possesses a moral dimension as well; it appears, among other things, as *a deep moral crisis in society*. A person who has been seduced by the consumer value system, whose identity is dissolved in an amalgam of the accoutrements of mass civilization, and who has no roots in the order of being, no sense of responsibility for anything higher than his or her own personal survival, is a *demoralized* person. The system depends on this demoralization, deepens it, is in fact a projection of it into society.

Living within the truth, as humanity's revolt against an enforced position, is, on the contrary, an attempt to regain control over one's own sense of responsibility. In other words, it is clearly a moral act, not only because one must pay so dearly for it, but principally because it is not self-serving: The risk may bring rewards in the form of a general amelioration in the situation, or it may not. In this regard, as I stated previously, it is an all-or-nothing gamble, and it is difficult to imagine a reasonable person embarking on such a course merely because he or she reckons that sacrifice today will bring rewards tomorrow, be it only in the form of general gratitude. (By the way, the representatives of power invariably come to terms with those who live within the truth by persistently ascribing utilitarian motivations to them—a lust for power or fame or wealth—and thus they try, at least, to implicate them in their own world, the world of general demoralization.)

If living within the truth in the post-totalitarian system becomes the chief breeding ground for independent, alternative political ideas, then all considerations about the nature and future prospects of these ideas must necessarily reflect this moral dimension as a political phenomenon. (And if the revolutionary Marxist belief about morality as a product of the "superstructure" inhibits any of our friends from realizing the full significance of this dimension and, in one way or another, from including it in their view of the world, it is to their own detriment: An anxious fidelity to the postulates of that world view prevents them from properly understanding the mechanisms of their own political influence, thus paradoxically making them precisely what they, as Marxists, so often suspect others of being—victims of "false consciousness.") The very special political significance of morality in the post-totalitarian system is a phenomenon that is at the very least unusual in modern political history, a phenomenon that might well have—as I shall soon attempt to show—far-reaching consequences.

There is no way around it: no matter how beautiful an alternative political model may be, it can no longer speak to the "hidden sphere," inspire people and society, call for real political ferment. The real sphere of potential politics in the post-totalitarian system is elsewhere: in the continuing and cruel tension between the complex demands of that system and the aims of life, that is, the elementary need of human beings to live, to a certain extent at least, in harmony with themselves, that is, to live in a bearable way, not to be humiliated by their superiors and officials, not to be continually watched by the police, to be able to express themselves freely, to find an outlet for their creativity, to enjoy legal security, and so on.

Anything that touches this field concretely, anything that relates to this fundamental, omnipresent, and living tension, will inevitably speak to people. Abstract projects for an ideal political or economic order do not interest them to anything like the same extent—and rightly so—not only because everyone knows how little chance they have of succeeding but also because today people feel that the less political policies are derived from a concrete and human "here and now" and the more they fix their sights on an abstract "some day," the more easily they can degenerate into new forms of human enslavement. People who live in the post-totalitarian system know only too well that the question of whether one or several political parties are in power, and how these parties define and label themselves, is of far less importance than the question of whether or not it is possible to live like a human being.

To shed the burden of traditional political categories and habits and open oneself up fully to the world of human existence and then to draw political conclusions only after having analyzed it: This is not only politically more realistic but at the same time, from the point of view of an "ideal state of affairs," politically more promising as well. A genuine, profound, and lasting change for the better can no longer result from the victory (were such a victory possible) of any particular traditional political conception, which can ultimately be only external, that is, a structural or systemic conception. More than ever before, such a change will have to derive from human existence, from the fundamental reconstitution of the position of people in the world, their relationships to themselves and to each other, and to the universe. If a better economic and political model is to be created, then perhaps more than ever before it must derive from profound existential and moral changes in society. This is not something that can be designed and introduced like a new car. If it is to be more than just a new variation on the old degeneration, it must above all be an expression of life in the process of transforming itself. A better system will not automatically ensure a better life. In fact the opposite is true: Only by creating a better life can a better system be developed.

The point where living within the truth ceases to be a mere negation of living with a lie and becomes articulate in a particular way, is the point at which something is born that might be called "the independent spiritual, social, and political life of society." This independent life is not separated from the rest of life ("dependent life") by some sharply defined line. Both types frequently coexist in the same people. Nevertheless, its most important focus is marked by a relatively high degree of inner emancipation. It sails upon the vast ocean of the manipulated life like little boats, tossed by the waves but always bobbing back as visible messengers of living within the truth, articulating the suppressed aims of life.

What is this independent life of society? The spectrum of its expressions and activities is naturally very wide. It includes everything from self-education and thinking about the world, through free creative activity and its communication to others, to the most varied free, civic attitudes, including instances of independent social self-organization. In short, it is an area in which living within the truth becomes articulate and materializes in a visible way.

And now I may properly be asked the question: What is to be done, then?

My skepticism toward alternative political models and the ability of systemic reforms or changes to redeem us does not, of course, mean that I am skeptical of political thought altogether. Nor does my emphasis on the importance of focusing concern on real human beings disqualify me from considering the possible structural consequences flowing from it. On the contrary, if A was said, then B should be said as well. Nevertheless, I will offer only a few very general remarks.

Above all, any existential revolution should provide hope of a moral reconstitution of society, which means a radical renewal of the relationship of human beings to what I have called the "human order," which no political order can replace. A new experience of being, a renewed rootedness in the universe, a newly grasped sense of "higher responsibility," a newfound inner relationship to other people and to the human community—these factors clearly indicate the direction in which we must go.

29

Antipolitics

György Konrád
1984

Politics cannot be explained in any context or medium but its own—the rich network of relationships that we call power. Politicians may have to reckon with economic interests, cultural conventions, and religious passions, but politics itself cannot be derived from economics, culture, or religion. Any approach to politics is bound to fail if it strays far from the standpoint of that political genius Machiavelli, who explained power by saying that power wills itself and that the prince wants not only to gain power but also to keep and enlarge it. That's his function—his obligation, if you like. Any philosophy of history will miss its mark if it tries to explain the riddle of political power in terms of economic interest, biological instinct, or religious enthusiasm.

For politics, anything that is not politics is merely an instrument, not a reason or a goal. If we don't reduce mysticism or money-making to something else, if we don't believe that a great painter paints because it's the way to God or riches, then why should we think that the great born politicians want power for some ulterior reason, good or bad, rather than for the sake of power itself? It's just as natural for them to love power as it is for a champion skier to love the slopes and the snow. Since humanity is hypocritical (and public opinion is particularly so), they have to pretend they love something more inspiring—their country, for example. If they succeed in making the public believe it, they are good politicians and deserve their power.

I don't believe that a new Central European identity will arise on the wings of emotionally charged movements, even mass movements, with the stormy popular tribunes and revolutionary personalities that typically go with them.

Our deepest feelings cannot be mediated by indignation, or anger, or passionate accusations. That is old stuff, yesterday's game, the style of thinking of the anachronistic left. It is the style of those who appeal melodramatically to others' overheated passions or to the inescapable commands of some historical agenda in order to acquire power for themselves—indeed, an emotionally overblown kind of power.

Nothing would be a bigger mistake for the Eastern European democratic opposition, nothing would hurt our real interests more, than falling captive to the style of thinking, rhetoric, and mythic tendencies of the Jacobin–Leninist tradition. I could only regard as a demagogue anyone who deemed himself a revolutionary today on our political soil.

The reality of Central Europe demands a form of conduct different from that of the communist tradition. In Central Europe, modernity means recognizing the abiding tendencies of our history and applying a sure intuition to extending them; it means recognizing processes that are unfolding and helping them mature, avoiding the clash of ideological and theatrical clichés. Such is the historic enterprise that presents a separate personal challenge to each and every one of us.

No thinking person should want to drive others from positions of political power in order to occupy them himself. I would not want to be a minister in any government whatever. I feel much better at my writing table than I would at any minister's desk, where I would have to puzzle over texts of official documents. I prefer to decide about words rather than people. Anyway, I suspect that ministers are more afraid of losing their portfolios to their deputies than to independent thinkers.

If the moral opposition tries to act like a political opposition, it may soon find that millions are standing behind it and asking, "Where do we go from here?" My worst nightmare is to have to tell millions of people what to do next. The opposition thinker is not a member of any shadow cabinet. He doesn't much care who the ministers are today or who the next ones will be. I would not want the government in power to feel threatened. If it is frightened, it is capable of casting aside all constitutional moderation and exchanging the methods of a conservative authoritarianism for those of totalitarian rule.

I ask the authorities not to feel themselves threatened by the independent intelligentsia. I ask the intelligentsia not to alarm the authorities. Grown people should not threaten; they should deal like sensible, well-brought-up Europeans. Bluster, arrogance, and conceit are never civilized behavior. It would be well for my friends—independent intellectuals, oppositionists, people on the fringes, dissidents, critics of the system, protesters, violators of the censorship, people who have been shown the door or banned—if the authorities themselves were to want some of the same things that we want. It doesn't say much for the reputation of our wares if we are unable to sell any of our ideas at all to those in power.

In fact, those who hold the leading positions are not the worst consumers of ideas. In the last analysis they are intellectuals, too: They enjoy reading interesting material—material not written under their control. They hope to find things in it that they too may be able to use sometime without losing their jobs.

In the market where ideas are exchanged, we are at their disposal, too (and also at the disposal of strike organizers, of course). We have to be clear about who is playing what game. If our role is clear, we can tolerate one another more easily. If our self-definition lacks precision, there can be no relative consensus. We can only give the advice we believe in, even if it is unwelcome advice. Everything goes to serve the beauty of the social game.

I am not calling for militant mass pressure against the politicians. It's not becoming for mature men to fear that they will be beaten; how much better if we can instill their superegos with our values. There's no reason why the executive intelligentsia should think exactly the same as the creative intellectuals, but is there any reason why they have to think the exact opposite?

We live in a crabbed society, and what I am most interested in is how we can make it less crabbed. I miss having a worldview adequate to our situation and affording some evidence of real self-knowledge. I take reality for a game and would like to understand the various strategies. I would like to know along what lines we could get in touch more productively.

It is also possible to conclude that we were born in an irredeemably ill-starred corner of the earth and that there is only one way to overcome this misfortune—by leaving it for some happier soil. The other way is to attempt the near impossible: even if our nation and our institutions have no autonomy, to try to work out our own.

I have chosen the latter. I have decided not to take leave of this country permanently. If I can, I will travel for a year or two, familiarizing myself with other cultures so as to view our conditions from a distance. I will cross the Iron Curtain, leaving most of myself here while a part of me sees the West. I am a Central European; here my attitudes are Western European, there they are Eastern European.

Some mad East Central European folly keeps me here; possibly the intoxication of inner freedom compensates for the painful absence of external liberty. At other times I think that this is the only place where there is really something to think about, since even geographically this is the center of Europe.

If Budapest, Bratislava, Prague, Cracow, Warsaw, and Berlin belong to Europe, then why not Leningrad, why not Moscow—indeed, why stop before Vladivostok? It is all part of Eurasia, there is no state frontier between. It is possible to think on a Eurasian scale, too. This is a more fitting perspective for the next millennium than that of little Western Europe, from where the life I live here seems an alien mythology. I would like to think of myself as some utopian son of Europe, able to touch the Pacific at San Francisco with one outstretched arm and at Vladivostok with the other, and keeping the peace everywhere within my embrace.

I have the Russians to thank for my life; of all the literatures of the world, that of Russia has affected me the most. Yet I see the role of the Russians in Europe as the biggest question mark for the cause of world peace. It would be foolish for me to pretend that we don't think about them. I know of no way for Eastern Europe to free itself from Russian military occupation except for us to occupy them with our ideas. Think about it: in a free exchange of ideas, who would colonize whom?

What is and what is not allowed in Hungary today? Thinking is allowed. Thinking for yourself seldom entails any unpleasant consequences; if it does, they can be lived through without any serious damage. These unpleasant consequences can even have an incentive effect: They spur one on to freer thinking. Who knows how much more intelligent the country would be if it were free to be intelligent, if there were no political repression at all?

When people cannot express something in one form, they express it in another. To understand a country is to examine what its inhabitants have had to give up and what they have compensated themselves with in return for their sacrifice. What doesn't work for them, and what does work for them instead? What makes them, by and large, just as happy as the inhabitants of other countries? If the values that seem fundamental elsewhere are less powerful here, there must be others that the inhabitants of this country explicitly or implicitly consider primary.

It seems to me that Hungary doesn't excel in the kinds of accomplishments that can be measured by any competitive yardstick. In the global statistics of technical achievements we are seldom near the top. In this area we do better than some Eastern European countries, but in selling our products on the world market we are only average. We do better at those intangibles that one might call the art of living: the cultivation of domestic comfort; an easygoing way of life; the art of getting on with one another; a certain worldly wisdom and a certain distance toward things that others consider vitally important; a healthy, pagan cynicism toward dedicated fanatics. It is as rewarding to sit in a well-kept garden at twilight drinking a quiet glass of wine with friends as it is to tear along a crowded eight-lane highway.

The game is at its most elegant when the players are not embittered. The important thing is that what we are doing should be good. The present is a special time. Enjoying each hour is in itself a struggle for liberation. Why should I do evil for the sake of good? I don't have to wait until I'm free to be happy. Right now I am trying to become free, and I am happy. We have basic groundwork to do on ourselves, for we are still a long way from the self-government of our own persons. If we strive for a state of internal détente, a relaxation of spiritual tensions, then we will meet with defeat less often, and the state will become less terrifying.

I am most likely to cultivate my freedom in the company of those I like. In organizations, too, small is beautiful; there one finds the solidarity of friends. I don't think I would ever want to name my circle of friends the National Association of Friends—much less the Hungarian State Association of Friends. I consider a network of informal circles of friends to be our natural form of organization. In large formal organizations either the parts pull the whole this way and that, or else a domineering minority—the central apparatus—imposes its authority on the parts. Those smaller, more easily encompassed circles are playing their own game. They add new gradations to the spectrum; they take responsibility for themselves and know how to make fine distinctions. I wish us the brightest good spirits, here and now. There is no need to wait for the distant triumph of our ideas. Friendship is everything; the final goal is a dream.

In our area the time has come for a kind of politics—or rather antipolitics, as I would call it—which doesn't just mean rising on the ladder of state office. It would not bring a better job, promotion, or jump in income. It would not bring an official car, a bodyguard, and a flock of secretaries. It would mean defending the place, the job, and the work we now have and want to keep. Antipolitics is not a dream of the future; it is respect for the present.

If an architect is an antipolitician, he will try to build better, according to his lights, with fewer constraints, rather than struggle up the official ladder to reach those offices where architects who don't design any more decide on the work of those who still do, generally only to make their work more difficult by burdening them with unnecessary regulations.

When our lives are bleak and we place our hopes in a change of government, we put our own tasks in the hands of a paternal authority; we delude ourselves, accepting the mythology of deputizing others to do our work for us. Why should we hope for more from a different party secretary or a different prime minister than from our friends and relations? I have never met a first secretary or a prime minister; I get along without them. I can find more interesting people among my friends.

If we didn't know what state socialism was like, we could still have hopes for it. As it is, we have no illusions about either capitalism or existing socialism. We cannot expect much good from politicians and political systems. The newspapers puff the chroniclers of the political class and cultivate in their readers the mythology of letting the state do it for them. The newspaper, whose lead story tells of some politician leaving on a trip or issuing a statement, is an accomplice in this self-trivialization of the reader; it is an instrument of the political class. The political discourse of the mass media raises up paternal idols before us and attributes profundity to the vacuities of power.

Autonomy's slow revolution does not culminate in new people sitting down in the paneled offices of authority. I cultivate in myself the illusion that the people who are working for autonomy in Eastern Europe have no desire to lounge in the velvet chairs of ministers, in front of microphones and cameras. I could be wrong: people are capable of strange reactions when an opportunity presents itself. Anyway I still say, let those remain in the government who have a weakness for power. My hope is that, since the dictatorship has already lost its revolutionary sheen, governments in Eastern Europe will learn to wield power more graciously.

A society does not become politically conscious when it shares some political philosophy but, rather, when it refuses to be fooled by any of them. The apolitical person is only the dupe of the professional politician, whose real adversary is the antipolitician. It is the antipolitician who wants to keep the scope of government policy (especially that of its military apparatus) under the control of civil society.

The antipolitician is not a representative of spiritual authority but, rather, its repository: His person and function are indivisible. The politicians and their intellectual employees pollute the intellectual environment in the hope that the population whom they target through the media will be unable to think in any terms other than the ones they present.

Their product is the cheerleader, the political dupe; the good party member (of any party); the loyal and unknown soldier who leaves the decisions to his superior while he charges to his death; the young people who can always be brought out for parades; the technicians of oppression who willingly commit atrocities because, if they have orders from above to do it, it cannot be an atrocity. Their product is the stultification of the average person.

What occupies our minds above all in Eastern Europe is not whether a policy is good or bad but the overabundance of policies everywhere. The state drags countless matters, questions, and decisions into politics that have no business there—private matters or technical questions with which, in the last analysis, the state has nothing to do.

Because politics has flooded nearly every nook and cranny of our lives, I would like to see the flood recede. We ought to depoliticize our lives, free them from politics as from some contagious infection. We ought to free our simple everyday affairs from considerations of politics. I ask that the state do what it's supposed to do, and do it well. But it should not do things that are society's business, not the state's. So I would describe the democratic opposition as not a political but an antipolitical opposition, since its essential activity is to work for destatification.

The antipoliticians—and in secret there are many of them—want to free biology and religion, rock music and animal husbandry from the pathological bloat of the political state. Wherever the number of informers, provocateurs, and police agents per thousand inhabitants is higher than it is in, say, Iceland, then it's time for the state to slim down. An antipolitician is someone who wants to put the state on a strict diet and doesn't mind being called antistate because of it.

The question is: More state or less? Those who want more state, stand over here; those who want less, over there. Possibly we have reached the point where even those who would like less will say they want more, because they don't trust their own minds any longer. They are state men, they have state minds; in their dreams the state rings the doorbell and takes them away. Yesterday's terror has become tonight's bad dream. We must push the state out of our nightmares, so as to be afraid of it less. That is antipolitics.

Theorists of revolution have long known that when a ruling group begins to lose confidence in the rightness of its dominant position, dramatic political change can occur. Economic privation, ideological barrenness, and nationalism did not cause Stalin's hand to tremble, nor did they make Nicolae Ceauşescu change his course. But Mikhail Gorbachev realized that despite its military strength the Soviet Union was in many ways a Third World country, unable to provide its citizens with what other Europeans consider the basic necessities of modern life. His solution, which held great short-term risks but enormous long-term potential, was to restructure the Soviet economy, which was tantamount to saying that he and his colleagues had lost their faith in the efficacy of Leninist strategies. In order to concentrate on his task, Gorbachev decided to permit the East European states to go their own ways, as long as they did not threaten the Soviet Union directly. The result was a turn toward pluralist politics in all the East European countries.

Oppositionists in Eastern Europe, as well as political theorists in the West, began talking in the late 1970s about the possibility of restoring politics in terms of reestablishing civil society. This line of thought suggested that the creation of autonomous organizations of all kinds would create a sphere in which people could act without reference to the political domination of the state. In Poland Adam Michnik called the process "new evolutionism," and in Czechoslovakia Václav Benda spoke of creating a "parallel polis." The dramatic, sudden emergence of Solidarity made for a much faster evolution than either Michnik or Benda believed possible and, because Leonid Brezhnev still ruled in the Soviet Union, made also for a vigorous reaction against Polish civil society in 1981.

After Solidarity achieved power, talk of recreating civil society died down, as Polish governments struggle with practical problems after forty years of mismanagement. In other words, Poland, along with all the other East European countries, is experiencing real politics in the 1990s: the struggle for public power by competing entities, whose outcome is uncertain. Efforts to find "hiding places," outcries against abuses of civil liberties, tortured redactions of sacred Marxist texts, and all the other features of East European opposition for forty years have given way to public struggle over the future. A fundamental problem this struggle must face, economic failure, is the subject of the first readings in this part, after which we turn to the place where the new politics began, Solidarity.

Economic Problems

The great variety of political energies that welled up in Eastern Europe in the 1980s was attributable in significant measure to the economic failures of the centrally planned economies. In the 1970s, the relative success of modest reforms and the infusion of large loans from the West helped Yugoslavia, Hungary, and Poland achieve, for a few years at least, higher standards of living. In Yugoslavia the feeling of prosperity peaked about 1978, in Hungary a bit later, and in Poland a bit earlier. During this relatively hopeful period, opposition continued, of course, but its ability to mobilize populations was limited by a feeling that economic improvements were occurring. Then in the 1980s the situation changed. Lowered standards of living, inflation, foreign debt, and shortages increased unrest and made the necessity for reforms more and more obvious.

One of the most influential analyses of the economic difficulties of centrally planned economies is János Kornai's study of the economics of shortage. Although much of Kornai's work is specialized and technical, one idea that underlies it can be gleaned from the brief condensation that follows. "Soft budget constraints" is another way of saying that in an economy administered by a centralized bureaucracy, success in obtaining investment capital and other benefits from the state is the main necessity for staying in business, not the satisfaction of social needs. Because the state can levy taxes and pass them on to managers who are successful politically, there is little need for industry to become efficient, to clear markets, or to compete effectively.

Lenin and Stalin appear to have had a static view of economic processes, believing that once the steel mills and generating plants that constituted modern industry in their youths were constructed, the job was done. Accordingly, after World War II, East European Communists emphasized heavy industry, creating an industrial plant that would have been modern in 1930 but by 1980 was not. An unintended consequence of this policy was the creation of extremely serious levels of pollution. In 1988, Greenpeace, the environmental action group, investigated the environmental situation in Poland. The following excerpt could easily describe other East European countries as well, particularly Czechoslovakia, where environmental damage is especially extensive.

30

Soft Budget Constraints

János Kornai

1980

Now let us start our examination of the actual subject of the present chapter: the instantaneous adjustment of the producer firm. It is assumed that the firm is interested in increasing production. The question is, what *constraints* are met in the course of increasing production? Three main groups of constraints can be distinguished.

1. *Resource constraints.*

These are *physical* constraints. Such are the material-, semifinished product- and part stocks instantaneously available to the firm, as well as workers of certain qualifications and of other particular abilities who are present instantaneously, functioning machines and equipment suitable for carrying out certain operations, and so on. These—and only these—are the physical resources that can be used for production.

2. *Demand constraints.*

The demand constraint exerts its effect on the producing workshop only in an indirect way. It is usually the firm's sales department that is in contact with the buyers. Employees of the firm in charge of sales forward the buyers' demand to the directors of the firm, or perhaps directly to the production managers. In any case the producing workshops will perceive, relying upon instructions received from the directors of the firm or upon information transmitted by the sales department, whether they should increase manufacture of the *j*th product, or reduce it, or perhaps stop it entirely. In this way, under definite conditions, demand may restrict fulfillment of intentions to increase production.

3. *Budget constraints.*

Under certain institutional conditions (e.g., in a socialist economy) not just one but several budget constraints exist. Separately "labeled" limits may be put on expenses to be spent on wages or on investments or on imports. If we do not mention a distinguishing attribute, we shall include under the heading, "budget constraint," the *total* of expenditures and the *total* of money available. In other words, the constraint formulates in a practical way the principle of "independent

Reprinted from János Kornai, *Economics of Shortage*, vol. A (Amsterdam: North-Holland, 1980), pp. 23–29, by permission of North-Holland Publishing Company and published by permission of Elsevier Science Publishers.

accounting of the firm": The firm has to cover its expenditures from its own proceeds.

The budget constraint, if it affects production, does so in an indirect way. It can prevent the firm buying physical resources: purchasing material and machines, employing workers.

For some constraints, given in the form of inequalities, equality holds in the solution. Production fully utilizes one or the other resource; sales may reach the limit of demand; expenses may exhaust the available financial resources. The constraint is *effective* because in fact it restricts the selected activities. Production would have been larger if it had not hit effective constraints. It can also be said that the effective constraint is in fact *binding*. For other constraints, however, inequality holds (they are "not exhausted") in the solution of the programming problem. They are *noneffective* from the point of view of the instantaneous solution. It is as if they were not there at all, they do not influence the choice, they are "redundant"; that is, they *do not bind* activities.

It is always the comparatively narrow constraints that are effective; it is they that restrict efforts at increasing production. Comparatively broad constraints are not effective.

Other distinctions will be needed, too. Resource constraints are of a *physical* nature. They express the trivial truth that it is impossible to make something out of nothing. It is possible to apply, instead of the first input–output combination, the second or third one; but some kind of combination of inputs will usually be needed, and this is constrained by the available quantities of resources. Therefore the resource constraints cannot be exceeded: They are hard as rock.

The situation is different with the demand and the budget constraints: These express not a physical necessity but a *behavioral* regularity. These are laid down by people, and people can transgress them. A program within the constraints is satisfactory for the decision maker, while he considers any overstepping unacceptable. This type of constraint may also be called an *acceptance constraint*. The output stock, waiting for sale, has, in normal circumstances, a tolerance limit. Yet if it is exceeded, then it is exceeded. Transgression of the budget constraint means insolvency: This can also happen. *It depends on concrete circumstances, that is, on social relations enforcing observation of the behavioral rule, how hard or soft the constraint is.* The hardness of the behavioral constraint has a graded *scale:* It can be almost as hard as the physical constraint, or of a medium hardness, or it can be expressly soft, that is it can be violated without trouble or consequence. A hard behavioral constraint may be effective, but it is not necessarily so—it depends on whether other constraints are relatively narrow or broad. On the other hand, a soft behavioral constraint (disregarding certain exceptional cases) can never be effective.

The constraint most often hit in the production of the firm, that is, which of the above discussed three types of constraints is effective, is deeply characteristic of the functioning of an economic system. First two "pure" types will be contrasted with each other. One is the "classical" capitalist firm. We are in the era before regular state intervention, that is, before Keynesian economic policy. We will disregard the peak of the upswing and will center our attention rather on the other phases of the cycle. The other "pure" type is *the firm functioning in the traditional socialist economic management system* (in the following called the *traditional socialist firm* for short). Its activities are controlled by detailed central instructions; it lives in an atmosphere of growth at a forced rate. The most important comparisons between these two pure types are summarized in Table 1.

The decisive difference is already revealed in the first two lines. *With the classical capitalist firm it is usually the demand constraint that is binding, while with the traditional socialist firm it is the resource constraint.* With abbreviated expression (and to a certain extent simplifying reality) the following contrast can be formulated: The functioning of the classical capitalist firm is basically *demand constrained,* and that of the traditional socialist firm is basically *resource constrained.* This proposition plays a central role in the whole train of thought of my book.

There is a close relationship between the third and the first two rows. The classical capitalist firm has a hard budget constraint. If it is insolvent, it will sooner or later become bankrupt. It can be granted a credit at best in advance of its future proceeds, which it has to pay back later with interest. It can buy only as much input as it can pay for from selling its products. Therefore it cannot produce more than it can expect to sell. It decides its production plans voluntarily at the level of demand constraints. ("At the level . . . " means that it produces approximately that volume; it might allow for some growth of its output stocks, but in the final account, it cannot depart much from expected selling possibilities.)

As opposed to this, the budget constraint of the traditional socialist firm is soft. If it works with a loss, that does not yet lead to real bankruptcy, that is, ceasing operation. The firm is helped out somehow: It receives additional credit, or its tax is reduced, or it is granted a subsidy, or the selling price is raised—and, finally, it survives financial difficulties. Accordingly, its demand is hardly constrained by solvency considerations. The firm, as *buyer,* tries to acquire as much input as possible in order that shortage should not hinder production. The other side of the same phenomenon is that the firm, as *seller,* faces an almost insatiable demand. At

TABLE 1   THE TWO PURE TYPES OF FIRM, AND TYPES OF CONSTRAINT

Types of constraint	Classical capitalist firm	Traditional socialist firm
Resource constraint	Rarely effective	Nearly always effective, more restrictive than demand constraints
Demand constraint	Nearly always effective, more restrictive than resource constraint	Rarely effective
Budget constraint	Hard	Soft
Production plan	Autonomous: the firm lays it down at the level of demand constraints; within resource constraints	Directive: prescribed by superior authority at the level of resource constraints; within demand constraints

least that is the situation with firms whose buyers are themselves firms: Demand from such buyers is almost impossible to satiate. This insatiable demand "pumps out" the product from the firm. What is more, the superior authority determining the plan would also like to encourage the firm toward the largest possible production. The final result is that the production plan of the traditional socialist firm is set at the level of resource constraints. "At the level of resource constraints" does not mean that every resource is always fully utilized. We only mean by this that with the given composition of available resources, in consideration of the existing bottlenecks and with the given managerial abilities and organization, no more can be done. In any case, this planned level of production usually remains below what buyers would be ready to accept.

31

Environmental Concerns in Poland

Sabine Rosenbladt

December 1988

The river around which the port city of Gdansk grew is called the Vistula. On its way through the heart of Poland, the Vistula passes through many large and small cities, most of which dump their raw sewage directly into it. Half of the 813 Polish communities that line the banks of the Vistula, including the capital city of Warsaw, have no sewage treatment facilities. Approximately ten thousand industrial polluters also do without waste treatment.

As a result, the Vistula is so polluted that along 81 percent of the river's length, the water is too dirty even for industrial use; it would corrode heavy machinery. The river flushes some ninety thousand tons of nitrogen and five thousand tons of phosphorus into the Baltic, along with eighty tons of mercury, cadmium, zinc, lead, copper, phenol, and chlorinated hydrocarbons.

The filth collects in the bay, where it is further enriched by the sewage from Gdansk, Gdynia, and Sopot. Polish newspapers report that the waters of the Baltic near Gdansk "exceed bacterial standards for waste water by at least one hundred times, due to sewage dumping." In 1981, the Polish newspaper *Szpilki* caricatured the Baltic as a gigantic toilet bowl.

This story is being repeated throughout Poland. In 1985, the Sejm, the Polish parliament, recognized four areas of the country, including Gdansk Bay, as "ecological disaster areas." The industrial district of Upper Silesia, the Krakow area, and the copper basin of Liegnitz/Glogow shared the distinction. "Disaster area" is meant literally. By Poland's own environmental standards, the regions are so contaminated with industrial and municipal pollution that the people living there should be evacuated. Evacuation is not an option, however, for these places are home to eleven million people, or 30 percent of Poland's population.

Gdansk's long sandy beaches have been closed for years. The seven nations that border the landlocked Baltic Sea have been poisoning it each year with about fifteen thousand tons of heavy metals, a million tons of nitrogen, seventy thousand tons of phosphorous, fifty thousand tons of oil, and highly toxic PCBs. While the Helsinki Convention of 1974 contains a pledge by these countries to limit damages "as much as possible, using the best possible methods," the promise remains unfulfilled. In 1988, 100,000 square kilometers of the seafloor were found to be biologically dead.

Extinction threatens seals, starfish, mussels, crabs, and gray seals. Algal blooms and dead fish float on the brackish waters.

Though Poland has an annual fishing quota of 200,000 tons, in 1984 Polish fishermen caught only 50,000 tons. In 1986, the catch declined to less than 28,000 tons. The last eels that were caught here were corroded by toxic chemicals, says Karola Palka, a resident of Sopot. "They looked like they were already cooked."

A few hundred pounds of sick flounder per night is all that the residents of Sopot, with their small boats and nets, can get out of the Baltic. Now they fear that even this will soon be forbidden. How contaminated are the fish? Palka displays her bare feet: Mosquito bites have swelled into purulent sores after contact with the Baltic seawater.

They still call what comes out of most Polish taps "drinking water," but only for reasons of nostalgia. According to 1984 official Polish environmental statistics, "71 percent of drinking water samples were disqualified by the national public health authorities for reasons of hygiene." By the year 2000, say some observers, not a drop of Poland's water will be clean enough to be used for anything.

Despite Eastern Europe's closed political atmosphere, a grass-roots environmental movement is blossoming. The latitude allowed these unofficial organizations varies between countries; Czechoslovakia and Romania tolerate little protest, if any, while independent environmentalists in Hungary and Poland have made surprising progress.

Of the literally hundreds of small regional groups in Poland, Polski Klub Ekologiczny (PKE), the Polish Ecological Club, is the acknowledged leader. Founded in 1980 in Krakow, it today has fifteen regional offices and six thousand members across the country. While it is recognized by the state as a legal opposition group, PKE consistently refuses official support. Government efforts to put Poland's budding environmental movement under one state-sponsored umbrella have been unsuccessful.

In 1981, the PKE and allies in the trade union succeeded in closing down the Skawina Aluminum Works, a plant nine miles south of Krakow whose fluorine emissions had so damaged the environment that cows in neighboring fields were no longer able to walk. In Upper Silesia, the club sees to it that local schoolchildren escape the extremely damaging, poisoned air at least once a year and get out into the country.

In Warsaw, club members have been locked in a hot battle with the local bureaucracy and construction industry over the fate of the last urban green spaces. In Miedzyrzecz, near Poznan, the club organized opposition to a planned nuclear waste site so effectively that the plans were shelved. And in Gdansk, the PKE is currently trying to prevent Poland's first nuclear power plant from being built.

Chernobyl turned Polish environmentalists from moderate supporters of nuclear power (coal is the principal source of Poland's air pollution) into determined antinuclear activists.[1] Both PKE and another prominent grass-roots peace and environ-

[1] In April 1986 a fire in one of the four nuclear reactors at the Soviet power plant in Chernobyl left thirty-one persons dead and released significant amounts of radiation that contaminated tens of thousands of acres of land in Byelorussia. Winds deposited considerable radioactive material on Poland and other European countries.

mental group, Freedom and Peace, have organized opposition to nuclear power plants and radioactive waste disposal plans. AKW Zarnowiec, which is currently being built near Gdansk and is scheduled to go into operation in 1992, has already been dubbed "Zernobyl" by locals.

"This thing is supposed to cost $5 billion, which is equivalent to the annual income of fifteen million Poles over three years," groans biophysicist Jerzy Jaskowski. "It's amazing! We need that money urgently in order to cope with the ecological disasters." At the beginning of 1988, two hundred scientists wrote an open letter to Prime Minister Zbigniew Mesner calling for a halt to construction at Zarnowiec.

Ministrations to this battered environment are desperately needed. Krakow's air, for example, is so contaminated as to defy description. The west wind blows in tons of toxic dust laden with heavy metals, sulfur, and nitrous oxide from Upper Silesia; when the east wind blows, the filth comes in even greater concentrations from Nowa Huta, the enormous steel complex in the eastern part of the city.

Krakow is enveloped in a stationary cloud of smog 135 days of the year. This causes the facades of the buildings in the medieval city center to crumble even faster; the corroding vapors have even decomposed the gold roof of the Sigismund chapel on the Wawel–Hugel. And in the old part of town, the oxygen content can drop from a normal of 21 percent to 17 percent, making the atmosphere literally fatal for heart patients, asthmatics, and old people.

The life span of Krakow residents is three to four years shorter than that of their fellow countrymen. The chances of developing lung cancer are twice as high here. PKE doctors have determined that the residents of this city suffer in disproportionately high numbers from allergies, chronic bronchitis, degenerative bone diseases, arteriosclerosis, and circulatory illnesses. And the infant mortality rate, at over 2.5 per thousand inhabitants, is more than one-and-one-half times the national average.

For the largest air polluter in Krakow, the Lenin foundry in Nowa Huta, the PKE drafted a plan to reform the production processes. Huta Lenina, as it is called, annually emits 400,000 tons of carbon monoxide, 50,000 tons of sulfur dioxide, and 60,000 tons of particulates. In addition, the antiquated plant uses two and a half times as much energy as modern foundries. In July, Krakow's environmental director, Bronislaw Kaminski, brought together the directors and the PKE experts for roundtable discussions about the PKE proposal. The enterprising Kaminski hoped "that in one to two years, we can begin to have actual ecological discussion about facilities like Huta Lenina."

But the conditions in Krakow are surpassed by those of Upper Silesia. This coal-producing and heavily industrialized region holds the uncontested world record for all kinds of pollution. Upper Silesia produces 60 percent of Poland's industrial waste, 40 percent of its gas emissions, and 30 percent of the toxic particulates. According to official statistics, in two-thirds of the region, all the emissions standards for particulates, gases, and heavy metals are continually broken by wide margins.

There is no improvement in sight. Until the year 2000, emissions will continue to rise, according to pessimistic assessments by the PKE. The sulfur dioxide content alone is expected to go from the current total of approximately 5 million tons annually to 9.1 million tons. Today, 60 percent of Polish forests are sick, and hundreds of thousands of hectares of ground are devastated.

"Do you have your gas masks with you?" asks PKE member Dr. Aureliusz Miklaszewski. Trained as a mining engineer and currently a lecturer at the technical high school, Miklaszewski offers this as a greeting before taking us into hell. "No? Then I advise you to suspend all breathing. We are about to inspect the site of legal murder."

We are in Siechnice, a chrome factory with annual production of 25,000 tons near Wroclaw. Here, the radiantly sunny day turns dark; a woolen gray fog cloud hangs over the cornfields. Through the mist, the shadowy outline of a huge industrial complex appears. Thick pipes, chimneys, and a mountain-high waste dump are wreathed in dead trees. Right next to the plant is a street with little houses. After a hundred meters, it disappears into the wisps of fog. "Chrome fog," says Miklaszewski. "People here have to live in this chrome cloud year in and year out."

The Szymanski family live at number two Kosciuzki Street. Alfreda Szymanski's face is marred by chrome-induced eczema; the hands of her husband Stefan are riddled with tumors. Yes, they know that chrome is toxic; they are always tired, they don't feel well, and their children are also sick; but what can they do? Last year, the factory paid them 2,800 zloty in damages for their ruined garden, about $6.50. "We don't care a hoot about the money!" But they are hoping that the PKE will help them complain about the plant. Despite a round of formal discussions about closing the facility in 1991, plant managers are currently looking for new workers. They want to increase production to 90,000 tons per year.

The drinking wells for Wroclaw are located just two hundred meters from Siechnice's waste dump. In addition to levels of lead, zinc, and copper well above normal, ground samples taken here contain up to 10.375 milligrams of toxic chrome per cubic meter. Legal limit: three milligrams per cubic meter.

The situation is much the same in Glogow, Poland's "copper basin." Here, copper ore is mined and melted down at several large facilities. Poland exports the semiprecious metal as a raw material, which is worth only pennies on the world market. Foreign companies reap the profits for refining the ore, while the pollution stays in Poland. The process of extracting copper from ore releases a host of toxins, including arsenic, while breathing large amounts of copper dust causes the so-called metal fever.

"Huta Miedzi Glogow II," says the street sign. Several years ago, some of the villages around Glogow were evacuated because of the highly contaminated soil. Abandoned under decree were Wroblin, Zukowice, Bogomice, Biechow, and Rapocin. In Wroblin, however, a surprise: People still live here, including several children. They are part of a group that wouldn't, or couldn't, leave.

In the midst of an apocalyptic scene, among ruins and piles of rubble from razed houses and dead vegetation covered with red dust, stand four or five buildings, intact. In the deserted village square, the crucifix is decorated with fresh, colorful ribbons. An old, tired man is leaning against the wall of a house.

A 1983 report from the government and the World Health Organization about the Glogow region predicts "emissions from the copper industry will double by 1990. It is therefore likely that public health standards will be seriously and frequently broken and that the health of the surrounding population will worsen."

Yet everywhere in the disaster area, contaminated fields continue to be farmed. The result: 20 percent of the food products tested were classified as hazardous to public health by the authorities. Among other things, vegetables were found to contain 220 times the limit for cadmium, 165 for zinc, 134 for lead, 34 for fluorine, and 2.5 times for uranium. Green lettuce, grown in the vicinity of the Boleslaw zinc plant near Krakow, contained 230 milligrams of lead per kilo. A kilo of cabbage held 30 milligrams of lead, a kilo of onions, 42. Lead causes brain damage, particularly in children. The 1983 report noted an "alarming increase" in the number of retarded children in Upper Silesia.

Poland in the Late 1970s

Surely the most dramatic initial response to economic distress was the emergence of the Solidarity movement in 1980. After the student revolt of 1968 and the Baltic strikes late in 1970, Edward Gierek replaced Władysław Gomułka as leader of the Polish United Workers party. Gierek hoped that by floating hard-currency loans in the West, Poland would be able to create the infrastructure necessary to get its economy moving. But Gierek's regime proved incapable of using in productive ways the sizable loans it received from Western banks. In effect the monies were simply passed on to the workers as a rising standard of living. Wages increased while the prices of food and other necessities remained artificially low.

In June 1976 Gierek tried to rebalance the situation by raising food prices. When workers in Radom and elsewhere protested, Gierek rescinded the price rises but severely repressed the strikers. To provide legal and material assistance to the families of workers imprisoned or unemployed because of the 1976 events, a group of intellectuals formed the Committee for the Defense of Workers (KOR). For the first time an organized group of intellectuals reached out directly to the workers. The innovation proved so successful that one year later KOR expanded its mission and added the title "Committee for Social Self-Defense" (KSS) to its name. During the next four years, until it voluntarily disbanded in 1981, KOR–KSS became an eloquent voice for the frustrations that Poles felt under Gierek. The portions that follow of KOR's "Appeal to Society," published in 1978, provide a summary statement of these feelings.

Poland has always been unique in East European lands for the continued strength of its Catholic church. During the interwar years, the church lost much of its support among the intellectuals, but it retained a strong hold on the masses. After the war the Polish church retained this hold by more or less accepting its new position under Communism, unlike the Croatian or Hungarian churches, which resisted and therefore suffered repression. By the 1970s, under the leadership of Cardinal Stefan Wyszyński, Catholics had begun to play a significant role in the battle against secular totalitarianism, and when Cardinal Karol Wojtyła was elected Pope John Paul II in 1978 the church's authority reached a new peak. The new pope's visit to his homeland in June 1979 produced, as one observer put it, a "psychological earthquake." John Paul II's tremendous personal appeal, as well as the nationalist overtones of the visit, which are apparent in the portions of one of his homilies that follow, helped create the conditions in which Solidarity could emerge a year later. After a generation of debasement of public rhetoric, the airing of John Paul's ethical, moral, and national appeals to literally millions of people in the face of official foot-dragging demonstrated to ordinary Poles that it was possible to discuss public affairs in a vocabulary that did not derive from the single-party state.

32

KOR's Appeal to Society
October 10, 1978

The workers' protest in June 1976 revealed a deep crisis in the economic and social life of our country. The two years that have elapsed since that time have been sufficiently long to warrant the expectation that the authorities would at least have sketched our directions for resolving the crisis. Unfortunately, during these two years the causes of the explosion have not been removed, and various new sources of tension have been introduced. Growing disorganization and chaos have ravaged the economic, social, and cultural life of the country. In this serious situation, we consider it our responsibility to present to Polish society an evaluation of the situation, together with an attempt to indicate what possible remedies are available to society. We would also like our statement to serve as a warning to the authorities against continuing their policy of deliberate disregard for genuine social problems and against their evasion of the responsibility for solving these problems. The results of such policies have on many occasions proven tragic for society, and the entire responsibility for this rests with the authorities.

I

1. The increase in prices for foodstuffs that was rejected by the public in 1976 has been replaced by hidden price increases. There exists a widespread practice of introducing more expensive goods labeled with new names onto the market, while eliminating cheaper goods. This tactic has been used with a number of industrial goods and with most foodstuffs, even including bread. The increase of prices in the state trade is also reflected in private trade, causing a severalfold increase in the prices of fruits and vegetables. The scale of this phenomenon is difficult to determine, but there is no doubt that together with the official price changes, inflation is actually much higher than one would conclude on the basis of official data.

Difficulties with supplies are constantly increasing, both in the area of industrial goods and of foodstuffs. It is impossible to purchase many items in the stores without standing in lines, an enormous waste of time, or engaging in bribery or nepotism.

The problem of supplying the population with meat has not been solved. It is difficult to consider the extensive network of commercial stores as a solution, since in these stores the price of a kilogram of sausage equals the daily wages of an average worker (150–200 zlotys per kilogram). Meat rationing has been introduced recently in several dozen industrial enterprises (e.g., the "Warszawa" Steel Mills and the Róża Luxemburg Enterprises). We do not know whether a system of meat rationing is necessary at this time. Until the state authorities publish full data on the availability of meat (production, export, and consumption), it will be impossible to adopt a position on this matter. It is certain, however, that any proposed rationing system should encompass the whole of society and be ratified by it. The hidden price increases and the supply difficulties have caused dramatic rises in the cost of living, and hit the poorest social strata particularly hard.

2. The state of health services is alarming. Chronic underinvestment over a period of years has recently been reflected in a decrease in the number of hospital beds (in psychiatry and obstetrics: *The Statistical Yearbook 1977*). The overcrowding and the technical conditions in a great many hospitals, which have never been renovated since the prewar period, create sanitary conditions that endanger the health of patients.

Insufficient nutrition and the lack of medications available in the hospitals and on the market are also obstacles to treatment.

The construction of a special modern government hospital for dignitaries in Międzylesie, and the special transport of medications, can be regarded in this context only as an expression of the full awareness on the part of the authorities insofar as the state of health services for the population as a whole is concerned; while the collection of contributions from the public for the Social Health Fund constitutes a cynical abuse.

3. The past several years have also brought about no improvement in the dramatic situation in housing. The number of people waiting for apartments grows larger every year, while the waiting period grows longer. This is coupled with a systematic increase in the cost of housing, which significantly burdens family budgets (monthly rent together with credit payments in housing cooperatives can run as high as three thousand zlotys).

4. The authorities are attempting to make up for the disorganization of the economy through an increased exploitation of the workers. The average working day of many occupational groups has often been lengthened. Drivers, miners, construction workers, many other occupational groups now work ten to twelve hours a day.

The fact that miners were deprived of free days to compensate them for free Saturdays, that work is required on Sundays, and that a single day's absence even for the most valid of reasons (such as death in the family or illness) leads to a loss of approximately 20 percent of a monthly salary—all this can be compared only with early capitalist exploitation.

5. A comparison of the daily earnings of a worker with prices in a commercial store reveals yet another worrisome fact: a growing social inequality. Earnings are overly differentiated (without much regard for qualifications). There are enormous differences in retirement benefits. We have now in Poland families who are strug-

gling under extremely difficult living conditions, and a small number of families who have no financial worries whatsoever. Another factor deepening social inequalities is the extensive system of privileges for groups associated with the authorities: privileged supplies, special health services, allocation of housing and building lots, foreign currency, and special recreational areas. These are only a few of the facilities available to small leadership groups. As a result, we are witnessing the growing social alienation of groups associated with the authorities, and their inability to notice the real social problems. When we learn that funds designated for the development of agriculture are being used to build a government center in Bieszczady and that in connection with this, local residents are being dislodged from the village of Wołosate, we are forced to view this fact as a proof that the authorities have lost all touch with reality.

More and more often, one can observe children inheriting the privileged position of their parents. The principle of equal opportunity for all young people is becoming illusory.

In a situation where the economic crisis threatens all of society, and especially the underprivileged groups, the assurance of special privileges to the governing groups provokes righteous anger and moral indignation.

6. The deepening crisis in agriculture is a fundamental factor in the economic, political, and social situation in the country. The consequences of a policy of discrimination and destruction of family farming, which has been conducted for thirty years, are now becoming visible. In spite of this, the production from one hectare of arable land in private hands is still higher than the production from one hectare of arable land in state agriculture. Still, gigantic investments are directed to the state agricultural farms and to production cooperatives despite the fact that the costs of maintaining state agricultural farms exceeds the value of their production.

Over the past several years, difficulties connected with the general state of the economy have been particularly evident: lack of coal, fertilizers, cattle feed, farming machinery, and building materials. This limits to a great extent the investment possibilities of peasant farms and leads to the exodus of young people to the cities.

Disorganization and corruption in the purchasing centers cause wastage of already produced farm goods.

At present, following the introduction of dues for retirement insurance for farmers, the financial responsibilities of the peasant farm to the state often exceed half of its income. The refusal by over 250,000 farmers throughout the country to pay retirement dues best illustrates the attitude of the peasants toward state agricultural policy.

7. The violations of the rule of law exhibited during the June events turned out to be a commonly used policy. Beatings of detainees by organs of the police are not isolated cases but constitute a form of police mob rule which is sanctioned by the higher authorities.

The materials gathered by the Intervention Bureau of the Social Self-Defense Committee "KOR" which have been published in the *Documents of Lawlessness* demonstrate the full impunity of the police and the security service. Even the most dramatic cases of murders of persons who were being detained does not result in any punishment of those functionaries guilty of such crimes. In the case of the murder of

Jan Brożyna, the desire to protect the real murderers went so far that the investigation was entirely fabricated, as was the court trial.[1] All this ended in the death in prison of a major witness, and in long prison sentences for two other people whose guilt was never proven.

The activities of the sentencing boards for misdemeanors, which have been greatly extended at the expense of the court system, do not respect even the appearances of legality. The Office of the Prosecutor General, in disregard of the law, does not react to complaints that are filed; while the Council of State, the Diet, and the Ministry of Justice remain deaf to all information about the degeneration and anarchy that prevails in the investigative agencies and the justice system.

8. The usurpation by the party of the exclusive and totally arbitrary right to issue and impose judgments and decisions in all areas of life without exception has created a particular threat to Polish science and culture. Drastic limitations of the extent and freedom of scientific research and the publication of its results, especially in the humanities and social sciences such as philosophy, economy, sociology, and history; the stiff demands of the imposed doctrine, which has lost all the characteristics of an ideology and been transformed into a system of dogmas and unrestricted commands dictated by the authorities; the staffing of scientific positions with incompetent people who simply comply with the directives of the rulers—all of this brings harm to Polish culture and not only hinders its development but also the preservation and cultivation of its former achievements. Literature, theater, and film—those branches of culture dominated by language—are especially vulnerable to the arbitrary throttling of the freedom of thought and to the annihilation of creative activities. Under these conditions, culture is being deadened, while literature, an enormously important element in the spiritual life of the nation, though unmeasurable in its effectiveness, is either reduced to the role of an executor of the orders of the authorities or forced to divorce itself completely from expressing the truth about the surrounding reality, or else is simply tolerated as a harmless "flower on the sheepskin."

The preservation of culture has been reflected for several years now in initiatives in support of publications beyond the reach of state control and a science independent of official and distorting falsehoods.

The system of preventive censorship harms not only culture and science but the entire social and economic life of the country. Censorship stifles not only all signs of criticism but also all authentic information that could equip society with self-knowledge about its actual situation, which could prove undesirable for the authorities. *The Book of Prohibitions and Directives of the Main Office for Control of the Press, Publications, and Performances* published by KSS "KOR" demonstrates the extent of the censor's interference in all areas of life. Ever-greater regions of silence, made infertile by the discrimination against living contemporary culture, are invaded by monstrously inflated and omnipresent ersatz products privileged by cultural policy: Multifaceted entertainments and numerous pop song festivals are

---

[1]In June 1976 Jan Brożyna was beaten to death by the authorities in the industrial city of Radom, scene of the largest protests against the price rises instituted by the Gierek government in that month. His death became a cause célèbre and an important mobilizing event in the creation of KOR.

shabby substitutes for culture. This constitutes in fact the main object of such popularization and fulfills its role by blocking the deeper cultural aspirations of society and by systematically debasing its spiritual needs.

The most distinguished representatives of science and culture are subject to prohibitions against publication. The more ambitious films are not allowed to be shown. Entire periods of contemporary history are passed over in silence or falsified. The Polish Episcopate, the highest moral authority in the land, has warned against this phenomenon, seeing in it a threat to the national and cultural identity of society. The threat to culture and art posed by the censorship has been discussed at Congresses of the Polish Writers' Union and the Polish Sociological Association and is the subject of a pronouncement by the Polish PEN Club.

The system of disinformation constitutes a vicious circle that does not spare even the authorities who created it. According to Życie Warszawy, 65 percent of the data supplied by statistical units reporting to the Main Office of Statistics is falsified, and this estimate must be regarded as optimistic. It is impossible to make correct decisions on the basis of false information. Under these circumstances, paralysis must overwhelm the entire life of the country.

The authorities fear society and are therefore unable to provide it with the truth about the current situation. The so-called economic maneuver propounded as a solution to the crisis turned out to be only a set of immediate, arbitrary, and uncoordinated interferences into the economic life of the country. The result of this policy is only an increasing disorganization of the economy:

- The freezing of investments has led to billions in losses because construction that had already started was never completed.
- Drastic limitations in imports have led to weeks of idleness in factories across Poland.
- The plunderous export of foodstuffs has increased shortages on the domestic market.
- The dissolution of the planning system, together with the simultaneous denial of the market economy and the retention of an anachronistic system of directing enterprises by order and commands, has eliminated all regulatory mechanisms from the economy.

The system based on arbitrary and irrevocable decisions by state and party authorities who see themselves as infallible has caused immeasurable damage to the social consciousness of the nation. The persecution of independent views, together with the use of coercion to extort an unconditional compliance with all directives coming from above, has formed attitudes that lack all ideals and has fostered duplicity; the spread of conformism, servility, and careerism has been encouraged throughout society. These characteristics serve as recommendations in the staffing of leadership positions. Competent, enlightened, and independently minded people are deprived of the possibility of advancement, and often even of a job.

The total lack of consideration for public opinion means that an overwhelming majority of the citizens have ceased to identify themselves with the state, and feel no responsibility for it.

Radical economic reform is necessary. But even the most thoroughly developed and most consistent reforms will not be able to change anything if they run up against a barrier of public indifference and despair.

The economy will not be revived by Conferences of Workers' Self-Governments which blindly obey the PUWP. Committees of Social Control selected from among the authorities, and at their service, will not reach down to the sources of inefficiency, corruption, and illegality. The only result of such actions will be to increase the disorganization of life throughout the country.

33

Pope John Paul II Speaks in Victory Square, Warsaw

Pope John Paul II

June 2, 1979

Dear fellow countrymen! Dear brothers and sisters! Fellow sharers in the Eucharistic Sacrifice that is being offered today in Warsaw's Victory Square!

I want to join you in singing a hymn of praise to God's providence that allows me to be here in the garb of a pilgrim.

We know that Paul VI, so recently deceased—the first pilgrim pope, after so many centuries—greatly *desired to set foot in Poland* and especially to go to Jasna Gora.[1] To the end of his life he kept this desire alive in his heart, and he took it with him to the grave. Now we see this desire—so powerful and deep-rooted that it lasted through a long pontificate—being fulfilled today and in a way that could hardly have been anticipated.

Let us, therefore, thank God for his providence in giving Paul VI so strong a desire. Let us thank him for the new type of pope—the pilgrim pope—that he brought into being by means of the Second Vatican Council.

Now that the entire church has acquired a renewed consciousness of being the people of God, a people that shares in Christ's mission, a people that carries this mission with it through history, a pilgrim people, the pope could not any longer remain the "prisoner of the Vatican." He too had to become once again a pilgriming Peter, like that first Peter who journeyed from Jerusalem via Antioch to Rome in order there to be a witness for Christ and seal his witness with his own blood.

Today, dear sons and daughters of my native land, it is granted to me to carry out in your midst the wish of our deceased Pope Paul VI. When in the inscrutable plans of divine providence, after the death of Paul VI and the short pontificate of my immediate predecessor, John Paul I, that lasted but a few weeks, the vote of the cardinals called me from the Chair of St. Stanislaus at Krakow to the Chair of St. Peter at Rome, I perceived immediately that *my duty was to carry out the desire*

---

[1]Częstochowa Monastery, founded in 1382, is in Jasna Góra and houses Poland's most famous national/religious painting, *Our Lady of Częstochowa*. The painting usually is referred to as "the Black Madonna" because of its dark coloration produced by years of exposure to smoke and dirt and to contrast it to the so-called White Madonna now in Lithuania.

Reprinted from *The Pope Speaks* 24(3), 1979:265–70, by permission of The Pope Speaks, 200 Noll Plaza, Huntington, Indiana 46750.

which Paul VI could not bring to fruition and to do so during the millennial anniversary of Poland's baptism.

Is not my pilgrimage to my native land during the year when the church in Poland is celebrating the ninth centenary of the death of St. Stanislaus, to be taken as a special symbol of our Polish pilgrimage through the history of the church, pilgrimage that has moved along roads which are not Poland's alone but those of Europe and the world as well?[2]

I leave aside here any consideration of myself as an individual; yet, I must ask myself, as all of you must ask yourselves, why it was that in the year 1978 (after so many centuries of a different and unbroken tradition in this matter) a son of the Polish nation, a son of Poland, should be called to the Chair of St. Peter. Christ required Peter, like the other apostles, to be his "witnesses in Jerusalem, throughout Judea and Samaria, yes, even to the ends of the earth." With these words of Christ in mind, are we not perhaps justified in thinking that *Poland in our time has become a land called to give an especially important witness?*

May we not think that here—at Warsaw, at Gniezno, at Jasna Gora, at Krakow, at every point in this entire historical pilgrimage which I have retraced so often in my life and have occasion to retrace again during these few days—we must proclaim Christ with singular humility but also with conviction?[3] That here in this land we must once again go on this pilgrimage and renew our insight into the testimony given by Christ's cross and resurrection? But if we accept all that I have just been so bold as to claim, what great duties and obligations it lays on us! Are we able to accept them?

To Poland the church brought the Christ who is *the key to understanding that magnificent* and utterly fundamental *reality which is the human person.* Apart from Christ it is impossible to understand the human person in a full and radical way. Or we might better say that the human person cannot understand himself fully and radically apart from Christ. He cannot grasp who he is or in what his true dignity consists or what his real vocation is or his ultimate destiny. He cannot understand any of these things fully apart from Christ.

It is impossible, then, to exclude Christ from the history of the human race anywhere in the world, in any geographical longitude and latitude. The exclusion of Christ from the history of the race is an attack on the person. Apart from Christ it is impossible to understand the history of Poland and, above all, the history of the men and women who have traveled and are now traveling the road of life in this land. A

---

[2]Poland celebrated the nine hundredth anniversary of the martyrdom of St. Stanisław, Poland's patron saint, in May 1979. Polish religious and folk tradition considers Stanisław a symbol of resistance against the excesses of royal or secular power, as he achieved martyrdom when he was killed by King Bolesław the Bold. After World War II the communists protrayed Bolesław as a progressive monarch attempting to limit the power of superstition, but this idea did not penetrate very deeply into the public mind. Originally, John Paul II wanted to officiate at the Stanisław celebrations, but the government refused to permit a visit at that time. During his visit one month later, however, John Paul II did not fail to praise St. Stanisław, whom on an earlier occasion he had called "an advocate of the most essential human rights, on which man's dignity, his morality, and his true freedom depend."

[3]Gniezno was the first capital of the Roman Catholic archdiocese of Poland. For this reason, and because its origin is attributed to Lech, the mythological founder of Poland, it holds a special place in the symbolism of Polish religious nationalism.

history of men and women—yes, the history of the nation is first and foremost a history of men and women. And the history of any and every human being unfolds in Jesus Christ. In him it becomes a history of salvation.

The history of a nation deserves an adequate evaluation in terms of the contribution it has made to *the advancement of the human person and the human race:* to the intellect, the heart, the conscience, for it is here that the deepest levels of a culture are to be found. Here, too, are a culture's most solid foundations, its very marrow and strength.

It is impossible, therefore, to understand and evaluate without reference to Christ the past contribution of the Polish nation to *the advancement of the human person and the person's very humanness* and the contribution it is still making today. "This ancient oak has grown as it has, and no wind has felled it, because its roots are in Christ." We must perceive what (or rather: who) Christ has been for the sons and daughters of this land through its many generations. I am referring here not only to those who have explicitly believed in him and professed the Church's faith in him but to those also who have apparently been far from him, outside the church, those who doubted or denied.

It is right, then, that we understand the history of a nation in the light of the person, that is, of every individual who has belonged to that nation. But in our day it is likewise impossible to understand the human person except in the context of the community which is the nation. The nation is, of course, not the only community, but it is a quite specific community, the one that is perhaps most intimately connected with the family and the one that is most important for the spiritual history of the human person. *Therefore, it is also impossible, without reference to Christ, to understand the history of the Polish nation,* this great thousand-year-old community that so profoundly shapes my existence and that of each of us. If we reject this key to the understanding of our nation, we expose ourselves to major misunderstandings of ourselves. We no longer understand what we really are.

Apart from Christ it is impossible to understand this nation with its past that has been so splendid and yet so terribly burdened. It is impossible to understand this city of Warsaw, the capital of Poland, that in 1944 resolved to wage an uneven battle with the aggressor, a battle in which its allies abandoned it, a battle in which it was buried under its own ruins—unless we bear in mind that under these same ruins was also buried the statue of Christ the Redeemer with his cross, which stood in front of the church in Krakowskie Przedmiescie.[4] It is impossible to understand the history of Poland from Stanslaus at Skalka to Maximilian Kolbe at Oswiecim, unless we apply to these men, too, the sole and *basic criterion of understanding* which bears the name of Jesus Christ.[5]

The millennial anniversary of the baptism of the Poland which bore St. Stanislaus as its first mature fruit—the millennial anniversary of Christ as part of our yesterday and our today—is the principal reason for my pilgrimage and for my

---

[4]The Church of the Holy Cross is located on Krakowskie Przedmieście, one of the main streets of Warsaw.

[5]Father Kolbe was beatified for saving the life of a Jew by voluntarily taking the man's place in the starvation bunker at Oświęcim (Auschwitz). Before the war Father Kolbe edited a rabidly anti-Semitic newspaper.

joining in a prayer of thanksgiving with all of you, my dear fellow countrymen, to whom Jesus Christ continues to teach the great cause of the human person; with you for whom Jesus Christ continues to be an open book of instruction about the person and his dignity and rights, as well as a book of knowledge regarding the dignity and rights of the nation.

Today, here in Victory Square in the capital of Poland, as I join you in the great Eucharistic Prayer, *may Christ continue to be for us an open book of life for the future,* for our tomorrow as Poles.

We stand here before the Tomb of the Unknown Soldier. In the history of Poland, ancient and modern, there is a special basis, a special reason, for this tomb. How many places there are in his native land where that soldier has fallen! How many places in Europe and around the world there are where by his death he has cried out that there cannot be a just Europe without Polish independence in concrete geographical form!

How many battlefields there are on which that soldier has fallen "for our freedom and yours" and thus borne witness to the rights of the person which are so closely interwoven with the inviolable rights of the people! "Where are your precious graves, O Poland? Rather, where are they not? You know the answer better than anyone, and God in His heaven knows it, too."

The written history of the fatherland takes us through the tomb of an unknown soldier!

I would like to kneel beside this tomb and pay homage to every seed that falls into the earth and, dying there, bears fruit. It may be the seed that is a soldier's blood shed on the field of battle or a martyr's sacrifice in a concentration camp or a prison. It may be the seed of hard daily toil and sweat in the fields, the factories, the mines, the foundries, the mills. It may be the loving seed of parents who do not refuse to give life to a new human being and to take on all the obligations of rearing it. It may be the seed of creative work in the universities, the schools of higher learning, the libraries, all the places that develop the national culture. It may be the seed of prayer, or of service to the sick, the suffering, the abandoned. In a word, it may be *"all that makes up Poland."*

All this is in the hands of the Mother of God who stands at the foot of the cross on Calvary and waits in the upper room for Pentecost.

All this makes up the history of a fatherland that has been shaped in the course of one thousand years by successive generations—including today's and tomorrow's—and by each of its sons and daughters, even though they be unknown and nameless like the soldier before whose tomb we now stand.

All this I embrace with mind and heart in this Eucharist and I include it in the one holy sacrifice of Christ, here on Victory Square.

And I cry out, I a son of Poland who am also John Paul II, Pope—I cry out of the depths of this millennium—I cry out on the Vigil of Pentecost:

> Let your Spirit come down!
> Let your Spirit come down!
> And let him renew the face
> of the earth—
> *this* earth! Amen.

Solidarity

The difficult situation brought about by Gierek's inability to solve Poland's eco-nomic decline, coupled with the increased sense that alternatives existed, produced in the summer of 1980 a series of strikes that led to a dramatic confrontation between government and strikers at the Lenin Shipyards in Gdańsk. After tense negotiations, the government, much to the surprise of everyone, capitulated almost completely to the workers' demands. A good many of the things the workers sought were traditional job-related gains, but some of their demands involved basic politi-cal issues. The portions of the Gdańsk accord of August 1980 by which the govern-ment accepted Solidarity as a legitimate political agent are printed here. This was the first time that a communist government recognized the independent existence of another political force in society.

During the next year and a half Solidarity acted less and less like a trade union and more and more as if it were a great national front preparing to assume power, perhaps first in local workers' councils and then eventually in parliament. The contradiction between Solidarity's trade union organization and its national goals, as well as the relatively moderate policies that its leader Lech Wałęsa pursued in order to lessen the chance of Soviet invasion, led Poles to call the movement a "self-limiting revolution." Nonetheless, in October 1981 Solidarity adopted a pro-gram that called for, among other things, the creation of a "self-governing re-public," a phase the party correctly interpreted as destructive of its "leading role." Portions of that program are excerpted here.

In 1981 General Wojciech Jaruzelski assumed leadership of the Polish party and state. After a series of demands that Solidarity cease its political activities, he imposed martial law, imprisoned most of the Solidarity leaders, and began a pro-cess of retrenchment he called "normalization." Reproduced here are portions of the speech in which he announced this policy.

34

The Gdańsk Agreement
August 31, 1980

The governmental commission and the Interfactory Strike Committee (MKS), after studying the twenty-one demands of the workers of the coast who are on strike, have reached the following conclusions:

On Point No. 1, which reads:
"To accept trade unions as free and independent of the party, as laid down in Convention No. 87 of the ILO and ratified by Poland, which refers to the matter of trade unions rights," the following decision has been reached:[1]

1. The activity of the trade union of People's Poland has not lived up to the hopes and aspirations of the workers. We thus consider that it will be beneficial to create new union organizations, which will run themselves, and which will be authentic expressions of the working class. Workers will continue to have the right to join the old trade unions, and we are looking at the possibility of the two union structures cooperating.

2. The MKS declares that it will respect the principles laid down in the Polish constitution while creating the new independent and self-governing unions. These new unions are intended to defend the social and material interests of the workers, and not to play the role of a political party. They will be established on the basis of the socialization of the means of production and of the socialist system that exists in Poland today. They will recognize the leading role of the PZPR in the state and will not oppose the existing system of international alliances.[2] Their aim is to ensure for the workers the necessary means for the determination, expression, and defense of their interests. The governmental commission will guarantee full respect for the dependence and self-governing character of the new unions in their organizational structures and their functioning at all levels. The government will ensure that the new unions have every possibility of carrying out their function of defending the interests of the workers and of seeking the satisfaction of their material, social, and

---

[1] The International Labor Organization (ILO) began as part of the League of Nations and after the war became the body of the United Nations concerned with labor issues around the world. Between 1977 and 1980 the United States withdrew from membership because it believed the organization had come under the control of Third World elements.

[2] PZPR is the Polish United Workers' party (Polska zjednoczona partia robotnicza).

Reprinted from Abraham Brumberg, ed., *Poland: Genesis of a Revolution* (New York: Random House, 1983), by permission of Denis MacShane, *Solidarity—Poland's Independent Trade Union*, trans. Labour Focus on Eastern Europe (Nottingham, England: Spokesman, 1981).

cultural needs. Equally it will guarantee that the new unions are not the objects of any discrimination.

3. The creation and the functioning of free and self-governing trade unions is in line with Convention 87 of the ILO relating to trade unions rights and Convention 98, relating to the rights of free association and collective negotiation, both of which conventions have been ratified by Poland. The coming into being of more than one trade union organization requires changes in the law. The government, therefore, will make the necessary legal changes as regards trade unions, workers' councils, and the labor code.

4. The strike committees must be able to turn themselves into institutions representing the workers at the level of the enterprise, whether in the fashion of workers' councils or as preparatory committees of the new trade unions. As a preparatory committee, the MKS is free to adopt the form of a trade union or of an association of the coastal region. The preparatory committees will remain in existence until the new trade unions are able to organize proper elections to leading bodies. The government undertakes to create the conditions necessary for the recognition of unions outside of the existing Central Council of Trade Unions.[3]

5. The new trade unions should be able to participate in decisions affecting the conditions of the workers in such matters as the division of the national assets between consumption and accumulation, the division of the social consumption fund (health, education, culture), the wages policy, in particular with regard to an automatic increase of wages in line with inflation, the economic plan, the direction of investment, and prices policy. The government undertakes to ensure the conditions necessary for the carrying out of these functions.

6. The enterprise committee will set up a research center whose aim will be to engage in an objective analysis of the situation of the workers and employees, and will attempt to determine the correct ways in which their interests can be represented. This center will also provide the information and expertise necessary for dealing with such questions as the prices index and wages index and the forms of compensation required to deal with price rises. The new unions should have their own publications.

7. The government will enforce respect for Article I of the trade union law of 1949, which guarantees the workers the right to freely come together to form trade unions. The new trade union will not join the Central Council of Trade Unions (CRZZ). It is agreed that the new trade union law will respect these principles. The participation of members of the MKS and of the preparatory committees for the new trade unions in the elaboration of the new legislation is also guaranteed.

On Point No. 2, which reads:
"To guarantee the right to strike, and the security of strikers and those who help them," it has been agreed that

The right to strike will be guaranteed by the new trade union law. The law will have to define the circumstances in which strikes can be called and organized, the ways in which conflicts can be resolved, and the penalties for infringements of the law. Articles 52, 64, and 65 of the labor code (which outlaw strikes) will cease to

---

[3]The Central Council of Trade Unions (Centralna rada związków zawodowych), the communist union movement, was dominated by the government.

have effect from now until the new law comes into practice. The government undertakes to protect the personal security of strikers and those who have helped them and to ensure against any deterioration in their conditions of work.

With regard to Point No. 3, which reads:

"To respect freedom of expression and publication, as upheld by the constitution of People's Poland, and to take no measures against independent publications, as well as to grant access to the mass media to representatives of all religions," it has been added that

1. The government will bring before the Sejm (parliament) within three months a proposal for a law on control of the press, of publications, and of other public manifestations, which will be based on the following principles: Censorship must protect the interests of the state. This means the protection of state secrets and of economic secrets in the sense that these will be defined in the new legislation, the protection of state interests and its international interests, the protection of religious convictions, as well as the right of nonbelievers, as well as the suppression of publications which offend against morality.

The proposals will include the right to make a complaint against the press control and similar institutions to a higher administrative tribunal. This law will be incorporated in an amendment to the administrative code.

2. The access to the mass media by religious organizations in the course of their religious activities will be worked out through an agreement between the state institutions and the religious associations on matters of content and of organization. The government will ensure the transmission by radio of the Sunday mass through a specific agreement with the church hierarchy.

3. The radio and television as well as the press and publishing houses must offer expression to different points of view. They must be under the control of society.

4. The press, as well as citizens and their organizations, must have access to public documents and, above all, to administrative instructions and socioeconomic plans, in the form in which they are published by the government and by the administrative bodies that draw them up. Exceptions to the principle of open administration will be legally defined in agreement with Point no. 3, paragraph 1.

On Point No. 10, which reads:

"To ensure the supply of products on the internal market and to export only the surplus,"

and Point No. 11, which reads:

"to suppress commercial prices and the use of foreign currency in sales on the internal market,"

and Point No. 12, which reads:

"to introduce ration cards for meat and meat-based products, until the market situation can be brought under control," the following agreement has been reached:

The supply of meat will be improved between now and December 31, 1980, through an increase in the profitability of agricultural production and the limitation of the export of meat to what is absolutely indispensable, as well as through the import of extra meat supplies. At the same time, during this period a program for the improvement of the meat supply will be drawn up, which will take into account the possibility of the introduction of a rationing system through the issue of cards.

Products that are scarce on the national market for current consumption will not be sold in the PEWEX shops,[4] and between now and the end of the year, the population will be informed of all decisions that are taken concerning the problems of supply.

The MKS has called for the abolition of the special shops and the leveling out of the price of meat and related products.

After reaching the above agreement, it has also been decided that

The government undertakes

To ensure personal security and to allow both those who have taken part in the strike and those who have supported it to return to their previous work under the previous conditions.
To take up at the ministerial level the specific demands raised by the workers of all enterprises represented in the MKS.
To publish immediately the complete text of this agreement in the press, the radio, the television, and in the national mass media.

The strike committee undertakes to propose the ending of the strike at 5:00 P.M. on August 31, 1980.

[4]PEWEX shops were retail stores that sold goods normally not available on the Polish market. They accepted only hard currency.

35

Solidarity's Program
October 16, 1981

I
WHO ARE WE AND WHAT ARE OUR ASPIRATIONS?

The independent self-governing trade union Solidarity emerged from the 1980 strike movement [as] the most massive movement in the history of Poland. Initiated among workers at large enterprises in various parts of Poland, that movement reached its historic peak in August 1980 on the coast. Within a year it engulfed all groups of the labor world: workers, peasants, the intelligentsia, and craftsmen. Our union originated simply from the needs of our country's common people, from their sufferings and disappointments, from their hopes and aspirations. Our union emerged from the rebellion of Polish society touched by the experience of over three decades of violations of human and civil rights, from the rebellion against ideological discrimination and economic exploitation. It was a protest against the existing system of exercising power.

What all of us had in mind were not only living conditions, although we lived poorly, worked hard and very frequently in vain; history has taught us that there is no bread without freedom. What we had in mind were not only bread, butter, and sausage but also justice, democracy, truth, legality, human dignity, freedom of convictions, and the repair of the republic. All elementary values had been too mistreated to believe that anything could improve without their rebirth. Thus the economic protest also had to be simultaneously a social protest, and the social protest had to be simultaneously a moral protest.

That social and moral protest did not occur overnight. Inherent in it was the heritage of blood shed by workers in Poznań in 1956 and on the coast in December 1970, of the 1968 students' rebellion, and the 1976 sufferings in Radom and Ursus. Inherent in it was the heritage of independent actions carried out by the workers, the intelligentsia and youth, of the efforts made by the church to preserve the values and the heritage of all struggles for human dignity in our country. Our union rose from those struggles and will remain loyal to them. We are an organization combining the features of a trade union and of a great social movement. The combination of those features makes our organization strong and determines our role in the life of the

Reprinted from Peter Raina, *Poland, 1981: Towards Social Renewal* (London: Allen & Unwin, 1985), pp. 326–29, 346–47.

entire nation. Owing to the formation of the powerful trade union organization, Polish society has ceased to be divided, disorganized and lost; while uniting under the slogan of solidarity, it has reconverted its strength and hopes. Conditions have been provided for an authentic national rebirth. Our union is the broadest representation of the working people in Poland; it wants to be, and will be, the causative force of that rebirth.

Solidarity unites many social trends and associates people adhering to various ideologies, with various political and religious convictions, irrespective of their nationality. We have united in protest against injustice, the abuses of power, and against the monopolized right to determine and to express the aspirations of the entire nation. We have united in protest against the treatment of the citizen by the state as if he were state property, against the deprivation of the working people of an authentic representation in their conflicts with the state, against the benevolence of those in power who know better how much freedom is to be allotted to those under their rule, and against awards for absolute obedience instead of initiative and independence in action. We have been united in repudiating hypocrisy and in objecting to the mismanagement of the results of the hard and patient toil performed by the people.

We are, however, a force capable not only of protesting. We are a force willing to build a just Poland for everyone, a force invoking common human values.

Our activity must be based on respect for man. The state should serve man and not rule over him. The state organization should serve society and not be identified with one political party. The state should be a real commonwealth belonging to the entire nation. Work is for man, and what determines its sense is its closeness to man, to his real needs. Our national and social rebirth must be based on the restored hierarchy of those goals. While defining its aims, Solidarity draws from the values of Christian ethics, from our national traditions, and from the workers' and democratic traditions of the labor world. Pope John Paul II's encyclical about human labor is for us a new stimulus to work.[1] As a mass organization of the working people, Solidarity is also a movement for the moral rebirth of the people.

We regard democracy as a principle that must not be desisted from. Democracy must not be rule exercised by groups placing themselves above society and claiming the right to determine the needs and to represent the interests of society. Society must be able to speak with its full voice, to express various social and political opinions; it must be able to organize in such a way as to guarantee a fair share in the material and spiritual achievements of the nation for all as well as to liberate all the nation's possibilities and creative forces. We aspire for the real socialization of the administration and management system. For this reason our objective is a self-governing Poland.

We value the idea of freedom and unqualified independence. We will support everything that consolidates national and state sovereignty, that helps freely develop

---

[1]In his encyclical *Laborem excercens,* issued on September 14, 1981, John Paul II argued that labor, as a fundamental dimension of human existence, is not an impersonal force opposed to capital. On the other hand, property is not an absolute right, for the Christian doctrine of work also implies rights for the workers.

national culture, and that hands down the heritage of history. We consider that our national identity must be fully respected. Having formed and acted under very difficult conditions, our union is advancing along a path not trodden by anybody. All who have important Polish questions at heart and who find no support or understanding anywhere else joined it from the very beginning and continue to join. Aware of its strength, of its social and moral prestige, people count on our union in every sphere. We must simultaneously fight for our union's existence, organize at all levels and learn—frequently from our own mistakes—the appropriate behavior and methods for the struggle for our goals.

Ours is a program for the struggle for the goals set, a program reflecting the aspirations and aims of our society, and a program rooted in these aspirations. It is a program pursuing long-term goals by setting more immediate problems. It is a program of our work, struggle, and service.

II
ATTITUDE TO THE COUNTRY'S PRESENT SITUATION

The formation of Solidarity, a mass social movement, has radically changed the situation in the country. It has given various independent public institutions, both new ones and those that until recently depended on the state authorities and have now won independence, a chance to develop. The formation of organizations independent of the state authorities is to be regarded as a fact fundamental for changes taking place in our country's sociopolitical relations. Owing to them, society is able to strive to realize its aspirations and effectively defend its rights.

Conditions for exercising power have thus changed. To exercise it effectively it is necessary to take into account the will of society and to act under its control in line with the requirements set forth in the Gdańsk, Szczecin, and Jastrzębie social accords.[2] It was necessary to introduce an economic reform and to reform the state and its institutions. We had the right to expect the state authorities to carry out such reforms.

Based on the omnipotence of the central party and state institutions, the way that we were ruled previously was leading the country to ruin. The holding back of changes, which has been continuing for a year, although it has been impossible to rule in the old way, has accelerated that process and is rapidly carrying us to catastrophe. After the Second World War, the economy did not sink anywhere in Europe as far as it did in our country under peaceful conditions. Notwithstanding the fatigue and disappointment in the past twelve months society showed enormous patience and, at the same time, determination. However, there is the danger that fatigue and disappointment will eventually turn into a blind destructive force or submerge us in helplessness. As a society, we must not lose the hope that it is possible to overcome the crisis. In the face of national tragedy Solidarity must no

---

[2]The Gdańsk agreement, part of which is printed in Document 34, was accompanied by similar agreements signed in Szczecin the day before and in Jastrzębie a few days later. Together they are known as "the social accords."

longer restrict itself to expectations and to exerting pressure on the authorities to keep obligations stemming from the agreements. For society we are the only guarantor of those agreements. For this reason the union considers it its fundamental duty to take every possible step, *ad hoc* or long term, to save the country from downfall and society from misery, apathy, and self-destruction. There is no other way to that goal than by reforming the state and the economy on the basis of democracy and universal public initiative.

We are fully aware that Polish society expects us to serve in such a way as to enable people to live in peace. The nation would not forgive anyone for treason against the ideals that brought Solidarity into existence. The nation would not forgive anyone's acts, even motivated by the best of reasons, if they result in bloodshed and in the destruction of our spiritual and material achievements. That awareness commands us to realize our ideals gradually, in such a way as to win public support for each consecutive task.

Responsibility compels us to see the system of powers that emerged in Europe after the Second World War. We want to continue the work of the great change, initiated by us, without violating international alliances. They must obtain better guarantees than those to date. Inspired by the profound feeling of dignity, patriotism, and its traditions, our nation can be a valuable partner only when it assumes obligations voluntarily and consciously.

The country's present situation has confronted us with the need to draw up a program with a different scope. This must be primarily a program for fast actions necessary to pass through the coming difficult winter season. At the same time, it must also be a program for an economic reform that is not to be postponed, a program for social policy and for reforming the country's public life, and a program for the path to a self-governing republic. [Sections III, IV, and V have been omitted.]

VI

SELF-GOVERNING REPUBLIC

Thesis 19: Pluralism of views and social, political, and cultural pluralism should be the foundation of democracy in the self-governing republic.

1. Public life in Poland requires profound and comprehensive reforms which should result in a permanent introduction of the principles of self-government, democracy, and pluralism. This is why we will seek both to transform the structure of the state and to create and support independent and self-governing institutions in all spheres of social life. Only such a direction of changes will ensure the agreement of the organization of public life with the needs of the human being, society's ambitions and the Poles' national aspirations. These changes are also necessary to overcome the economic crisis. We regard pluralism, democratization of the state, and the opportunity to make full use of constitutional freedoms as the basic guarantee that the working people's toil and sacrifices will not be once again wasted.

2. Our union is open to cooperation with various social movements, above all with the other unions that were set up after August 1980 and belong to the common

movement of Solidarity—the Independent Self-governing Trade Union of Private Farmers, the Independent Self-governing Trade Union of Artisans, the Independent Self-governing Trade Union of Private Transport Drivers, and the independent, self-governing trade unions of those groups of employees who, because of the regulations in force, have not been able to join Solidarity. These regulations should be changed. The freedom to form trade unions and the employee's freedom to choose his trade union is of fundamental importance in Poland today. Hence we attach the greatest importance to the trade union law, which should guarantee these freedoms.

3. Our union has close links with the Patronat, the Independent Union of Students, with the independent scout movements, and other organizations that are helping implement the August agreements and Solidarity's statutory tasks.[3]

These organizations and associations are meeting difficulties in their activities and in obtaining registration. This is why we think it necessary to pass a new law on associations to ensure the full freedom of citizens to form associations.

4. We take the view that the principles of pluralism must be applied in political life. Our union will support and protect civic initiatives whose aim is to present to society various political, economic, and social programs and to form organizations in order to implement such programs. On the other hand, we are against the notion that our union's statutory authorities should form organizations, the character of which is that of political parties.

5. Our union professes the principle of pluralism in the trade union movement and sees the possibility for loyally coexisting with other trade unions.

6. Pluralism will always be threatened if we fail to carry through an overall reform of the penal law—a reform of the general rules of punishment and, in particular, of those regulations of the penal law and other penal decrees that were or can be applied to smother civil freedoms.

[3]The Patronat was a Catholic institution that "extended educational and financial help to prisoners and their families, and helped 'resocialize' them after their release from prison." See Joanna M. Preibisz, *Polish Dissident Publications: An Annotated Bibliography* (New York: Praeger, 1982), pp. 57–58.

36

Jaruzelski Declares Martial Law

Wojciech Jaruzelski

December 13, 1981

Citizens of the Polish People's Republic!

I address you today as a soldier and as the head of the government of Poland. I address you on matters of paramount importance.

Our country stands at the edge of an abyss.

The achievements of many generations, the Polish house raised from the ashes, are collapsing. The structures of the state are failing to operate. Fresh blows are continuously being dealt to the flagging economy. The people are finding it increasingly difficult to bear the burden of living conditions.

Distressing lines of division run through every workplace and through many Polish homes. The atmosphere of interminable conflict, controversy, and hatred is sowing mental devastation and mutilating the traditions of tolerance. Strikes, strike alerts, and protest actions have become the rule. Even schoolchildren are being drawn in. Yesterday evening, sit-ins were being staged in many public buildings. Calls are heard for a physical showdown with "the Reds," with people of differing views. Acts of intimidation, threats, and moral lynching, as well as direct violence, are multiplying.

A wave of audacious offenses, assaults, and burglaries has swept across the country. Growing fortunes running into millions of zlotys are being made by leaders of the economic underworld. Chaos and demoralization have assumed disastrous proportions. The nation has reached the limits of mental endurance. Many people have been seized by despair.

A national catastrophe is no longer days but only hours away.

How long can one wait for reason to prevail? How long can the hand extended in accord be met with a clenched fist? I say this with heavy heart, with enormous bitterness. It could have been different in our country. It should have been different.

Any further continuation of the present state of affairs would inevitably lead to catastrophe, to complete chaos, to poverty and hunger. The severe winter could multiply the damage and claim many victims, especially among the weakest, whom we are most anxious to protect.

In this situation, inactivity would be a crime toward the nation. We have to say: That is enough.

Reprinted from Robert Maxwell, ed., *Jaruzelski: Prime Minister of Poland* (Oxford, England: Pergamon Press, 1985), pp. 28–30.

The road to confrontation, which has been openly forecast by Solidarity leaders, must be avoided and obstructed. It is today, precisely, that this must be announced, when we know the date of imminent, mass political demonstrations, some of them in the center of Warsaw, to be organized in connection with the anniversary of the December events.[1] That tragedy must never be repeated. We must not, we have no right to, permit the projected demonstrations to become the spark which could ignite the whole country. The nation's instinct for self-preservation must be allowed to take control; the hands of the troublemakers must be tied before they push the homeland into the abyss of fracticidal warfare.

The burden of responsibility which falls upon me at this dramatic moment in Polish history is great. It is my duty to shoulder this responsibility, for what is at stake is the future of Poland, for which my generation fought on all the war fronts and to which it gave the best years of its life.

I hereby announce that today a Military Council of National Salvation (WRON) has been constituted.

In conformity with the provisions of the constitution, at midnight tonight the Council of State proclaimed martial law throughout the whole country.

---

[1] "The December events" refers to the mass protests of December 1970 over food prices that led to the resignation of Gomułka and the coming to power of Gierek.

Central Europe

Outside Poland, politics in the other East European countries was relatively un-
eventful as the 1970s turned into the 1980s. Even in Yugoslavia, where Tito died in
the spring of 1980 at the age of eighty-eight, the transition to the post-Tito period
seemed to go smoothly. When Leonid Brezhnev died in 1982, he was not replaced
by young reformers but by two semi-invalids, both of whom died a little more than a
year after taking office. In these static circumstances, in which "normalization"
seemed normal, a nostalgia began to develop for the Austro-Hungarian Empire in
those parts of the region that formerly had been part of that empire. Milan Kun-
dera, who now lives in France, has absolutely no interest in returning to the kitsch
of Hapsburg times, nor is he favorably disposed to modern kitsch, but one of the
most widely read and influential articles of the pre-Gorbachev 1980s was his
discouraged effort to suggest that the postwar tragedy of Central Europe was part
of a larger European loss of direction and meaning. The version reprinted here is
somewhat condensed.

37

The Tragedy of Central Europe

Milan Kundera
April 26, 1984

In November 1956, the director of the Hungarian News Agency, shortly before his office was flattened by artillery fire, sent a telex to the entire world with a desperate message announcing that the Russian attack against Budapest had begun. The dispatch ended with these words: "We are going to die for Hungary and for Europe."

What did this sentence mean? It certainly meant that the Russian tanks were endangering Hungary and with it Europe itself. But in what sense was Europe in danger? Were the Russian tanks about to push past the Hungarian borders and into the West? No. The director of the Hungarian News Agency meant that the Russians, in attacking Hungary, were attacking Europe itself. He was ready to die so that Hungary might remain Hungary and European.

Even if the sense of the sentence seems clear, it continues to intrigue us. Actually, in France, in America, one is accustomed to thinking that what was at stake during the invasion was neither Hungary nor Europe but a political regime. One would never have said that Hungary as such had been threatened; still less would one ever understand why a Hungarian, faced with his own death, addressed Europe. When Solzhenitsyn denounces communist oppression, does he invoke Europe as a fundamental value worth dying for?

No. "To die for one's country *and* for Europe"—that is a phrase that could not be thought in Moscow or Leningrad; it is precisely the phrase that could be thought in Budapest or Warsaw.

In Central Europe, the eastern border of the West, everyone has always been particularly sensitive to the dangers of Russian might. And it's not just the Poles. Frantisek Palacky, the great historian and the figure most representative of Czech politics in the nineteenth century, wrote in 1848 a famous letter to the revolutionary parliament of Frankfurt in which he justified the continued existence of the Hapsburg Empire as the only possible rampart against Russia, against "this power which, having already reached an enormous size today, is now augmenting its force beyond the reach of any Western country." Palacky warned of Russia's imperial ambitions; it aspired to become a "universal monarchy," which means it sought

Reprinted from Milan Kundera, "The Tragedy of Central Europe," trans. Edmund White, *The New York Review of Books*, April 26, 1984, pp. 33–38, by permission of Milan Kundera.

world domination. "A Russian universal monarchy," Palacky wrote, "would be an immense and indescribable disaster, an immeasurable and limitless disaster."

Central Europe, according to Palacky, ought to be a family of equal nations, each of which—treating the others with mutual respect and secure in the protection of a strong, unified state—would also cultivate its own individuality. And this dream, although never fully realized, would remain powerful and influential. Central Europe longed to be a condensed version of Europe itself in all its cultural variety, a small arch-European Europe, a reduced model of Europe made up of nations conceived according to one rule: the greatest variety within the smallest space. How could Central Europe not be horrified facing a Russia founded on the opposite principle: the smallest variety within the greatest space?

Indeed, nothing could be more foreign to Central Europe and its passion for variety than Russia: uniform, standardizing, centralizing, determined to transform every nation of its empire (the Ukrainians, the Belorússians, the Armenians, the Latvians, the Lithuanians, and others) into a single Russian people (or, as is more commonly expressed in this age of generalized verbal mystification, into a "single Soviet people").

And so, again: Is communism the negation of Russian history or its fulfillment?

Certainly it is both its negation (the negation, for example, of its religiosity) *and* its fulfillment (the fulfillment of its centralizing tendencies and its imperial dreams).

Seen from within Russia, this first aspect—the aspect of its discontinuity—is the more striking. From the point of view of the enslaved countries, the second aspect—that of its continuity—is felt more powerfully.

But am I being too absolute in contrasting Russia and Western civilization? Isn't Europe, though divided into east and west, still a single entity anchored in ancient Greece and Judeo-Christian thought?

Of course. Moreover, during the entire nineteenth century, Russia, attracted to Europe, drew closer to it. And the fascination was reciprocated. Rilke claimed that Russia was his spiritual homeland, and no one has escaped the impact of the great Russian novels, which remain an integral part of the common European cultural legacy.

Yes, all this is true; the cultural betrothal between the two Europes remains a great and unforgettable memory. But it is no less true that Russian communism vigorously reawakened Russia's old anti-Western obsessions and turned it brutally against Europe.

But Russia isn't my subject and I don't want to wander into its immense complexities, about which I'm not especially knowledgeable. I want simply to make this point once more: On the eastern border of the West—more than anywhere else—Russia is seen not just as one more European power but as a singular civilization, an *other* civilization.

This is why the countries in Central Europe feel that the change in their destiny that occurred after 1945 is not merely a political catastrophe: It is also an attack on their civilization. The deep meaning of their resistance is the struggle to preserve their identity—or, to put it another way, to preserve their Westernness.

There are no longer any illusions about the regimes of Russia's satellite countries. But what we forget is their essential tragedy: These countries have vanished from the map of the West.

Why has this disappearance remained invisible? We can locate the cause in Central Europe itself.

The history of the Poles, the Czechs, the Slovaks, the Hungarians has been turbulent and fragmented. Their traditions of statehood have been weaker and less continuous than those of the larger European nations. Boxed in by the Germans on one side and the Russians on the other, the nations of Central Europe have used up their strength in the struggle to survive and to preserve their languages. Since they have never been entirely integrated into the consciousness of Europe, they have remained the least known and the most fragile part of the West—hidden, even further, by the curtain of their strange and scarcely accessible languages.

The Austrian empire had the great opportunity of making Central Europe into a strong, unified state. But the Austrians, alas, were divided between an arrogant Pan-German nationalism and their own Central European mission. They did not succeed in building a federation of equal nations, and their failure has been the misfortune of the whole of Europe. Dissatisfied, the other nations of Central Europe blew apart their empire in 1918, without realizing that in spite of its inadequacies it was irreplaceable. After the First World War, Central Europe was therefore transformed into a region of small, weak states, whose vulnerability ensured first Hitler's conquest and ultimately Stalin's triumph. Perhaps for this reason, in the European memory these countries always seem to be the source of dangerous trouble.

And, to be frank, I feel that the error made by Central Europe was owing to what I call the "ideology of the Slavic world." I say "ideology" advisedly, for it is only a piece of political mystification invented in the nineteenth century. The Czechs (in spite of the severe warnings of their most respected leaders) loved to brandish naively their "Slavic ideology" as a defense against German aggressiveness. The Russians, on the other hand, enjoyed making use of it to justify their own imperial ambitions. "The Russians like to label everything Russian as Slavic, so that later they can label everything Slavic as Russian," the great Czech writer Karel Havlicek declared in 1844, trying to warn his compatriots against their silly and ignorant enthusiasm for Russia. It was ignorant because the Czechs, for a thousand years, have never had any direct contact with Russia. In spite of their linguistic kinship, the Czechs and the Russians have never shared a common *world:* neither a common history nor a common culture. The relationship between the Poles and the Russians, though, has never been anything less than a struggle of life and death.

Joseph Conrad was always irritated by the label "Slavic soul" that people loved to slap on him and his books because of his Polish origins, and, about sixty years ago, he wrote that "nothing could be more alien to what is called in the literary world the 'Slavic spirit' than the Polish temperament with its chivalric devotion to moral constraints and its exaggerated respect for individual rights." (How well I understand him! I, too, know of nothing more ridiculous than this cult of obscure depths, this noisy and empty sentimentality of the "Slavic soul" that is attributed to me from time to time!)

Nevertheless, the idea of a Slavic world is a commonplace of world historiography. The division of Europe after 1945—which united this supposed Slavic world (including the poor Hungarians and Romanians whose language is not, of course, Slavic—but why bother over trifles?)—has therefore seemed almost like a natural solution.

So is it the fault of Central Europe that the West hasn't even noticed its disappearance?

Not entirely. At the beginning of our century, Central Europe was, despite its political weakness, a great cultural center, perhaps the greatest. And, admittedly, while the importance of Vienna, the city of Freud and Mahler, is readily acknowledged today, its importance and originality make little sense unless they are seen against the background of the other countries and cities that together participated in, and contributed creatively to, the culture of Central Europe. If the school of Schönberg founded the twelve-tone system, the Hungarian Béla Bartók, one of the greatest musicians of the twentieth century, knew how to discover the last original possibility in music based on the tonal principle. With the work of Kafka and Hasek, Prague created the great counterpart in the novel to the work of the Viennese Musil and Broch. The cultural dynamism of the non-German-speaking countries was intensified even more after 1918, when Prague offered the world the innovations of structuralism and the Prague Linguistic Circle. And in Poland the great trinity of Witold Gombrowicz, Bruno Schulz, and Stanislas Witkiewicz anticipated the European modernism of the 1950s, notably the so-called theater of the absurd.

A question arises: Was this entire creative explosion just a coincidence of geography? Or was it rooted in a long tradition, a shared past? Or, to put it another way: Does Central Europe constitute a true cultural configuration with its own history? And if such a configuration exists, can it be defined geographically? What are its borders?

It would be senseless to try to draw its borders exactly. Central Europe is not a state: It is a culture or a fate. Its borders are imaginary and must be drawn and redrawn with each new historical situation.

Central Europe therefore cannot be defined and determined by political frontiers (which are inauthentic, always imposed by invasions, conquests, and occupations), but by the great common situations that reassemble peoples, regroup them in ever new ways along the imaginary and ever-changing boundaries that mark a realm inhabited by the same memories, the same problems and conflicts, the same common tradition.

Sigmund Freud's parents came from Poland, but young Sigmund spent his childhood in Moravia, in present-day Czechoslovakia. Edmund Husserl and Gustav Mahler also spent their childhoods there. The Viennese novelist Joseph Roth had his roots in Poland. The great Czech poet Julius Zeyer was born in Prague to a German-speaking family; it was his own choice to become Czech. The mother tongue of Hermann Kafka, on the other hand, was Czech, while his son Franz took up German. The key figure in the Hungarian revolt of 1956, the writer Tibor Déry, came from a German-Hungarian family, and my dear friend Danilo Kis, the excellent novelist, is Hungario-Yugoslav. What a tangle of national destinies among even the most representative figures of each country!

And all of the names I've just mentioned are those of Jews. Indeed, no other part of the world has been so deeply marked by the influence of Jewish genius. Aliens everywhere and everywhere at home, lifted above national quarrels, the Jews in the twentieth century were the principal cosmopolitan, integrating element in Central Europe. They were its intellectual cement, a condensed version of its spirit, creators of its spiritual unity. That's why I love the Jewish heritage and cling to it with as much passion and nostalgia as though it were my own.

Another thing makes the Jewish people so precious to me: In their destiny the fate of Central Europe seems to be concentrated, reflected, and to have found its symbolic image. What is Central Europe? An uncertain zone of small nations between Russia and Germany. I underscore the words: *small nation*. Indeed, what are the Jews if not a small nation, *the* small nation par excellence? The only one of all the small nations of all time which has survived empires and the devastating march of History.

But what is a small nation? I offer you my definition: The small nation is one whose very existence may be put in question at any moment; a small nation can disappear and it knows it. A French, a Russian, or an English man is not used to asking questions about the very survival of his nation. His anthems speak only of grandeur and eternity. The Polish anthem, however, starts with the verse: "Poland has not yet perished. . . ."

Central Europe as a family of small nations has its own vision of the world, a vision based on a deep distrust of history. History, that goddess of Hegel and Marx, that incarnation of reason that judges us and arbitrates our fate—that is the history of conquerers. The people of Central Europe are not conquerers. They cannot be separated from European history; they cannot exist outside it; but they represent the wrong side of this history; they are its victims and outsiders. It's this disabused view of history that is the source of their culture, of their wisdom, of the "nonserious spirit" that mocks grandeur and glory. "Never forget that only in opposing History as such can we resist the history of our own day." I would love to engrave this sentence by Witold Gombrowicz above the entry gate to Central Europe.

Thus it was in this region of small nations who have "not yet perished" that Europe's vulnerability, all of Europe's vulnerability, was more clearly visible before anywhere else. Actually, in our modern world where power has a tendency to become more and more concentrated in the hands of a few big countries, *all* European nations run the risk of becoming small nations and of sharing their fate. In this sense the destiny of Central Europe anticipates the destiny of Europe in general, and its culture assumes an enormous relevance.

Today, all of Central Europe has been subjugated by Russia with the exception of little Austria, which, more by chance than necessity, has retained its independence, but ripped out of its Central European setting, it has lost most of its individual character and all of its importance. The disappearance of the cultural home of Central Europe was certainly one of the greatest events of the century for all of Western civilization. So, I repeat my question: How could it possibly have gone unnoticed and unnamed?

The answer is simple: Europe hasn't noticed the disappearance of its cultural home because Europe no longer perceives its unity as a cultural unity.

In fact, what is European unity based on?

In the Middle Ages, it was based on a shared religion. In the modern era, in which the medieval God has been changed into a *Deus absconditus* [hidden God], religion bowed out, giving way to culture, which became the expression of the supreme values by which European humanity understood itself, defined itself, identified itself as European.

Now it seems that another change is taking place in our century, as important as the one that divided the Middle Ages from the modern era. Just as God long ago gave way to culture, culture in turn is giving way.

But to what and to whom? What realm of supreme values will be capable of uniting Europe? Technical feats? The marketplace? The mass media? (Will the great poet be replaced by the great journalist?) Or by politics? But by which politics? The right or the left? Is there a discernible shared ideal that still exists above this Manichaeanism of the left and the right that is as stupid as it is insurmountable? Will it be the principle of tolerance, respect for the beliefs and ideas of other people? But won't this tolerance become empty and useless if it no longer protects a rich creativity or a strong set of ideas? Or should we understand the abdication of culture as a sort of deliverance, to which we should ecstatically abandon ourselves? Or will the *Deus absconditus* return to fill the empty space and reveal himself? I don't know, I know nothing about it. I think I know only that culture has bowed out.

The last direct personal experience of the West that Central European countries remember is the period from 1918 to 1938. Their picture of the West, then, is of the West in the past, of a West in which culture had not yet entirely bowed out.

With this in mind, I want to stress a significant circumstance: The Central European revolts were not nourished by the newspapers, radio, or television—that is, by the "media." They were prepared, shaped, realized by novels, poetry, theater, cinema, historiography, literary reviews, popular comedy and cabaret, philosophical discussions—that is, by culture. The mass media—which, for the French and Americans, are indistinguishable from whatever the West today is meant to be — played no part in these revolts (since the press and television were completely under state control).

That's why, when the Russians occupied Czechoslovakia, they did everything possible to destroy Czech culture. This destruction had three meanings: First, it destroyed the center of the opposition; second, it undermined the identity of the nation, enabling it to be more easily swallowed up by Russian civilization; third, it put a violent end to the modern era, the era in which culture still represented the realization of supreme values.

This third consequence seems to me the most important. In effect, totalitarian Russian civilization is the radical negation of the modern West, the West created four centuries ago at the dawn of the modern era: the era founded on the authority of the thinking, doubting individual, and on an artistic creation that expressed his uniqueness. The Russian invasion has thrown Czechoslovakia into a "postcultural" era and left it defenseless and naked before the Russian army and the omnipresent state television.

While still shaken by this triply tragic event which the invasion of Prague represented, I arrived in France and tried to explain to French friends the massacre of culture that had taken place after the invasion: "Try to imagine! All of the literary and cultural reviews were liquidated! Every one, without exception! That never happened before in Czech history, not even under the Nazi occupation during the war."

Then my friends would look at me indulgently with an embarrassment that I understood only later. When all the reviews in Czechoslovakia were liquidated, the entire nation knew it, and was in a state of anguish because of the immense impact of the event. If all the reviews in France or England disappeared, no one would notice it, not even their editors. In Paris, even in a completely cultivated milieu, during dinner parties people discuss television programs, not reviews. For culture has already bowed out. Its disappearance, which we experienced in Prague as a catastrophe, a shock, a tragedy, is perceived in Paris as something banal and insignificant, scarcely visible, a nonevent.

After the destruction of the Austrian empire, Central Europe lost its ramparts. Didn't it lose its soul after Auschwitz, which swept the Jewish nation off its map? And after having been torn away from Europe in 1945, does Central Europe still exist?

Yes, its creativity and its revolts suggest that it has "not yet perished." But if to live means to exist in the eyes of those we love, then Central Europe no longer exists. More precisely: in the eyes of its beloved Europe, Central Europe is just a part of the Soviet empire and nothing more, nothing more.

And why should this surprise us? By virtue of its political system, Central Europe is the East; by virtue of its cultural history, it is the West. But since Europe itself is in the process of losing its own cultural identity, it perceives in Central Europe nothing but a political regime; put another way, it sees in Central Europe only Eastern Europe.

Central Europe, therefore, should fight not only against its big oppressive neighbor but also against the subtle, relentless pressure of time, which is leaving the era of culture in its wake. That's why in Central European revolts there is something conservative, nearly anachronistic: They are desperately trying to restore the past, the past of culture, the past of the modern era. It is only in that period, only in a world that maintains a cultural dimension, that Central Europe can still defend its identity, still be seen for what it is.

The real tragedy for Central Europe, then, is not Russia but Europe: this Europe that represented a value so great that the director of the Hungarian News Agency was ready to die for it, and for which he did indeed die. Behind the Iron Curtain, he did not suspect that the times had changed and that in Europe itself Europe was no longer experienced as a value. He did not suspect that the sentence he was sending by telex beyond the borders of his flat country would seem outmoded and would not be understood.

The Return of Solidarity

As the 1980s ended, the full impact of the normalization process imposed by Jaruzelski in 1981 became apparent. Rather than containing the opposition, the necessity to crush it by force demonstrated with utmost clarity the bankruptcy of the regime. Jaruzelski's policy, after lifting martial law, was to find some way that he could co-opt the leaders of Solidarity while at the same time controlling them. The climax of this process came in 1989 with the convening of a roundtable discussion of the main parties, led by the Communists and by Solidarity, in which the antagonists worked out an electoral arrangement whereby the Communists would retain their domination but Solidarity would have a voice in the government. The Communists were to control the lower house of the legislature, and the upper house would be elected freely. Before the election—held in June 1989 and preceded by a chaotic but vigorous campaign—no one predicted the outcome: an almost complete victory of the Solidarity elements. In addition, no one predicted that the previously completely subservient "opposition" parties, which the Communists had permitted to operate under their control since the 1940s, would see the handwriting on the wall and suddenly switch sides to Solidarity. The stunning result was the creation in September 1989 of a government dominated by Solidarity and its allies.

One reason this could happen was that Solidarity always pursued a policy of realistic politics, rather than succumbing to the radical elements within it that sought to push for confrontation. Lech Wałęsa was the charismatic leader who fought for such a policy, but many others favored it as well. In the following reading, for example, Adam Michnik, active at the center of oppositionist politics since his leadership of the student strikes of 1968, recommends that Solidarity pursue a politics of accommodation, even though he is writing from prison during the period of normalization.

In the second reading, the new prime minister of Poland, Tadeusz Mazowiecki, a former Catholic activist and Solidarity ally, presents his vision of the tasks that lay ahead in his first speech on becoming Poland's first non-Communist prime minister in fifty years.

38

Letter from Gdańsk Prison

Adam Michnik

1985

Why did Solidarity renounce violence? This question returned time and again in my conversations with foreign observers. I would like to answer it now. People who claim that the use of force in the struggle for freedom is necessary must first prove that in a given situation it will be effective and that force, when it is used, will not transform the idea of liberty into its opposite.

No one in Poland is able to prove today that violence will help us to dislodge Soviet troops from Poland and to remove the communists from power. The U.S.S.R. has such enormous military power that confrontation is simply unthinkable. In other words, we have no guns. Napoleon, upon hearing a similar reply, gave up asking further questions. However, Napoleon was above all interested in military victories and not building democratic, pluralistic societies. We, by contrast, cannot leave it at that.

In our reasoning, pragmatism is inseparably intertwined with idealism. Taught by history, we suspect that by using force to storm the existing Bastilles we shall unwittingly build new ones. It is true that social change is almost always accompanied by force. But it is not true that social change is merely a result of the violent collision of various forces. Above all, social changes follow from a confrontation of different moralities and visions of social order. Before the violence of rulers clashes with the violence of their subjects, values and systems of ethics clash inside human minds. Only when the old ideas of the rulers lose this moral duel will the subjects reach for force—sometimes. This is what happened in the French Revolution and the Russian Revolution—two examples cited in every debate as proof that revolutionary violence is preceded by a moral breakdown of the old regime. But both examples lose their meaning when they are reduced to such compact notions, in which the Encyclopedists are paired with the destruction of the Bastille, and the success of radical ideologies in Russia is paired with the storming of the Winter Palace. An authentic event is reduced to a sterile scheme.

In order to understand the significance of these revolutions, one must remember Jacobin and Bolshevik terror, the guillotines of the sans-culottes, and the guns of the commissars. Without reflection on the mechanisms in victorious revolutions that gave birth to terror, it is impossible to even pose the fundamental dilemma facing contemporary freedom movements. Historical awareness of the possible consequences of revolutionary violence must be etched into any program of struggle for freedom. The experience of being corrupted by terror must be imprinted upon the consciousness of everyone who belongs to a freedom movement. Otherwise, as Simone Weil wrote, freedom will again become a refugee from the camp of the victors.

Solidarity's program and ethos are inextricably tied to this strategy. Revolutionary terror has always been justified by a vision of an ideal society. In the name of this vision, Jacobin guillotines and Bolshevik execution squads carried out their unceasing, gruesome work. The road to God's Kingdom on Earth led through rivers of blood.

Solidarity has never had a vision of an ideal society. It wants to live and let live. Its ideals are closer to the American Revolution than to the French. Its thinking about goals is similar to that of the resistance against Franco in Spain or against the "black colonels" in Greece; it is unlike the thinking of those who strive to attain doctrinal goals. The ethics of Solidarity, with its consistent rejection of the use of force, has a lot in common with the idea of nonviolence as espoused by Gandhi and Martin Luther King, Jr. But it is not an ethic representative of pacifist movements.

Pacifism as a mass movement aims to avoid suffering; pacifists often say that no cause is worth suffering or dying for. The ethics of Solidarity are based on an opposite premise: that there are causes worth suffering and dying for. Gandhi and King died for the same cause as the miners in Wujek who rejected the belief that it is better to remain a willing slave than to become a victim of murder.[1] In this belief Solidarity activists consciously reject the idea of adhering to doctrinal consistency at all cost. Following the teachings of the Polish pope—and hating war the way he does—they will nevertheless admit the possibility of armed defense of freedom against aggressive despotism. It was no accident that one of the most prominent creators of contemporary Polish culture (Leszek Kołakowski) wrote an essay titled "In Praise of Inconsistency."

Having said this, I should add that Solidarity has not been wholly immune to totalitarian temptations. Organized as a social movement struggling against the totalitarian state, composed of people who grew up in the Leading System and were shaped by its totalitarian structures, Solidarity has always been torn between trying to influence administrative decisions and attempting to restrict the omnipotence of the state. In fact, this conflict was the seed of a dramatic dilemma that faced the movement: whether it should seek to become an alternative to the authorities or instead renounce such aspirations and concentrate on a struggle to limit the scope of their power. Solidarity, and every other freedom movement in the communist system, will have to confront this dilemma in the days to come. The future of postcommunist societies will depend on how it is resolved. The struggle for state power must lead to the use of force; yet in the struggle for a self-governing republic,

---

[1]Three days after the declaration of martial law, the police fired on protesting strikers at the Wujek mines and killed several of them.

according to the resolution passed at the memorable Solidarity congress in Gdańsk, the use of force must be renounced.

But ethics cannot substitute for a political program. We must therefore think about the future of Polish–Russian relations. Our thinking about this key question must be open; it should consider many different possibilities. Thus we must not rule out the possibility of a change in Soviet foreign policy that would bring compromise within the realm of the attainable. Let us remember that compromise between the Soviet Union and Finland was preceded by a war between these two countries.

The Soviet state has a new leader; he is a symbol of transition from one generation to the next within the Soviet elite. This change may offer an opportunity, since Mikhail Gorbachev has not yet become a prisoner of his own decisions. No one can rule out the possibility that an impulse for reform will spring from the top of the hierarchy of power. This is exactly what happened in the time of Alexander II and, a hundred years later, under Khrushchev. Reform is always possible, even in the face of resistance by the old apparatus. Leaders of the Kremlin may wish to take on the challenge of modernity; they may begin searching for a new model of relations with Soviet satellites. Polish political thought must be prepared for this contingency. Phobias and anti-Russian emotions provide no substitute.

No one can be a prophet in his own house. Rationally, it is possible only to say that no source of tensions has yet been eliminated and that none of the critical problems has been solved. Normalization, in the sense of reaching an understanding, turned out to be an illusion. Normalization as pacification became an unmitigated disaster. So what can now happen?

The "fundamentalists" say, no compromises. Talking about compromise, dialogue, or understanding demobilizes public opinion, pulls the wool over the eyes of the public, spreads illusions. Wałęsa's declarations about readiness for dialogue were often severely criticized from this point of view.

I do not share the fundamentalist point of view. It is true that a compromise cannot be achieved by begging and that it is futile to explain to the communists why a compromise would be a sensible solution. This is why the appeals by "neo-realists" are so pitiful and empty; their authors should beware of crossing the thin line that divides political speculation from collaboration. When Wałęsa declares the need for compromise he unmasks the intentions of the authorities; when the same is being said by a neorealist who avoids mentioning the word *Solidarity* like the plague, he sends word to the authorities of his own readiness to take part in murdering our union.

The logic of fundamentalism precludes any attempt to find compromise, even in the future. It harbors not only the belief that communists are ineducable but also a certainty that they are unable to behave rationally, even in critical situations—that, in other words, they are condemned to suicidal obstinacy.

This is not so obvious to me. Historical experience shows that communists were sometimes forced by circumstances to behave rationally and to agree to compromises. Thus the strategy of understanding must not be cast aside. We should not assume that a bloody confrontation is inevitable and, consequently, rule out the possibility of evolutionary, bloodless change. This should be avoided all the more inasmuch as democracy is rarely born from bloody upheavals. We should be clear in our minds about this: The continuing conflict may transform itself into either a dialogue or an explosion. The TKK and Wałęsa are doing everything in their power to make dialogue possible.[2] Their chances of success will be greater if the level of self-organization of independent Polish society increases. For street lynchings, angry crowds are enough; compromise demands an organized society.

[2]Solidarity activists founded the underground Temporary Coordinating Committee (TKK) a few months after the declaration of martial law, in an effort to keep the movement alive after the government imprisoned many of its leaders. Despite this disadvantage, underground Solidarity was phenomenally successful in maintaining its organization and especially in distributing publications of all kinds, including videotapes. For example, its newspaper *Tygodnik Mazowsze*, which came out once a week in an edition of fifty thousand copies, did not miss a single issue.

39

A Solidarity Government Takes Power

Tadeusz Mazowiecki

August 24, 1989

Mr. Speaker, High Chamber:

I want to form a government capable of acting for the good of society, the nation, and the state. Today such a task can be undertaken only by a government open for cooperation of all forces represented in parliament and based on new political principles. The history of our country is accelerating. It has happened due to a society which does not agree to continuing life as it has been until now. One has to return to Poland the mechanisms of normal political life. The transition is difficult, but it does not have to cause shaking. On the contrary, it will be a path to normalcy. The principle of struggle, which sooner or later leads to elimination of one's opponent, must be replaced by a principle of partnership. We will not pass from the totalitarian system to [a] democratic one in any other way. The current philosophy of the state must be changed. It cannot take care of everything and guarantee everything. It should facilitate and regulate activities. The most important role for the government and administration at this moment is opening possibilities for common actions and individual actions.

I want to be the prime minister of all Poles, regardless of their views and convictions, which must not be a criterion for dividing citizens into categories. I will undertake efforts so that the principles of constructing the government will be clear to all. I am especially obliged to do that for Solidarity. Helpful will be the understanding of the church, which has always stood in defense of human rights and has felt the worries of the nation as its own. The church was and is a stabilizing force in Poland. The future government must be truthful to society. It must also create mechanisms which will allow it to hear the voice of public opinion. We will pass certain problems to its judgment. If sacrifices are necessary, all must know their sense, understand them, and be able to express their opinions on the problems occurring.

High Chamber,

The most important issue for society is the condition of the national economy, which now has to be considered critical. How bad it is and why—already everything has been said about it. The problem is how to get out of it. I am fully aware of the great effort that repairing the economy will require of the new government and everybody. The long-term strategic goal of government's activities will be restoring to Poland economic institutions long known and tested. I understand by this a return

Reprinted from *Miami Herald,* August 27, 1989, by permission of the Associated Press.

to a market-oriented economy and a role for the state similar to that in economically developed countries. Poland cannot afford ideological experiments any longer.

Any changes, on which the nation's prospects and citizens' welfare depend, are blocked today by inflation and the lack of an economic balance manifested by poor market supplies and queues, a state budget deficit, and an unbalanced balance of payments. Restoring equilibrium and stifling inflation is a task of utmost economic importance, as well as political and social significance. Disequilibrium and inflation, increasing social tensions, can undermine the Polish march to freedom. With high inflation there can be no discussion about creating normal working conditions for the nation, on which its material existence mainly will depend.

The government, sensing an absolute and urgent need to challenge inflation, will prepare a package of required measures, utilizing what has been tried so far in Poland and in other countries, as well as by referring to the experience of international experts and financial organizations. We will start without delay demonopolizing the structures serving the food market, the excessive growth of which is one of the causes of high prices and halting rural development. Struggling with inflation and restoring market balance has always and everywhere been risky for government and painful for society. Keeping in mind the effectiveness of the anti-inflation operation, the government will do everything to make it as painless as possible. One cannot promise, however, that it will not be felt at all. Nobody responsibly can make such an offer.

Poles themselves have to solve Polish problems. Our own ingenuity, work, and patience—our own effort—will determine our success. This does not mean that we are doomed to be alone in this difficult undertaking. The world is watching the transformations taking place [in Poland] with sympathy and hope. The government will aim energetically at obtaining as much economic support for Poland from the international community as possible, in all possible forms, according to existing procedures and customs. We will not apply for privileges denied others in a similar situation to ours. We will, however, expect the maximum possible support of our efforts to cure the economy. Governments by themselves do not create economic success for their nations and do not alone end economic crises. Many a government, by stifling the initiative of citizens and trying to direct everyone and everything, effectively overpowered the country economically. However, there have been and there are governments that release the economic energy dormant in talented and diligent people. My greatest wish is that the present coalition government could open to Poles the possibility of lifting up the country economically. We need efficient, economic means which will give enterprising people a feeling of security about their activity and let everyone find a moral and material sense of their work.

The problem of law and rule of law is of basic importance. For forty-five years the law has been treated cavalierly in Poland, subordinated to the current political aims. And citizens did not have a sense of freedom of conscience, that the law protects them and that it is the same for all. It is necessary to introduce the rule of law, by giving every citizen the rights accordant with international pacts, agreements, and conventions. Citizens must have a feeling of freedom, security and coparticipation. They can have such a feeling only in a law-abiding state, in which every action by authorities is based on the law and through legislation, contents and interpretation of its provisions correspond with the social feeling of justice. Only law aiming at the common good may enjoy respect and social authority. We will not form an entirely new army or police. What matters is creating legal guarantees so that everyone, including those inside those institutions, feels they serve society.

Professional administration functions effectively when appointments are based on competence and bound by loyalty to the state, not as currently by loyalty to particular parties. In relations between the government and citizens, the mass media play an irreplaceable role, especially radio and television. Today they must be pluralistic. I consider transition from a monopoly to pluralism in this field indispensable.

High Chamber,

I am convinced that Poland can fulfill an important role in the political, economic, and cultural life of Europe. The extremely difficult economic situation of the country does not bode optimistically in the field of international relations. A gap is growing in the level of civilization between Poland and societies of highly developed countries. This increases Poles' weariness, as expressed among other ways through emigration, especially by young people. Poland's friends should understand that one cannot wait until we are sinking. Economic reconstruction will serve not only our country but also the whole European community.

Europe is one, including the East as well as the West. Transformations in the Soviet Union arouse our lively sympathy. We understand their significance for the political opening in our country as well. We desire to maintain good-neighborly, friendly relations with the Soviet Union. For the first time, a chance is appearing for the relationship between our nations to be based on friendship and cooperation between the societies and not just among a single party. This is a great opportunity which cannot be wasted. We understand the significance of obligations resulting from the Warsaw Pact. To all its members, I state that the government that I will form will respect this treaty.

High Chamber,

The change in Poland's political situation stems from the fact that the new government is formed on Solidarity's initiative in agreement with the United Peasants party and the Democratic party. This is perceived as an extraordinary event in our political life. The possibility that every force in parliament could form the government must become something completely normal. The government I am forming does not assume responsibility for the legacy it inherits. However, that influences the circumstances in which we must function. We separate ourselves from the past with a thick line. We will be responsible only for what we have done to lift Poland from the present state of collapse.

I am aware that for my compatriots today the most important question is whether it could be better. We will all reply to this. The success of the activities of the future government depends on whether it will be accepted and understood by the society. All social and political forces represented in the parliament and those existing outside must define their position in the face of the new situation. It poses a challenge for everyone and especially for the young generation, which must take notice of a great opportunity to solve the challenges we face. The government will not cure anything. We must do it together. Poland will be different if everybody wants it.

New Visions in Hungary

Throughout the 1970s Hungary had a reputation as being, along with East Germany, the most successful communist state in Eastern Europe. Although János Kádár became the Hungarian leader as an agent of Soviet repression in 1956, he managed to find a separate path for Hungary on the basis of his reconciliatory motto, "Those who are not against us are for us." His New Economic Mechanism, which was supposed to permit a certain amount of privatization, did not work too well, but he restored good relations with the West, found hard-currency loans, and permitted an expansion of civil liberties. By the mid-1980s, however, Kádár's program had run its course. The Hungarian economy, though not as decrepit as the Polish and not nearly as devastated as the Romanian, was suffering under the highest per-capita debt in Eastern Europe, rising inflation, and increasing unemployment.

Under the Gorbachevian dispensation, these problems had two important political consequences. The first was the emergence of a reform movement in the party, which led not only to the deposition of Kádár but also to the capture of the party leadership by reform elements led by Imre Pozsgay. In 1989, seeking to put its communist past behind it, the party renamed itself the Hungarian Socialist party and emerged with only 30,000 members rather than the approximately 800,000 it had before its reorganization. The second was the proliferation of a enormous variety of political organizations. Most popular among the intelligentsia was the Alliance of Free Democrats, whose program called for the full-scale implementation of Western liberal politics and full integration of Hungarian industry into the international system of trade. The following excerpts from "The New Social Contract" are an early version of ideas that stimulated this movement. What the authors were attempting to do in the still-restrictive circumstances of 1987 was to find roles for both the Communist party and the opposition, by instituting a classic separation of powers among the executive (communists), legislative (opposition), and judicial (independent) branches of government. Adam Michnik proposed a similar solution for Poland in a 1989 article entitled "Their President; Our Premier."

The strongest Hungarian opposition movement at the end of the 1980s, however, was not the Alliance of Free Democrats but the Democratic Forum. The forum favored democracy but tended to be considerably more nationalistic than the Free Democrats, favoring a slower pace of privatization. Its populist wing adheres to a policy, taken from theorists of the 1930s, called the Third Way that asserts Hungary should be neither collectivist nor capitalist but a mixed system shaped by the traditions of the Hungarian past. In the following condensed article, Iván Szelényi, who does not consider himself a member of the Democratic Forum, outlines an economic strategy appropriate to the Third Way.

232

40

A New Social Contract

János Kis, Ferenc Kőszeg, and Ottilia Solt

January 1987

There is no simple solution to the Hungarian economy's present problems. It is not enough to say, as it was said in 1953, something to the effect that if the artificial forcing of investment in heavy industry were stopped, there would immediately be more for the consumers. Abandonment of the spendthrift industrial policy would adversely affect also the population in the short term. Even the best program of consolidation and growth would produce temporary unemployment and a decline of the living standard and would create tensions between social strata, industries, and districts.

What could the leadership do about these conflicts? One possible course of action would be to attempt to compensate the masses with social, national, or racial demagoguery. By launching order-restoration, mobilization, and centralization drives, in combination with political hysteria. A sort of northwestern Romania. But we see where that leads.

Another course of action would be to enforce the requirements of a market economy and to suppress with an iron hand any manifestation of society's dissatisfaction. A police state in combination with free competition, some Hungarian version of South Korea. But Hungary is not in Southeast Asia. Here the very institutions from whose grip the market has to be pried would harden back into dictatorship.

The third and final course is to proceed from the breakdown of the tacit consensus to open negotiations. A social contract, instead of a mobilizing or disarming dictatorship. Working out the compromises with the participation of those concerned.

There will be no advancement for the nation without a social contract.

Hungary last received a political program in 1956. The present authors share the opinion that history has not made obsolete the basic demands of October 1956:

- Political pluralism and representative democracy in government.
- Self-management at the workplace and local government in the settlements.
- National self-determination and neutrality in foreign policy.

Reprinted from a mimeographed version by Radio Free Europe from the special issue of *Beszélő*, no. 20, June 1987.

However, we are convinced that these demands cannot be placed on the agenda in the country's present political situation, which will probably not change significantly for a long time to come. But the conditions have improved for the similar compromise solutions that the remnants of the democratic parties and the workers' councils proposed in November 1956.

After all, what we have today it is not a defeated revolution fighting its rearguard action against a restorational regime that is settling in. The development since consolidation also counts: Mass consumption has gained acceptance; the patterns of market behavior are more acceptable than before; several collectives of Western orientation have been formed in the social sciences; the official ideology has been relaxed, and specialized knowledge has gained in prestige; and the gap between the new generation of cadres and the professional elite has narrowed. The external conditions have also improved: Hungary is more open to the West than thirty years ago; the possibility of Soviet intervention has declined; and the Soviet Union's leaders are more tolerant.

Starting out from these premises, we are considering ways to shape the growing dissatisfaction into goal-oriented political demands. We accept, must accept as given, one-party rule and certain executive prerogatives of the party. We are investigating how we could finally raise anew, within this framework, the basic political questions that have been deferred continually since the revolution's suppression.

For it is time to raise them anew.

We are proposing compromise solutions that fall short by far of what the people are aspiring for. But these compromises would produce changes perceptible already now in the relationship between the power structure and society. And their implementation would permit orderly further progress toward a democratic, autonomous, and independent Hungary.

The constitutional principle of popular sovereignty requires that supreme state power be vested in bodies elected by direct vote (Constitution, Section 2, paragraphs 2 and 4). The party's "leading role" (Section 3) limits popular sovereignty, and it must be recognized as a limitation, as an arrangement for allocating executive powers to guarantee the Soviet Union fulfillment of the country's external commitments and the social system's continuity.

The party's special role is not an obstacle to making the political system constitutional or to introducing elements of political pluralism that are protected by law, provided the party is integrated into the state's legal system.

Two basic solutions present themselves.

One of the solutions has emerged from the internal debates within political science: The Presidential Council would be abolished and replaced by a head of state who is independent of the National Assembly. Power would be divided between the head of state and the National Assembly. This was the constitutional arrangement in the Hungarian People's Republic from 1946 until 1949. The difference now would be that the party nominates the [candidate for] head of state.[1]

Under the other solution, some governing body of the party would exercise executive powers directly. It seems expedient to choose the Central Committee for this role. Among the party's permanent bodies, the Central Committee comes

---

[1]This is the solution actually adopted in 1989.

closest to the National Assembly in terms of representativeness and mode of operation. The Central Committee can be expected to make executive decisions in public session and to publish in the press its resolutions that are binding on the state administration.

The advantage of the head-of-state solution is that constitutionally it is the more simple and provides a flexible framework for the separation of the party and state, which is to be continued in future. Its drawback is that the party's governing bodies retain their opportunity to administer the state from behind the scenes.

The other solution is constitutionally more cumbersome. But it includes the statutory regulation of the party's executive powers, which we regard as a decisive advantage. Of course, a combination of the two solutions is also conceivable.

Whether the party's executive powers are vested in a head of state serving at the party leadership's pleasure or in the Central Committee, statutory definition of these prerogatives would end the illusion that the National Assembly is the sole repository of supreme state powers. But this way the legislative branch would at least exclusively possess some supreme powers.

This possibility will become reality when the National Assembly develops into a strong institution to which the government and its apparatuses are accountable.

Power to regulate fundamental legal relationships must be restored to the National Assembly.

- It must be the National Assembly's prerogative to enact regulations that affect civil rights or the interests of larger social groups. Decrees of the executive branch should not substitute for laws enacted by the National Assembly.
- Laws should not confine themselves to outlining the principles of regulation, leaving actual regulation to the executory instructions of government agencies.

The government and its apparatuses must be accountable to the National Assembly.

- The Council of Ministers could assume office only upon a vote of confidence in the National Assembly.
- The cases will have to be defined when the government must ask for a vote of confidence (for example, when the government's program, medium-range plan, annual budget or its report on the fulfillment of any of the preceding is voted down). Deputies should be able to introduce motions of no confidence in other instances as well.

The organizational and procedural prerequisites must be ensured for the emergence of a strong National Assembly.

- The Presidential Council's role as a substitute National Assembly must cease. It should not have authority to issue law decrees or to modify the laws enacted by the National Assembly. Its role should be confined to representing the state as its head, to deciding appeals for clemency, to ordering referendums, and to convening the newly elected National Assembly. This solution is in accord with the variant under which the Central Committee directly exercises the party's prerogatives. If the head of state were endowed with these prerogatives, the status of the Presidential Council would have to undergo essential change. It could not be an organ of the National Assembly, and it would be expedient to elect its president by direct popular vote.

- The National Assembly must hold more and longer sessions than are now customary.
- The National Assembly must have its own staff of experts. It needs also a staff to draft legislation, so as to end its reliance on the experts of the Ministry of Justice. Any deputy should have access to the National Assembly's experts.

The electoral system must be modified.

- We need a national list of candidates one order of magnitude larger than at present. The voluntary public, professional, and interest-representing organizations with public-law status would enter their candidates on this list. In other words, all the organizations that are enumerated in the constitution or whose founding is regulated by separate statute. The party, too, would enter its candidates on the national list. An agreement on each organization's proportional share of candidates on the national list would be concluded through the PPF.[2]

We need an independent judiciary functioning under public scrutiny.

- Paternalistic control by the Ministry of Justice over the judiciary must cease. It should not be the ministry that nominates candidates for election as professional judges or assigns the judges to specific courts.
- The rule must be enforced that court proceedings are open to the public. Unless the judge orders a closed trial, anyone interested must be given an opportunity to be present. The openness of the trial also means that the public must not be prevented from making notes or tape recordings. The judge who fails to ensure the requirements of openness or who orders a closed trial contrary to the provisions of the law commits a disciplinary offense.
- The disciplinary code for judges must be made public. It should be possible to transfer a judge against his will and to demote or recall him (unless he has become incapable of serving on the bench) only for a disciplinary offense, but not for political reasons. It should be a disciplinary offense for a judge to violate the rules of procedure or to show partiality unscrupulously or in any other way. Any party in a case before the court should be able to institute disciplinary proceedings. If the defendant or the defense attorney (in a criminal case) institutes disciplinary proceedings, or if either of the parties or their counsel (in a civil lawsuit) does so, he may be present at the disciplinary proceedings.
- A Constitutional Court should be established as the court of last instance for deciding fundamental problems of constitutional law. The Constitutional Council of the National Assembly does not yet qualify as such a court. Its members are not professional judges, and its authority to hand down decisions is limited. It is wrong to allow only a specified circle of institutions and organizations to refer matters to the Constitutional Council; any Hungarian citizen should be able to do so. Furthermore, keeping the public informed likewise requires regulation; citizens have the right to know which statutory regulations were submitted for review of their constitutionality, what the decision was, and what were the reasons adduced. Public exposition of the minority opinion on so fundamental questions of legal principle is also warranted.

---

[2]The People's Popular Front was the official mass organization of communist Hungary. The suggestion that seats be delegated proportionally in advance is similar to the rules under which the election of 1945 was held in Hungary and under which the Poles held their election in 1989.

41

The Third Way

Iván Szelényi (translated by Iván Szelényi)
September 1989

In this article I try to achieve three tasks: First, I describe the current state of socioeconomic transformations in Eastern Europe; second, I assess alternative scenarios for the future development in this part of the world; and third, I suggest what I regard as the least risky or costly future of Eastern Europe. This future may not be all that different from what was called the Third Way by progressive social theorists during the interwar years in Hungary and other countries.

Theorists of the Third Way during the interwar years insisted that those who claim that countries in this region could choose only between a Soviet-style collectivization of agriculture or a capitalist, plantation type of transformation of the semifeudal manorial estates offered a false alternative. They argued that the proletarianization of the entire peasantry is not inevitable and that it would be possible and even desirable to transform some of the peasants into family farmers and some of the urban artisans into industrial entrepreneurs.

Those who subscribe to the Third Way today similarly give priority to the development of a domestic bourgeoisie. Today the Third Way suggests a strategy that encourages peasant-workers and workers involved in the second economy to become proper entrepreneurs. This is indeed a "Third Way," an alternative between the reform communists, who insist that the only way out of the current crisis is through the rationalizing power of large firms, and the classical liberals, who hope that Eastern Europe—by opening its windows to the fresh air of the market and inviting a massive importation of Western capital—can jump into Western Europe and become an equal partner of the countries of the European Community.

Whatever strategies we eventually pursue, one thing we know: An epoch is coming to its end. The character of the epoch that is now behind us is not that easy to define, but I call it communism, and I recommend the cautious use of the term *transition to postcommunism*, or perhaps *transition to a socialist mixed economy*, for the changes now taking place in Poland, Hungary, Czechoslovakia, Yugoslavia, and East Germany.

During the period of communism the state enjoyed a monopoly of production. The "means of production" were public property, and almost the entire population was employed by the state. Today this system is disintegrating; the importance of

Reprinted from Iván Szelényi, *Hitel*, no. 18, September 1989. Shortened English version contributed by the author.

the private sector of production is increasing; and a newly dynamic private sector is in the making.

The social structure of communist society resembled a hierarchical pyramid. At the peak of the pyramid were those whose loyalty was unquestionable and whose educational credentials were in order. At the bottom of the pyramid were the uneducated whose loyalty was in doubt. The former constituted the cadre-intellectuals, and the latter, the proletarians. But during the past few years this structure has become more complex, as a second pyramid, one with a more classlike structure, has begun to impinge on the first. At the top of this second pyramid we find the entrepreneurs, and at its bottom, the wage laborers. The majority of the Hungarian population today occupies the middle of this second pyramid, including semiproletarians, peasant-workers, part-time entrepreneurs, in short all those who have tried their luck in the second economy.

If we were to characterize the events of the past few months, the best term we could find is *embourgeoisement* or *bourgeoisification*. The process of embourgeoisement in Hungary began long before 1988, as entrepreneurs took advantage of spaces provided by the Kádár regime of the 1960s and the 1970s. But by the mid-1980s the Kádár regime gradually lost its original willingness and ability to compromise, and the petty bourgeoisie found itself facing legal and political limits more characteristic of corrupt and arbitrary Ottoman times than of modern economies. What has happened quite recently is the coming together of the process of bourgeoisification with the drive for legal–political reform. This has created more favorable circumstances than have existed since the *ausgleich* of 1867 for entering a developmental trajectory that can both build on national traditions and at the same time move Hungary toward a European model of civilization.

Restoration of the communist system, even if there is a conservative turn in the Soviet Union, does not seem to me very likely, since embourgeoisement is an organic, historical process that has already deeply transformed both the society and the economy in Hungary. Even the cadre-intelligentsia has become bourgeoisified and has lost the will to reimpose a communist system. They live in luxurious private villas furnished with antique furniture; they send their children to English-language schools; and they dream of sending these children to college in England or the United States.

In what direction will the transforming countries move? I am quite certain of one thing: The economies of postcommunist societies will be mixed systems in which the state sector will be complemented by a dynamically growing private sector, although it is impossible to tell at this point what proportions of the total economy the two sectors will have in twenty years. The main task facing these societies is the creating of a new private sector. Until recently, reformers focused on reforming the "economic mechanism," but during the past few years many economists have begun to realize the need for a transformation of ownership relations. There is no market economy without individual private property. The idea of a "socialist market economy," in which collectivist forms of ownership retain a monopoly, is unattainable. The great puzzle, therefore, is this: How is it possible to create a private sector in a society in which there is no propertied bourgeoisie and where there is no private capital?

Two alternative strategies present themselves. The first is *reprivatization,* in which public property passes into private hands. The second I call *deregulation*, which means the elimination of the government's regulation and restriction of private economic activities. The main aim of deregulation is to create spaces that will stimulate the creation of new private firms and thereby encourage dynamism in the national economy. Clearly both strategies will be used, but emphases can differ.

Reprivatization is achievable in two ways. The first way, which I call *multinational reprivatization*, is to sell public firms to foreign companies. At present in Hungary there are no restrictions on such multinational reprivatization. Foreigners, whether they be multinational concerns, former owners, or wealthy émigrés, may own 100 percent of Hungarian enterprises. Multinational reprivatization has two important advantages. First, it creates access to Western technology, managerial expertise, and contacts with the world market. Second, it has a potential for reducing Hungary's international debt. A leading Hungarian economist recommended a year ago that Hungarian firms should be offered for sale to the banks that hold Hungarian debt. Given the difficulties Hungary will have paying these debts, the banks might be willing to trade relatively inexpensive Hungarian enterprises for obligations they feel unlikely to be paid off.

The second, less adventurous, strategy of reprivatization I call *managerial reprivatization*. Those who advocate this strategy recommend transforming Hungarian state firms into Hungarian private firms. Some have recommended that since there is no private Hungarian capital to purchase these firms, they should be simply given to their managers. An advantage of this strategy is that it gives the cadre-intelligentsia—who are, after all, the managers who would become the private owners—a stake in the radical process of ownership reform. In this way the most dangerous enemies of reform in the last decade might become the most enthusiastic supporters of radical reform.

But massive and rapid reprivatization would also have serious negative consequences. In both versions of reprivatization the new managers, whether foreign concerns or Hungarian cadre-intelligentsia, will only be interested in purchasing profitable companies. Currently about half of the Hungarian economy is operating profitably, and half not. During the last budgetary year the state received 238 billion forints from state firms, and it spent 235 billion forints subsidizing state firms. For the sake of argument, let us assume that the firms that produced the 238 billion forints are privatized. What will the state do with the firms that produced the 235 billion forints in losses? If it closes down the nonprofitable firms, it may leave up to half the work force without jobs.

A South Korean–style leap to the cutting edge of capitalist competition promises to have very high social costs, which foreign investors are unlikely to pay. Foreign firms are not interested in underwriting failing East European enterprises. They have to be attracted by concessions such as low wages, low taxes, industrial peace, and no militant labor unions. Eastern Europe may have little choice but to accommodate them. To create a South Korean economic miracle, one may have to pay a South Korean political price.

The punch line is that whereas both reprivatization strategies offer certain benefits, mindless implementation of either one or both could have devastating consequences.

A third alternative, a Third Way, exists, however. In order to consider deregula-

tion as an alternative to rapid and large-scale reprivatization we may have to begin
to think in radically new ways about our developmental strategies. The Third Way
strategy will require public policies that are not merely permissive but that are
supportive. In Eastern Europe today it is not sufficient to offer equal opportunities to
private entrepreneurs and public firms. After four decades of public policies that
guaranteed a virtual monopoly to the public sector, a domestic capitalist sector can
be formed only if for one or two decades postcommunist governments adopt policies that not only permit but positively encourage domestic entrepreneurship.

The most promising development in Hungary over the last two decades has been
the evolution of a new petty bourgeoisie. In the "school of the second economy" a
large potential pool of future entrepreneurs has developed. Some half a million
Hungarian entrepreneurs already exist ready to put their skills to work if they are
permitted to do so. But today in Hungary private entrepreneurs must pay a tax of 40
percent on their profits, after which each employee pays almost half of his or her
salary in social security taxes. The postcommunist societies desperately need public
policies that encourage domestic primary accumulation. Such policies need to include long-term tax concessions, a lessening of the social security burden, encouragement of foreign trade ventures, and a more flexible credit policy. In the past East
European regimes borrowed from Western banks for public firms. Now the regimes
should negotiate loans to assist their private entrepreneurs.

The primary aim of economic policy should not be to get rid of the public sector
as fast as possible, but to deregulate with a view to creating new spaces for private
entrepreneurs. But this aim raises the question of what one will expect from the
public sector in the postcommunist system. In this regard perhaps it is not such a
devastating result that the Hungarian state received 238 billion forints from its
enterprises last year while subsidizing them with 235 billion forints. Why should it
be considered a problem that the public sector in fact covered its costs? It is the job
of the private sector to generate profits. The public sector should provide inexpensive services to the public and secure high levels of employment. If it can do that
while covering its costs, it is effective. The absurdity of the East European economies is not that its public sector only covers costs but that this public sector employs
about 95 percent of the work force, rather than 10 to 50 percent. If this public sector
were to be complemented by a dynamic private sector, a public sector that covered
its costs, even if quite large, would be an acceptable or even a good idea.

An economic policy that gives priority to deregulation over reprivatization
would reduce the public sector gradually, closing down or selling public firms only
if the emergent new private sector is able to absorb most of the resulting
unemployment.

The major shortcoming of the Third Way of deregulation is that it does not
promise the successful integration of high-technology industries into world markets.
It is a policy that would create an economy characterized by small and medium-
sized firms. Is this another version of a "small is beautiful" utopia? I think not. The
world economy has been evolving in two opposite directions. On the one hand,
economies of scale are producing massive international companies. But while this is
happening, smaller and medium-sized firms, oriented toward quality production,
have found niches in which they are proving to be perfectly viable. Is it utopian to

assume that the East European economies could enter the West European market effectively with products specifically aimed at the needs of the upper middle classes of the advanced countries? This seems to me a much more plausible formula for success than to attempt to compete with the multinational giants.

The public policy strategy of the Third Way suggests that countries in this part of the world learn how to live with being Central rather than West European. After forty years of being pushed toward the East, Poland, Hungary, and Czechoslovakia are beginning to move back to the *center*. It would be major progress if Eastern Europe could become Central Europe again.

The Revolutions of 1989

As of mid-1989, four East European states continued to reject the drift toward pluralism that Gorbachev's more tolerant policies were permitting in Poland and Hungary. The most adamant of these was Romania, where the government of Nicolae Ceauşescu had completely eliminated any semblance of resistance to its rule, making his one of the most repressive regimes in the world and one whose future at Ceauşescu's death remained problematical. Surrounding himself with members of his own family, Ceauşescu squeezed the already none too developed Romanian economy in order to pay off Romania's foreign debt, which he accomplished in 1989. At the same time he devoted enormous resources to grandiose building projects, such as reconstructing the center of Bucharest into a homage to himself, and to forcibly resettling peasants from their village homes into "modern" agrocomplexes. The result was an economic downturn in which room lighting was limited to one small bulb per room, winter temperatures in urban apartments were kept in the fifties, and food supplies were extremely limited. None of this weakened Ceauşescu's faith in the Stalinist model, and until the outbreak of violence in December 1989 ended in his execution by firing squad he remained the most extreme example of that once-strong current in Eastern Europe that passionately rejected pluralism.

Three other rejectionist states experienced dramatic and spontaneous repudiations of their neo-Stalinist regimes in the month of November 1989. The great symbolic event of these revolutionary movements was the opening of the Berlin Wall. In August 1961 the German Democratic Republic suddenly imposed travel restrictions on East Germans, who were fleeing their country through Berlin at the rate of two thousand to three thousand a week, and constructed a wall between the eastern and western sections of Berlin to enforce the restrictions. The wall, which eventually grew to formidable proportions and became over one hundred miles long, became the symbol of repression in the east and of the permanence of the division of Europe. The unexpected and fundamental transformations in the German Democratic Republic, Czechoslovakia, and Bulgaria late in 1989 began with the events in East Germany described in the New York Times *article reprinted here.*

The opening of the Berlin Wall on November 9, 1989, surely one of the most emotional and symbolically important European events of the postwar era, had rapid repercussions. Apparently under urgings from Moscow, on November 10 Todor Zhivkov, who had been Bulgaria's leader for thirty-five years, resigned, and a new leadership promised changes. A little more than one week later protesters began to take to the streets in Czechoslovakia, demanding freedom and democracy. At first the government, which had controlled the country with an iron hand since the Soviet invasion of 1968, insisted that it would not relax its control, but on November 24 massive demonstrations forced it to resign. A million demonstrators crowded the streets of Prague to cheer Alexander Dubček, the hero of 1968, and Václav Havel, the leader of Charter 77, as they jointly announced the changes. As in East Germany, the new Czechoslovak government, with Havel as its president and Dubček as the head of the parliament, removed the provision in its constitution that guaranteed the leading political role to the Communist party and began the process of turning Czechoslovakia toward pluralism. On New Year's Day 1990 Havel, who had been in office for only a few days, addressed his people in tones that have rarely been heard in Eastern Europe, or, for that matter, in Western Europe and the United States. A slightly shortened version is printed here.

42

The Opening of the Berlin Wall

Craig R. Whitney, David Binder, and Serge Schmemann
November 19, 1989

The frustration that erupted in October had been long in gathering. Mikhail S. Gorbachev, the Soviet president, had set loose yearnings for change throughout Eastern Europe, but in East Germany the old loyalists around Mr. Honecker sat entrenched in their isolated villas on Lake Wandlitz, refusing to see any reason to change.

The words *perestroika* and *glasnost* could not be uttered over the airwaves or printed in the official East German press, either in Russian or German, and Soviet publications were also banned.

East Berlin continued to flaunt its rigidity. Local elections on May 7 were plainly rigged. After the massacre in Tiananmen Square in Beijing on June 4, Mr. Krenz sent a message to the authorities in China congratulating them on their firmness.

But a new threat was growing in the south: the rapid drives by Poland and Hungary toward Western models of democracy. When Hungary began to snip away at its stretch of the East–West divide, the East German Interior Ministry warned the Politburo in a report that such action could spell serious trouble for East Germany, many of whose citizens vacationed in Hungary.

The Politburo took no action, evidently afraid that closing its borders with Hungary would be more dangerous than allowing a few East Germans to flee. And at first the exodus was a trickle—a few East Germans sneaking across the border, a few others seeking asylum at the West German embassy in Budapest.

Soon East Germans were filling West German embassies in Prague, Warsaw, and East Berlin. By late August, thousands of East German refugees were camped in Budapest. The Hungarians declined to send them home by force. Then, in a decision announced on September 10, Budapest said it would let the émigrés go to the West in defiance of a 1967 agreement with East Berlin to prevent East Germans from doing so without East Berlin's authorization.

Hungary's decision marked a momentous breach in Eastern European unity. For the first time, a Communist government declared that international covenants on human rights were more important than treaties with other Warsaw Pact nations.

The gates were open. Eventually, more than 30,000 East Germans swept out to West Germany through Hungary. In all, more than 200,000 have left East Germany.

Mr. Honecker was back at work, and his attention was fixed on the gala celebrations planned for October 7, the fortieth anniversary of the German Democratic Republic. Mr. Gorbachev was to lead a retinue of Communist leaders to East Berlin.

But the moment of triumph was shaping rapidly into a disaster. East Germany had quickly curtailed travel to Hungary, and Czechoslovakia remained the only Eastern European country where East Germans could go without permission. Before long, thousands of would-be émigrés seeking permission to travel to West Germany via Czechoslovakia were jammed into the West German Embassy in Prague.

Desperate to clear the West German Embassy in Prague before his guests arrived, Mr. Honecker granted permission on October 1 for the refugees to leave the embassy, although he insisted that they ride special trains through East Germany to satisfy East Berlin's demand that they first return home.

That solution proved disastrous. Even as the first group left, more East Germans flooded the embassy in Prague, forcing Mr. Honecker to authorize a second release and finally to shut his southern border.

Worse, the trains riding through Dresden drew thousands of East Germans desperate to join the exodus. On October 4, violent clashes erupted with the police, who tried to clear the Dresden station, and the trains were sealed to prevent them from being mobbed by others hoping to flee.

Against that backdrop, Mr. Honecker went to Schönefeld Airport on October 6 to greet Mr. Gorbachev, walking with a deliberate jauntiness to show that he was in good health.

Mr. Gorbachev seemed intent, publicly at least, not to inflame the opposition. But it did not take much. It was enough that he said that East Germany had to decide its own future to signal to many that Soviet troops would not interfere, and when he said that those who did not change with the times would see life punishing them, the comment was seen as a direct reference to Mr. Honecker. Wherever he went, the crowds chanted "Gorby! Gorby!"

Mieczyslav Rakowski, the Polish Communist party leader, sat next to Mr. Gorbachev on the reviewing stand at the October 7 military parade. He later said with some irony that when he heard the chants he remarked to Mr. Gorbachev, "It looks as if they want you to liberate them again."

The Soviet leader was more direct when he met in private with the East German Politburo. According to an East German diplomat, Mr. Gorbachev did not try to prescribe what the East Germans should do. "He made it very clear that the spectacle of thousands of people running away from the country and of violence being the only way to keep them in was not helping him in his own difficult situation," he said.

According to a wide range of party insiders, Mr. Honecker was incapable of grasping the situation. He reacted with stubborn insistence that he was on the right course and would brook no leniency. He told a Chinese visitor that any attempt to change his course was "nothing more than Don Quixote's futile running against the steadily turning sails of a windmill."

On Saturday night, October 7, as Mr. Gorbachev was leaving for Moscow, tens of thousands of East Berliners moved from the anniversary ceremonies to Alexanderplatz, the vast square at the heart of the city. Bearing candles and torches, they began chanting slogans demanding change.

The East German police, armed with riot sticks, chased them out of the square and north into the heavily populated, dilapidated Prenzlauer Berg section, hotbed of the growing New Forum opposition group. Hundreds were beaten and jailed. The scene was replayed on Sunday night in the same area of East Berlin, as well as in Leipzig and Dresden.

Mr. Krenz, at fifty-two the youngest member of the Politburo, was hardly a predictable architect of change. He had followed Mr. Honecker's path from the Communist youth league to take charge of security and youth affairs, and his statements had given no sign that he was anything but a hard-liner.

But he was considered sharp, and he was young. And it was he who took the fateful step on October 9 to avert violence in Leipzig. [Mr. Honecker earlier had authorized local commanders in Leipzig to respond with force in case of "provocation," but Mr. Krenz provided the key last-minute permission to local leaders to let the demonstrations proceed peacefully, which they had already intended to do.]

Back in East Berlin, the Politburo gathered for its regular Tuesday meeting. Nobody knew how Mr. Honecker or his ideological allies would react to the unilateral order by Mr. Krenz barring the Leipzig crackdown.

It was Erich Mielke, the tough eighty-two-year-old security chief, who told Mr. Honecker, "Erich, we can't beat up hundreds of thousands of people."

But the seventy-seven-year-old Communist leader would not be swayed. Earlier in the day, three members of the Central Committee had handed Mr. Honecker a report on the unrest among the country's youth and its causes, with a request for a special session of the leadership to deal with it. Mr. Honecker had flown into a rage, calling the report "the greatest attack on the party leadership in forty years."

Now Kurt Hager, the seventy-seven-year-old chief ideologist, raised his voice. The young people were right, he said. The mood on the streets was more defiant that he had ever seen it. Günter Schabowski, the respected party secretary for East Berlin, concurred.

Only two members firmly took Mr. Honecker's side: Günter Mittag, the sixty-three-year-old secretary for the economy, who had dominated East German economic planning since the era of Walter Ulbricht, the first party chief, and Joachim Hermann, the sixty-one-year-old secretary for propaganda.

Others wavered or kept silent. With the Politburo deadlocked, the secretaries of East Germany's fifteen districts, including Hans Modrow, the party chief for Dresden who had a reputation as a reformer favored by Moscow, were called in for an unusual expanded meeting of the leadership. The meeting went late into the night of October 10 and continued on October 11.

"The district leaders said that the grass-roots wouldn't stand for things to continue the way they were," a Central Committee member said.

The leaders began discussing a conciliatory statement to the nation. According to several accounts, Mr. Honecker resisted this too, fuming instead about his betrayal by Hungary.

Over his objections, the statement was issued October 11, declaring that the

Politburo was ready "to discuss all basic questions of our society" and acknowledging that those who had fled may have had valid reasons.

From that day, the press suddenly became more open, with panel discussions on major public complaints. The small "parties," traditionally subservient to the Communists, suddenly gained a voice of their own, and Mr. Gerlach, the Liberal party chairman, even suggested in his party paper that the "leading role" of the party should be reconsidered.

The Politburo met again on October 17. By now it was clear to most of the other seventeen Politburo members that Mr. Honecker no longer understood what was happening. One Communist official said Mr. Honecker had been so infuriated by Mr. Gerlach's statement and considered taking action against him.

This time, several Central Committee members said, only Mr. Mittag and Mr. Hermann still supported Mr. Honecker. Some officials said Mr. Mittag was holding out in the hope of securing the party leadership for himself, after having filled in for the ailing Mr. Honecker through the summer.

An important defector was Mr. Hager. "Without Hager, nothing would have gone through in the Politburo," a party official said.

Finally, Willi Stoph, the seventy-five-year-old prime minister, told Mr. Honecker that the time had come for him to resign, a Central Committee member said.

That was the decisive push. On the next day, October 18, Mr. Honecker announced to the Central Committee that he was resigning for reasons of health, and the Politburo moved that Mr. Mittag and Mr. Hermann be ousted. Mr. Krenz was the new party chief, head of state and chairman of the Defense Council.

The meeting was brief. Mr. Krenz read a speech promising an "earnest political dialogue" and then urged the Central Committee to quickly close its proceedings so he could go on nationwide television.

Mr. Krenz immediately set about trying to establish himself, within the party and outside, as the leader of real change. "We see the seriousness of the situation," he said. "But we also sense and recognize the major opportunity we have opened for ourselves to define policies in dialogue with our citizens."

The pace quickened. Mr. Krenz and other Politburo members took to the factories and streets to meet with people. On October 27, the government announced that it would restore free travel through Czechoslovakia, for people wanting to go to West Germany. On November 1, Mr. Krenz flew to Moscow to meet Mr. Gorbachev and endorsed a version of perestroika—economic and social restructuring—in East Germany.

Still, demonstrations swelled. Huge crowds marched in Leipzig, East Berlin, Dresden, and other major cities, and thousands of East Germans perhaps seeing this as their last chance to flee resumed their efforts to get into the West German Embassy in Prague.

Finally, on November 4, Mr. Krenz announced that East Germans who wanted to settle in West Germany could travel freely through Czechoslovakia. More than ten thousand a day began quickly surging across the border into the West.

That same day, more than a half million East Germans demonstrated for democracy in the largest protest that East Berlin or East Germany had ever seen. The crisis was not over.

Hoping to slow the exodus, the government hastily drafted a law on travel that said East German citizens would be free to go abroad, but for only thirty days a year and after applying at police offices. The bill was promptly denounced, and in a sign of the rebellious mood, the Legal and Constitutional Committee of the normally docile parliament dismissed it as unacceptable.

The pace of change gathered speed. On November 7, the entire Council of Ministers resigned and called on parliament to choose a new government. The Central Committee convened on November 8, and this time the entire Politburo resigned, to be replaced by a smaller group, still headed by Mr. Krenz, with five new members. Among them was Mr. Modrow, the party leader from Dresden, who would soon become the next prime minister.

Thousands of Communist party members demonstrated outside, demanding a party congress to install an entirely new leadership.

On November 9, a Thursday, the Central Committee continued to sweep the ranks of the leadership. Four new members of the top leadership were swept out after their regional party organizations rejected them.

Mr. Mittag came under intense criticism and was expelled from the Central Committee for "the most egregious violations of internal party democracy and of party and state discipline, as well as damaging the reputation of the party."

In the evening, Günter Schabowski came to brief reporters. Toward the end of the session, he announced that a new travel law had been drafted, giving East Germans the right to leave the country through any border crossings. The Berlin wall, already circumvented, was beginning to crumble.

The measures had been drafted by the Politburo, officials later said. It was still fresh, and the details were not immediately clear, although it later became evident that citizens did have to obtain exit visas from local police stations before going across. But when Mr. Schabowski was asked directly if East Germans could freely go West, his answer was yes.

Soon after, a young East German couple went to the Invalidenstrasse crossing to test the announcement. To their amazement, the guards, who had heard Mr. Schabowski and had no instructions, let them cross. After twenty-eight years, two months, twenty-seven days, and the deaths of eighty killed trying to cross it, the wall was open.

43

New Year's Day Speech, 1990

Václav Havel
January 1, 1990

Dear fellow citizens. For the past 40 years on this day you have heard my predecessors utter different variations on the same theme, about how our country is prospering, how many more billion tons of steel we have produced, how happy we all are, how much we trust our government, and what beautiful prospects lie ahead of us. I do not think you appointed me to this office for me, of all people, to lie to you.

Our country is not prospering. The great creative and spiritual potential of our nation is not being used to its full potential. Whole sectors of industry are producing things in which no one is interested, while the things we need are in short supply.

The state, which calls itself a state of the working people, is humiliating and exploiting the workers. Our outdated economy is squandering energy, of which we are in short supply. A country that could once be proud of the standard of education of its people spends so little on education that today it occupies seventy-second place in the world. We have laid waste and soiled the rivers and the forests that our forefathers bequeathed to us, and we have the worst environment in the whole of Europe today. Adults in our country die earlier than in most other European countries.

Allow me to tell you about a little personal experience of mine. Flying to Bratislava recently, I found time during various meetings to look out of the window. What I saw was the Slovnaft [oil refinery] complex and the Petrzalka suburb immediately beyond it. That view was enough for me to understand that our statesmen and politicians had not even looked—or did not even want to look—out of the windows of their planes. None of the statistics available to me would have enabled me to understand more quickly or more easily the situation we have gotten ourselves into.

But not even all of that is the most important thing. The worst thing is that we are living in a decayed moral environment. We have become morally ill, because we have become accustomed to saying one thing and thinking another. We have learned not to believe in anything, not to have consideration for one another, and only to look after ourselves. Notions such as love, friendship, compassion, humility, and forgiveness have lost their depth and dimension, and for many of us they merely represent some kind of psychological idiosyncrasy, or appear to be some kind of

Reprinted from Federal Broadcast Information Service, East Europe, 90-001 (Washington, D.C.: U.S. Government Printing Office, January 2, 1990).

stray relic from times past, something rather comical in the era of computers and
space rockets. Few of us managed to cry out that the powerful should not be all-
powerful and that the special farms which produce ecologically sound and high-
quality foodstuffs for them should send their produce to the schools, children's
hostels, and hospitals, since our agriculture is not yet able to offer this to everyone.

The previous regime, armed with its arrogant and intolerant ideology, denigrated
man into a production force and nature into a production tool. In this way it attacked
their very essence and the relationship between them. It made talented people who
were capable of managing their own affairs and making an enterprising living in
their own country into cogs in some kind of monstrous, ramshackle, smelly machine whose purpose no one can understand. It can do nothing more than slowly but
surely wear itself down, and all the cogs in it.

When I talk about a decayed moral environment, I do not mean merely those
gentlemen who eat ecologically pure vegetables and do not look out of their airplane
windows. I mean all of us, because all of us have become accustomed to the
totalitarian system, accepted it as an unalterable fact, and thereby kept it running. In
other words, all of us are responsible, each to a different degree, for keeping the
totalitarian machine running. None of us is merely a victim of it, because all of us
helped to create it together.

Why do I mention this? It would be very unwise to see the sad legacy of the past
40 years as something alien to us, handed down to us by some distant relatives. On
the contrary, we must accept this legacy as something that we have brought upon
ourselves. If we can accept this, then we will understand that it is up to all of us to
do something about it. We cannot lay all the blame on those who ruled us before,
not only because this would not be true, but also because it could detract from the
responsibility each of us now faces—the responsibility to act on our own initiative,
freely, sensibly, and quickly.

Let us not delude ourselves: not even the best government, the best parliament,
or the best president can do much on their own, and it would be profoundly unjust to
expect them alone to put everything right. Freedom and democracy, after all, mean
that we all have a part to play and bear joint responsibility. If we can realize this,
then all the horrors that the new Czechoslovak democracy has inherited will suddenly cease to appear to be terrible. If we can realize this, hope will return to our
hearts.

In putting right the general state of affairs, we already have a sound footing on
which to build. The recent times, and especially the last six weeks of our peaceful
revolution, have shown what an enormous generally humane, moral, and spiritual
charge and what high standards of civic maturity lay dormant in our society under
the mask of apathy that had been forced upon it. Whenever anyone talking to me
began to put categorical labels on our people, I always pointed out that society is a
very mysterious creature and that it is never wise to trust only the particular fact that
it is presenting to you. I am glad to have been proved right.

Throughout the world, people are surprised that the acquiescent, humiliated,
skeptical Czechoslovak people who apparently no longer believed in anything suddenly managed to find the enormous strength in the space of a few weeks to shake
off the totalitarian system in a completely decent and peaceful way. We ourselves are

also surprised at this, and we ask where do the young people, in particular, who have never known any other system, find the source of their aspirations for truth, freedom of thought, political imagination, civic courage, and civic foresight? How is it that their parents, the generation that was considered lost, also joined in with them? How is it even possible that so many people immediately grasped what had to be done, without needing anyone else's advice or instructions?

I think that this hopeful aspect of our situation today has two main reasons. Above all, man is never merely a product of the world around him, he is always capable of striving for something higher, no matter how systematically this ability is ground down by the world around him. Second, the humanistic and democratic traditions—which are often spoken about in such a hollow way—nonetheless lay dormant somewhere in the subconscious of our nations and national minorities, and were passed on quietly from one generation to the next in order for each of us to discover them within us when the time was right, and to put them into practice.

Of course, for our freedom today we also had to pay a price. Many of our people died in prison in the 1950s; many were executed, thousands of human lives were destroyed, and hundreds of thousands of talented people were driven abroad. Those who defended the honor of our nations in the war were persecuted, as were those who resisted totalitarian government, and those who simply managed to remain true to their own principles and think freely. None of those who paid the price in one way or another for our freedom today should be forgotten. Independent courts should justly assess the appropriate guilt of those responsible, so that the whole truth about our recent past comes out into the open.

Neither should we forget that other nations paid an even higher price for their freedom today, and thus they also paid indirectly for us too. The rivers of blood which flowed in Hungary, Poland, Germany, and recently also in such a horrific way in Romania, as well as the sea of blood shed by the nations of the Soviet Union, should not be forgotten, primarily because all human suffering affects every human being. But more than that, they must not be forgotten because it was these great sacrifices which weaved the tragic backcloth for today's freedom or gradual liberation of the nations of the Soviet bloc, and the backcloth of our newly charged freedom too.

Without the changes in the Soviet Union, Poland, Hungary, and the German Democratic Republic, the developments in our country could hardly have happened, and if they had happened, they surely would not have had such a wonderful peaceful character. The fact that we had favorable international conditions, of course, does not mean that anyone was helping us directly in those weeks. For centuries, in fact, both our nations have risen up by themselves, without relying on any help from more powerful states or big powers.

This, it seems to me, is the great moral stake of the present moment. It contains the hope that in the future we will no longer have to suffer the complex of those who are permanently indebted to someone else. Now it is up to us alone whether this hope comes to fruition, and whether our civic, national, and political self-confidence reawakens in a historically new way.

Self-confidence is not pride. Quite the contrary. Only a man or a nation self-confident in the best sense of the word is capable of listening to the voice of others, accepting them as equal to oneself, forgiving one's enemies, and regretting one's own mistakes. As such people, let us try to introduce self-confidence into the life of our community and as nations into our conduct on the international arena. Only thus shall we regain self-respect and respect for each other, as well as the respect of other nations. Our state should never again be a burden or a poor relation to anyone else. Although we have to take a great many things and learn many things from others, we must do this, after a long period of time, as equal partners who also have something to offer.

Our first president wrote "Jesus and not Caesar." In this he followed up both on Chelcicky and Komensky.[1] This idea has once again been reawakened in us. I dare say that perhaps we even have the possibility of spreading it further, thus introducing a new factor in both European and world politics. Love, desire for understanding, the strength of the spirit and of ideas can radiate forever from our country, if we want this to happen. This radiation can be precisely what we can offer as our very own contribution to world politics.

Masaryk founded his politics on morality. Let us try, in a new time and in a new way, to revive this concept of politics. Let us teach both ourselves and others that politics ought to be a reflection of the aspiration to contribute to the happiness of the community and not of the need to deceive or pillage the community. Let us teach both ourselves and others that politics does not have to be the art of the possible, especially if this means the art of speculating, calculating, intrigues, secret agreements, and pragmatic maneuvering, but that it also can be the art of the impossible, that is the art of making both ourselves and the world better.

We are a small country, but nonetheless we were once the spiritual crossroads of Europe. Is there any reason why we should not be so again? Would this not be another contribution through which we could pay others back for the help we will need from them?

The home mafia—those who do not look out of their airplane windows and eat specially fed pigs—are still alive, true, and make trouble from time to time, but they are no longer our main enemy, and international mafias are even less of an enemy. Our worst enemy today is our own bad qualities—indifference to public affairs, conceit, ambition, selfishness, the pursuit of personal advancement, and rivalry—and that is the main struggle we are faced with.

I would like to conclude by saying that I want to be a president of action rather than words, a president who not only looks out of the windows of his airplane

---

[1]Czechoslovakia's first president was Tomáš Masaryk (1850–1937). Masaryk was a professor of philosophy in Prague and always took an interest in ethical and national issues, clearing a Jew of a charge of ritual murder, befriending the Slovaks, and inspiring the Croatian secession. The most prominent Czech political figure before World War I, Masaryk agitated for the creation of a Czechoslovak state during the war, and when that event came to pass he became the country's first president. Peter Chelčický (1390–1460) was the foremost thinker of the Czech reformation movement founded by Jan Hus at the turn of the fifteenth century. His pacifist and utopian teachings gave rise to the Protestant movement called the Bohemian Brethren, the last leader of which was Jan Ámos Komenský [John Amos Comenius] (1592–1670). Komenský said, "I love my country and its language and my greatest wish is that it be cultivated." At the same time he felt himself a citizen of Europe and believed in the unity of humankind. Czech patriots consider the moral strength of these men a constituent part of Czech national character.

carefully, but one, above all, who is consistently present among his fellow citizens and listens to them carefully.

Perhaps you are asking what kind of republic I have in mind. My reply is this: a republic that is independent, free, and democratic, with a prospering economy and also socially just—in short a republic of the people that serves the people, and is therefore entitled to hope that the people will serve it too. I have in mind a republic of people with a well-rounded education, because without such people none of our problems—whether human, economic, environmental, social, or political—can be tackled.

One of my most distinguished predecessors began his first speech by quoting Comenius. Allow me to end my first speech with my own paraphrase of that same statement: People, your government has returned to you!

The revolutions of 1989, as well as the collapse of the Soviet Union in 1991, ended not just one but many eras of European history. They completed the post–World War II era known as the cold war. Relationships created by forty years of superpower confrontation suddenly became obsolete, transforming the entire period from current events into history. The end of the Soviet Union also ended the experiment in communist government and centrally planned economies begun by the Bolshevik Revolution of 1917. And in a sense, 1989 completed a two-hundred-year phase of European confrontation with the ideals of the French Revolution. During the twentieth century, both communism and nazism rejected these ideals in different ways. The defeat of nazism in 1945 and the collapse of communism in 1989 and 1991 left democratic governments and liberal economies, the rivals that both nazism and communism despised, as the primary surviving secular ideologies in the world.

During the period of the cold war, it was relatively easy to grasp the fundamentals of East European events, since each country had to adopt Stalinism and then adapt to it. East Europe's peripheral position to European concerns, and even to Russian concerns, was clear. After 1989, however, all certainties vanished. Each East European country is now developing its own political culture and its own economic strategies. Whereas in 1985 one could think of one Soviet Union and seven East European countries, today we encounter a fractured Russia and at least eighteen states in a region that could be called Eastern Europe. Each of them faces not only the normal problems facing every modern country but also the far more complex problems of identity, economic structure, and political organization. It is not possible in this section even to mention the scope of these issues. Two difficult problems, however, have attracted worldwide attention: nationalism and the collapse of Yugoslavia. Accordingly, in this last section, we turn to these difficult issues.

The final two texts are by the man whose reforms in the Soviet Union opened the door to changes in Eastern Europe. Had the Poles and Hungarians not been prepared to take advantage of the opening that Mikhail Gorbachev provided, events would not have moved as they did. But, with a different Soviet leader perhaps events would not have moved at all. Our book ends with Gorbachev's vision of a common European home and his resignation speech on Christmas Day 1991.

Nationalism

Nationalism is not just a post-1989 phenomenon. The political use of the idea of nation goes back at least to the French Revolution. The countries of Eastern Europe that came into existence after World War I were the fruits of nationalist aspirations dating back several generations. During the 1930s, nationalist jealousies were one of the main reasons that the countries of Eastern Europe could not sustain their economies and their democracies. When the communists came to power, they claimed that they would eliminate nationalism in favor of proletarian internationalism. In actuality, however, most communist regimes encouraged nationalism as circumstances permitted. In Bulgaria, this meant not speaking out against Russian domination but keeping the aspiration for Macedonia alive, and in Romania it meant promulgating the idea of an alleged two-thousand-year-long Romanian desire for national unity.

Two of the four readings in this section are from the pre-1989 period, and two are from after the revolutions. The first consists of two pieces by the Roman author Ion Lăncrănjan. Lăncrănjan was writing for a Romanian audience in a context of increasing friction between Hungary and Romania over Transylvania and strident nationalism on the part of Nicolae Ceaușescu. The articles emphasize some of the characteristics common to nationalist discourse, such as heroism and self-sacrifice coupled with victimization. But they also provide a striking example of the genderization of nationalist rhetoric in which the country is seen as the passive female receptacle for its active male inhabitants.

The second reading in this section is a portion of a speech by Stanko Todorov, president of the Bulgarian parliament, discussing what the Bulgarians called the "reconstruction of names." In 1984 and 1985, after thirty years of increasing pressure on its Turkish-speaking Muslims (about 10 percent of the population), Bulgarian authorities suddenly began forcing them to change their Turkic- and Arabic-sounding names to Bulgarian-sounding ones. In doing so, the authorities used an argument similar to one that the Serbs and Croats used later in Bosnia and Herzegovina: that the Turks were actually Bulgarians forcibly converted to Islam four hundred or five hundred years ago. Underneath their Turkic culture, therefore, they were "really" Bulgarians.

In 1989, the Bulgarian authorities forced more than 300,000 ethnic Turks across the border into Turkey, where they gathered in refugee camps. Late in that year, when Todor Zhivkov resigned and Bulgaria began to change, it was Stanko Todorov who tried to appease the Turks demonstrating outside the national parliament in Sofia by announcing that ethnic freedom would henceforth be the law of the land. Since that time a new Turkish political party has played a significant balancing role between the almost equally divided former communists and the democratically inclined Union of Democratic Forces.

The third reading in this section comes from post-1989 Hungary. In it the vice-president of the Hungarian Democratic Forum, the leading party in Hungary's first democratically elected government, attacks his own party for its poor decisions and the opposition for its links to the old communist regime and to world Jewry. Anti-Semitism has been a powerful element in East European nationalism since the nineteenth century. Today, because of the Holocaust and the postwar emigration of most survivors, few Jews remain in Eastern Europe. Even some of the old signs of anti-Semitism are disappearing. But there remains a fringe element that continues to try to make political capital out of anti-Semitism. Csurka's article thus created a firestorm of public commentary and concern in Hungary, and eventually the Hungarian Democratic Forum was forced to drop Csurka. When the separate party he formed ran in the elections of 1994, it received less than 2 percent of the vote.

The final reading is another Bulgarian selection, this one by President Zhelyu Zhelev concerning Macedonia. The breakup of Yugoslavia created a new state that calls itself The Republic of Macedonia. Greece has vigorously opposed its use of this name, to which the Greeks claim exclusive rights. Surprisingly, however, Bulgaria has not used the ensuing tensions to press its historic claims to Macedonia, even though it occupied the region twice in this century and argues that the people who lived there in the nineteenth century were Bulgarians. Zhelev's speech provides a salutary example of a relatively stabilizing kind of nationalism that is neither overtly aggressive and nor blatantly irridentist.

44

Patriotism: A Vital Necessity

Ion Lăncrănjan (translated by Katherine Verdery)
1982

As a child, you think the world begins and ends with the threshold of the house where you were born, with the edge of the village or town in which you first saw the light of day, with the light that first set the boundaries of your sight. As an adolescent, you think that your first love is your only true and great love, in comparison with which the stars in the sky grow pale and the lilies fade, along with everything that is alive and mortal, for, or so you then think, only this love of yours, around which everything else turns, even the land and the waters, is undying. Things change after that, you realize the world is bigger and more comprehensive, and loves succeed one another endlessly, yet over them all there arises out of nothing, when you aren't even aware of it, a single and inextinguishable love[1]—love of your country (*patria*), love of your native land and of the places of your birth and of the nation (*neam*)[2] you come from, that unstinting love that overpowers, time and again, that grows and opens itself to the light as you yourself grow and are clarified in and toward the world, a love that intersects with and fraternizes with your first love and with all your other loves, for only those who are capable of love are able to love their country and their people, only those who are good and generous, only those who know the weightiness of speech and the earthquake of self-abandon can raise themselves up to the height of this profound and powerful sentiment.

We will see, if we look back, that the most notable sons of the Romanian people, the most enlightened and gifted, the best and most just, the most honest and sincere, the most daring, passed through the fire of this sentiment, gave themselves to it without restraint, gave themselves in fact to the country and the people they were descended from. The life and work of Eminescu,[3] for instance, are inconceivable without this self-giving, without this sacred love, which his genius purified for all time, raising it up into the undying light of eternity, and in its light he himself was pulverized, without stopping to waver, without awaiting sustenance or payment from somewhere, carrying everything through as if preordained to happen thus, so

[1]The word used here (*dragoste*) has carnal as well as spiritual connotations.
[2]Meaning both group of kin and people or nation in the ethnic sense.
[3]A nineteenth-century Romanian romantic poet whose early death cut short a brilliant career.

Katherine Verdery, "From Parent–State to Family Patriarchs: Gender and Nation in Contemporary Eastern Europe," *East European Politics and Societies* 8 (Spring 1994): 224–47. From Ion Lăncrănjan, *Cuvînt despre Transilvania* (Bucharest, 1982), pp. 69–71, 81–84.

that our country, Romania, and our ancestral language, our culture, in its entirety, might acquire a new and deeper self-awareness. The pathos of the life of this great poet, whose feet trod all the regions inhabited by Romanians so as to hear their speech and know their aspirations and legends, his tremendous labor, of inestimable value, everything that this superb man wrote and did, stood under the sign of his great and earthshaking love, for in his unique and exemplary case, things took a dramatic if not indeed tragic turn, so deep was his ardor, so pure, so unhesitating, so total, that it was transformed at last into an undying flame.

The same things can be said also about Bălcescu, about Iorga, and about Sadoveanu.[4] Bălcescu, especially, can be compared only with Eminescu, for the same fire consumed him too, he too put above everything, above satisfactions and glory, his love for his people and his country, where he would have wanted to die but where he did not manage to return, dying instead in the loneliness of strangers and entering thus into eternity. The other two men, Iorga and Sadoveanu, seem less legendary, being closer to us in time. But the pathos of their lives also stood under the sign of love of their country and people, which both of them served in their own ways, with self-abnegation.

Nor should we forget, besides the example of these notable men and of so many others—the always-fresh and ever-unsullied example of the man of the people, the example of the people itself, for it was the parent and the teacher of all, it ascended the "Golgothas" of the centuries, bleeding and gnashing its teeth, believing so much in its own star, having such strength in its manner of being—its beauty, and sensibility, and intelligence, and vivacity, and love, and longing—that it overcame everything in the end: centuries of hostility, subjugation, and dependency, being itself that which its most important men were: the people of an earthshaking, profound, and pure love. . . .

Love, any love, raises up and purifies, and love of country, love of your places of birth, of your people, gives another meaning to everything, raising everything up onto the high platform of all accomplishments, making of yesterday's child a daring and clearheaded man, transforming the adolescent into a hero, as has so often happened, as will happen again, and as ought to happen.

Romania is my natal land, the land of my dreams, the land of my longing . . . Romania is my land of origin, it is the old song of the flute and the quiet whisper of the plowed field that is almost ripe, . . . it is the far-away and almost forgotten tinkling of the shepherd's pipe that brightens the mountainsides of an evening—it is the land with the name of a girl and the fiery soul of a fiery man! . . .

Romania is the land that paid with sweat and tears—and often, much too often, with blood—for whole days and years of its tumultuous history; it is the land across which came massive waves of fire and smoke; it is the land that always refound its being in its own soil, in its mountain springs, in the quiet of its glades, in the fascinating journey through its fascinating landscapes, in its just and honest judgment, owing to which no one can push you aside or destroy you if you rely on what

---

[4]Three important figures of Romanian history, the first a revolutionary, the second a politician and historian, and the third a writer.

is yours, if by your work and your struggle you have become one with the soil on which you tread! . . .

Romania is the land whose boundaries give it the shape of the sun, "plump," as our unforgettable poet Blaga would have said; it is a land with so much beauty, so rich and so good, so generous and credulous and endowed so bountifully—that you can't capture it in words, you can't paint it on paper in all its true and radiant splendor, you keep missing something: a leaf that is dying, a flower opening its corolla toward the sky, the rumbling of a mountain storm or the endless calm of the sea, the deep breathing, barely perceptible and barely felt, of the plain at sunset, the peaceful song of the regions between the Carpathians and the East, the silver trill of the swallow!

Romania is the land of some unforgettable men, the land of Bălcescu, the land of Horea and Iancu, of Michael the Brave and Stephen the Great, the land of the Basarabs, of Gelu and the Mușatins,[5] the land that never let itself be conquered, that met difficulty with quiet and patience—and how often that was! . . .

Romania is a hardworking and capable land, exceedingly capable, with the most diverse and unexpected inclinations, and even if it was also often sad, in a distant and not-so-distant past, the reason is that the fruits of this industriousness were often taken from it, outright or indirectly through the usual base perfidy, and was left more often than not only with tears and weeping. . . .

Romania is the land of the truest independence, a land now geared into a profound process of renewal; it is a land penetrated from one end to the other by the manly, powerful, and rising hum of machines; it is a land that adds to its old jewels other more valuable ones, a land that makes the strong waters into current and electric light, a land in which fires burn constantly—at the [steel mills in] Hunedoara, Galați, Reșița, and other places! . . .

Romania is the land of friendship, a hospitable land full of understanding and of respect for everyone, eager to assimilate all that is good and beautiful, wanting only to be respected, understood, and appreciated justly for its hard work! . . .

Romania is the eye of the world, an eye that is clear and watchful, sensitive to the finest nuances of the light, deep, and vibrant, with rustling eyelashes of rustling grain stalks, with melancholy eyelids, and with rough hiding places of a rough audacity, with the clearness of great and calm waters, with undreamt-of openings toward the future! . . .

Romania is my natal land, the land of my origin, with which I am so much and so fervently in love that if I should happen to die who knows where, in a distant and foreign place, I would rise up again on my feet, and I would walk back here, to my country, to these loved and known places! But let us not speak of death, now when it is more appropriate than ever to speak of life, of that which was and will remain imperishable in the soul of this land with the name of a girl and the rough steadfastness of a rough man.[6]

---

[5] All of these were famous figures, most of them princes and rulers.

[6] For an explication of this text and the issue of gender and nation in Eastern Europe, see Katherine Verdery, "From Parent–State to Family Patriarchs: Gender and Nation in Contemporary Eastern Europe," *East European Politics and Societies* 8 (Spring 1994): pp. 225–55.

45

Name Changes in Bulgaria

Stanko Todorov (translated by Gale Stokes)

March 12, 1985

One of our greatest achievements is the continuous strengthening of the moral and political unity of the Bulgarian people, and of our national homogeneity. The Bulgarian socialist nation has consolidated itself and grown stronger, especially since the April plenum of 1956.[1] And our homogeneity has grown. This has taken place through struggle against the forces and tendencies that are hostile to socialism.

A powerful effect of the party's April line was the thwarting of a plot against the Bulgarian national consciousness among the population of the Pirin area. This brought trust and peace to the people, who had been the object of scandalous [Yugoslav] claims on their national self-consciousness. Anyone who travels in the Pirin region of our fatherland today is impressed by not only its great progress but also the people's high level of patriotic Bulgarian consciousness in the Blagojevgrad region.[2]

A great success is also that the descendants of the forcibly Islamized Bulgars of the Smoljan, Pasardschik, and Blagojevgrad regions [the Pomaks] have reconstructed their Bulgarian names.[3] One or two decades have passed since that happened. Any unprejudiced person can see how quickly the economy of those areas developed, how the culture and education of the people improved, and how promising management emerged. The Bulgars of the Rhodope regions have shaken off their Islamic fanaticism, liberated themselves from the influence of conservatism in their lives, and strengthened their Bulgarian patriotic consciousness.

At the end of 1984 and the beginning of 1985 there appeared in our country a new force, a spontaneous and comprehensive process of reconstructing the Bulgarian names of our compatriots who had Turkish–Arabic names. This process was

[1]The April plenum of the Bulgarian Communist party held in 1956 established the fundamental policy on nationalities that Bulgaria followed until recently. This policy essentially was to assimilate all minority peoples into the Bulgarian nation.

[2]The Pirin area, which includes the Blagojevgrad region, borders on Macedonia, which since 1945 has been one of the six constituent republics of Yugoslavia. After 1956 the Bulgars, who believe that Macedonia was originally ethnically Bulgarian and therefore have been trying since their creation as a state in 1878 to obtain it, refused to accept the existence in the Pirin area of any persons called "Macedonian."

[3]Pomaks are Bulgarian-speaking Muslims.

Taken from Stanko Todorov, "Namenswechsel—ein historischer Akt!" *Osteuropa Archiv,* October 1986, pp. 478–80, from *Slivensko delo,* March 12, 1985.

completed throughout the country in two or three months, and in some areas and settlements in a few days. Why did this measure occur so spontaneously and painlessly? Above all because the working people reconsidered their own past and became conscious of their Bulgarian origins and their membership in the Bulgarian nation. This was a historic choice of people who understand that only unity with the Bulgarian people offers opportunities for their development and well-being. The people understand that the changing of names is a historic measure, a new birth that opens space for their comprehensive development and for their complete realization in life.

Now everyone knows better that the People's Republic of Bulgaria is a mononational state. It includes in its territories no foreign lands; no portions of other peoples and nations are contained in the Bulgarian people.

But the Bulgarian people have, as you know, experienced a bitter historical fate. Foreign conquerors have cut off living parts of our national strength [i.e., Macedonia]. There are numberless historical examples that entire regions of strategic significance were forcibly Turkicized, that young Bulgars, stolen from their parents' homes as young boys, were enrolled in the Janissary corps.[4] Assimilation in the Islamic imperium was a standing policy of the state, whose goal was to take national consciousness from our people.[5] Thus a portion of our people was forcibly Turkicized. One can see from their way of life, folklore, speech, and clothing that Bulgarian citizens of the Islamic faith are the descendants of Bulgarians.

One would have expected that this population would have united with its own Bulgarian people quickly after the liberation of Bulgaria. But the shortsighted policy of the Bulgarian bourgeoisie pushed this population back and left them completely under the influence of the *hodžas* and of bourgeois Turkish nationalism.[6] After the victory of the socialist revolution this population became ever more integrated into the Bulgarian people. Many mistakes, hindrances, and hurdles had to be overcome for the truth to reach the hearts of these people and to strengthen the self-consciousness among them that they are Bulgars, children of the Bulgarian people.

Exactly for that reason, the reconstruction of Bulgarian names is a historic act, a revolutionary measure that shows that these our compatriots, who a short time ago found themselves in a complicated contradiction, have thrown off their shackles. They worked and are working for the construction of socialism in their own land; they constructed their own well-being. But at the same time they were exposed to the intensive working over of bourgeois Turkish propaganda, which created nationalism, religious confusion, and a conservative life-style. The reactionary forces in neighboring Turkey made futile efforts to speak in the name of the citizens with

---

[4]The *devşirme*, or boy-levy, of Ottoman times took young boys from Balkan families to Istanbul, where they were converted and enrolled in the sultan's service. A few of them rose from this humble beginning to the highest civil rank in the empire, grand vizier, but many others became soldiers in the sultan's professional army corps, the Janissaries.

[5]Actually, the Ottomans were quite tolerant of both the Christian and Jewish religions, as they consider both to be faiths "of the book," that is, inferior earlier versions of God's final revelation through Mohammed. The surprising thing about the Ottoman occupation of the Balkans—which in Bulgaria lasted for more than five hundred years—is that so relatively few persons converted.

[6]Hodža is the term for local Muslim religious leader.

Turkish–Arabic names living in Bulgaria and arbitrarily to draw them into the Turkish nation. The reconstruction of the Bulgarian names will contribute to withdrawing the reactionary Turkish influence from our cocitizens so that they can live peacefully and without contradiction.

The completion of the process of drawing this population into the Bulgarian nation has not only national but also international significance. It strengthens the position of the People's Republic of Bulgaria as an outpost of the Warsaw Pact on the Balkan peninsula. It also objectively serves the cause of peace and good neighborliness in this region, and it creates the conditions for developing our mutual relations with Turkey on a healthy, clear basis.

The fact that in the entire land the reconstruction of names went peacefully shows that it was a historically mature event.[7] It gave the class enemies a chance for some rabble-rousing propaganda, but they found no support among the working people. We expected that our enemies abroad would fabricate the most improbable lies and slanders. They accuse us of assimilation. These reproaches come from the reactionary circles of bourgeoise Turkey, in which over ten million Kurds, over one million Armenians, and over two million Arabs live deprived of their rights. Turkish reactionary circles are conducting a true civil war against their national minorities in gross violation of international agreements and conventions.

Nothing like that is occurring here. There is no forcible drawing of foreign ethnic groups or foreign regions into the Bulgarian nation, but rather a return of that which is due us, which was torn from the hearts of our people by blood and violence. With full justice we can say that we are returning to our Bulgarian family our dear brothers and sisters for whom the conqueror had darkened the national consciousness for centuries. This people is blood of our blood, flesh of our flesh.

[7]In fact, eyewitness accounts reported bitter resistance and considerable bloodshed.

46

A Few Thoughts

István Csurka

August 20, 1992

It should be obvious that a small country like ours, which was tossed to Stalin at Yalta with such ease and which was let down so hideously in 1956, cannot be as independent as it would like to be. This is not only known to, but also instinctively felt by, those who, to their misfortunes, were born as Hungarians. Nevertheless, there is a minimum level of effort to achieve independence that must be made primarily in the field of domestic policy and in setting basic national goals, and the people must be told if that effort cannot, or is not permitted to, be made. The government has not made this minimum effort and has not even made an attempt to explain why it has not. It was unable to give such an explanation because it could have done so only if the government had its own press and media, which breathed together with the government. But the government handed over the press and the media to the opposing forces as part of its first bad improvisation. Since then, however, it gives this constant, constrained excuse of not being able to achieve its goals because the press is hostile and misinterprets or fails to report the government's intentions.

The process that took place was something like the process that had taken place in 1945 and 1946. At that time, the Interior Ministry and the political police—the only possible repressive organ in those days—had been grabbed away from the Smallholders party, the winner in the elections, and then used to crush democracy. In the ensuing forty-five years the banking system and finances have acquired the kind of significance the police had in those days, and the preservation of this system provided the same kind of security for the Kadar-era power elite and the nomenklatura in 1990 as the political police had provided in 1945–46. In those days Vorosilov's Allied Control Commission and the Red occupation army stood behind communist henchmen, murderers, and people who urinated in people's mouths and tore out their fingernails; today the IMF stands behind the financial elite of the era of system change.

As early as September 28, 1987, the day after the Lakitelek camp meeting, the *New York Times* published a commentary charging that the Lakitelek gathering had been nationalistic and anti-Semitic. Sandor Csoori, one of the founders, happened to be out there at the time, and the same charges also began pouring to his address.

Condensed from JPRS-EER-92-132-S, a publication of the United States government, pp. 2–8, 10–11, 13.

Csoori himself has already written about these events. It seemed that these charges were fueled by the fact that a few members of the democratic opposition who had played an important role at the previous joint meeting in Monor were not invited to Lakitelek.[1]

In reality, however, the problem was that we dared to form *our own* organization. The MDF was based precisely on a recognition that the various strata of the Hungarian people that had hung around outside the fences of power and had never before been organized, needed their own organization *by all means*, one that was not formed to serve some international interest group or to salvage those in power but, instead, to directly resolve the vital issues of the Hungarian people.

The charge of anti-Semitism has followed the MDF from the first moment on. The government, too, has been forced to continuously defend itself against this charge.

The idea that the MDF included anti-Semites was not invented by the democratic opposition; they only inherited it from idea-men operating in Aczel's agit-prop division.[2]

It is enough to tell this story beginning in 1945. At that time, following the German occupation, a significant number of Hungarian Jews returning to a terribly decimated Hungary, or daring to reemerge from hiding, envisioned the Communist party as the sole guarantee for starting a new life and for preventing a return of conditions similar to those of 1944. This expectation was based not only on the fact that every member of the Moscovite quartet that had grabbed power had been Jewish but also on the financial support provided to the Left in Hungary, to the communist remnants, by the former liberal, bourgeois Jewry.

Quite naturally, the Rakosi system that settled in and soon turned into a wild beast robbed the Jews, too, of their private property and did not exempt a person from deportation merely because of Jewish origin, as long as an AVO [State Security Division] official cast his eyes on the villa of such a person. Following the example provided by Stalin, Rakosi would also have ventured to arrange for a Jewish physicians' trial, but nevertheless the bottom line was: The Jews concluded that a period of emergency could not be expected, there was no threat, and the Rakosi system had to be accepted.

In the end, Hungarian Jewry developed a greater sense of being at home in the Kadar system than ever before. The fact that an overwhelming part of the nation's non-Jewish majority had simply forgotten about the Jewish question or, as in the case of the younger generation, had not even learned about the Jewish question, contributed to this situation. While Romania sold out its Jewish citizens, causing

[1]The Hungarian Democratic Forum (MDF), which led the first post-communist government in Hungary from 1990 to 1994, grew out of meetings of opposition intellectuals that took place in Monor in 1986 and Lakitelek in 1987. Sándor Csoori is a populist poet whose summer home provided the venue for the second meeting. Whereas some liberal oppositionists who later formed the Alliance of Free Democrats (SZDSZ) attended the first meeting, they did not attend the second due to their political differences with the right of center oppositionists.

[2]György Aczél was the member of the Hungarian politburo who presided over cultural issues. *Agit-prop* refers to the Agitation and Propaganda Section of the Central Committee Secretariat of the Communist party of the Soviet Union, which was replicated throughout Eastern Europe in the Stalinist period. The term was not common in Hungary during Aczél's era.

substantial damage to culture and civilization in Transylvania and in all of Romania, only a negligible number of people emigrated from Hungary to Israel after 1956. In this sickly era that outlived its own time, Budapest and Vienna were the two major cities where Jewry had a say and could exert overt or covert influence and where it could be a decisive element.

Both the Aczel-type liberals of the MSZMP [Hungarian Socialist Workers party] and the members of the democratic opposition who maintained close communications with them felt that this hegemonic situation was threatened when the MDF [Hungarian Democratic Forum] was established. If a newly formed organization's leadership did not include a delegate from this group, so that there was no certainty that a signal would be given if any steps were contemplated that threatened the hegemonic position of Hungarian Jewry, then such an organization was dangerous. Accordingly, both the party of those days and the democratic opposition considered the MDF the chief danger.

The fact that the day after Lakitelek a writing that analyzed the MDF's anti-Semitism—in reality a warning threat—was published in New York must not be attributed solely to the good connections and efficiency of the democratic opposition. This kind of action required cooperation with the already described former banking connections, with the consulate, and with secret channels that had been developed much earlier.

[Elections in 1990 brought an MDF-led coalition to power.] Negotiations concerning a pact that had been going on previously between the SZDSZ [Alliance of Free Democrats] and the MDF accelerated, and even before a government was formed, one of the most contradictory and, in its effects, most damaging agreements of Hungarian political history was reached. The pact produced tragic consequences, primarily from the standpoint of system change. Only one of the parties to the agreement was what the MDF was. It negotiated and agreed to the bargain as a force empowered to govern, one that intended to implement system change its own way. The method of changing the system was supported by a majority [of Hungarian voters]. In contrast, the other party entered into the agreement not in order to accomplish a system change but to sustain the conditions of power that had continuously existed ever since 1945 and to slow down system change. That side had lost the elections and yet acquired the highest public office.

Yielding the office of the president of the republic would have caused no particular problem had it been yielded to a real opposition party, one that wanted a system change but in a different way. But as it was, by giving this post to Arpad Goncz, whom the SZDSZ hard core controlled, the pact made it above all possible to restrict the independence of system change and the commitment to Hungarian national interests. The goal was not to change the system but to secure the most important personal interests of those whose continuous rule has prevailed since 1945. The nomenklatura is the only real winner as a result of the pact.

One had to wait until all this was unquestionably proven by the actions of the president of the republic and of the hard core of the SZDSZ. Proof?

Based on a law adopted by a majority of the National Assembly, the government wanted to appoint three vice-presidents to the radio and three to the television [stations]. The candidates were selected so that they would also be acceptable to the opposition parties. The president refused to sign the letters of appointment on the grounds that the prospective vice-presidents would scuttle the illegally and illegitimately structured intendant system, which served as an accessory to antigovernment sentiments and to the preservation of safety features built into the pact to protect the nomenklatura. Goncz said no, because the communist, reform communist, liberal, and radical members of the nomenklatura, the liaisons between Paris, New York, and Tel Aviv had ordered him to do so.

The full discrediting of the MDF and the open mockery of Hungarian values began. The internationalist leaders of the nomenklatura staff discovered that if they let the MDF retain the hard-fought privilege of serving national values, the bases of respect constructed even before the system change, the love of Hungarians beyond our borders—in brief, if it let the MDF keep the national-Christian-Center—then the resurrection of the MDF was possible. For this reason, a volley had to be fired at everything that was national, populist, and Hungarian. Traditions had to be discredited, common treasures had to be thrown away, everything that was created by the hands of the people had to be declared outdated, and everyone who dared to declare himself Hungarian had to be humiliated and cast out of his job. Unbridled terror began at the newspapers, at the television, and in every place where professing to be Hungarian could be part of the operations. Education, upbringing, the ministry itself, and the minister himself; religious life, the churches, the return of church property, the functioning of parochial schools; compensation, credit policies, the irregularities of obtaining credit and of the tax system, and the hindering of the Existence loan and Start loan funds;—all this is only an incomplete and sketchy listing of all the clashes the government must bleed from and recover from each and every day.

What else could a humiliated, poor government without means do? It manufactures ideas, improvises, spins, retreats, proclaims flexible disengagement, throws in its successful international relations, amends laws, seeks allies, courts anyone it can, strikes hard at its own following just to silence the opposing side, listens and falls silent, swallows the insults, and wipes the filth off its face.

Accordingly, the final assessment of the pact is as follows: Great political wisdom manifested itself in making this pact, which was forced into being, but in its afterlife it produced and continues to produce tragic consequences from the standpoint of the Hungarian people.

It destroyed the Hungarian people's ability to see through (alien) people; it concealed the intolerable injustices of privatization; it helped return Hungarian public communications into the hands of those who had usurped it during the Kadar–Aczel era; and finally, it *disarmed the MDF, and the MDF became surrounded as a result.*

The task to be performed by the government and by what remains of the MDF flows from the above: There is only one possible way to survive and to resolve the vital issues of the Hungarian people: *We must break free.*

We must not—and cannot—dispute that those on the opposite side, on the other end of the "Line," have the exact same legitimacy in parliament as we do, because like us, they, too, were elected, and therefore they, too, are entitled to everything that flows from being elected. Instead, we must guard against a situation in which the Hungarian people elect them again without knowing where they come from, who they really are, and what they want to do in this country.

Accordingly, breaking free means a total break with the comfort of pactism, softness, and gullibility, and a break from constant mournful retreat. We cannot remain silent any longer.

47

Esteemed Compatriots

Zhelyu Zhelev

August 21, 1993

Esteemed Compatriots, patriotic men and women of Bulgaria: There are events in the history of every nation that should never be forgotten, events that determine that nation's historic fate, that not only form that nation's past but also predetermine its future. Only a nation with a strong historical memory and a strong national feeling is able to cope with the vicissitudes and trials of the changing times and take up a worthy place among other nations and win their trust.

One of the brightest pages in our modern history was written by the Bulgarians of Macedonia and eastern Therace through their fight to preserve their nationality and to win liberty and independence.

From the Ilinden–Preobrazhensko Uprising [1903] and from the three national disasters that Bulgarian men and women have experienced this century, one can draw many important lessons. One of them is that Bulgaria must follow its own sovereign and independent foreign policy. It is no accident that we were the first to recognize the independence and state sovereignty of the Republic of Macedonia, together with the other three former Yugoslav republics—Slovenia, Croatia, and Bosnia–Herzegovina. This fact demonstrates yet again that in 1993 the Republic of Bulgaria must begin to develop its own autonomous and independent foreign policy, bearing in mind only its own national interests [cheering] and the principles and norms of international law.

We were the first to recognize Russia as an independent state, by signing a protocol on establishing diplomatic relations even before the Soviet Union had disintegrated. Gorbachev, who was president at that time, was very angry about this and did not want to meet our delegation; our American friends were very uneasy about this Bulgarian diplomatic move. They, like the representatives of the EC, nurtured the hope that the decommunization and democratization of this multinational state could take place within the framework of the empire itself, without its dissolution. A similar illusion was held in relation to the Federation of Yugoslavia. We, however, held the opposite view and were therefore the first to recognize the right to self-determination of all the peoples forming the population of our western neighbor, and we subsequently, when the referendums were held, recognized their state sovereignty.

I remember how, soon after we recognized the Republic of Macedonia, an old

FBIS-EEU-93-161, a publication of the United States government, pp. 10–11.

man from Vardar [region in the Former Yugoslav Republic of Macedonia] addressed an appeal to me, that we should show more understanding toward the populace of the new sovereign state, because, in his own words, Macedonia is a child of Bulgaria. By this, he evidently wanted to stress our common ethnic roots and cultural and historical traditions.

One cannot but remember the ancient parable of the judgment delivered by King Solomon, when he had to judge in a dispute between two quarreling women and decide to which of them a child belonged. One of them claimed that the child was hers, while the other would not yield in her claim that the child belonged to her. Then the wise judge said: Because there is no way to find out to whom the child belongs, and I want to be fair, I will order the child to be severed in two, so that each of you will receive her own half. Then one of the women cried out: Do not cut the child in half, give the child to her! In this way King Solomon found out who the true mother was and gave the child to her, because a true mother can wish nothing but good for her own child; most of all that it should remain alive and well.

The Republic of Bulgaria naturally has no intention of claiming maternity rights or imposing any other kind of patronizing relationship on Macedonia. The parable that I have related expresses instead the good feelings and partiality of the Bulgarians toward the Republic of Macedonia. However, bearing in mind that policies between two neighboring states can never be built on nationalist prejudices, on the basis of bias, but only on sensible principles, our aims regarding the Republic of Macedonia are as follows: to assist in consolidating its state sovereignty and territorial integrity; to help Macedonia to become a member of the principal European and world structures and organizations; and to help it build up democratic institutions and establish democratic principles in its social life, by developing as widely as possible economic, political, and cultural cooperation between our two countries and by expanding links between state institutions at all levels.

Only on the basis of universal, completely free interchange between our two countries, to the extent that the border becomes merely a token barrier, can we achieve a real drawing together of the people, by revealing our common roots, our common history, our common culture, common religion, and common language. Today, this is the only realistic and reasonable policy that can be pursued in relation to the Republic of Macedonia. It corresponds both to our national interests and to the principles and norms of international law. I believe that it also completely conforms to the present state interests of the Republic of Macedonia. Today, anyone who isolates the settlement of the Bulgarian national question from the country's internal development, from the level of democracy and the market economy, and from the overall prosperity and concern for the Bulgarians outside the country's borders cannot achieve anything in practice.

Incidentally, we also propose such a policy of free movement of people, goods, capital, and cultural values across borders to our other neighbors—Greece, Turkey, Romania, and Serbia; naturally, when the embargo is lifted.

There is no other country in the Balkans so strongly interested in free borders and free movement across them as Bulgaria, which borders with Bulgarians on every side. At the end of the twentieth century and on the threshold of the new millennium, the Balkan peoples have no other possibility than to try to copy the model set by Western Europe, to follow the example of the EC member countries by renouncing war and the forcible acquisition of territories, to act in such a way as their borders unite and draw them closer together rather than separate them, so that the strength and greatness of every state is judged not by its size and the aggressiveness of its army but by its development of democracy and the market economy, by the rights and freedoms that individuals enjoy, and by the real wealth that its people have created.

Only in this way can we defend and continue in a worthy manner the cause of national unification of the heroes of the Ilinden–Preobrazhensko Uprising. Eternal glory to the heroes of the Ilinden–Preobrazhensko epic! Homage to their bright memory!

The Collapse of Yugoslavia

The most disastrous series of events in Eastern Europe after 1989 was the collapse of Yugoslavia. The disintegration of this multiethnic country began with the emergence of Slobodan Milošević in Serbia. Milošević brought old-line communists and military officers together under a banner of militant nationalism. His rallying cry was to regain control of Kosovo. This region was the center of Serbian culture in medieval times, but by the 1980s its population was 90 percent Albanian. After 1945 Kosovo, along with Vojvodina, had become an autonomous region within Serbia. By the Yugoslav constitution of 1974 these autonomous regions had obtained the power to influence federal legislation that was equal to Serbia itself. Milošević rallied millions of Serbs with the demand that Serbia no longer acquiesce to this limitation on its power. He succeeded in reasserting Serbian control over both Kosovo and Vojvodina, but in the process he made the other Yugoslav republics very nervous. In Slovenia, a movement of intellectuals both inside and outside the party began to demand rights for Slovenia, and in Croatia a well-known nationalist dissident from the 1960s formed a political party for a similar purpose.

With the Soviet bloc collapsing, the six Yugoslav republics moved toward their own reforms. All six republics held elections in 1990, and all of them elected leaders with nationalist programs. As each republic began to go its own way, first the League of Yugoslav Communists collapsed, and then the central government itself. Both Milošević and his counterpart in Croatia, Franjo Tudjman, turned to increasingly vitriolic forms of nationalist invective while the Slovenes systematically moved to disengage themselves from the Yugoslav federation.

Despite peace efforts by the leaders of Macedonia and Bosnia and Herzegovina, when Slovenia declared its independence on June 25, 1991, the Yugoslav army attempted to subdue the Slovenians, but without success. Meanwhile, when Croatia also declared its independence, armed conflict broke out between the Croatian government and its sizable Serbian minority. Soon the Yugoslav National Army, whose officer corps was predominantly Serb, intervened on the side of Serbia. Assisted by semiprivate armed bands, they brutally occupied about one-third of Croatia. The European powers decided to recognize Croatian and Slovenian independence, and the United Nations sent a force (UNPROFOR: United Nations Protection Force) to maintain a separation between the new Serbian Republic of Krajina (in Croatia) and the Croats.

In the spring of 1992, Bosnia and Herzegovina also declared its independence, at which point its Serb minority rose up in revolt against the new state. The Bosnian Serbs, with the help of Milošević, occupied about 70 percent of Bosnia and Herzegovina. The United States and the European Union were not able to find a formula that would stop this war, despite economically blockading Serbia, prohibiting arms shipments to Bosnia, and even threatening air strikes.

The four documents reprinted here provide material for understanding the feelings of the parties involved. The first is shortened version of a memorandum that was under preparation in the Serbian Academy of Sciences (SANU) in 1986 when it was leaked to the press. It remains a controversial document, but there is little doubt that it represented the position of a significant number of Serbian intellectuals at the time. Since then, the views of most of the persons associated with the SANU memorandum have hardened even more.

The second document is an adaptation of an article that appeared in Slovenia shortly after the SANU memorandum. The author, Dimitrij Rupel, contributed the article to a special issue of the journal Nova Revija (New review). The editors asked a number of prominent Slovenian writers and scholars to write about the situation of the Slovenian nation. The fact that the journal published these articles at all created a sensation among Slovene intellectuals and was an important milestone in accelerating Slovenia's turn away from communism. Rupel later became the foreign minister of Slovenia.

The third document is the preface to the Croatian constitution of 1990. Croatia's first postcommunist election in 1990 brought politicians to power who believed that Croatia should be primarily a Croatian state, not a multiethnic one. This preface to the constitution presents their argument that throughout history, Croatia had always been an autonomous actor. The preface distinguishes between Croats, for whom the state has been established, and others, who are citizens also. Insensitivity to Croatia's large Serbian minority was an important contributing factor, along with Milošević's hectoring, in producing war in Croatia.

The final document is a speech by Haris Silajdžić, at the time foreign minister of Bosnia and Herzegovina, to the United Nations conference on human rights held in Vienna in June 1993. Silajdžić's emotional speech goes beyond the dry political programs of the other documents to evoke in a small way the tragedy that the war in Bosnia has become. Ethnic cleansing undertaken by all sides, but primarily by the Serbs, sent hundreds of thousands of people into flight, and massacres killed tens of thousands more. Silajdžić's speech galvanized his audience but had little effect on the willingness or the ability of the international community to undertake the costly measures needed to bring a halt to the fighting.

48

Memorandum of the Serbian Academy of Sciences (SANU)

Translated by Denison Rusinow

1986

Many of the misfortunes suffered by the Serb nation originate in circumstances that are common to all the Yugoslav nations. However, other calamities also burden the Serb nation. The long-term lagging-behind in the development of the economy of Serbia, undefined state and legal relations with Yugoslavia and the provinces [Kosovo and Vojvodina], and also genocide in Kosovo have appeared on the political scene with a combined force which have created a tense if not also explosive situation. The crucial nature of these three tortured questions, which derive from a long-term policy toward Serbia, threaten not only the Serb nation but also the stability of Yugoslavia as a whole. They must therefore be given central attention.

Extensive knowledge and data are not required to confirm the longstanding lagging-behind of the Serbian economy. . . . Throughout the postwar period the Serbian economy suffered from lopsided terms of trade. A primary example is the low price for electrical energy, which is supplied in large quantities to other republics. Economic instruments and measures taken in credit and monetary policies, and especially the contribution to the federal fund for the economic development of inadequately developed regions, have lately been the most important factors in its relative retardation. With the addition that the most developed republics, because of Serbia's lack of capital, have penetrated her economy (agriculture, food-processing industry, commerce, and banking) with their capital, the picture is one of a subordinated and neglected economy in the framework of the Yugoslav area.

The economic subordination of Serbia cannot be fully understood without its politically inferior position, which also determined all relations. For the CPY [the Communist party of Yugoslavia] the economic hegemony of the Serbian nation between the wars was not disputable, although the industrialization of Serbia was slower than the Yugoslav average. Thinking and behavior with a dominant influence on later political events and internationality relations were formed on the basis of that ideological platform. Slovenes and Croats created their national Communist parties before the war and achieved decisive influence in the CC [Central Commit-

From *East European Nationalism in the Twentieth Century*, edited by Peter F. Sugar, published by The American University Press, 1995. Copyright © 1995 by The American University Press.

tee] of the CPY. Their political leaders became the arbiters of all political questions
during and after the war. These two neighboring republics shared a similar history,
had the same religion and desire for ever-greater independence, and, as the most
developed, had common economic interests, all of which supplied sufficient reason
for permanent coalition in an attempt to realize political domination. This coalition
was solidified by the long-lasting cooperation of [Josip Bnoz] Tito and [Edvard]
Kardelj [respectively a Croat and a Slovene], the two most prominent personalities
of postwar Yugoslavia, who enjoyed unlimited authority in centers of power. A
cadre monopoly allowed them essential influence over the composition of the political apex of Yugoslavia and all the republics and provinces. The exceptionally great
contribution of Edvard Kardelj in preparing and carrying out the decisions of
AVNOJ [Anti-Fascist Council for the National Liberation of Yugoslavia] and of all
postwar constitutions is well known to all.[1] He was in a position to build his
personal views, which could not realistically be opposed, into the foundation of the
social order. The determination with which Slovenia and Croatia today oppose any
constitutional change shows how much the Constitution of 1974 suits them.[2] Views
concerning the social order had no chance of being accepted if they were different
from the conceptions of [those] two political authorities, and it was not possible to
do anything even after their deaths, given that the Constitution insured against any
such change by granting [each republic and autonomous region] the possibility of a
veto. In view of all of this, it is indisputable that Slovenia and Croatia established a
political and economic domination through which to realize their national programs
and economic aspirations.

The attitude toward the economic lagging-behind of Serbia demonstrates that a
revanchist policy toward her did not weaken over time. On the contrary, nourished
by its own success, it became ever-stronger until it finally expressed itself also in
genocide. It is a politically unacceptable discrimination that citizens of Serbia,
because of equal representation by the republics [and autonomous regions], have
less access than others to positions as federal functionaries and delegates to the
federal parliament and that the votes of voters from Serbia are worth less than those
of any other republic or province. In this light Yugoslavia does not appear as a
community of equal citizens or equal nations and nationalities, but as a community
of eight equal territories. However, even this equality does not hold for Serbia
because of its special legal–political situation, which supports a tendency to keep
the Serb nation under constant control. The dominant idea of such a policy has been
"a weak Serbia, a strong Yugoslavia," advanced under the influence of the view that
if the Serbs, as the most numerous nation, were permitted rapid economic development, that would represent a danger for the other nations.

[1]The Slovene Edvard Kardelj was the main theorist of Yugoslav communism. Serbs generally
consider him responsible for the constitutional arrangements to which they objected in Kosovo. Tito
created the AVNOJ in 1942 to serve as the broad political front backing the efforts of the communist
Partisans to resist the Germans and to seize power in postwar Yugoslavia.

[2]In 1974 Yugoslavia adopted a constitution that gave to two autonomous regions included in the
Republic of Serbia, Kosovo and Vojvodina, political rights almost equal to those enjoyed by the rest of
the Yugoslav republics, even though they remained within the boundaries of Serbia. It also permitted
each republic and autonomous region to veto, or at least significantly delay, any federal legislation to
which it objected.

Serbia is in fact divided in three parts by the Constitution of 1974. The autonomous provinces are equivalent to republics in everything except that they are not defined as states and do not have the same number of representatives in some federal organs. They compensate for this deficiency through their ability to intervene in the internal affairs of Narrow Serbia [i.e., Serbia without the two autonomous provinces] through a common republican parliament, while their own parliaments are totally autonomous. The political–legal situation of Narrow Serbia is completely undefined; it is neither a republic nor a province.

Relations between Serbia and the provinces are not only and not primarily a matter of formalistic–legal interpretation. It is primarily a question of the Serb nation and its state. A nation, which after a long and bloody battle again achieved its own state, which itself opted also for bourgeois democracy, and which in the last two wars lost 2.5 million conationals, had an arbitrarily constituted party commission establish that, after four decades in the new Yugoslavia, only it [among the nations of Yugoslavia] does not have its own state. A worse historical defeat in peace cannot be imagined.

The exile of the Serbian people from Kosovo is a spectacular testament to its historic defeat. In the spring of 1981, the Serbian people received a declaration of open and total war [from the Albanians in Kosovo]. This war was waged skillfully with not only passive but even active support from various political centers in the country. This support was even more fatal than that coming from neighboring countries. This unconcealed war, which we have yet to face clearly or call by its true name, has been going on for almost five years. It has thus lasted much longer than this country's entire war of liberation—from April 6, 1941, to May 1945. The rebellion of the Balisti in Kosovo and Metohija at the very end of the war, begun with the help of Nazi units, was militarily crushed between 1944 and 1945, but it was not politically beaten.[3] Its present form, disguised in a new context, has been developing more successfully and has been approaching a victorious outcome. Therefore a true reckoning with neofascist aggression never occurred. All measures taken to date have only hidden it from view and in fact have strengthened its irrevocable goals, which are motivated by racism.

The physical, political, legal, and cultural genocide of the Serbian population in Kosovo and Metohija is the worst defeat in the Serbian-led battles of liberation from Orašac in 1804 to the 1941 uprising.[4] Responsibility for this defeat falls primarily on the Comintern heritage present in the policy of the Communist party of Yugoslavia and the loyalty of the Serbian communists to this policy, on the extremely costly ideological and political delusions, ignorance, immaturity, or already incorrigible opportunism of the generation of Serbian politicians who arose after the war, who are always defensive and always care more about what other people think of them and their timid "postings" of Serbia's status than about the objective facts which determine the future of the people they govern.

---

[3]"Balisti" refers to the Albanian nationalist organization Bali Kombetar (National front) that collaborated with the Germans during World War II in hopes of creating a large Albanian state in the Balkans. Metohija is the western part of Kosovo. Serbs use the term because it has a historical resonance for them, but Albanians use only the term Kosovo (or *Kosovë* in Albanian) for the entire province.

[4]The first Serbian uprising against Ottoman rule, which began a successful struggle for independence in the nineteenth century, began in the village of Orašac.

The Serbs of Kosovo and Metohija have not only their past, personified in precious cultural–historic monuments, but also living spiritual, cultural, and moral values: They have the motherland of their historic existence. The violence which has, over the centuries, thinned out the Serbian population in Kosovo and Metohija is—in this, our time—entering its relentless end game. The emigration of Serbs from Kosovo and Metohija in socialist Yugoslavia exceeds in numbers and in character all former phases of this great exile of the Serbian people. Jovan Cvijić in his time estimated that in all migrations, beginning with the great one under Arsenije Čarnojević in 1690 to the first years of our century, more than 500,000 Serbs had been exiled; of that number between 1876 and 1912 about 150,000 Serbs had to leave their hearths under the ruthless terror of the local and privileged Albanian basibazuks [irregular Ottoman military forces].[5] In the course of the last war, over 60,000 Serbian colonists and natives were exiled, but after the war this wave of emigration really reached its crest: In the last twenty or so years, 200,000 Serbs left Kosovo and Metohija. The remaining Serbian people are not only leaving their land at an undiminished pace, but being persecuted by oppression and physical, moral, and psychological terror, they are preparing for their final exodus, according to all sources of information. In less than the next ten years, if the situation does not change considerably, there will no longer be any Serbs in Kosovo, and an "ethnically clean" Kosovo—that unequivocally expressed goal of the "Greater-Albanian" racists established in the programs and actions of the "Prizren League" as early as 1878–1881—will be completely fulfilled.

Kosovo is not the only region in which the Serbian people has found itself under the pressures of discrimination. Not only the relative but the absolute decline in the numbers of Serbs in Croatia is evidence enough for the above claim. According to the census of 1948, there were 543,795 Serbs in Croatia, that is, 14.48 percent of the Croatian population. According to the 1981 census, these numbers had diminished to 531,502 which was 11.5 percent of the entire population of Croatia. During the thirty-three years of peace, the number of Serbs in Croatia had declined even in relation to the immediate postwar period, when the first census was carried out and when the consequences of World War II on the number of Serbs were well known.

Lika, Kordun, and Banija have remained the least-developed regions in Croatia, which greatly motivated Croatian Serbs to migrate to Serbia as well as to other regions of Croatia, where Serbs, as a minority group of newcomers and a socially inferior people, were extremely susceptible to assimilation. The Serbian people have been, in general, exposed to a sophisticated and efficient assimilation policy. A consistent part of this policy is a ban of all Serbian societies and cultural institutions in Croatia, which were part of a rich cultural tradition during the reign of the Austro-Hungarian Empire and the Kingdom of Yugoslavia between the wars. This policy also includes the imposition of an official language, which is named after another people (Croatian), thus signifying national inequality. That language was, through a constitutional act, made obligatory for all Serbs in Croatia. Also, nationalistically inclined Croatian language experts, through systematic and extremely

[5]Jovan Cvijić was Serbia's greatest geographer. His ethnic maps, often skewed by political considerations, played an important role in the Paris Peace Conference after World War I.

well organized action, have been distancing that language from the language spoken in other republics where Serbo-Croatian is the mother tongue, which contributes to the weakening of connections between Serbs in Croatia and other Serbs. In order to achieve this goal, the Croats are ready to sacrifice the continuity of their own language and lose from it international terms necessary for communication with other cultures, especially in the fields of science and technology. Moreover, the Serbian people in Croatia are not only culturally cut off from the mainstream of the Motherland, but the Motherland has no possibility of informing itself—to nearly the extent that other nations who live in Yugoslavia are connected with their fellow peoples—about the Serbian people's economic and cultural position in Croatia. The question of the integrity of the Serbian people and their culture in all of Yugoslavia is a fateful one for their survival and progress.

Except for the period of the existence of the NDH [the Independent State of Croatia], Serbs in Croatia were never so endangered as they are today.[6] The solution of their national position imposes itself as a first priority political question. Unless a solution is found, the consequences can be damaging in many ways, not only for the situation in Croatia, but for all of Yugoslavia.

Under the influence of the ruling ideology, the cultural heritage of the Serbian people is being alienated, usurped, invalidated, neglected, or wasted; their language is being suppressed; and the Cyrillic alphabet is vanishing. The field of literature in this sense serves as a main arena for arbitrariness and lawlessness. No other Yugoslav nation has been so rudely denied its cultural and spiritual integrity as the Serbian people. No literary and artistic heritage has been so routed, pillaged, and plundered as the Serbian one. The political maxims of the ruling ideology are being imposed on Serbian culture as more valuable and stronger than scientific and historic ones. While Slovenian, Croatian, Macedonian, and Montenegrian culture and literature are today being integrated, Serbian culture and literature alone are being systematically disintegrated. It is ideologically legitimate and in the spirit of self-management to freely divide and disperse the Serbian literary heritage and attribute it to authors from Vojvodina, Montenegro, or Bosnia and Herzegovina. Serbia's best authors and most significant literary works are being torn from the Serbian literary canon so that new regional literatures can be artificially established.

The Serbian people have a historic and democratic right to establish fully national and cultural integrity independently, regardless of the republic or province in which they live. The acquisition of equality and independent development have a deeper historic meaning for the Serbian people. In less than fifty years, within two consecutive generations, twice exposed to physical annihilation, forceful assimilation, religious conversion, cultural genocide, ideological indoctrination, invalidation, and denunciation of their own tradition under the imposed complex of guilt, intellectually and political disarmed, the Serbian people were exposed to temptations that were too great not to leave deep scars on their spirit. We cannot allow

---

[6]During World War II, the Independent State of Croatia (NDH) pursued a brutal policy of purifying Croatia—which at that time included Bosnia—of its "unhealthy" elements: Jews, gypsies, Muslims, communists, and Serbs. About one-sixth of the Serbs living in Croatia and Bosnia lost their lives during the war.

49

The Slovene National Question

*Dimitrij Rupel (translated by Meta von Rabenau
and Carole Rogel)*
1987

In the past, it seems, [religious] conversion was a major instrument of Slovene liberation. Conversion means replacing gods, saints, morals, and cultures. It constitutes a social upheaval that overturns values, ideas, rules, and laws. Conversion from one faith to another has been a characteristic of the Slovene nation from the very beginning. It began when the Slovene Prince Borut asked the Bavarians for help during their war against the Avars [and the Bavarians required the Slovenes to convert to Christianity]. This is documented in the first historical account of the Slovenes, *Conversio bagoariorum et carantanorum* [from the ninth century]. [After the baptism of the Slovenes] Prince Inko hosted converted Slovene peasants at his table with gold-plated goblets, leaving unconverted noblemen in the courtyard to eat like dogs. In its retellings, this story of the conversion of the Slovenes from barbarians into Christians acquired a mythical character. The paradigmatic character of this event was confirmed more than a thousand years later when it became a focal point of [Francè] Prešern's only epic poem *Baptism at the Savica*. In 1986 Jan Makarović, in analyzing this poem, wrote that the physical defeat of the Slovenes became "at the same time their spiritual victory."

The next major cultural forward thrust was also related to a religious conversion, this time from Catholicism to Protestantism. In the sixteenth century [Primož] Trubar [who had converted to Protestantism] translated more than twenty religious and literary pieces into Slovene, thus legitimizing Slovene as one of Europe's civilized languages. The next opportunity for a conversion [this time a secular one] came with the creation of the Illyrian Provinces under Napoleon Bonaparte. Napoleon enriched the Slovene experience linguistically and culturally. During the revolutionary year of 1848 the Slovenes experienced one of their most important cultural–political conversions, this time to liberalism. Even though this happened to be a German concept, and not really suitable for Slovenes considering their subordinate sociopolitical relationship to Germans, it helped Slovene liberal intellectuals to develop many useful and successful political and cultural programs, including the Slovene novel.

The most recent Slovene conversion was to (belligerent) atheism. The protago-

Adapted from Dimitrij Rupel, "Odgovor na slovensko narodno vprašanje," *Nova revija* 57 (1987): 57–73. Published with the permission of the author.

nists of this conversion were liberals, social democrats, and communists, all of whom took part in twentieth-century developments. This conversion reached its climax after 1945. Atheization and, later, bolshevization were mixed blessings for the Slovenes. The international and class emphasis of these concepts, especially the Stalinist version, meant a neglect of the national question. Nevertheless, some common sense lay behind the concepts, which had democratic and even populist features that prevented the creation of a totally unitary or centralized state in postwar Yugoslavia. Without question, the creation of a sovereign Slovene state within its ethnic territory constitutes the most developed form of the Slovene nation thus far, the one closest to an ideal form.

None of the major conversions pushed the Slovenes backward. On the contrary, they permitted survival and progress. On the other hand, living with conversions involves the development of a particular mentality or national spirit. Provisionally, this mentality could be labeled a spirit of adjustment, compromise, and sublimation, as well as of rationality and openness. In politics Slovenes often followed the path of small steps, uneasy alliances, and elasticity, which sometimes earned them harsh and moralistic criticism. This mentality also led to resignation expressed in out-migration and a high level of suicides.

Numerous data dealing with the current Slovene situation show a possible change in this traditional behavioral pattern, that is, a reordering of the Slovene national question:

1. Due to the diminished importance of class identification generally taking place among developed European nations, national–ethnic identification is becoming stronger and more real.

2. In contrast to the situation in the ninth century, Slovenes today are not threatened by any great power that would necessitate seeking help from another great power.

3. Today, Slovenes deal with internationally comparable and analogous nation-states.

4. The knot that tied Slovenes to a nationally liberated and yet revolutionary society after World War II is beginning to unravel.

The opportunity of European nations to establish national states emerged in 1848. We missed our chance then. The opportunity reemerged during World War I, and we made use of it only halfway, which is why we joined the national liberation struggle [during World War II]. At that time, because of all sorts of circumstances, political revolution overshadowed national liberation. Political revolution temporarily legitimized class goals as primary, when they actually are secondary.

The problems of untying the knot are not simple, but I think that the old values built by the history of conversions are declining, while the primary values, such as national belonging, state dignity, and personal integrity, are on the rise. Among the encouraging phenomena are the demands for civil society, the new alternative movements, examples of cultural pride, less restraint in practicing religion and in making public statements, and demands for political pluralism.

Past Slovene conversions abandoned state, political, and religious traditions, but they retained the Slovene character, which was maintained in the language and numerous national and cultural habits. Conversion was not assimilation. The Slovene language today is probably much less in danger than ever before while at the same time we are aware of alarming assessments about language endangerment even among well established nation-states, such as France. That means that we are dealing with new language problems, in particular with the problem of minority languages and the problem of languages in nationally mixed states.

Relations in Yugoslavia would certainly be ideal if the Slovenes knew Serbo-Croatian, perhaps even Serbian and Croatian as separate languages, and possibly also Macedonian; if the Serbs and Croats knew Slovene and Macedonian; and if the Macedonians knew one or two languages in addition to their own. In practice, the Slovenes do try to maintain such a relationship. For example, Slovene children learn the Serbo-Croatian language in elementary schools as a compulsory subject. Serbs and Croats, however, do not usually learn the Slovene language in elementary school. This means that we unconsciously apply the principle [of language equality] one-sidedly. Slovene is a second-class language in Yugoslavia, a fact that is confirmed by a superficial survey of the situation and about which there are thousands of anecdotes. Serbs and Croats are aware that knowledge of the Slovene language is not a strict necessity for them. Their contacts with Slovenes teach them that Slovenes are willing to speak to them in their own language on most occasions. I imagine that a Croat or Serb presented with the thought that he should learn Slovene asks himself the very logical question: Why should I learn Slovene when I can use this time to learn a language that could be used for something more urgent, which presses on me in daily life, and on which my prosperity and progress depends?

Many Slovenes, especially those working in federal jobs, think that a knowledge of Serbo-Croatian is their moral obligation, in the hope that by their example they will convince other citizens that they should learn Slovene. I think that this view is wrong, and that in the end Slovenes too should ask themselves, as others do: Why should I learn Serbo-Croatian if I could use this time to learn some more important language? Why should not Slovenes learn English, German, or Russian, instead of Serbo-Croatian?

The answer lies in fear, which has been characteristic of Slovenes for a thousand years. Imagine a Slovene abroad in a diplomatic delegation or in the army. Suddenly he finds that he is completely alone before an assembly of Serbo-Croatian–speaking representatives of the country. The only possible conclusion is that he stands before [representatives of] a *Serbo-Croatian–speaking country,* not individual representatives of the Serbian or Croatian nations. The language question becomes a question of patriotism and even ultimately of treason.

To this terrifying fear we must add something else. A Slovene speaks Serbo-Croatian out of fear for his own language. If the state guarantees language rights, Slovenes have to pay this state their highest respect, which is to adapt to its language. To be able to speak Slovene at home, the Slovenes have to speak Serbo-Croatian with the state. Otherwise there is a danger that the state will not understand them, that it will consider them to be even worse citizens than they already are.

And now one of the most important questions arises: How is it possible to speak face to face with the state if you are overwhelmed with fear? Everyone has had such experiences. Before the commander, the governor, the strict teacher—sooner or later you can only stammer. Slovenes stammer in the Yugoslav language. Only at home can they speak fluently, in the family and in home institutions.

The principle that says people in multinational states become equal if they know two or more languages is thus shown to be disputable. It can be adhered to in a one-sided manner, and even this one-sided respect of the principle is not free from inner contradictions. In saying this, we have also said that *Yugoslavia is not a country of equal nations and languages* and that, considering the practicalities, *it cannot become one.*

The language problems listed [in other parts of the article not reproduced here] do not mean that the Slovene national question starts with the language issue. The fact that we deal with it so intensely suggests just the opposite, that we are more and more sober, deliberate, and professional about our language accomplishments. Our detailed involvement with language problems and dilemmas is witness to our high level of achievement to date. This list of problems is to be used to plan relationships in our multinational society, as long as it still remains the best framework for the realization of Slovene national interests.

At this level of development, one needs to count on the expansion of Slovenization and its impregnation of all sectors of Slovene society. What the Slovenes inherited from history and what remains in spite of all conversions, which were instruments of minimal national preservation, has to be projected into all levels of social life. In the past this task was given up to foreign states, international projects, churches, and ideologies. The Slovene mentality of conversion weakened substantially during the national liberal struggle, but certain elements of limitation can be observed even today. It seems that the time has come when these elements can be removed, when we can say farewell to the conversion strategy and abandon the kind of activity captured in the term *the national question*. From now on our questions will be modernization, international participation on an equal level, efficiency, political life, and [achieving] as high a level of accomplishment and as high a quality of life as possible. With the resolution of the national question, we will assume much more difficult tasks than we have had so far, those that were postponed due to inappropriate priorities. Any new conversion, let us say to an "eastern" mentality, or even to the third world of Islam or Orthodoxy, would mean catastrophe for the Slovenes, since it would be the only backward step in our thousand-year history.

50

The Constitution of the Republic of Croatia
December 22, 1990

The thousand-year-long national identity and state existence of the Croatian nation, confirmed by the course of its entire historical experience in various state forms and preserved by the development of the state-creating idea of the historical right of the Croatian people to full state sovereignty, manifested itself:

- In the formation of Croatian principalities in the seventh century.
- In the independent medieval state of Croatia founded in the ninth century.
- In the Kingdom of Croats established in the tenth century.
- In the preservation of the subjectivity of the Croatian state in the Croatian–Hungarian personal union.
- In the autonomous and sovereign decision of the Croatian Sabor [to sign] the Pragmatic Sanction in 1712.
- In the conclusions of the Croatian Sabor of 1848 regarding the restoration of the integrity of the Triune Kingdom of Croatia under the power of the Ban, on the basis of the historical, state, and natural right of the Croatian nation.
- In the Croatian–Hungarian Compromise of 1868 regulating the relations between the Kingdom of Dalmatia, Croatia, and Slavonia and the Kingdom of Hungary on the basis of the legal traditions of both states and the Pragmatic Sanction of 1712.
- In the decision of the Croatian Sabor of October 29, 1918, to dissolve the legal state relations of Croatia with Austria-Hungary and the simultaneous affiliation of independent Croatia, invoking its historical and natural right as a nation, with the State of the Slovenes, Croats, and Serbs, proclaimed on the former territory of the Habsburg Monarchy.
- In the fact that the Croatian Sabor never sanctioned the decision of the National Council of the State of Slovenes, Croats, and Serbs to unite with Serbia and Montenegro in the Kingdom of Serbs, Croats, and Slovenes (December 1, 1918), subsequently (October 3, 1929) proclaimed the Kingdom of Yugoslavia.
- In the establishment of the Banovina of Croatia in 1939 by which Croatian state identity was restored in the Kingdom of Yugoslavia.
- In laying the foundations of state sovereignty during the Second World War through decisions of the Antifascist Council of the National Liberation of Croatia (1943), as counter to the proclamation of the Independent State of Croatia (1941), and subsequently in the Constitution of the People's Republic of Croatia (1947) and several later constitutions of the Socialist Republic of Croatia (1963–1990).

At the historic turning point marked by the rejection of the communist system and changes in the international order in Europe, the Croatian nation, in its first

Based on the English version supplied by the Embassy of the Republic of Croatia.

285

democratic elections (1990), confirmed by its freely expressed will its thousand-year-long statehood and its resolution to establish the republic of Croatia as a sovereign state.

Proceeding from the historical facts presented above, from generally accepted principles in the modern world, and from the inalienability and indivisibility, non-transferability, and nonconsumability of the right of the Croatian nation to self-determination and state sovereignty, including the inviolable right to secession and association, as the basic preconditions for peace and stability of the international order, the Republic of Croatia is hereby established as the national state of the Croatian nation and a state of members of other nations and minorities who are citizens: Serbs, Muslims, Slovenes, Czechs, Slovaks, Italians, Hungarians, Jews, and others, who are guaranteed equality with citizens of Croatian nationality and the realization of ethnic rights in accordance with the democratic norms of the United Nations Organization and the countries of the free world.

Respecting the will of the Croatian nation and all citizens, resolutely expressed at free elections, the Republic of Croatia is hereby formed and will develop as a sovereign and democratic state in which the equality and freedoms and rights of man and citizen will be guaranteed and ensured, and their economic and cultural progress and social welfare promoted.

51

Human Rights in Bosnia and Herzegovina

Haris Silajdžić
June 15, 1993

Allow me to join those who express their gratitude to the Government of Austria for their warm hospitality. For my part, I thank those who speak on behalf of the victims of Bosnia and Herzegovina. Bosnia and Herzegovina is a blooodstain on your TV screens today. Bosnia and Herzegovina is genocide. Bosnia and Herzegovina is everything that human rights are not. I want you to keep in mind the name of one town in eastern Bosnia. The town is called Gorazde and I will come back to that town in a while to make a proposal to this conference.

Twenty thousand people dead, over 1.5 million displaced persons, refugees, 25,000 children dead, now hundreds of thousands in Bosnia at this moment starving to death. Thousands of children maimed, legless, handless, armless, parentless, to remind the international community forever of the international crime in which the international community is an accomplice. Bosnia and Herzegovina is not a natural disaster, it is not a crime. It is a genocide by people, a regime in Belgrade that attacks not only Muslims and Croats in Bosnia, but Croats in Croatia, Albanians in Kosovo, Muslims in Sandzak, Hungarians in Vojvodina, all in broad daylight, in front of all of you, in front of those who were handed the banner of might and justice in the international community. They are not punished. We are punished because we believed in justice, we believed in the international community, and we are guilty because we have resisted for so long. We have become an embarrassment to such a degree that high officials of the United Nations do not even mention Bosnia in their speeches—do not even mention Bosnia.

I will not speak long. I want once more to draw your attention to the town of Gorazde in eastern Bosnia that is now, as we speak, being savagely attacked by the Serbian forces. The Serbian forces from Serbia proper, an attack on Bosnia which is not a place but which, for those who do not know, has been a country, a state, a kingdom for one thousand years. For Bosnia knew about human rights hundreds of years ago when Jews, Hungarians, and other who sought refuge in Bosnia were given refuge and who have lived as first-rate citizens there ever since.

Until when shall we tolerate this? I know, and I am speaking on behalf of those who cannot speak because they have been denied the right to speak, they have been denied the right to eat, they have been denied the right to live for fifteen months with almost no action on the part of the international community. So how can we

Based on a transcript provided by the Embassy of the Republic of Bosnia and Herzegovina.

talk about human rights? Theoretically we should speak about the mechanisms to implement the human right to punish the tyrants wherever they are. This means Gorazde today: Sixty thousand people are awaiting death, as we speak now—an hour from here by airplane—people are dying in the hospitals, in the schools, in the houses, in the streets. Hundreds lie dead in the streets now as we speak about human rights here and as we go on with the so-called peace process—the process in which not only the regime in Belgrade is accused but also the international community (whatever that means) for allowing genocide to go on shamelessly.

Human rights. Where are the human rights? Where is the political will? And then the question: What can we do? I propose today, and I hope, Mr. President, that I will be listened to, that this conference at least appeals to the Security Council to stop the genocide of the people in Gorazde. At least bear this in mind: Twenty thousand children in Gorazde are going to be killed. There is no doubt about it. So I repeat, let us make an appeal today from this conference to the Security Council; let us demand on behalf of the participants, on behalf of humanity—because this is a crime against humanity—to stop, to take all necessary measures (UN resolutions entitle the Security Council to take such measures) to stop the genocide in at least one town, Gorazde.

This is a test. If this is not done, I don't think that there will be any credibility left for any of us—for the international community or for the United Nations. Those calling from the United Nations for the downtrodden and for the dispossessed would be right. Is this what we want? Why double standards so blatant, so open, so bloody, and so deadly for us? But this is the message of the people of Bosnia and Herzegovina: We are going to fight and defend ourselves because it is our inherent right—one of the oldest human rights—to defend ourselves, despite the fact that the international community has tied our hands while we are being killed, while 30,000 women are being raped, while children are being maimed.

I appeal to you again to demand that the Security Council take all necessary measures in Gorazde in order to restore credibility to this conference, to the United Nations and to the international community.

I thank you very much.

Gorbachev's Legacy

Mikail Gorbachev is almost a forgotten man in Russia today, and when he is remembered, it is not with approval. Russians consider him responsible for the collapse of the Soviet Union. But Gorbachev was not at fault. The Soviet Union fell, as the nineteenth-century Slavophile Alexei Khomiakov remarked, "even as old trees which have lost all their vital sap but still have just recently withstood a severe storm sometimes fall, thundering and booming, on a still night when there is not movement enough in the air to stir a leaf on the healthy tress." Gorbachev understood that the Soviet Union had lost its vital sap, and he tried to do something about it. To win the intelligentsia for his policy of restructuring the economy (perestroika), he instituted greater openness (glasnost), and when that did not work, he tried to bring the people into the process with elections and parliaments (demokratsia). In foreign policy, he and his brilliant foreign minister, Edvard Shevardnadze, introduced "New Thinking," which included scaling back nuclear weapons and trying to find a way to cooperate with Europe rather than to confront it. But these efforts failed. Gorbachev underestimated the power of nationalism, did not understand market mechanisms, and miscalculated his ability to bring his party and his people along with him on his journey of reform.

In trying to save socialism, Gorbachev destroyed the Soviet Union. But as Mikhail Bakunin, an anarchist contemporary of Khomiakov, put it, "The passion for destruction is a creative passion." Out of the rubble of the Soviet Union, new states and nations are emerging. They suffer the wounds of seventy years of mismanagement and excess, but at least the movement of possibility has replaced the stasis of conformity. No one can predict where the new paths will lead, but the past is gone and important events are at hand.

The first of the two readings in this section presents Gorbachev's conception of "a common European home." Delivered after the Polish elections of 1989 and before the collapse of the rest of the East European states, it is Gorbachev's vision for the future of Europe. The last reading in this section, and in the book, is Gorbachev's resignation speech, delivered two years to the day after the killing of Ceauşescu. When we read of the difficulties that the former Soviet states are undergoing today, we must not forget what preceded them. Put in another way, we should not underestimate the importance of Mikhail Gorbachev.

52

A Common European Home

Mikhail Gorbachev

July 6, 1989

It is not enough now simply to state that the European states share a common fate and are interdependent. The idea of European unity must be collectively rethought, in a process of creative collaboration among all nations—large, medium, and small.

Is such a formulation of the question realistic? I know that many in the West see the presence of two social systems as the major difficulty. But the difficulty actually lies elsewhere—in the widespread conviction (sometimes even a policy objective) whereby overcoming the split in Europe means "overcoming socialism." But this is a policy of confrontation, if not worse. No European unity will result from such approaches.

The fact that European states belong to different social systems is a reality. And recognition of this historical given and respect for the sovereign right of every people to choose a social system at its own discretion constitute the most important prerequisite for a normal European process.

Social and political orders in one or another country have changed in the past and may change in the future. However, this is exclusively the affair of the peoples themselves; it is their choice. Any interference in internal affairs and any attempts to restrict the sovereignty of states—either friends and allies or anyone else—are inadmissible.

Differences between states cannot be eliminated. They are, as I have said on more than one occasion, even beneficial—provided, of course, that the competition between the different types of societies is oriented toward creating better material and spiritual conditions of life for people.

Thanks to restructuring the U.S.S.R. will be able to be a full-fledged participant in this kind of honest, equitable, and constructive competition. Despite all our current shortcomings and lagging, we are well aware of the strong aspects of our social system that stem from its essential characteristics. And we are sure that we will be able to use them for the benefit of both ourselves and Europe.

It is time to relegate to the archives the postulates of the cold war, when Europe was viewed as an arena of confrontation divided into "spheres of influence" and somebody's "forward defense areas," and as an object of military opposition—a theater of military operations. In today's interdependent world, geopolitical notions born of another epoch are just as useless in real politics as the laws of classical mechanics are in quantum theory.

Meanwhile, it is on the basis of outdated stereotypes that the Soviet Union continues to be suspected of hegemonistic plans and intentions to tear the United States away from Europe. Some people would even like to place the U.S.S.R. outside of Europe from the Atlantic to the Urals, by limiting Europe to the expanse "from Brest to Brest." The U.S.S.R. is allegedly too big for coexistence: Others, it is said, would not feel very comfortable next to it. The realities of today and the prospects for the foreseeable future are obvious: The U.S.S.R. and the United States are a natural part of the European international political structure. And their participation in its evolution is not only justified, but also historically determined. . . .

[Our idea of a common European home] arose from an awareness of the new realities, from an understanding that a linear continuation of the path along which inter-European relations have been developing up to the last quarter of the twentieth century no longer corresponded to these realities.

The idea is connected with our internal economic and political restructuring, for which new relations were needed, above all, in the part of the world to which we, the Soviet Union, belong and with which for centuries we have had more ties than with anyone else.

We also took into consideration the fact that the colossal burden of armaments and the atmosphere of confrontation were not only hindering Europe's normal development but, at the same time, were obstructing—economically, politically, and psychologically—the full-fledged inclusion of our country in the European process and were introducing deforming impulses into our own development.

Those are the motives behind our decision to sharply step up our European policy, which, incidentally, was always of value to us in and of itself.

The philosophy of the concept of a "common European home" rules out the probability of an armed clash and the very possibility of using force or the threat of force, above all, military force—alliance against alliance, within alliances or wherever. To replace the doctrine of deterrence, it offers a doctrine of restraint. This is not just a game of ideas, but the logic of European development dictated by life itself.

Now for the economic content of the common European home. We consider the formation of a vast economic expanse from the Atlantic to the Urals, with a high level of interconnection between its eastern and western parts, to be a realistic prospect, though not an imminent one.

The Soviet Union's transition to a more open economy has fundamental importance in this respect. And not just for us ourselves, for increasing the efficiency of the national economy and satisfying the demands of consumers. It will increase the interdependence of the economies of East and West and, consequently, will have a favorable effect on the whole complex of general European relations.

Similar features in the practical functioning of economic mechanisms, strengthening of ties and economic interest, mutual adaptation, and training of the appropriate specialists—all of these are long-term factors in the course of cooperation, and a pledge of the stability of the European and international process as a whole. . . .

53

We Opened Ourselves to the World

Mikhail Gorbachev

December 25, 1991

Dear compatriots, fellow citizens, as a result of the newly formed situation, creation of the Commonwealth of Independent States, I cease my activities in the post of the U.S.S.R. president.

I am taking this decision out of considerations based on principle. I have firmly stood for independence, self-rule of nations, for the sovereignty of the republics, but at the same time for preservation of the union state, the unity of the country.

Events went a different way. The policy prevailed of dismembering this country and disuniting the state, with which I cannot agree. And after the Alma-Ata meeting and the decisions taken there, my position on this matter has not changed. Besides, I am convinced that decisions of such scale should have been taken on the basis of a popular expression of will.

Yet, I will continue to do everything in my power so that agreements signed there should lead to real accord in the society [and] facilitate the escape from the crisis and the reform process.

Addressing you for the last time in the capacity of president of the U.S.S.R., I consider it necessary to express my evaluation of the road we have traveled since 1985, especially as there are a lot of contradictory, superficial, and subjective judgments on that matter.

Fate had it that when I found myself at the head of the state it was already clear that all was not well in the country. There is plenty of everything: land, oil, and gas, other natural riches, and God gave us lots of intelligence and talent, yet we lived much worse than developed countries and keep falling behind them more and more.

The reason could already be seen: The society was suffocating in the vise of the command-bureaucratic system, doomed to serve ideology and bear the terrible burden of the arms race. It had reached the limit of its possibilities. All attempts at partial reform, and there had been many, had suffered defeat, one after another. The country was losing perspective. We could not go on living like that. Everything had to be changed radically.

That is why not once—not once—have I regretted that I did not take advantage of the post of [Communist party] general secretary to rule as a czar for several years. I considered it irresponsible and amoral. I realized that to start reforms of such scale

Reprinted from the *Washington Post,* December 26, 1991, by permission of the Associated Press.

in a society such as ours was a most difficult and even a risky thing. But even today I am convinced of the historic correctness of the democratic reforms that were started in the spring of 1985.

The process of renovating the country and radical changes in the world community turned out to be far more complicated than would be expected. However, what has been done ought to be given its due. This society acquired freedom, liberated itself politically and spiritually, and this is the foremost achievement—which we have not yet understood completely, because we have not learned to use freedom.

However, work of historic significance has been accomplished. The totalitarian system that deprived the country of an opportunity to become successful and prosperous long ago has been eliminated. A breakthrough has been achieved on the way to democratic changes. Free elections, freedom of the press, religious freedoms, representative organs of power, a multiparty [system] became a reality. Human rights are recognized as the supreme principle.

The movement to a diverse economy has started; equality of all forms of property is becoming established; people who work on the land are coming to life again in the framework of land reform; farmers have appeared; millions of acres of land are being given over to people who live in the countryside and in towns.

Economic freedom of the producer has been legalized, and entrepreneurship, shareholding, privatization are gaining momentum. In turning the economy toward a market, it is important to remember that all this is done for the sake of the individual. At this difficult time, all should be done for his social protection, especially for senior citizens and children.

We live in a new world. The cold war has ended; the arms race has stopped, as has the same militarization that mutilated our economy, public psyche, and morals. The threat of a world war has been removed. Once again I want to stress that on my part everything was done during the transition period to preserve reliable control of the nuclear weapons.

We opened ourselves to the world, gave up interference into other people's affairs, the use of troops beyond the borders of the country, and trust, solidarity, and respect came in response. We have become one of the main foundations for the transformation of modern civilization on peaceful democratic grounds.

The nations and peoples [of this country] gained real freedom of self-determination. The search for a democratic reformation of the multinational state brought us to the threshold of concluding a new union treaty. All these changes demanded immense strain. They were carried out with sharp struggle, with growing resistance from the old, the obsolete forces: the former party–state structures, the economic apparatus, as well as our habits, ideological superstitions, the psychology of sponging and leveling everyone out.

They stumbled on our intolerance, low level of political culture, fear of change. That is why we lost so much time. The old system collapsed before the new one had time to begin working, and the crisis in the society became even more acute. I am aware of the dissatisfaction with the present hard situation, of the sharp criticism of authorities at all levels, including my personal activities. But once again I'd like to stress: Radical changes in such a vast country, and a country with such heritage, cannot pass painlessly without difficulties and shakeup.

The August coup brought the general crisis to its ultimate limit. The most damaging thing about this crisis is the breakup of the statehood. And today I am worried by our people's loss of the citizenship of a great country. The consequences may turn out to be very hard for everyone.

I think it is vitally important to preserve the democratic achievements of the last years. They have been paid for by the suffering of our whole history, our tragic experience. They must not be given up under any circumstances or any pretext; otherwise all our hopes for the better will be buried. I am saying all this straight and honest. It is my moral duty.

Today I'd like to express my gratitude to all citizens who supported the policy of renovating the country, got involved in the implementation of the democratic reforms. I am grateful to statesmen, public and political figures, millions of people abroad, those who understood our concepts and supported them, turned to us, started sincere cooperation with us.

I am leaving my post with apprehension but also with hope, with faith in you, your wisdom, and force of spirit. We are the heirs of a great civilization, and its rebirth into a new, modern and dignified life now depends on one and all.

I wish to thank with all my heart all those who have stood together with me all these years for the fair and good cause. Some mistakes could surely have been avoided. Many things could have been done better. But I am convinced that sooner or later our common efforts will bear fruit, our nations will live in a prosperous and democratic society.

I wish all the best to all of you.